T0313864

PLANE QUEER

Phil Tiemeyer   ·   PLANE QUEER

Labor, Sexuality, and AIDS in the
History of Male Flight Attendants

University of California Press

Berkeley   Los Angeles   London

University of California Press, one of the most
distinguished university presses in the United
States, enriches lives around the world by advancing
scholarship in the humanities, social sciences, and
natural sciences. Its activities are supported by the UC
Press Foundation and by philanthropic contributions
from individuals and institutions. For more information,
visit www.ucpress.edu.

University of California Press
Berkeley and Los Angeles, California

University of California Press, Ltd.
London, England

Library of Congress Cataloging-in-Publication Data

Tiemeyer, Philip James, 1970–.
    Plane queer : labor, sexuality, and AIDS in the
. history of male flight attendants / Phil Tiemeyer.
        p.   cm.
    Includes bibliographical references and index.
    ISBN 978-0-520-27476-1 (cloth : alk. paper)
    ISBN 978-0-520-27477-8 (pbk. : alk. paper)
    ISBN 978-0-520-95530-1 (ebook)
    1. Flight attendants—United States—History.
2. Flight attendants—Labor unions—United
States.   3. Gays—Employment—United States.
4. Sexual orientation—United States.   5. Civil
rights—United States—History.   I. Title.
    HD6073.A432T54   2013
    331.7'61387742—dc23   2012041959

Manufactured in the United States of America

21   20   19   18   17   16   15   14   13
10   9   8   7   6   5   4   3   2   1

CONTENTS

ILLUSTRATIONS

ACKNOWLEDGMENTS

In the absence of ample archival sources, this book could not have been written without the help of former flight attendants. These men and women sat down with me, sometimes for hours, and recounted their histories with riveting honesty. They detailed not only the highlights of their careers but the many slights they had endured as well. The gay men were particularly insightful, sharing otherwise unrecorded stories of coming out and falling in love on the job, at times fearing ridicule and at other times enjoying the connections of friendships that spanned the globe. When it came to stories of loss—especially during the AIDS crisis—they also shared their pain, and sometimes even guilt, for surviving when their loved ones didn't. Whatever this book has accomplished in detailing this career owes more to these men and women than to my own work.

I am also indebted to a cadre of archivists across North America who helped me string together various loose threads into a solidly researched narrative. I especially thank Craig Likness at the University of Miami for helping me co-discover my topic in the first place, Bill Gulley at the Walter Reuther Labor Archives in Detroit for patiently explaining the intricacies of labor union structures, the staff at the ONE Archives in Los Angeles for chewing over my topic at lunches that were informative and full of laughter, Cilla Golas at the Association of Professional Flight Attendants Archives for bringing American Airlines' flight attendant history alive with humor and depth, and James Folts and his colleagues at the New York State Archives for their persistence in tracking down obscure legal files. Thanks also to the following institutions for their generous support: the University of Texas for a Continuing Fellowship, the New York State Archives for a Hackman Research Fellowship, Philadelphia University for a Faculty Research Grant and various other forms of financial support, and the Smithsonian National Air and Space Museum for a Guggenheim Fellowship.

One of the joys of writing this book is that I now belong to intellectual institutions where the pursuit of knowledge has overlapped seamlessly with the forging of friendships. The Department of American Studies at the University of Texas at Austin was a fantastic intellectual flight school. My dissertation chair, Janet Davis, is a living example of the flight attendants I so admire. She guided me safely through a PhD program with the charm, humor, and devotion that surely made her a great Northwest Airlines stewardess before becoming a historian and, later on, the devoted steward for my academic career. I also couldn't ask for better colleagues than those I have at Philadelphia University, especially those of us in Ravenhill Mansion. Our assemblage of liberal arts and social science scholars makes for the right blend of synergy and independence that allows fine scholarship and stellar teaching to thrive. My colleagues at the Smithsonian National Air and Space Museum found the most gentle ways to invite this social historian of sexuality into their fascination of machinery, without ever making me an outsider. I especially thank curators Dom Pisano and Martin Collins, who made my year as a Guggenheim Fellow so collegial. I am also indebted to my friend Collette Williams at NASM, who always had a way of keeping me grounded when my intellectual gears came unhinged. Finally, I am grateful to my editor at the University of California Press, Niels Hooper, for retaining his enthusiasm for my project from our first meeting until today. Even when our collaboration encountered unexpected turbulence, Niels reassured me with a combination of calm and persistence, coupled with genuine personal warmth, that kept this project flying.

My grandma is ultimately responsible for this book. When I was six years old, she took me on my first flight, whisking me away from my backyard in St. Louis to the desert landscape of New Mexico. All these years later, our time there stands out less in my memory than my flight on TWA with Grandma by my side. She loaded me up with gum to keep my ears from popping and only let out the slightest chuckle when I asked her, quite concerned, if our jet was going to do flips like the ones I saw on TV. Grandma held my hand all the way to Albuquerque and let me fall asleep in her lap, giving me just the security I needed to plant the seeds of a lifetime love affair with travel.

Over the years, Mom and Dad have nurtured this love affair. Often confused as a homebody, those of us who love Dad know that he's most in his element driving a car on a family vacation. He's at his funniest and most revealing with eyes on the road and hands on the wheel, destination westward, mountains just coming into sight. Meanwhile, Mom taught me that it's okay to explore even more distant horizons. She showed me Europe for the first time and remains my favorite travel companion to this day. Most importantly, Mom and Joan, my "second mom," showed me that I would still be loved even if I pursued my passions far away from home. The suburban backyards of St. Louis weren't for everyone, and Mom would come find me wherever I ended up. She has, and so has Dad. In my life's various changes of course and the occasional emergency landing, they've held my hand, just like Grandma on my first flight. And that backyard in St. Louis is still there, too, nurtured by Mom and Dad's fifty-year love affair.

I owe tremendous gratitude to Charlie for taking me deeper into love than I ever dared to dream as a child. We had a great voyage together, to places as disparate as Minneapolis, Newfoundland, and Austin. I'm delighted that we still get to travel together as family, if not as co-pilots. We'll probably settle down close by each other in a fabulous flight attendant getaway, ideally on the set of the Golden Girls, still fighting over which of us gets to be Dorothy. It's me, by the way, and you're Rose, and Brian is our Blanche.

As I mature, I find myself increasingly enamored by history's voyagers who chart a new course halfway through their lives. In the process, some of them discover a second naïveté, a deep sense of exhilaration every bit as wonderful as their first adventures. Falling in love with you, Shaun, has made me one of these fortunate characters. With my hand in yours, I'm a little kid again, venturing out on a TWA flight from St. Louis to who-knows-where. When you smile at me the way Grandma did, and I fall asleep in your arms, I know we belong on this voyage together forever. I think of our wonderful times in D.C., Philly, Colombia, and—most especially— Montreal, and proclaim with the joy of a newly minted flight attendant in aviation's gayest years: *Tu me donnes des ailes.*

March 22, 2012, Philadelphia, PA

Introduction

The idea for this book came to me back in 2004, while I was sifting through a box of materials in the Pan American Airways Archives at the University of Miami. Among the archives' vast collection of papers, I found dozens of folders, enough to fill an entire box, marked "Stewardesses." One folder in this box jumped out at me: a relatively thin one marked "Stewards," whose contents, though not extensive, were fascinating. I first noticed newspaper clippings from the late 1960s, which spoke of a court case filed by a young Miami man named Celio Diaz Jr. Diaz invoked the clause of the 1964 Civil Rights Act that forbade "sex discrimination" when Pan Am refused to hire him, or any other man, as a flight attendant. He thereby began a legal assault on the corporate sphere's gender norms, one complemented by far more numerous efforts from female plaintiffs. Hundreds of women were fighting at the Equal Employment Opportunity Commission (EEOC) and in federal courts to gain access to higher-paying male-dominated professions, while Diaz and a few dozen other men demanded entry into female-only service sector jobs.

When Diaz finally won his case in 1971, a new era for flight attendants was born: not only Pan Am but all other U.S. airlines were forced to integrate men into their flight service crews. This was a little-known, highly controversial consequence of the landmark civil rights legislation passed in 1964. A clipping from the *Wall Street Journal* cast the ruling as an affront to America's heterosexual, male-privileged hierarchy that kept flight attendants young, female, and attractive: "To the extent male stewards replace glamorous stewardesses," the *Journal* scornfully mused, "the

[*Diaz*] case . . . may prove to be one of the more controversial interpretations of the 1964 law among members of the male-dominated Congress."[1]

Deeper in the folder, I found much older photographs of Pan Am's first flight crews from the 1920s and '30s. Interestingly, the entire crew were men: pilots, co-pilots, *and* stewards. It turns out that this most storied of U.S. airlines didn't hire a single stewardess until the labor shortage of World War II, and it continued to hire stewards in sizable numbers well into the 1950s. Only in 1958 did Pan Am switch to the female-only hiring policy that Diaz successfully challenged a decade later. The same was true of another of America's great legacy carriers, Eastern Air Lines, which imitated Pan Am by introducing all-male flight crews in 1936 and continuing to hire a sizable number of stewards until the mid-1950s.

Once again, the photos were remnants of a history I had never heard before: I was unaware that male flight attendants had been in the career even before stewardesses, the first of whom had started in 1930, a couple years after Pan Am's first steward. This small folder's contents held tremendous promise to uncover a seemingly forgotten history, chronicling how one group of men struggled to maintain their foothold in a profession that gradually went from being originally male, to almost exclusively female, to sexually integrated by the 1970s.

Excited by my discoveries, I walked into the office of Dr. Craig Likness, then the university's head archivist, to discuss the folder on stewards. I told him how men seemed to have played a key role in various moments of the career and turned to him plaintively for more records. Surely this material was rich enough to warrant more folders—or, ideally, boxes—on stewards. First came the bad news: Craig was familiar enough with the collection to know that everything explicitly about stewards was in the meager folder. Then came the good news: he too was fascinated by my findings, both what they revealed and the promise of all the things they concealed. "Well, it sounds like you've found a great book topic," he smilingly concluded.

From that day onwards, with the help of devoted archivists and patient former flight attendants who sat for hours of interviews, I have been cobbling together the history of the male flight attendant. Though far from exhaustive, this book reconstructs the key contours of this history, all the while demonstrating how male flight attendants have held a broader significance beyond aviation history. The fact that these men have been treated as gender misfits and suspected homosexuals since their debut makes them an important case study of gender discrimination and homophobia in an American workplace. *Plane Queer* thereby offers nearly a century of civil rights history that typically has been overlooked, especially examining the various successes and setbacks flight attendants experienced in striving for queer equality in the United States.[2]

Thanks to social norms that took root in the early 1930s, the male flight attendant has stood out, as the book's title suggests, as *plainly queer* for almost the full run of this profession. After all, these were white men who performed what large segments of U.S. society deemed servile "women's work" or "colored work" and who thereby invited scrutiny as failed men and likely homosexuals. According to Kathleen Barry, whose book *Femininity in Flight* is the most authoritative history of the career to date, "The flight attendant occupation took permanent shape in the 1930s as 'women's work,' that is, work not only predominately performed by women but also defined as embodying white, middle-class ideals of femininity."[3] The historical record confirms this finding, as stewards in the late 1930s constituted just one-third of the nation's flight attendants. Thereafter, their numbers declined significantly, receding to a mere 4 percent when *Diaz v. Pan Am* was being argued in the late 1960s.[4]

Yet a countervailing fact is also true: men have persisted in this career from its first day to the present, often in surprisingly large numbers. Indeed, their status as men that society perceived as queer—a good many of whom also self-identified as gay—who were also unionized, working-class employees in a relatively high-profile, public relations-oriented profession makes them particularly important historical actors in a larger struggle to combat sexism and homophobia in the American workplace.

Male flight attendants' contributions to queer equality developed in an ever-widening spiral, as they quietly sought acceptance first from fellow flight attendants and other coworkers, then from airline managers and union officials, and then—in the most far-reaching examples—in groundbreaking legal fights that influenced the larger trajectory of gender-based and sexuality-based civil rights in the United States. *Plane Queer* uncovers these moments when male flight attendants successfully expanded civil rights, focusing especially on *Diaz v. Pan Am*, legal actions filed by flight attendants to protect the work rights of people with HIV/AIDS, and the gradual bestowal of domestic partner benefits and other "gay-friendly" workplace rules that arose in the 1990s.[5]

At the same time, I also focus on moments of retreat, when sexism and homophobia prevailed over queer equality, as when Pan Am and Eastern stopped hiring stewards in the late 1950s. Equally devastating for men in the career was the AIDS crisis of the 1980s, when various airlines exploited public panic to ground flight attendants with HIV/AIDS, even when medical experts dismissed the potential of such employees to endanger passengers' health and safety. In particular, Air

Canada flight attendant Gaëtan Dugas, known more often by his media-imposed alias "Patient Zero," demonstrated the potential of male flight attendants to elicit fear and anger at this panicked time. Despite a distinct lack of proof, gay journalist Randy Shilts succeeded in planting the idea among readers of his 1987 book *And the Band Played On* that this attractive, gay, unabashedly promiscuous flight attendant was the origin of America's AIDS epidemic.[6] Shilts interlaced accounts of "Patient Zero" throughout his 630-page tome on the early history of AIDS, all the while promoting the salacious theory that Dugas was responsible for the virus's entry into the United States and its initial spread from coast to coast.

While queer flight attendants today enjoy fuller equality than they did in the 1950s or 1980s, their accomplishments are still in jeopardy. At first glance, the benefit parity that airlines offer to gay, lesbian, and even transgender workers is impressive, including domestic partner health care coverage and travel benefits. At the same time, however, these same employers over the past decade have dramatically reduced wages and benefits, often using court-protected bankruptcy proceedings to rewrite labor contracts to the disadvantage of workers. Thus the expansion of benefits to queer employees has occurred in a climate that increasingly deprives all flight attendants—female and male, straight and gay, gender conforming and otherwise—of the financial means necessary to secure a middle-class standard of living. Consequently, the quest for queer equality that flight attendants have undertaken through the last eighty-plus years of commercial flight has been fraught with ups and downs and today is in a nosedive (to use a graphic aviation metaphor), propelled by the neoliberal economic pull of lower ticket prices at the expense of workers' livelihoods.

I am not the first to write of flight attendants' contributions to the U.S. civil rights legacy. In fact, I hope readers will examine my work alongside accounts by Kathleen Barry and Georgia Panter Nielsen.[7] These scholars have accentuated how this career became an important locus of "pink-collar" labor and activism, where stewardesses fought against work rules that kept them underpaid and oversexualized. Indeed, stewardesses were among the first women to flood the EEOC with sex-based discrimination complaints once the 1964 Civil Rights Act came into effect, and their legal efforts helped to professionalize this career and many other female-dominated workplaces. Quite reasonably, stewards are neglected in these histories, since they never endured the same indignities: rigorous weight checks, forced retirement upon marrying or reaching age thirty-two, pregnancy bans, and employer-sanctioned sexual harassment.[8]

Yet these preexisting histories thereby overlook the full extent of discrimination faced by flight attendants, including stewards' virtual banishment from the job at midcentury and increased scrutiny during the AIDS crisis. Recovering these additional experiences highlights how gender nonconformists and homosexuals endured pernicious inequality of their own (alongside that faced by the young, attractive, gender-conforming stewardess corps) and fought just as vigorously to overcome it. Often, queer rights and disability rights are deemed auxiliary pieces to America's civil rights legacy, which primarily foregrounds race-based struggles and women's rights efforts. By recovering the steward's neglected history dating back to the 1920s, we find that homophobia has been intimately entwined (and just as enduring) as sexism and that AIDS phobia, while more recent, has been just as intense.

Like Barry's *Femininity in Flight*, my work also occasionally follows flight attendants' struggles for equality beyond the workplace and into venues such as labor union deliberations, congressional records, EEOC proceedings, and courtroom arguments. *Plane Queer* highlights previously overlooked chapters in legal history that pertain to the plight for queer equality, from the rise of the "homosexual panic" defense (used in 1954 at the expense of an Eastern Air Lines steward named William Simpson), to the entanglement of homophobia with sex-based civil rights in the wake of the 1964 Civil Rights Act, and onward to the fight for equal workplace rights for people with HIV/AIDS.[9]

Legal scholars to this day treat *Diaz v. Pan Am* as a groundbreaking interpretation in gender discrimination law, since it forced greater scrutiny on employers' decisions to hire only one gender of employees for a certain job. But less familiar, even to many of these scholars, is *Diaz's* standing as one of the first and most successful gender discrimination cases brought by a man. While the mainstream media and right-wing commentators during the *Diaz* trial ridiculed the notion of male gender discrimination as a bizarre misappropriation of the law, some feminist legal scholars were intrigued. In particular, future Supreme Court justice Ruth Bader Ginsburg, who headed the ACLU's Women's Rights Project in the early 1970s, began to argue more cases on behalf of male plaintiffs. She envisioned a new and ultimately only partially accomplished legal goal: removing all government support for sexual stereotypes, whether for women undertaking notionally male roles or men like Diaz aspiring to notionally female roles.[10] *Plane Queer* thus offers a unique rendering of feminist legal history, which gains new texture by foregrounding male flight attendants and other similarly situated men.

Just as male flight attendants' history deepens our understanding of civil rights and legal history, so too does it complement previous scholarship on the origins of

America's gay subculture. These histories have detailed the genesis of a gay community in realms as diverse as the medical world, homophile activist circles, federal government policy, and, perhaps most importantly, the nightlife in industrialized U.S. cities.[11] The case of male flight attendants and their contributions to gay society suggests a new and as yet overlooked venue for gay community building: the workplace.[12] For gay flight attendants (and the passengers who suspected their stewards of being gay), the aisles and galleys of airplanes, as well as crew hotels and crash pads, served the same role that other gays and lesbians found in bars: a place where they could meet others like themselves and even embrace their same-sex desires for the first time.

This fact suggests a secondary meaning for the book's title: much as gay men forged a foothold in cities' bohemian scenes, they appropriated the airplane as a space where they belonged and secretly thrived. Planes—one of America's cherished symbols of progress and modernity—acquired a gay presence, thanks especially to the stewards who worked in them. In other words, stewards made the *plane queer*. The book proceeds from the fact that a sizable cadre of gay men worked in the skies to their gradual agitation for queer equality. In this way, this workplace follows a script that queer historians have noted in the gay nightlife circles that cautiously prospered in postwar America: numerous individuals' ostensibly apolitical motive of seeking out a place to belong ended up creating communities that could increasingly function as power bases in the fight for queer equality.[13]

Connected with reflections on flight attendants' contributions to gay life in America are two common sets of questions posed about my topic: *Just how gay has the male flight attendant corps been through the years? And how and why did the profession get to be so gay?* These are difficult questions to tackle. For one, there has never been a formalized effort to count gay or straight airline employees. After all, such figures are not required under federal or local employment laws and are not easily attained without infringing on workers' civil liberties. That said, I found that some gay flight attendants in various decades involved themselves in gossip aimed at discerning their coworkers' sexuality. Likewise, others I interviewed were quite willing to estimate the percentage of gays they worked with. According to their conclusions, between 30 and 50 percent of male flight attendants were gay in the 1950s, and between 50 and 90 percent in the 1970s. Speculation on today's corps of gay flight attendants tends closer to 50 percent, with lesbian and transgendered colleagues being a small but more prevalent contingent than ever before. Sometimes, too, as at Pan Am's San Francisco base in the 1950s, straight stewards took it upon themselves to make lists of gay flight attendants in the hopes that management would then weed out the men they uncovered. Such efforts were unsuccessful, however, as Pan Am's managers refused to act on these complaints.

A more successful, though less empirical, way to address these questions is to follow the line that historian Allen Bérubé developed in his work on queer ship stewards. His understanding of how and why certain careers become gay identified stresses the relationship between sexual identity and regimes governing gender and race in the workplace. Ship stewards, like airline stewards, performed work that was notionally feminine, primarily undertaking servile tasks to comfort customers. One ship official, when asked why his company hired so many gay men, simply replied, "If it wasn't for these boys, who else would we get to do this kind of women's work."[14] Yet as Bérubé aptly adds, men of color could also credibly perform such work in trains, hotels, and wealthy homes without raising suspicions of queerness. Indeed, the work that the all-male corps of African American railroad porters performed was quite similar to air and ship stewards' work, though porters never developed a reputation as gay.

Only when white men undertook such work did it become a noticeably queer job. Thus the air steward's gayness—presumed for all stewards and true for a good many of them—relied on U.S. airlines' racist hiring policies that largely remained in effect until after the 1964 Civil Rights Act. For several decades, no member of the flight crew at any airline could be African American or another racial minority, except for light-skinned Latinos whom Pan Am hired for their Latin American Division or Hawaiian-born stewards hired by United for their Honolulu flights after 1950. The result, as Bérubé states of ship stewards, was that "white gay men on the liners learned to racialize gay as white."[15] Simply stated, queer careers arose out of America's Jim Crow past. It took a series of exclusionary choices based on both gender and race for white men like flight attendants to stand out as gay. Indeed, for these men to become *plainly queer*, they first had to enter workplaces that were notionally feminine and predominantly white. When this career became queer is thus something we can pinpoint, even without knowing the details of how stewards identified sexually: it occurred in the very first decade of U.S. commercial aviation—in the 1930s—when stewardesses began to outnumber stewards and African American applicants were uniformly turned away.

The chapters of this book detail the undulations of tolerance and discrimination experienced by male flight attendants from the dawn of commercial aviation in the late 1920s through the post-AIDS crisis years of the late 1990s and 2000s. The development of the career shows that these men experienced sexism and homophobia as fluid, ever-changing variables. At certain times, male flight attendants—and, more specifically, gay male flight attendants—enjoyed a modicum of tolerance from the public and their coworkers. At other times, the animosity they faced threatened their livelihoods. While we might think that queer equality developed in history along a progressive trajectory, starting with very little traction in the earliest years and gaining increasing momentum as time went by, this is not the case. The deeper reality is that each decade has experienced a tenuous interplay between progress and regression. Even in ostensibly homophobic decades like the 1950s, flight attendants made impressive strides toward forging a gay-tolerant career. Yet at the very same time male flight attendants risked becoming objects of ridicule for segments of society that pushed back against such gains. Thus flight attendants' hard-won achievements toward gaining tolerance were rarely ever decisive, and even their most stellar victories, such as the *Diaz* court case, often were tinged with regressive characteristics as well.

Chapter 1 considers the late 1920s through the beginning of World War II. These years were the de facto heyday of stewards, even as stewardesses gradually became established as the preferred employees for this job. The 1930s saw varied reactions to stewards, from tolerance and even playfully campy portrayals of stewards as dapper fashion icons to deeply phobic responses to these seemingly unmanly men. In trying to explain this variety of responses, I place early aviation within its upper-class social milieu: the "gay" (in the sense of over-the-top and fun) nightlife of Prohibition-era cities. Since the airlines drew their customers from the cosmopolitan elite who frequented this opulent and flirtatiously androgynous nightlife, Pan Am and Eastern enjoyed greater freedom to hire stewards and promote them as dapper and sexually desirable. But especially as World War II loomed on the horizon a deeper discomfort with stewards surfaced, including the first evidence in the media and from airline archives that stewards fostered homophobic derision and animosity.

Chapter 2 is the first of two chapters that examine the steward's demise in the post–World War II era. This chapter focuses on the economic rationale behind the steward's expulsion, linking it to the cold war's military-industrial complex that took hold after the war. In the immediate postwar era, civil aviation settled into a second-class status versus military aviation in terms of aircraft development and supply. The airlines inherited thousands of decommissioned military planes, creating a vast oversupply of aircraft that altered their financial strategies considerably, forcing every airline to become more cost-efficient. I argue that stewards were the indirect casualties, "collateral damage," if you will, of this militarization of the industry. The oversupply of aircraft brought on by the war meant that stewards, with their higher salaries and longer tenures, were now less cost-effective than stewardesses. By reshaping the flight attendant corps as female only, postwar airlines realized significant payroll savings. The more the career was treated as women's work, the less the airlines had to pay flight attendants. Airlines were then also free to impose egregious work rules on stewardesses that men would never be expected to tolerate, including marriage bans and forced retirement in their mid-thirties.

Chapter 3 examines a related social development, the rise of homophobia in the postwar era, which also led to the steward's demise by the close of the 1950s. As normative models of American manhood increasingly embodied the ruggedness and adventuring of a soldier, stewards raised more eyebrows as failed men. In the early 1950s, insinuations against stewards circulated not only in rumor mills but also in salacious front-page headlines. Miami's newspapers took the lead, sensationalizing a gay sex tryst gone wrong: the murder in 1954 of an Eastern Air Lines steward, William Simpson, at the hands of two young male hustlers on a lovers' lane. The antigay hysteria in Miami following the murder solidified the link between gender transgression (men doing women's work) and sexual perversion, and it portrayed stewards as threats to normalcy and decency. In this climate, pressure grew on Eastern and Pan Am—both with strong ties to the Miami market—to stop hiring stewards. The career, seemingly, had become irretrievably feminized and the stewards too tied to homosexuality in the public's eyes. This homophobic stance was also adopted in the legal world, as the jury for the Simpson case acquiesced to the defense's claims of "homosexual panic" and refused to find his killers guilty of first-degree murder. This legal argument, effectively refuting gay men's standing as equal under the law, serves as important background for the civil rights legal discussions in the ensuing chapters.

Chapter 4 describes the social shock waves generated by the return of male flight attendants to the job after Celio Diaz successfully used the 1964 Civil Rights Act to reverse the airlines' female-only hiring practices. Diaz's legacy, though virtually unknown today, attests to queer Americans' deep investment in the civil rights moment of the 1960s, even though they were often seen as unwelcome in this movement. While many citizens were increasingly ready in the 1960s to extend legal equality to African Americans, they were far more reluctant to extend the same guarantees to women. Meanwhile, the idea of extending equality to homosexuals or gender nonconformists like male flight attendants was typically greeted with alarm. Incidents like the Simpson murder just a decade earlier had conditioned many to believe that gays and lesbians had no claim to equality, regardless of how neutrally the laws themselves were written. The awkward legal standing of queers becomes evident as the chapter traces the entanglements of Celio Diaz and male flight attendants with civil rights law from the dawn of the 1964 Civil Rights Act to the final decision in *Diaz v. Pan Am*.

In this light, I treat the *Diaz* case as a vitally important precursor to future queer equality victories. Even though Diaz himself wasn't gay, his victory in the courts helped establish limits on social conservatives' use of homophobia to block gender-based civil rights and prevent the inclusion of gays and lesbians into mainstream civil society. Of course, Diaz's victory also opened the doors for countless numbers of gay men to enter a relatively high-paying, unionized, and public relations-oriented career. The flight attendant corps would become a new sort of workplace by the 1970s, increasingly responsive not only to women's rights but also to queer rights.

Chapter 5 examines the flight attendant corps of the 1970s, paying particular attention to how the workplace changed with this new influx of gay men. With thirty-five years of hindsight since first hiring a man, a former member of American Airlines' hiring committee nowadays identifies a deeper import to the post-*Diaz* flight attendant corps: "The collision of women's liberation and the outing of sexuality created an explosion that changed the airline industry beyond recognition."[16] To a certain degree, the whole of American society experienced a similar explosion in the 1970s, the heyday of women's liberation and maturation period of gay rights. But because the flight attendant corps was disproportionately female and gay male, it experienced this culture shock much sooner and more acutely than the rest of U.S. society. Flight attendants were in the avant-garde of this major social upheaval. This chapter covers this "explosion" in greater detail, examining how women and gays cooperated—and sometimes fought—in both the workplace and the union hall to find common ground that respected all employees: male or female, straight or gay.

I also link these developments with the considerable backlash against a feminist, progay ethic, whether from airline executives or larger conservative social movements. These increasingly severe skirmishes in the culture war also influenced the legal legacy of *Diaz v. Pan Am*, as conservatives continued to portray women's rights initiatives like the Equal Rights Amendment as backdoor pathways for queers to gain equal rights. Meanwhile, as progressives like Ruth Bader Ginsburg made male plaintiffs key to her legal strategy in the 1970s, others increasingly bemoaned such support for men as misguided and counterproductive. By the close of the decade, *Diaz* risked being orphaned even by champions of women's rights and gay rights.

Chapter 6 begins to examine the most heart-wrenching, darkest days of the flight attendant corps. All of the flight attendants I interviewed regard AIDS as a deeply personal tragedy that took from them coworkers and dear friends. The workplace was filled with talk—though most of it still hushed—of funerals, extended sick leaves, new therapies, and the occasional hopeful signs of recovery. Tears still well up in many of my interviewees over a decade after the worst of the dying has ended. "AIDS was devastating for us," was the common refrain.[17] Male flight attendants also became more acutely aware than other workers of how AIDS was a political, not just a personal, tragedy. After all, their careers were being threatened both by the epidemic's health dimensions and by the political response of conservatives seeking to use AIDS as a bludgeon against gay civil rights. The demonization of Air Canada steward Gaëtan Dugas, better known as "Patient Zero," illustrates the ways that flight attendants became embroiled in these pitched social battles over AIDS. This chapter details the facts of Dugas's life and the state of the "Patient Zero" myth circa 1984, before Shilts circulated the myth in his book.

I also chronicle the plight of another flight attendant with AIDS, whose legacy—while less known—warrants equal attention. United Airlines flight attendant Gär Traynor was also diagnosed with AIDS very early in the crisis. But his response to his diagnosis ultimately offered a more positive basis for overcoming AIDS phobia. When his employer, citing passengers' and coworkers' fears of contagion, permanently grounded him in June 1983, Traynor and his union fought back. In a key 1984 legal victory, Traynor became one of the first people with AIDS (PWAs) in the United States to win the right to return to work, a precedent that was replicated in subsequent court decisions and in the 1990 Americans with Disabilities Act.

Chapter 7 traces these two rival legacies regarding AIDS and flight attendants—Dugas's castigation as a scapegoat and Traynor's role as an advocate combating marginalization—into the 1990s. The chapter begins with the 1987 release of Randy Shilts's book *And the Band Played On* and his portrayal of Dugas as the origin of the epidemic in America. My analysis confirms long-standing assertions by scholars and AIDS activists that Gaëtan Dugas was not the first American with AIDS.[18] Instead, Shilts's editor, Michael Denneny, confirmed to me that Shilts manipulated the "Patient Zero" narrative to garner media publicity for the book. Denneny claims that the subsequent media frenzy saved *And the Band Played On* from obscurity, vaulting it onto the best-seller list. With so much attention focused on Dugas, flight attendants—though they certainly did not ask for such a role—were now implicated in the larger social and political battles over AIDS, post-Stonewall gay sexual practices, and workplace rights for PWAs. Flight attendants and their employers were more passive actors than Shilts, social conservatives, and AIDS activists in this fight, but they helped determine whether PWAs would be quarantined out of the public sphere.

Indeed, the airlines ultimately helped to defuse the hysteria embodied by "Patient Zero." Just months after Shilts released his salacious account, United Airlines finally stopped its long-established practice of grounding flight attendants with AIDS. And by 1993, American Airlines was working hard to overcome its previous AIDS-phobic and homophobic reputation to become the United States' first self-proclaimed "gay-friendly" airline. Such practices didn't completely dispel the indignation directed at Gaëtan Dugas and his fellow male flight attendants, but it did decisively marginalize social conservatives, at least in the corporate boardroom and in corporately administered public spaces like airplanes. Airlines like American and United had rather abruptly switched allegiances in the culture war, even as AIDS hysteria was still potent.

Chapter 8 examines the increasingly gay-friendly era of aviation since the 1990s, during the peak of America's neoliberal economic policies. Gay and lesbian flight attendants won more benefits as the 1990s progressed, including flight privileges for their domestic partners and, by 2001, health benefits for partners. While such developments seem to make the 1990s the ideal conclusion to the topsy-turvy history of male flight attendants and their encounters with homophobia, they are not as one-dimensionally optimistic. Indeed, following work of other queer scholars, I explain how expanding gay civil rights via the private sector is fraught with danger.[19] Just as gay flight attendants have attained parity with their straight peers, all of them have endured unprecedented pay cuts and the loss of collective bargaining power. Along these lines, I consider the plight of disgruntled JetBlue flight attendant Steven Slater, who became an instant celebrity in 2010 when he walked off his job by deploying the plane's emergency slide and sauntering across the JFK Airport tarmac toward his waiting car. Slater embodies how male flight attendants, even if they are no longer discriminated for being gay or HIV positive, nonetheless experience their work as undignified and underpaid in the cutthroat economic age of deregulation, airline bankruptcies, and court-monitored reorganizations.

The conclusion summarizes my findings on the quest for queer equality in the eighty-plus-year career of the male flight attendant. It especially focuses on this fact: while these men have always stood out as *plainly queer* in the long expanse of commercial aviation history, the intensity of the animus directed against them has shifted considerably through the years. Certain decades stand out as particularly sexist and/or homophobic, while others have been more tolerant. These undulations, I conclude, are consequences of deeper economic and legal factors. Sexism and homophobia became most pronounced when there was economic gain to be had by marginalizing these men. Similarly, tolerance predominated when the airlines stood to benefit from treating these men well. All of these financial calculations took place amid a similarly evolving legal landscape; the expansion of civil rights laws tended to alter the financial calculus of discrimination to stewards' benefit, while legal innovations like "homosexual panic" had the opposite effect.

Overall, this investigation of a queer workplace exposes how sexism and homophobia are undergirded by deeper economic and legal developments. It is not enough to countenance male flight attendants as just *plain queer;* they are also people with fluid legal standing and evolving economic value. Recounting the history of male flight attendants and the quest for queer equality allows us to consider these multiple factors—queerness, economics, and the law—in tandem, arguably even more effectively than in the ways queer community histories have been written to date.

From histories of the flight attendant profession it would be easy to come away
with the notion that America's first flight attendant was a woman. Many accounts
describe how a savvy Iowa nurse, Ellen Church, approached executives at Boeing
Air Transport (the predecessor of United Airlines) in 1930 and prevailed on them
to usher in a new female member of their flight crews who would keep passengers
comfortable and assist them in emergencies. Far fewer accounts mention that such
jobs actually existed before Church and that men, not women, held them. Pan Am's
inaugural flight between Key West and Havana on January 16, 1928, could be just
as immortalized in flight attendant histories as Church's first flight over two years
later. An artist's rendering of the 1928 flight (figure 1) shows the airline's very first
flight attendant, a nineteen-year-old Cuban American named Amaury Sanchez,
standing in his black-and-white uniform and greeting passengers as they board the
Fokker F-7 plane. While a few other men served before him, Sanchez was the first
U.S. flight attendant on a so-called "legacy carrier," and in that sense he represents
the beginning of a line of men and women who would make their careers as airborne
ambassadors of reassurance, charm, and service.[1]

Over time, however, Ellen Church's hiring has been remembered and Sanchez's
almost entirely forgotten. After all, the more familiar understanding of the profession as female dominated begins with Church. Labor historian Kathleen Barry
has correctly noted that the flight attendant career "took permanent shape in the
1930s as 'women's work.'"[2] Certainly, by the 1950s, popular media like the *Satur-*

FIGURE 1.

Artist John T. McCoy Jr.'s rendering of "Pan American's first passenger flight—Key West, Florida, to Havana, Cuba, January 16, 1928—Fokker F-7," 1963. Courtesy Smithsonian National Air and Space Museum.

day Evening Post could matter-of-factly misreport the origins of the career: Ellen Church "was hired by United to work their flight between two Western cities, and to recruit other girls for similar duty. She did so and a profession was started."[3] Indeed, when Eddie Rickenbacker, then CEO of Eastern Air Lines, introduced his plans for a male-only flight attendant corps in late 1936, the *Washington Post* went so far as to belittle these men as "male hostesses," suggesting they were interlopers in an already well-established female realm. "Capt. E. V. Rickenbacker confessed yesterday he is simmering in a nice kettle of fish," the reporter noted, "because he proposes to install flight stewards or, if you prefer, male 'hostesses' on Eastern Air Lines planes."[4] In just half a decade, even as men like Sanchez still held all positions in Pan Am's flight attendant corps, Eastern's stewards were seen as gender misfits.

Rickenbacker withstood these attacks, and significant numbers of men continued to take the job. In fact, Eastern maintained a male-only corps of flight attendants up until the labor shortage of World War II, and Pan Am did the same, from the time of Sanchez's hiring until 1944. Thanks to these two airlines, men during the 1930s constituted around one-third of flight attendants.[5] Thus, compared to the female-dominated fields of nursing or typing, where women in the 1930s held over 95 percent of positions, the flight attendant profession was still an extensively gender-integrated space.[6] But these publicly disparaged "male hostesses" were clearly flying into cultural headwinds. As all-white or light-skinned Latino men performing servile work customarily reserved for women or men of color, they elicited deep anxieties surrounding the evolution of gender and sexuality norms in Jim Crow America.

It is anachronistic to speak of a "gay" flight attendant corps that endured "homophobia" in the 1930s. In those years, unlike the postwar years, homosexuality was a barely choate identity category. It found expression mainly in scientific tomes as a sexual pathology and in a rather limited urban nightlife that grew up alongside the other illicit pleasures of Prohibition-era America.[7] In addition, explicit sources such as memoirs or corporate records on homosexuality in the steward corps do not exist, which means I have no ability to assess stewards' actual sexual behaviors and attitudes.

To speak of "homophobia" is also, therefore, problematic. In fact, even if stewards' sexual identities were known, it would be enormously difficult to discern when they experienced discrimination based on sexuality rather than gender. As these men walked the tenuous cultural line identified by Barry—and, more polemically, the *Washington Post*—that sought to cleanly divide male and female realms, we know they experienced discrimination that belittled these men as women. This cultural response is easily construed as homophobic, and I do, in fact, use the term in this manner.[8] Yet such discrimination actually depended on the culture's sexism that rigidly restricted male and female social roles. Similarly, the fact that the African American men performing the same servile tasks as Pullman porters on trains never elicited derision as "male hostesses" shows that such epithets depended on America's racism as well.

My primary focus in this chapter is stewards' unconventional gender performance in the 1930s. I especially scrutinize remnant public relations materials, assessing the degree that stewards were portrayed as either appropriately masculine or deficiently so. I also examine what links may have existed between the steward's public image and the nascent gay (homosexual) subculture of the 1930s. The first half of this chapter examines the steward within his socioeconomic milieu, as an employee designed to appeal to the white, wealthy, cosmopolitan urban dwellers who made up the lion's share of air travelers in the 1930s.[9] These customers, who were predominantly men, had already acclimated themselves to what I call the "gay"—in quotation marks—lifestyle that arose in the Prohibition era, where opulence comingled with illegality and sexual adventure.[10] While this social scene was not "gay" in a sense synonymous with "homosexual," participants did embrace a softer version of masculinity that emphasized the pursuit of libidinal pleasure, and some homosexual encounters were tolerated, even if only a fraction of men chose to engage in them. While the steward could not aspire to participate fully in this eccentric lifestyle because of his working-class status, he was groomed by Pan Am's and Eastern's public relations departments to cater to this softer upper-class masculinity. In this sense, stewards of the day belonged—at least aesthetically, from an examination of their uniforms and other public relations materials—to the more fluid gender and sexuality norms that typified the "gay" life of the urban elite.

The second half of the chapter examines the first stirrings of homophobia (in the sense of a virulent sexism) directed at the steward. Interestingly, more than just external observers like the *Washington Post* journalist belittled stewards for their inadequate masculinity. Eastern's and Pan Am's own public relations materials betrayed a degree of apprehension that at times surpassed the *Post*'s. This section examines both an Eastern article on a steward's "diaper drama" (changing a baby's diaper in flight) and a violently demeaning comic published by Pan Am in their respective in-flight magazines. As indicated by the discomfort that even their employers displayed, stewards of the 1930s had undertaken a troubling social role, even if they were spared the more explicit homophobia of the postwar moment.

The chapter also details how technology played a vital role in casting the steward as a social outcast. Here my work relies heavily on previous historians, who have begun to stress the "mutual shaping" that occurs between technological and social innovation.[11] In terms of gender, historians now realize that "the boundaries between how people designated male are expected to behave and how people designated female are expected to behave are sometimes redefined, negotiated, or violated" by technology.[12] Regarding flight attendants, I add one important element to Kathleen Barry's work stressing the feminization of the career in the 1930s: I show how new technology, when coupled with the culture's sexism, helped render stewards ever more queer as the decade progressed.

The release in 1936 of the two most advanced pre–World War II aircraft—the DC-3, heralded as the first modern passenger aircraft, and the Pan American Clipper, the largest passenger plane to date—played a particularly important role in defining stewards as unmanly. These innovations allowed the airlines for the first time to credibly domesticate the cabin and assert this realm as decidedly feminine.[13] Airplanes were now safe and comfortable, thereby permitting an influx of new female passengers and even children. With his work increasingly devoted to catering to customers as they reclined in spaces more evocative of their own living rooms, the steward seemed increasingly out of place. Technology was thus central to ostracizing this group of men, opening them to derision as laughable "male hostesses."

"GAY" TAKES OFF

It was sheer coincidence that the 1920s marked both the rise of commercial aviation and one of the most formative moments for gay male communities. Yet the location of both these innovations in America's largest cities increased the likelihood that they would become intertwined. As historian George Chauncey points out, the term *gay* held multiple meanings during this period. When referring to the lifestyle of America's Prohibition-era elites, it connoted flamboyance, awareness of cultural fashion, fun, and transgressions that could be enjoyed by straights and gays alike. It also held strong overtones of illegality, because of patrons' indulgence in alcohol and their dabblings in sexual vice, including renowned Broadway "pansy shows."[14] The sexual connotations of the term go back at least to the nineteenth century, when *gay* referred to female prostitutes and brothels. In the 1920s and 1930s, however, the term was innocent enough that a morally upstanding person could use it to express her enjoyment of a night out at the theater, but still edgy enough to suggest sexual illicitness.

For men in this upper-crust "gay" culture, traditional notions of masculinity were being reworked. Prohibition-era cosmopolitan men were expected to indulge in customarily feminine activities: they knew how to dress well, manicure themselves, and dance like Fred Astaire. Their social lives often revolved around Broadway shows, speakeasies, and, for some, brothels, all venues that tolerated more promiscuous heterosexual and/or same-sex desires. As Chauncey summarizes, these men lived in a "time when the culture of the speakeasies and the 1920s' celebration of affluence and consumption . . . undermined conventional sources of masculine identity."[15]

Note that these "gay" developments were affecting heterosexual men at the time, ostensibly having nothing to do with one's sexual object choice. That said, homosexuals moved in the 1920s and 1930s to appropriate *gay* as a self-identifier, regardless of their class status. The more effeminate so-called "fairies" were the first to do so, since they more fully embodied the traits of fashionability, gender transgression, and emotional excess that the term denoted even in the larger culture. Thus, by the early 1930s, at least in major cities like New York, *gay* maintained two separate but closely related meanings. It was now synonymous with *fairy* but also retained a nonhomosexual meaning of frivolity, whose potential impact was to increase effeminacy in all men.[16]

The airlines saw an influx of "gay" culture from two different sources. First, the same wealthy patrons of the "gay" nightlife were also the airlines' core customer base, which is hardly surprising given air travel's status as a prohibitively expensive luxury in the 1930s. Only the very rich could afford to pay the significant premium over rail tickets. And only men were expected to be daring enough to fly on airplanes, much less be gainfully employed by the few corporations willing to pay for plane tickets. In addition to these wealthy cosmopolitan customers, Pan Am hired male flight attendants, who became "gay" icons themselves, because the airline proceeded to ensconce them in the style and opulence expected by the elite men they served. Following the example of other white male service professionals in cities—think of bellhops, doormen, ship stewards, and elevator attendants—Pan Am stewards became fashionable accessories catering to this elite, adorned in military-inspired suits, and changing into white sport coats and gloves when serving meals aboard planes.

Stewards' fashionable dress and access to high-society clientele, even if they didn't share their customers' exalted class status, also probably drew envious attention from some in the "fairy" community. In his study of early twentieth-century gay erotica, art historian Thomas Waugh notes a particular fascination with men in service-related jobs. He asks rhetorically: "What to make of the recurring iconography of young men in service occupations such as bellhops?"[17] Waugh is particularly struck by the contrast with post-World War II pornography. While this later material emphasizes more macho imagery, the prewar items tend to fetishize male softness. Something about a man's servile softness stood out, to many "fairies" at least, as deeply homoerotic.

Ideas about male softness and homoeroticism aside, the work aboard airplanes in commercial aviation's earliest years was a mixture of both notionally masculine and feminine tasks. For this reason, it would be inaccurate to see early stewards as transgressors into a decidedly feminized realm. Air transport until the mid-1930s was quite dangerous and downright unpleasant. One early customer on a twelve-passenger Ford tri-motor plane, one of the first planes large enough to accommodate a flight attendant, confessed: "When the day was over, my bones ached, and my whole nervous system was wearied from the noise, the constant droning of the propellers and exhaust in my face."[18] The cabins were not heated or air conditioned, nor were they soundproofed or pressurized. Vomiting was so prevalent that all passengers were furnished with "burp cups" akin to spittoons. Facing such unpleasantness while paying a premium over the cost of rail travel, early air passengers surely welcomed the added touch of a flight attendant to cater to their comfort. But airline executives were uncertain whether the hostile environment required a flight attendant with manly fortitude or the comforting touch of a woman.

Reflecting how this job rested atop America's gender fault line, the initial flight attendant work descriptions, whether at Pan Am or at airlines like United that hired only women, were more varied than in later years. All flight attendants were expected to pitch in on notionally manly ground duties. As Inez Keller, an original stewardess at United in 1930, remembers, "We had to carry all of the luggage on board. . . . Some of us had to join bucket brigades to help fuel the airplanes [and] we also helped pilots push planes into hangars."[19] Along these lines, Pan Am's stewards also were responsible for rowing passengers ashore from their seaplanes (which the airline favored until after World War II), handling customs paperwork, and buying provisions in South American markets for the return flight.

Once everyone was on board, however, the job description was more tied to comforting passengers: after assigning seats, flight attendants passed out packages of cotton for the droning noise and chewing gum for the altitude shifts. They then served food, which in the earliest years was typically a boxed lunch of cold or steamed chicken. Other than that, as Pan Am's first steward, Amaury Sanchez, noted, "My only instructions were to keep people happy and not too scared."[20] This rather open job description led flight attendants to improvise a great deal and undertake a wide variety of tasks that straddled the nebulous line between men's work and women's work: changing diapers, shining shoes, reassuring nervous flyers, or playing a quick game of gin rummy.

These service-oriented tasks drew far more attention from the airlines' public relations departments than flight attendants' safety roles or physically demanding work. This was especially true of the stewardesses, all of whom were required to have a nursing certificate to better prepare them to assist in emergencies. Yet any focus on nursing skills reinforced just how dangerous even routine air trips could be. Public relations departments therefore preferred to highlight stewardesses' regard for passengers and their sexual availability. With an assist from Hollywood's first of many stewardess movies, *Air Hostess*, in 1933, female flight attendants became associated with comfort and sexuality. The film's advertising poster contained the provocative moniker, "She went up in the air for romance and thrills . . ."[21]

While *Air Hostess* marked the beginning of America's decades-long and well-publicized heterosexual love affair with stewardesses, the flip side of this erotic fascination has so far remained undocumented: starting in 1933, stewards also were marketed as alluring sex objects. The fictitious public relations persona known as "Rodney the Smiling Steward" became the most famous male steward of the 1930s (figure 2).

1,000,000
SILENT SALESMEN
On the Road for Pan American

Pan American salesmen—one million of them—waiting in travel bureaus, and railway stations, standing at the counter in telegraph offices and consolidated airline ticket offices! Silent, suave, persuasive, eloquent, ready to nab the prospective traveler and sell him a ticket "via Pan American" before he knows what has happened to him.

This is the latest step in the campaign to divert to Latin America a share of that stream of tourist traffic and tourist dollars which year after year flows across the ocean to the old world.

"The new idea in winter travel," is the name of these new salesmen. Each is a gay little booklet, bright with the color of sunshine and filled with pictures designed to tell people more convincingly than words can do, the story of color-filled countries and glamorous cities a few hours from northern icebound lands.

That they are putting new ideas in people's minds, is indicated by the increasing traffic and the growing interest shown in the system, both by travelers and by travel agencies.

Pleasure travelers in greater numbers are beginning to think in terms of the West Indies, Mexico, Central and South America. Commercial travelers are beginning in greater numbers to turn naturally to Pan American as the logical transport system to carry them to the important commercial markets of the southern republics.

The first step in sending out these silent salesmen was a letter campaign to travel agents, designed to tell them where our routes are, how to use our services, and how to sell them.

Next, the leading telegraph companies were interested in selling our services. Travel agents and railway and airline ticket offices were induced to distribute many thousands of the booklets, and the two telegraph companies requested an additional half million for their own use. The result is that one out of every twelve Americans at a conservative estimate this year is reading the story of winter travel "via Pan American".

To aid in the distribution, striking photographic cutouts of a steward in Pan American uniform were devised.

"RODNEY," THE SMILING STEWARD, WHOSE MISSION IN LIFE IS TO GIVE AWAY THE "NEW IDEA" BOOKLET

ONE OF THE MILLION "SILENT SALESMEN" NOW ON THE ROAD FOR PAN-AMERICAN.

...The new idea in winter travel

These life-sized figures stand in leading railway terminals, travel agencies, and ticket offices. Each one, courteously smiling, offers a small box filled with the booklets.

The same figure in a smaller size stands on the counter of many agencies, bowing, smiling and distributing booklets so rapidly that it almost requires the services of a real man to keep them supplied with booklets to give away.

As a further means of attracting attention, a few giant copies of the book have been made photographically for use in the windows of travel agencies. Here, a live "steward" stands behind the book and turns the pages as the crowds outside stare and learn of Pan American.

This campaign has attracted much attention and discussion, all of which helps to spread the Pan American story.

15

FIGURE 2.

"Rodney the Smiling Steward." *Pan American Airways Magazine*, March 1933, 15. Courtesy of Special Collections, University of Miami Libraries, Coral Gables, FL.

The "Rodney" marketing campaign involved placing hundreds of life-sized, full-color cutouts of the steward in train stations and travel agencies all along the East Coast and as far west as Chicago. The goal of the promotion was the same as most airline marketing strategies through the 1950s: to lure the wealthy clientele of train and ship lines to Pan Am's international air routes. But the use of a male steward as the company's publicity ambassador would never again be replicated at Pan Am until after the 1970s, reflecting just how unique the steward's moment of visibility was. Rodney's short life span and his subsequent consignment to public relations obscurity both testify to his softer version of masculinity, which for a brief while in the 1930s enjoyed a higher degree of social acceptability among Pan Am's wealthy prospective clientele.

The "Rodney" campaign accentuated the steward's softer features, especially his dashing good looks and elegance when adorned in his formal black-and-white uniform with red highlights. With his smile and slightly cocked head, Rodney combined both youthful attractiveness and an approachability that invited people to size him up, thereby placing him in the notionally feminized role of alluring sex object. According to Pan Am's corporate newsletter, Rodney had tremendous potency in this regard, at least in its own offices: "From all the comments, Rodney has made quite a hit. . . . We thought he would, ever since the first day he was brought into the office for final inspection, suntanned, shoes shined, close-shaved and all, and the ladies deserted their typewriters to flock around."[22]

Stewards shared these alluring physical qualities with other working-class men in the service industry, but their role as icons of style stood out against more widespread images of working-class masculinity: the exceptionally muscular images of white male factory workers and agricultural laborers (think of those popularized in WPA art), or the renderings of doting but safely asexual black train porters, busboys, and the like. The conflation of the steward's white skin and his job's fashionable servility drew him closer toward the aesthetic excesses of the dandified urban "fairies." His suntan, dapper dress, and well-manicured face emulated those of the wealthy (largely heterosexual) playboys of high-society Midtown or Harlem speakeasies, while his class status placed him in a more passive role of serving other men and using his charm to accrue favor. A 1938 interview that *Washington Post* columnist Tom McCarthy conducted with Eastern Air Lines steward Bill Hutchison again emphasized these same characteristics seen in the "Rodney" campaign, highlighting the job's emphasis on male physical beauty. "Besides having to pass rigid physical examinations," the article notes of stewards, "they've got to watch their diet as closely as a movie star. When the needle on the weighing machine goes beyond 150 pounds they're likely to have outgrown their job." Coupled with this rigorous weight regimen came a preoccupation with suntanning: "What Bill was worrying about, particularly, when I saw him was not what he'd do when he got tired of being a flight steward, but rather what the March winds were going to do to his red and painful Florida sunburn."[23]

Stewards' white skin was an essential physical trait that reinforced their softness, or, if you will, their "gayness." In the very train stations where Pan Am placed the life-sized Rodney cutouts, thousands of African American men held very similar jobs but never attained the status of sexualized public relations agents. Indeed, the railroads chose these men in part because of their supposed sexual undesirability. In his study of Pullman train porters, journalist and author Larry Tye notes that porters' dark skin—when coupled with the predominant racism of the time—meant that "passengers could regard them as part of the furnishings rather than a mortal with likes, dislikes, and a memory." This ability to effectively become "an invisible man" allowed porters intimate access to the sleeping quarters and changing rooms of white men and women.[24] Thus, just as he never attained the status of a sex object, the Pullman porter also never became an ambassador of the newly crystallizing "gay" subculture that arose in America's largest cities during the pre–World War II era.

The sexual history of stewards and stewardesses on planes was quite a different story. In their workplace, the primary object of 1930s sexual desire, white skin, was placed in arm's length of the passenger. Since no airline hired African Americans as flight attendants until the civil rights era of the late 1950s, the entire career was dominated by white women and men.[25] Stewardesses bore the brunt of this newly unleashed sexual desire. Many male passengers showered affection on these women and also sought out their company once the plane landed. A stewardess from 1939 noted, "You never have a trip that two or three or four men won't ask you to dinner or a luncheon."[26] Hollywood only stoked the notion of stewardesses' sexual availability. The famed actress Joan Bennett, who played a stewardess in the 1936 film *Thirteen Hours by Air*, enticed men by giving them advice on how to score a date with a real stewardess. Her words advanced a prevailing view and also exposed the galling willingness of the airlines to force their stewardesses into sexual roles: "If you ask her for a date," commented Bennett, "she is obliged to say, 'Yes, sir,' and accept. It is a company rule on all airlines!"[27]

Nothing of the sort would be expected of male stewards, given deeply entrenched social codes that required men to initiate sexual advances with women and forced male-male sexual encounters to play out with furtive exchanged glances and the subterfuge of double entendres (including the term *gay* itself). Such codes ultimately made stewards much more difficult to deploy as erotic ambassadors for the airlines, just as stewardesses' nursing skills were hard to market in delicate and appealing ways. Thus, in relatively short order, Rodney and other steward-centered public relations efforts were overshadowed by efforts from Hollywood, newspapers, and the airlines themselves to promote stewardesses as the most enchanting sexual newcomers of the decade. But that is not to say that the steward immediately disappeared as a public relations ambassador. Instead, his role simply became more limited. Meanwhile, with the rise of new aviation technology, these marketing attempts centering on stewards became even more suspect as "gay," at times suggesting outright homoeroticism.

GREAT STRIDES IN TECHNOLOGY, GREAT MISGIVINGS ABOUT MASCULINITY

The year 1936 featured phenomenal advances in civilian air travel, empowered by significant innovations in aircraft technology. It saw the introduction of the world's most successful (in terms of being the longest serving, safest, and most widespread) aircraft of the pre–World War II era: the Douglas Corporation's DC-3. Indeed, the DC-3 dominated the skies for the next two decades, becoming the workhorse for the world's major airlines well into the 1950s and serving as the preferred transport plane for the Allied militaries in World War II. An even grander plane debuted that same year: the Pan American Clipper (a seaplane originally manufactured by Sikorsky and later by Boeing), which boasted the largest payload and longest range of any civilian vessel. The Clipper was the world's first flying behemoth and allowed Pan Am to initiate service all the way from San Francisco to China. The DC-3 and the Clipper could fly transcontinental or overseas routes, increasing flight times from just a couple hours in the air to full overnight trips. In fact, Pan Am's record-long 2,400-mile nonstop flight from San Francisco to Honolulu would spend almost a full day in the air. These new planes also doubled capacity, accommodating at least twenty-one passengers each.

Air travel after 1936 was consequently a very different experience than before, for both passengers and flight attendants. Both of the latest aircraft offered passengers greater comforts, starting with a smoother ride, a climate-controlled environment, and a cabin with improved soundproofing. The lack of air pressure still required pilots to stay below a ten-thousand-foot ceiling, which made for a bumpy ride at times, but the aerodynamics of the DC-3 in particular (with its wings integrated in the body of the aircraft) significantly lessened the risk of accidents. Seeking to emulate the luxury of rail travel, the airlines commissioned top industrial designers like Raymond Loewy and Donald Deskey to outfit the new planes' interiors. Passengers now enjoyed stylish and comfortable touches, including fancy sitting lounges with plush reclining seats, designated dining tables, sleeping chambers with bunks more spacious than those on trains, warm meals prepared in-flight, and movies projected on the front wall of the cabin.[28] While still not a perfect emulation, airplane interiors increasingly invoked the opulence of ship or train interiors and permitted many of the creature comforts of one's own home.

As historian David Courtwright notes, this move toward greater safety and comfort permitted the first significant diversification of airlines' clientele. Airline marketing executives promoted their new planes as female-friendly and child-safe, hoping to cash in on their easiest growth demographic: wives and families of the wealthy businessmen who already were frequent flyers. After all, these potential customers enjoyed the same class status as their wealthy husbands and fathers, making them uniquely able to afford the airlines' prohibitively expensive product. Thus airlines like United created a simple marketing strategy designed to appeal foremost to women: "Tell them how comfortable they'll be, how delicious the meals are, how capable the stewardesses are, how luxurious their surroundings will be, and you can 'sell' women on air travel. Leave the 'revolutions per minute' to the men."[29]

As this quote suggests, flight attendants' jobs were increasingly tied to more feminine tasks like cooking and providing comfort to passengers. For the first time, stewards and stewardesses were expected to prepare full meals in flight, as both the DC-3 and the Clipper boasted galleys fully stocked with ovens and refrigerators. Meanwhile, the work of providing for passengers' comfort also increased the potential for passengers and flight attendants to establish erotic ties, albeit in subtle ways. This increase in erotic potential may well have led more customers—over 75 percent of whom were men—to prefer stewardesses over stewards.[30] After all, as airplanes approached the opulence of Pullman cars, flight attendants now might touch their passengers when passing them a pillow or tucking them under a blanket. Their gazes might also be palpable to passengers disrobing behind curtains in Pan Am's or United's sleeper cabins. Some first-time travelers' raw nerves offered other opportunities for intimate touch. One steward noted in a 1938 *Washington Post* article that his gender actually benefited him in this regard, since a good number of these new fliers were women. He recounted that nervous female passengers often wanted him to hold their hands: "Now, I'd been instructed on how to make a nervous passenger feel at ease. But they never told me I ought to hold the lady's hand."[31]

At the same time, some aspects of these technological innovations actually made the flight attendant's job stand out as more masculine. Most important in this regard, with passenger capacity now doubled and a myriad of new tasks the job became more complex and hierarchical. Two or three attendants now staffed flights, and their work roles were increasingly varied. Some executives like Eastern's CEO Eddie Rickenbacker, the famed World War I fighting ace, found men to be the obvious choice for this more complex job. In October 1936 he made the decision to hire only men as flight attendants for the dawn of the DC-3 age, even though the company had hired only women a few years earlier.[32] His reasoning was grounded in traditional sexism rather than some novel desire to promote gender transgression: "Women have shown themselves extremely heroic in emergencies. Nobody can take that away from them. . . . But planes are getting bigger, there is more to do in them, and men are the logical answer."[33]

This raw invocation of male privilege did not go unchallenged. In fact, Rickenbacker's announcement placed his company—and the flight steward—in the heart of a public relations battle over gender and work. One *Washington Post* reporter referenced Rickenbacker's World War I heroics to emphasize the magnitude of public displeasure, which, in his words, "promises to make his toughest battle with an enemy plane appear tame before this 'steward vs. hostess' war is over."[34] Yet the adversaries in this so-called "war" were more difficult to identify than the *Post* article made it seem. The reporter suggested that the discontent came from feminist circles. The headline stated that "feminists" were "aroused" by Eastern's plan, while the article itself employed even more colorful language: "When Rickenbacker revealed his line was planning to add stewards, feminists lost no time in hopping on his weatherbeaten neck. What was the idea, they wanted to know, hiring men for work that women have proved they can do capably?" While the article certainly references a plausible feminist grievance, the reporter offers no names and fails to quote anyone espousing these views.

Eastern was quick to tamp down concerns about stewards by inviting First Lady Eleanor Roosevelt, America's most politically connected woman, who later became outspoken on feminist issues, aboard an early flight. According to Eastern's in-house publication, the *Great Silver Fleet News*, Mrs. Roosevelt "comes right out and says what she thinks." And in this case, stewards received her seal of approval: "The flight stewards," she noted, "are most courteous and helpful."[35]

Just as likely as a feminist critique of stewards is another possibility: that men who enjoyed being served by stewardesses were deeply upset with the airline's decision.

The same article suggesting feminists' arousal actually was placed in the *Post's* Section X, an addendum to the Sports section. Littered with college football scores and advertisements for men's clothes, the section clearly had an overwhelmingly male readership. Moreover, the article's cheeky tone is reminiscent of fraternity-house conversations, as it starts off with the previously quoted description of stewards as "male hostesses." Thus, even before Eastern's stewards made their inaugural voyage, other men were already ridiculing them for their perceived effeminacy.

Rickenbacker's decision exposed a rift within male chauvinist circles. Despite invoking sexist reasoning for his male-only policy, Rickenbacker had alienated a demographic essential for the airline's survival: the macho pilot corps and the unchaperoned businessmen who were his core customers. In this internecine war among chauvinists, Rickenbacker mixed economic reasons and aggressive bravado to defend his actions, always sidestepping the claim that stewards were failed men. At a closed-door meeting, facing a hostile crowd of his own pilots who wanted to know why he had changed the policy, Rickenbacker baldly replied, "Because you bastards are making enough dough to buy your own pussy!"[36] And in reference to the laments of his core customer base of businessmen, he noted, in slightly less colorful terms, "If passengers want to fool around with girls, let 'em do it at their expense, not mine."[37]

His comments, while flippant, expose an underlying economic reality behind the commodification of stewardesses' bodies: selling female sex appeal could become prohibitively expensive for the airlines. Stewardesses actually commanded the same wage as men during the 1930s.[38] This parity was unusual for the time, but it reflects the fact that these women held superior credentials in the form of their nursing degrees. All female flight attendants thus had completed at least two years of college and also held valuable skills in the case of a health emergency on board. Meanwhile, stewards at Pan Am and Eastern needed only to possess the equivalent of a high school degree and a few years' experience in a customer service field like ship stewarding, bell-hopping, or waiting tables. "Even filling station attendants will not be overlooked in the search for personnel," noted one article covering Rickenbacker's choice of stewards.[39]

All told, stewardesses actually cost the airlines more on average than stewards. Rickenbacker bemoaned how his company, when it had hired stewardesses before 1934, had spent one thousand dollars training each employee, only to have them quickly get married and leave.[40] Of course, he could have undone this problem by allowing married stewardesses to continue working, like his all-male pilot corps and even his stewards. But such thinking was seemingly beyond him and all other airline executives in the 1930s. Instead, Eastern embraced a male-privileged orthodoxy: "When a flight-steward marries he is more valuable to the company because his stability increases, whereas the stewardess who marries gains a husband and loses her job."[41]

Because Eastern had very little competition on its most lucrative routes, Rickenbacker did not need to give his straight male customers (much less his pilots) the costly amenity of attractive stewardesses. Eastern competed with companies like American and Delta within the triangle connecting Chicago, New York, and Atlanta. However, its most lucrative route—the busy vacation and convention corridor between New York and Miami—remained an Eastern monopoly.[42] Thus there was no pressing economic rationale for Rickenbacker to raise his costs by hiring stewardesses without the hope of increasing his revenue. The other major airline to hire men, Pan Am, similarly faced little competition before World War II. The airline's primary destinations in the 1930s were in the Caribbean and South America, with the China route opening in late 1936. After having been awarded every contract with the U.S. Postal Service to carry mail to its destination countries, Pan Am was guaranteed to be the only U.S. airline that could make money on these routes. Meanwhile, competition from South American airlines was largely thwarted by Pan Am's aggressive monopolistic practices.[43]

Overall, then, the dollars and cents of selling stewardesses as sexual icons broke down this way: domestic airlines facing more competition on their most lucrative routes hired stewardesses and were more likely to use them in their marketing. They did so even though the company might lose much of their thousand-dollar start-up investment in a stewardess if she married early. But both Eastern and Pan Am, which had a certain degree of protection from competition, chose the less fetishized stewards, thereby securing a flight attendant corps that would remain on the job longer than the average stewardess. The trade-off was that stewards' customer appeal was more restricted to niche markets, including some travelers who preferred male employees and others—both female and male—who found stewards sexually desirable.

As to Eastern's steward corps itself, two somewhat ironic caveats warrant attention. First, these stewards owed their jobs to a male chauvinist executive who was responding to the technological innovation of the DC-3 in a way that he felt would reinforce the patriarchal order of U.S. society, placing men in workplaces that were deemed complex and hierarchical. And second, the airline willingly surrendered the opportunity to sell sex in its most obvious and widespread form: by commodifying female bodies for the sake of heterosexual men. Rickenbacker's public statements basically presumed that his steward corps would thereby stand out as asexual when compared to his domestic competitors like United, Delta, and American, who used stewardesses on their flights.

The reality of Eastern's stewards was, however, quite a bit different. Indeed, these men embodied even more of the "gay" traits seen in Pan Am's previous "Rodney" campaign, and the airline promoted them as men who remained intriguingly desirable, especially to female customers, whom the airline hoped to attract. Eastern's most adventurous attempts to eroticize stewards involved their vibrant uniform design, which stood in marked contrast to the more conservative attire worn by stewardesses. Stewardess uniforms of the 1930s were very different from their later manifestations in the 1960s, when they became scanty, bright, form-fitting, fashionable outfits that highlighted the woman's sexual appeal. Instead, the uniforms of United's first stewardesses and all other female uniforms from the decade obscured their form. United commissioned a traditional long skirt coupled with a blazer and a knee-length cape for cold weather. The material was cut generously to conceal the woman's body under layers of drab gray fabric.

Meanwhile, the steward uniforms at Eastern had the opposite effect, accentuating the man's broad shoulders and tight waist (figure 3). Stewards looked thin and muscular, as the jacket's wide shoulders tapered off to a more compact lower torso. The pants, starting tight on the waist, then continued this sleek, ever-slimming line all the way down to the ankles. Even the overlap of the coat and the pants was skin-tight. The overall effect was not just to accentuate the steward's form but also to ensconce him in the most modern and sophisticated style of the day: streamlined design, which celebrated aerodynamic features.[44] It was surely more than a coincidence that these uniforms accomplished the same sort of tight body-sculpting on the steward as the DC-3's sleek chrome exterior and integrated wings accomplished on the aircraft's form. Eastern's stewards, far more than stewardesses of the day, were at the pinnacle of modern style.

The steward's streamlined uniform, with its inspiration from other service uniforms found in upper-class urban society (bellhops, doormen, elevator attendants, and ship stewards), very much belonged to the elite "gay" world. And like its counterparts in these other service professions, the Eastern uniform drew attention for its use of color just as much as its cutting-edge form. After all, it was a dazzling color burst in the otherwise stark airplane cabin. The steward's white coat already stood out, but the designers took it one step further, accenting the lapel and sleeves with red zigzag piping. The resulting ensemble contrasted sharply with most other forms of professional dress. However, as designer Gilbert Rohde suggested in 1939,

FASHION PREVIEW

EASTERN AIR LI...

A custom-built white jacket with smart red piping and lettering; dark blue trousers, blue tie, and white and blue cap—the Eastern Air Lines Flight-Steward is formally presented.

FIGURE 3.

"Fashion Preview" for Eastern steward uniform. *Great Silver Fleet News*, November 1936, 8. Courtesy Eastern Air Lines.

this use of color was in the avant-garde of men's fashion: "No longer does [the man of the future] submerge his personality and stifle his imagination in the monotony of the twentieth-century business suit. He, too, is gay, colourful, and different. . . . In the nineteenth century, something happened in our Western World, and he gave up his gay dress without a struggle. In the twenty-first century, the strange custom of dressing like a monk will have disappeared."[45]

Eastern bought into this futuristic idea that "gayness" needed a space in men's fashion. Interestingly, however, it limited its uniform makeover to stewards, not the more traditionally manly pilot corps. Pilots, after all, derived their manliness from technical prowess and, quite often, a military or barnstorming background, not a career devoted to service and style. The pilots were shrouded in drab navy blue military-style suits, not streamlined to show off their bodies.

In their public relations materials, Eastern marketed their stewards with the same techniques that one might expect of female stars in the pages of *Vogue*. The airline's public relations magazine the *Great Silver Fleet News* introduced the new uniforms in November 1936 under the headline "Fashion Preview."[46] Below the photo of the steward modeling his uniform came a detailed piece-by-piece description of the outfit. The description itself was more terse than one might expect of an analysis of women's clothes: the jacket, for example, was efficiently described as "a custom-built white jacket with smart red piping and lettering." Yet the overall effect was for readers to view the steward as a fashion model whose clothes and looks they could scrutinize and enjoy.

Follow-up stories had a similar emphasis; a month after the uniform's unveiling, an Eastern steward "led the style parade in his jaunty uniform at the 10th Anniversary Fashion Show."[47] It seems strikingly unusual that a man would "lead a style parade" at a major fashion show, especially as these were heavily female-dominated events, usually occurring in department store parlors and restaurants where middle-class women spent their days.[48] A decade later, thousands of men would lead parades, but these would be in honor of their military valor in the war, not their looks and clothing.

Another glamorous sighting in the steward's first year included a night of publicity at the elite Rainbow Room nightclub atop New York's Radio City, where a steward awarded a lucky attendee a free flight to Washington, D.C. The Rainbow Room, with its commanding views of the city and bold use of color and streamline motifs, typified the cosmopolitanism and over-the-top style of the 1930s upper-class "gay" nightlife. The club itself was not particularly known for being sexually libertine, attracting instead an upper-crust crowd looking for a night of fun in

EAL INVADES
GOTHAM P. M. LIFE

Gay guests at the Rainbow Room, Radio City's smart nightclub, recently were jolted pleasantly out of their top-hat, white tie complacency when EAL zoomed in and took over several of Manhattan's swankiest spots in connection with an amusing contest involving free trips to Washington. Lovely Florence Saunders, the winnah, is shown here with orchestra leader, Ruby Newman, and EAL flight-steward, Thomas Davis.

FIGURE 4.

A suggestively playful photo and blurb employing homosexual innuendo in Eastern's company magazine. *Great Silver Fleet News*, June 1937, 3. Courtesy Eastern Air Lines.

opulent surroundings with good music and ample alcohol. That said, historian George Chauncey identifies it as one of several new upper-class clubs opening at the time that "were heavily—but covertly—patronized by gay men and lesbians."[49]

Eastern's description of the steward's visit to the Rainbow Room played quite flirtatiously with how its attractive and fashionable stewards were perceived in this "gay" nightlife environment, even potentially suggesting male-male eroticism (figure 4). The company's magazine laid out the story with a photo at the top of the page depicting a dapper steward in his stylish uniform presenting the free trip to a female attendee. Just below the photo is the headline "EAL [i.e., Eastern Air Lines] Invades Gotham P.M. Life." The headline and the photo together stress that the steward, as the main public relations representative for the company, took the leading role in this nightlife "invasion."

The article begins just below the headline with an unusual choice of words, given the steward's prominence in the evening's festivities: "Gay guests at the Rainbow Room, Radio City's smart nightclub, recently were jolted pleasantly out of their top-hat, white tie complacency when EAL zoomed in."[50] Of course, those in the audience wearing top hats and ties were the men, not the women. So, what about Eastern's presentation would have aroused them? If the passage is read in a nonsuggestive way, these male guests, having a perfunctorily good time, started to really enjoy themselves (and thus could be identified as "gay guests") when Eastern enticed them with a free ticket to Washington. Arguably, men could be "jolted pleasantly" when presented with a chance to fly on an airplane.

Yet, among the sexually savvy in 1930s New York, another more flirtatious reading of the text would be obvious: the good-looking, fashionably dressed steward is jolting the "gay guests" among the men. Without question, the steward would have made quite an impression not only on straight women in the audience but on the gay men as well. But whether this interpretation dawned on more than a few readers, and perhaps a clever copywriter, is impossible to know. The word *gay* had definitely acquired its double meaning by the late 1930s, but only for those knowledgeable about the homosexual underworld. At the very least, the homoerotic juxtaposition of a male steward arousing even male patrons among the evening's "gay guests" probably struck many readers as peculiar. At the most, though, it suggests an awareness of the polymorphous sexual desires that Eastern's fashionable steward corps incited.

THE RISE OF HOMOPHOBIA:
CASTING THE STEWARD AS ANTIHERO

As stewards increasingly straddled the lines between masculine/feminine and straight/gay with the rise of new aircraft technology, they also became lightning rods for a very real but still inchoate homophobia. This homophobia was expressed in more subtle ways than outright accusations of sexual impropriety or full-throated castigations of the stewards' gender performance. Instead, it was often cloaked in humor and sarcasm, marking it as more muted and less violent than America's outbursts of the 1950s, when gay bashings and other forms of vigilante justice become prominent. Surprisingly, the public relations materials from Eastern and

Pan Am—the same media that promoted the steward as attractive, dapper, and doting—also partook in the steward's hazing. Both airlines devoted pages of their in-house publications (circulated both among employees and passengers) to poking fun at stewards for their gender-nonconforming work and persona. Even stewards' employers recognized that their softened masculinity, while advantageous for luring female passengers onto their increasingly safe and comfortable planes, was out of sync with much of the culture.

Just a few months after Eastern unveiled their stewards, the airline's public relations department playfully poked fun at their compromised masculinity. The humorously sensationalized article "Flight Steward Reveals Drama" from the April 1937 edition of the airline's in-flight magazine actually covers the mundane activity—when not performed by a man, that is—of changing a baby's diaper. The "drama" of the story involved a six-week-old baby who was traveling with his father and grandfather and whined incessantly until the doting steward realized he had a wet diaper.

Playing the proper male-privileged role, the child's father and grandfather were completely unaware of how to change a diaper. "Their knowledge of diaper technique, I soon learned, was minus nil," noted the steward who penned the article. "Well, *something* had to be done." For the steward, acting heroically in this scenario meant exposing himself as someone able to do the womanly work of changing diapers. So potentially emasculating was this onerous duty that he chose to withhold his name for the article. At the same time, he desperately—to the point of agitation—clung to his manhood by suggesting his status as a dad had given him this gender-bending ability: "The flight-steward who contributes the following picture out of his gallery of memories prefers to remain anonymous, but submits that he is a father in his own right as proof positive of his knowledge of the details described below. 'What certificate,' he asks a trifle aggressively, 'what certificate can serve better than a marriage certificate as a diaper diploma?' "[51] A marriage certificate certainly provided some cover for the steward. At the very least, it allowed him to present himself as a conventionally heterosexual man despite his feminine skill set. Yet the baby's father and grandfather also presumably had marriage certificates and had managed to keep their manly reputations unscathed by the burdens of child care.

What drove this steward to the abjection of anonymity was the tension between his own masculinity and the airline's financial success in the age of the DC-3. The airline sought to assure its ever-diversifying clientele that stewards could assist with the "motherly" tasks of changing diapers or feeding babies, even though the steward's gender made many passengers suspect he would perform them poorly.

At the same time, such work raised eyebrows among other men, who sensed that stewards' manliness was more deficient than they had initially suspected. In lieu of their stewards' enduring this concern unchecked, the airline opted to poke fun at the situation, surely hoping that laughter would defuse the tension between their stewards' role and society's more chauvinistic notions of acceptable manly behavior.

An even more striking example of homophobic humor is the short-run comic *Tale Wind*, found in the *Pan American Air Ways* magazine that was distributed to Pan Am employees and customers (figure 5). In the summer of 1938, an in-house artist named Vic Zimmerman published the first of eight comic strips that followed the travails of Barney Bullarney, a fictitious Pan Am steward. Already with his debut, the reader learns that Barney is a lightning rod for other employees' aggression. The first comic strip portrays a pilot looking for "our glib young ambassador of good will" as he passes through the hangar where mechanics and copilots are busy playing cards. Noticing that Barney is actually approaching the hangar from the other direction, the mechanics prepare to welcome him by hurling wet sponges at his face. Meanwhile, Barney's foremost nemesis, the mammoth mechanic Blimp McGoon, gives the reader a grand introduction just as Barney sets foot in the room: "Well, here he is, folks—That dizzy young dean of stewards, with 687,000 passenger smiles to his credit—Folks, we give you Barney Bullarney!" The following frame shows the "dizzy" (a term laden with feminine connotations) Barney with a smile on his face and a big wave, as though the repeated hellos and good-byes aboard the aircraft had been fixed in his muscular memory. Barney, who is round-faced, with pronounced dimples, and dressed impeccably in his three-piece steward uniform, is completely unaware of the sponge soaking that awaits him. Instead, he greets the men warmly, calling out, in a peculiar dialect, "My frans!"

The publication date of early July 1938 means Barney Bullarney debuted within days of a far more famous comic strip character, Superman. With his premiere at Action Comics on June 30, the Man of Steel ushered in a new genre of comic book hero, a man so strong and possessing such otherworldly skills that he came to be known as a "superhero." In comparison to this flying superhero, Barney was far inferior. In fact, rather than heroic, he was coded in multiple ways as a classic "screwball" character, whose appeal to audiences was his zany behavior and his ability to evoke laughter.[52] Barney's screwball contemporaries were the cartoon film stars Daffy Duck, Bugs Bunny, and Elmer Fudd, who premiered at roughly the same time.[53] Each of these screwballs, like Barney, shared a peculiar speech impediment that softened him to the extent that he couldn't be taken seriously. The only "superhuman" trait of screwball characters was their masochistic ability to endure endless

FIGURE 5.

The debut of *Tale Wind*. *Pan American Air Ways*, July–August 1938, 10. Courtesy Smithsonian Institution Libraries.

abuse and violence without ever showing its effects. (Daffy and Elmer in particular would be shot in the head, dropped off cliffs, or beaten to a pulp in nearly every film.) These tropes are already evident in Zimmerman's first depiction of Barney, who comes across as dim-witted and unmanly as he walks right into a hostile crowd of men ready to unload on him.

In two of the other seven installments of *Tale Wind*, Barney endures more demeaning physical insults than in his debut (figure 6). Both depict the burly mechanic Blimp McGoon bending Barney over his knee and spanking him or punching him in the rear, much to the delight of an onlooking crowd of Pan Am coworkers. The impetus for the punishment in each case is a so-called "bright idea" that Barney thinks up, which is met by the other members of the Pan Am staff as foolishly funny. These men then turn Barney over to Blimp for his ritual punishment. Blimp's abuse of Barney as the snickering crowd of other Pan Am employees look on, conjures up images of a sadistic gang rape, replete with anal penetration. It also highlights the chasm between traditionally manly working-class roles (the mechanic) and the more effete man working in service professions. Yet, as though Barney embodied all the masochistic qualities of the most timid victim, he returns in each subsequent episode of *Tale Wind* as chipper and accepting of his co-workers as ever.

While completely fictional, *Tale Wind* nonetheless served as a cautionary tale for real-life stewards. Some coworkers and members of the public—especially the most macho and chauvinistic men—would inevitably greet them as dim-witted "screwballs" worthy of ridicule. And the main trait that made Barney so vulnerable was true of real-life stewards: unlike the other men at the airlines, their embodiment of manhood was not tied to their physical skills or management prowess. Instead, they were soft and dapper, relying on good looks, charm, and servile work for their livelihoods. The quasi-gang rape scenes in *Tale Wind* thereby stand out as alarming artifacts of a very real homophobia that flew just under the radar.

REARMING MASCULINITY

Historians of gender highlight World War II as a watershed moment. Mobilization allowed women to occupy positions in the workplace that men otherwise held. These women's gender bending was celebrated in the war years, allowing many of them to connect with long-suppressed yearnings to hold a job on par with men. Less notable but equally true is that some men—at least in the male-only regular corps of the military—found themselves in notionally feminine jobs, working as

FIGURE 6.

Abuse of a steward by his coworkers in *Tale Wind* installment. *Pan American Air Ways*, November–December 1938, 7. Courtesy Smithsonian Institution Libraries.

cooks, secretaries, or nurses. Wars, after all, are moments when societies relinquish various fictions regarding proper gender roles: men become largely self-sufficient on the front, while women become equally autonomous and multi-capable at home.[54]

Nonetheless, predominant notions of manliness tend to harden during wars. Whatever room war creates for men to enter women's work doesn't prevent the masculine ideal from becoming more tied to aggression, risk taking, and exposure to death and violence. Along these lines, the steward's softer masculinity of the 1930s was increasingly out of place as America moved toward war in 1940 and 1941. As most stewards joined the sixteen million men who registered for the draft in October 1940, Eastern rushed to envelop its stewards in military-inspired rhetoric and jettison their "gay" public image.

In June 1941, just months before Pearl Harbor, the airline's in-flight magazine carried its most thorough justification yet of Eastern's all-male flight attendant corps. Most notable is how the airline now disavowed notions of style. Entitled "Eastern Carries the Male!," the article noted that Eddie Rickenbacker's choice of stewards was based "on the premise that air transport had grown up and that service rather than glamour or silk stockings was needed to keep the clientele pleased."[55] The article then stressed that the steward corps possessed a military-like discipline and sense of purpose. It recounted the World War I heroics of Walter Avery, Eastern's head of stewards, who had famously downed one of Germany's Red Barons while serving on the Western front. By emphasizing that the flight attendants were led by two World War I flying aces, Captain Eddie Rickenbacker and Walter Avery, the article cast stewards as the loyal foot soldiers of distinguished military men.

Despite their misgivings, the war ultimately forced even Rickenbacker and Pan Am's CEO Juan Trippe to abandon their all-male flight attendant corps. Eastern began to address its male labor shortage in 1943 with its first female hires since the company's earliest years of passenger service. Pan Am followed in 1944 when it hired seven women in March, then an additional twelve a few months later. Just as much as United's first stewardesses from 1930, these new hires were trailblazers. They fulfilled all the duties of their male counterparts, including loading mailbags into the plane's cargo hold, rowing passengers to the docks, and handling customs forms. A member of Pan Am's first stewardess class, Genevieve Baker, recalls her instructor saying, "You will be paid on the same basis as men stewards. You will have the same chances of promotion but—don't use your sex as an excuse. Never say, 'You can't expect a woman to do that!' "[56]

Only in one key way did Pan Am distinguish between its male and female flight attendants. Given the fear that women would not be able to work the sustained hours demanded on long-haul routes, the company's stewardesses were concentrated on shorter trips from Miami to Havana and Nassau, while men were still exclusively used on the routes to the Canal Zone, Brazil, and Buenos Aires. Over time, these gender-based restrictions would give way as stewardesses proved their abilities even to the originally dubious Rickenbacker and Trippe. Their success, when coupled with the more intense homophobia and continuing technological advances of the postwar era, further led the 1930s steward toward historical obsolescence.

THE 1930S STEWARD: A POSTMORTEM

As workers who were also public relations tools for one of America's most technologically advanced industries, stewards and stewardesses in the 1930s embodied an idealized future that was supposedly being wrought by the high-tech machine age. In this sense, they were vessels for the aspirations of what all of U.S. society would strive to look like once the pain of the Depression gave way to new prosperity, thanks to new technologies like the airplane. No wonder, then, that both stewards and stewardesses captured the imaginations of ordinary Americans. Hollywood fell in love with these women who could gallivant from New York to Los Angeles, exhibiting poise, professionalism, and alluring beauty along the way. Meanwhile, in the mode of the dapper "Rodney the Smiling Steward" and his confreres at Eastern Air Lines, stewards found financial stability and access to a high-society lifestyle despite being low-skilled workers in the heart of the Depression. These men enjoyed the same exhilarating mobility that stewardesses did—both a geographic and socioeconomic reach beyond what their education, skill set, and financial resources would otherwise permit.

The steward's appeal was very much grounded in a social milieu peculiar to the 1920s and 1930s urban elite. Airlines' clientele at the time were exclusively America's very rich, and the companies hiring men actively sought to ensconce the steward in the "gay" leisure world these passengers already knew. Thus stewards were servile but also sophisticated and fashionable. Their natural good looks could be used to sell air travel. Their cutting-edge, dapper uniforms granted them access to upper-crust venues like fashion shows and nightclubs where they could promote air travel as glamorous, just as opulent and exotic as a night out on the town. Of course, in some ways, the steward was no more than a bit player in the "gay" social scene of these upper-crust elites. It wasn't his privilege to overindulge in the life of good food, fine alcohol, dancing, sexual excess, and opulent locales. Yet just as the elite men who partook in this charmed life were more feminized by their surroundings, so too was the steward vis-à-vis other working-class men. His livelihood depended primarily on his looks and style, and he was even less credentialed than the nurses who worked as stewardesses.

The composition of the 1930s flight attendant corps depended on complex interactions of cultural notions of gender and sexuality, technological advances, racial segregation, and economic considerations that at times favored stewards and at other times compromised their viability in the job. On the whole, stewards garnered a fairly generous amount of tolerance, even as they were dandied up and promoted as inviting sex objects by their respective employers. This tolerance suggests an easiness with white masculinity norms in the prewar era that would virtually vanish with the onset of hostilities and would be ghettoized after the war, prospering almost exclusively in the gay male subculture.

At the same time, however, the sadomasochistic cartoons chronicling the abuse of the fictional steward Barney Bullarney point to an aggressive homophobia brewing in 1930s society. These images, while just cartoons, expose a visceral desire among some to maintain a more macho code of manhood. This trend would only intensify after World War II and would lead the flight attendant corps to become increasingly a female-only domain. Indeed, as planes became even more comfortable after the war and the culture grew more aggressively homophobic, the ratio of stewards in the flight attendant corps began its precipitous decline from one-third to well below one-tenth.

Not surprisingly, by the mid-1950s both historians and journalists had begun to misremember flight attendants' history. Amaury Sanchez and his peers from the 1920s were virtually forgotten, and United's stewardesses hired in 1930 were now hailed as America's very first flight attendants. Also overlooked were the Pan Am and Eastern stewards hired before the war, some of whom continued to live—and even work—for several more decades. Equally neglected was these men's deeper historical significance for gender and sexuality history: that a gender-bending, potentially homosexual cadre of "gay" stewards had thrived for an entire decade.

CHAPTER TWO · The Cold War Gender Order

The airplane's success as a piece of military hardware during World War II had a profound impact on postwar civil aviation, stimulating immense growth for the industry. Wartime output included vast supplies of the airlines' favored DC-3 aircraft, modestly modified for military purposes, which became a major workhorse · for deploying troops and replenishing supplies across Europe and the Pacific. When the war ended, the military decommissioned many of these planes, selling them at discount prices to a variety of airlines and charter services, some of them founded before the war and others entirely new start-ups. This glut of newly available seats helps to explain the jump in air passengers after the war. U.S. airlines in 1941 had carried roughly five million passengers. Despite the decline of commercial air travel during the war itself, fifteen million people flew in 1946, and almost fifty-five million did so by 1958. Thus, by the close of the 1950s, air travel had expanded more than ten times over levels at the end of the 1930s.[1] A new era of mass air transportation had begun, with airlines now competing with trains and ships for a larger chunk of the traveling public.

As an expanded airline culture consolidated in tandem with the economic and geopolitical order of the cold war, the flight attendant culture changed radically as well. But it did so in response to two countervailing impulses regarding gender in the aftermath of World War II. One impulse was to reward men, especially those who fought in the armed forces, with well-paying, unionized jobs that would remain lifelong careers.[2] Consistent with these norms, various airlines—not just Pan Am and Eastern—welcomed men into the flight attendant corps after the war. And as victories at the bargaining table were won by newly organized flight attendant labor unions, the profession actually became slightly more male and better paid, at least in the immediate postwar years. Indeed, many of the stewards hired in these years stayed in their jobs for decades (in some cases into the 1980s), as their jobs offered stable wages, solid health coverage, lucrative travel benefits, and supposedly secure retirement pensions.

But a stronger and ultimately more lasting employment trend pulled the demographics of the profession in a very different direction, toward becoming an almost exclusively female domain by the close of the 1950s. While seemingly contradictory, this dynamic was also a consequence of white men's growing privileges in middle-class and unionized jobs after the war, and it was coupled with the war-induced longing for a return to more traditional gender roles for men and women. As historian Elaine Tyler May points out, marriage and child rearing ticked upwards for almost two decades after the war, and white middle-class women were increasingly expected to seek fulfillment in tending to family needs at home rather than seeking out careers.[3] That said, May also notes that women's employment did not decline in the postwar years. Instead, the types of work women undertook changed, mainly for the worse. Gone were the stable and high-paying factory jobs of the war years, the ones valorized by the fictitious but compelling image of the strong and independent Rosie the Riveter. Instead, women entered workplaces that ostensibly complemented their primary roles as wives and mothers. Such work was poorly paid and overwhelmingly part time or temporary. Full-time working women typically held such jobs only in the years between high school and marriage.

In workplaces geared toward these younger women—with airline stewardessing a prime example—employees were expected to provide precisely the type of emotional work required of good wives and mothers. Serving meals and drinks, looking after sick passengers, soothing the nerves of worn-out businessmen, and changing dirty diapers—all done with boundless charm and alluring feminine beauty—made the stewardess's role an ideal proving ground for marriage and motherhood. The stewardess had become a counterversion of Rosie the Riveter for the 1950s, an image of white feminine strength and working prowess that mainly reinforced a woman's conformity to the traditional roles of wife and mother and did not challenge the male privileges of higher wages and stable long-term careers.

The image of the cold war–era stewardess is so emblazoned on the historical memory—one need only peruse films and television shows about these years—that it is easy to overlook how her status was briefly challenged by the paradigm of a male-privileged flight attendant corps.[4] In this chapter, I retrieve this overlooked reality, examining how and why the stewardess, thanks to a combination of economic and cultural factors, ultimately became predominant in this profession. In doing so, I help nuance the customary understanding of the gender-based labor market retrenchment after World War II that focuses on the banishment of female laborers back to the home. Considering the plight of stewards helps isolate distinct groups of employees who languished under the cold war gender order: not only working women, who remained underpaid and shut out of notionally male careers, but also white men who attempted to maintain a foothold in service-oriented workplaces. Men who aspired to be stewards, like women seeking work in male-dominated professions, faced increasing likelihood of rejection as the 1950s progressed and, as we shall see, also risked greater derision as gender failures and suspected homosexuals.

Certainly, female flight attendants were also victimized by this corporate-imposed gender segregation. The successes of unionizing and collective bargaining, which bore fruit immediately after the war, were increasingly neutralized over time, thanks in part to stewardesses' lack of clout tied to their gender. The airlines never revived the prewar practice of hiring skilled nurses as flight attendants, replacing them instead with women who possessed no health or safety qualifications and whose most valued assets were their youth, good looks, and charm. Additionally, they found ways to ensure that stewardesses would not accrue significant seniority, which would have allowed them to command the higher wages and more lucrative benefits that longer-serving stewards enjoyed. Most gallingly, many airlines added new mandatory retirement ages on top of the marriage bans that already existed back in the 1930s. American Airlines started this trend in 1953, followed by Northwest in 1956 and TWA in 1957; each of these airlines now forced stewardesses to retire at the still-sprightly age of thirty-two or thirty-five.[5] Stewardesses were part of a familiar trope in American corporate practice: as in many low-skill professions, employers sought to feminize their workforces so as to enjoy greater leeway in keeping these jobs short term and low paying.

Stewards, meanwhile, also faced discrimination as the years progressed. By 1958 both Pan Am and Eastern had completely reversed their prewar policies of hiring only men and instead refused to accept them for such jobs. Thereafter, only a small New York–based airline, Trans Caribbean, which flew primarily between New York and San Juan, hired men as stewards, while TWA and Northwest hired a limited number of male pursers for their international routes throughout the 1960s. Another exception was United's small cadre of Hawaiian men, who, starting in 1950, served as both flight attendants and cultural ambassadors on flights from the mainland United States to Honolulu. By and large, however, male flight attendants by the 1960s had virtually disappeared from domestic flights. They also were heftily outnumbered and put in supervisory positions requiring less interaction with passengers on U.S. carriers' international flights.

All the while, stewards and male applicants for the job faced an even more virulent form of homophobia than had existed in the 1930s. As gay historian John D'Emilio notes, World War II amounted to a national "coming out" experience for gays and lesbians.[6] The gender segregation and increased mobility during the war years helped bolster the size of gay and lesbian communities around the country, while simultaneously elevating straight society's awareness of homosexuals. In response to this increasing sexual fluidity, U.S. society largely chose to clamp down, creating a variety of novel legal and extralegal mechanisms to stigmatize homosexuality. Stewards were again castigated as effeminate men, even more than their predecessors before the war. And gay stewards, who by the 1950s represented a sizable percentage of the male flight attendant corps, endured an extra dose of suspicion. Far from being auxiliary to the economic factors I discuss, the more virulent homophobia of the 1950s played an equally important role in making the career less amenable to men as the decade progressed. I consider homophobia and the flight attendant corps explicitly in chapter 3, after first examining here how financial and gender-based cultural pressures coalesced to nearly banish the steward from the job.

RE-MANNING THE FLIGHT ATTENDANT CORPS

In the immediate postwar moment, airlines, like most other employers in the country, felt obliged to reward veterans by accommodating them in the workforce. The flight attendant corps was not immune from this trend, especially at Pan Am and Eastern. Both airlines claimed during the war that their companies' first female flight attendants had been hired to relieve men for war duty, so there was strong pressure to rehire the men once they were decommissioned. This sense of obligation pertained first and foremost to former employees, and Eastern was gearing up for a potential logistical nightmare in late 1945. As chief executive Eddie Rickenbacker noted, "There will be approximately 1,200 men returned from the Armed Services. The majority will want to come back and we want to be in position to absorb them in a manner that will be beneficial to them and the company."[7] The company further committed itself to new hires, even offering work to one thousand wounded veterans, who might otherwise face tremendous difficulty finding a job.[8]

The overall effect of these veteran-friendly employment policies, while certainly noble in intent, was to place many women at a disadvantage in the application process. Priority given to male veterans meant that well-qualified women were overlooked. Rickenbacker codified female applicants' secondary status in a 1947 conversation with managers: "Don't hire women unless you have to, but if you do hire women, hire women with brains. There are plenty of middle-aged women who have obligations and responsibilities, who want to do a good job, and there you will find the answer to some of your problems."[9] His words contradict themselves, as he accepts that the abilities of certain women will benefit the company in crucial ways but nonetheless tells his managers to place their applications at the bottom of the stack. Executives like Rickenbacker were willing to forego workplace efficiency in order to prioritize men over women.

The flight attendant corps was one of the positions at Eastern and other airlines that saw such favoritism for white men. Aviation historian Robert Serling claims that Rickenbacker briefly imposed an "edict banning the hiring of any more women as replacements for departing stewardesses," which in turn led to higher percentages of men in the flight attendant corps by 1950.[10] But thanks to the rapid increase in seating capacity after the war, all airlines, including Eastern, continued to hire stewardesses. Starting in January 1946, men reappeared at Eastern's flight attendant training school, with many partaking in a retraining program established for former stewards who had served in the military. Photos of the first reintegrated class show that women outnumbered men by a 3-to-1 margin in a class of fifty, but this ratio evened out over the next few years as decommissioning progressed.[11] Pan Am by the end of 1946 had a flight attendant corps that was roughly half male and half female and was training more men than women, at least in its Atlantic Division, which serviced its newly opened routes between New York and Europe.[12] Even as late as February 1951, Pan Am's graduating class in the Latin American Division included seven women and five men.

However, 1951 also exposed the considerable downside of men's privileged status as soldiers and veterans. Even as Pan Am's corporate newsletter celebrated the new class of flight attendants that February, it also noted that this mixed-gender makeup could soon end. The reason was that men's availability for work was thrown into doubt by the military's unanticipated engagement in Korea. It noted that "the five newest stewards . . . probably will be the last men hired for this job until the international situation clears."[13] Indeed, another man who applied at the Seattle base just a few months later discovered that Pan Am was not hiring men at all. Despite a strong personal interview and extensive experience as a steward on charter airlines, applicant Jay Koren was told, "We don't anticipate the Ivory Tower giving us the go-ahead to hire [men] until the fall."[14] The Ivory Tower—Pan Am's New York headquarters high up in the Chrysler Building—did, however, rescind the no-males directive later in 1951. Once conflict on the front lines in Korea had stalemated by early 1951, the labor market at home stabilized as well. Now confident that the military would not require all able-bodied men, Pan Am hired Koren and several other stewards.

The pre-1951 moment represented perhaps the most expanded hiring of male flight attendants before the 1970s. Not only were Pan Am and Eastern hiring again, but several other airlines started doing so for the first time. On the one hand, this was a response to the national priority to hire more veterans, but, like Eddie Rickenbacker's decision to hire stewards with the advent of the DC-3 in 1936, it also reflected a desire to establish a more patriarchal order in the plane's cabin. The first generation of post–World War II airplanes doubled passenger capacity once again, and the work of flight attendants was getting more complex and hierarchical. The DC-4, DC-6, Boeing Stratocruiser, and Lockheed Constellation all seated more than fifty passengers; therefore, there were now as many as four flight attendants serving passengers on any given flight. The response of several airlines was to create a new rank in the flight attendant corps, the purser, who delegated responsibilities to the other attendants. Pursers also handled communications with the cockpit and relieved pilots of some paperwork duties, which were also becoming more demanding. On international flights, they processed customs forms and interacted with border officials.[15] They also earned significantly more money: a 40 percent premium over the regular flight attendant salary at Pan Am.[16]

This high-paying supervisory position was just the veneer of male privilege that some airlines needed to hire men. Seizing on the Truman administration's efforts to increase competition on international air routes, a series of U.S. airlines were finally able to challenge Pan Am with flights to South America, Asia, and Europe. TWA, Northwest, and Braniff all appointed men to serve as pursers, and reserved this position for men only, once their international flights began. Delta Air Lines also introduced male pursers in 1946, despite being only a domestic carrier. Thus, between 1946 and 1949, a whole new male-only set of jobs was created, even at airlines that had never hired stewards.[17]

Eastern also created a purser position after the war and reserved it exclusively for men. In addition to getting basic training in safety and hospitality, men learned about personnel management and paperwork, while women increasingly were trained in hygiene and beauty. Despite the airline's attempts in the 1930s to market its stewards as handsome and desirable, the glamour aspect of the job was now female only. Male trainees were exempt from exercises like this one described in its corporate magazine: "Each Saturday during the training course the stewardess trainees attend Dorothy Gray's salon on Fifth Avenue where they are coached by experts on intelligent make-up, hair-do, speech and posture—a 'charm' course that would cost the private client $25."[18] Placing men automatically in the position of purser meant that they were better paid and held authority over the rest of the flight attendant crew, even over women with considerably more seniority. This hierarchical imbalance was also expressed in the plane's cabin, where the men remained in the galleys for much of the flight. According to new company policy, "A Purser will prepare the food and a Stewardess will serve."[19]

The steward's new status as manly and militarized was perfected by a drastic uniform change from the 1930s (figure 7). Gone was the white double-breasted, form-fitting coat that had made the steward a fashionable presence. Also gone were the ginger-bread red piping and the bow tie, both of which had markedly divorced the earlier uniform from its military roots. Instead, the May 1946 innovations remilitarized the steward, as he was now outfitted from head to toe in navy blue, with gold piping on the hat and a gold star and stripe on the sleeve designating his rank (one of each, rather than the head pilot's four). The steward was now virtually indistinguishable from the pilot—or a soldier in his dress uniform. Eastern's public relations described this new uniform with the lackluster adjectives *neat* and *business-like*.[20] There was no attempt to glamorize the steward, as the airline had done in the 1930s and continued to do with its charm school–trained stewardesses. The uniform instead emphasized a militaristic form of manliness, highlighting the steward's role as a leader in the cabin. While perhaps consistent with the cold war militaristic ethos, this uniform choice was, as we shall see, out of sync with airlines' attempts to make air travel more appealing to new female and children customers.

MALE PRIVILEGE AND UNIONIZING

In tandem with airlines' embrace of the steward came moves to upgrade the profession into a secure, middle-class livelihood. Male flight attendants benefited disproportionately from the first contracts negotiated by newly organized flight attendant labor unions that led to wage increases, better health benefits, and retirement pensions. These moves were consistent with larger economic priorities promoted by New Deal Democrats and supported by the Eisenhower administration at the dawn of the cold war. Many industries emulated the status quo that took hold in America's

FIGURE 7.

Eastern's first pursers, 1946, in pilot-inspired military uniforms. *Great Silver Fleet News*, July-August 1946, 35. Courtesy Eastern Air Lines.

burgeoning armaments industries: in exchange for lucrative subsidies to contractors, the federal government established the expectation that companies would pay their workers a family wage and allow union representation to guarantee this. In turn, union leaders, especially those at the United Auto Workers (UAW) and the International Association of Machinists (IAM), used their increasing influence to help unionize workers in a wider swath of industries beyond those tied directly to the military-industrial complex. For flight attendants, the money and know-how for organizing came primarily from preexisting unions within the American Federation of Labor (AFL), especially from the pilots' union, the Air Line Pilots Association (ALPA). Starting with United's stewardesses in August 1945, flight attendants at airlines across the country (save for those at Delta) quickly unionized, becoming members of ALPA's newly formed Air Line Stewards and Stewardess Association (ALSSA). Only Pan Am's flight attendants opted for the Congress of Industrial Organizations (CIO)-affiliated Transportation Workers Union (TWU).[21]

Both the ALSSA and the TWU had immediate success at the bargaining table, securing substantial raises for employees in every pay grade. But flight attendants with greater seniority and those who ascended to the purser position were the biggest winners under these contracts. Male stewards were overrepresented in both of these categories, since they were unaffected by the airlines' marriage and age restrictions on stewardesses and could easily—even automatically at some airlines—become pursers. For those promoted to purser, unionizing bestowed a twofold benefit: they enjoyed the across-the-board increases shared by others, plus a promotion into the even higher-paying category. Pan Am's Miami-based TWU Local 500 was so proud of its first flight attendant contract in late 1946 that it boasted to all the airline's rank and file, even the mechanics: "During your lunch or smoke period try to visit with some of the Flight Stewards or Stewardesses. Ask them how the CIO tackled the problem of wages AND reclassifications. Fully 118 (or some 36% of Flight Service) Flight Stewards and Stewardesses, shortly after their contract was signed, were immediately reclassified into Pursers with an average $72 per month increase."[22] Male flight attendants throughout the industry were enjoying similar double raises, especially since airlines reserved the new purser position for their male personnel.

Back in the 1930s, female flight attendants cost the airlines more than men in the same position. With the job's relatively low wages that were equal for both men and women, the primary cost difference stemmed from stewardesses' being forced out of the job when they married, thereby leading airlines to pay an additional $1,000 to train a replacement. But the rise of contracts negotiated through collective bargaining, coupled with the adoption of the purser category, changed the airlines' financial calculations. The new pay scales meant that airlines were paying their veteran pursers quite a bit more than junior flight attendants, often for work that was only negligibly different.[23] New employee training was still expensive, and airlines still deemed the rapid turnover of stewardesses to be a financial drain; however, the cost of long-serving flight attendants had increased considerably.

Men who entered the job and gained seniority were now commanding a family wage. In addition, they also garnered extra pension payments, greater scheduling autonomy, and increased sick leave, all of which altered the gender-based financial calculus for airline executives. By the mid-1950s, Captain Rickenbacker's concern from the 1930s that women were too costly had flipped; men now were far more expensive. Cold war economic and gender expectations were coalescing to create an imbalance in the flight attendant corps: stewards now enjoyed a middle-class income and a potentially lifelong career, while stewardesses faced sexist work rules that forced them out when they married or reached their midthirties.

DOMESTICATING MILITARY HARDWARE

On the whole, stewards after World War II benefited from the militarization of U.S. society. They earned priority in hiring because of their status as veterans, and they gained disproportionately from the larger trend toward unionization that accompanied the cold war economic cooperation between government and private industry. Yet in other crucial ways they suffered from the entwinement of aviation with the militarism of the day. Following the work of historian Elaine Tyler May, it is important to recall that cold war militarism had a strong cultural counterbalance: a desire to downplay, even ignore, the existential threats to American security by embracing traditional gender roles and an idealized home life. May argues that "cold war ideology and the domestic revival [were] two sides of the same coin: postwar Americans' intense need to feel liberated from the past and secure in the future."[24] Indeed, middle-class Americans effectively hid the geopolitical anxieties of the 1950s behind a curtain of domestic bliss; the nation's muscular foreign policy was balanced—at least psychologically—by a feminine domestic sphere. A similar balancing of masculine and feminine was required by airlines in the postwar moment, especially as their quest for profits increasingly required them to diversify their clientele. This need ultimately left the steward in a vulnerable position vis-à-vis the stewardess.

To appeal to women and children, airlines needed to find a way to play down the militarized connotations of the airplane itself. Airplanes have always been a product of intense cooperation between the military and private industry. Before the war, a vast majority of planes were purchased by the U.S. military, as would also be the case after World War II.[25] However, commercial airliners and military aircraft advanced in tandem during the prewar years, since aviation research and development were shared via a common governmental agency. Innovations that might have been developed as part of a government contract (more powerful engines, lighter-weight fuselages, etc.) were quickly adopted in commercial aircraft. At times, airlines such as Pan Am—not the U.S. military—spearheaded the advance of aviation technology. When hostilities broke out in late 1941, Pan Am acquiesced to the military's lease of its largest and most advanced aircraft, the oversized Pan Am Clippers, since the military possessed nothing of the sort. Likewise, Douglas Aircraft simply modified its DC-3 to create the backbone of Allied military aircraft during World War II, the C-47 transport plane.

The war, however, radically reworked this relationship between military and commercial aviation. In the lead-up to World War II, the aircraft industry changed drastically. Military aircraft output soared, from roughly 2,000 planes in 1939 to 18,466 in 1941, finally peaking at over 96,300 in 1944.[26] Aircraft manufacturers also devoted their research and development almost exclusively to the military's fleet, which became far more technologically advanced than that of the airlines. Manufacturers produced impressive technological innovations in a very short period of time. Boeing's B-29 Superfortress bomber became the new mammoth of the skies, boasting enough cargo capacity to carry an atomic bomb (as it did, in August 1945). It also was one of the first planes with a pressurized cabin, an innovation that finally allowed cruising altitudes in excess of ten thousand feet without oxygen masks.

Perhaps the most radical invention of the war years was the jet engine, which debuted in 1944. While still too novel to be of practical use during the war itself, jet technology—which ultimately tripled the speeds even of transport planes—became the cornerstone of military aviation development throughout the late 1940s and 1950s. It was military aircraft, not civilian carriers, that first possessed this awe-inspiring technology and heralded the onset of the "jet age" that captured Americans' imagination. While some military inventions like pressurized cabins were quickly introduced into commercial use (1946), the jet engine remained military-only technology in the United States until 1958. This lag between military and civilian use firmly established that airplanes were now primarily products of the armaments industry. Throughout the cold war, aviation research and development depended primarily on the consortium of congressmen, military generals, and manufacturing executives that dominated the military-industrial complex.

Furthermore, as previously noted, airlines experienced yet another adjustment thanks to military decommissioning after World War II: a sudden glut of transport planes that the military offered at cut-rate prices. While the airlines possessed 397 aircraft at the war's end, another 5,000 transport planes converted from military use, mostly C-47s, soon entered the civilian market.[27] This sudden and dramatic increase in seat inventory forced the airlines to radically alter their business plans, leaving them little choice but to attract new customers. Aviation innovators like Juan Trippe of Pan Am embraced the new oversupply and introduced new pricing schemes, including a cheaper, less luxurious coach class and even more economical night flights. Trippe believed that his company's future lay in democratizing access to air travel: "Air transport has the very clear choice of becoming a luxury service to carry the well-to-do at high prices—or to carry the average man at what he can afford to pay. Pan American has chosen the latter course."[28]

These novelties led airlines to evolve from a solely elitist mode of transport to a product appealing to different types of customers with different price points. Of course, for most middle-class Americans, Trippe's promise still rang hollow: the "average man" still found air travel prohibitively expensive—or a once-in-a-lifetime indulgence—until after deregulation in 1979. However, even in the 1950s, airlines were instituting multitiered pricing schemes and also gained approval from the Civil Aeronautics Board (CAB, the government-run board that set prices for the industry) to engage in cut-throat pricing on a few select routes. Thus even cash-strapped economic migrants from Puerto Rico became consumers of air travel, since a San Juan–to–New York air ticket was now cheaper than passage by boat. They thereby became the first wave of economic migrants in history to arrive in the mainland United States by plane.[29] New York's newest airport, Idlewild (later renamed Kennedy), opened in 1948 and soon became an Ellis Island of the jet age.

In addition to democratizing air travel in key ways, airlines continued their efforts from the 1930s to attract more women and children. While businessmen remained the airlines' core passengers, their spouses and families were increasingly coveted as a secondary revenue stream. Thus the postwar airlines sought to reinforce the proclivities of wealthier Americans to travel, especially fostering a passion for summer vacationing, while also expanding interest in the more customary winter sojourns to Florida or Cuba. Convention travel for spouses boomed, the airlines and other boosters began marketing hot climates like Florida for summer travel, and trips to Europe became status symbols for America's growing upper and middle classes. A significant sum of these newly available travel dollars—by-products of

America's cold war prosperity—flowed from women (or at least spending choices they initiated) to the airlines.

Yet just as in the 1930s women and children first had to be convinced that air travel was safe and comfortable. The airplane's role in World War II and Korea as military weaponry made this sales job more challenging. Potential customers were regaled with stories of pilots' heroics from these wars, Hollywood films replete with dogfights and ghastly crashes, and news reports of the first combat missions for jet planes over Korea. The situation was exacerbated on August 7, 1955, when Boeing executives showed off their prototype of the 707 commercial airliner to a delegation of airline executives. Test pilot Alvin "Tex" Johnston, unbeknownst to Boeing personnel, had decided to send the plane into a barrel roll during the test flight. The sight of the first passenger jet plane flying upside down was an instant media hit, replayed often on television and reproduced in newspapers throughout the country. Yet, as much as this vision of adventuring masculinity and over-powering technology wowed the public, it also caused many to wonder whether commercial jet travel would be safe and comfortable.[30] With former military heroes in the cockpit and jet engines perched under the wings, commercial aircraft by the late 1950s risked alienating customers by virtue of associations with the dangers and the heroic maneuvers of combat.

Airlines effectively had to conceal their machines' muscular engineering potential (no more barrel rolls) and instead disguise them as cozy, warm spaces akin to the family living room. Designers thus sought to create a symbiosis between masculine and feminine elements, compensating for an exterior that projected mechanical power with an interior that was excessively luxurious and comfortable. If the plane's technology and all-veteran pilot corps evoked militarism, then the cabin would have to evoke both domestic tranquillity and femininity.

Ads such as that shown in figure 8, from National Airlines in 1956, do more than place cute little girls and sharply dressed women in the fold of appropriate airline passengers. They also rewrite the relationship between technological innovation and masculinity. The cozy plane, with relaxed passengers sitting cross-legged in plush seats, even allows a fragile little girl to harmlessly saunter down the aisle—thanks to the technological innovation of radar. The plane is now a cross section of white America: young and old, male and female, all relaxed and enjoying the sight of the little girl as though sharing a joyful moment in a communal living room. Now that the DC-7 aircraft can detect turbulent air pockets by a radar system embedded in its nose, the little girl can roam the plane as freely as she would her own home. In the process, a piece of military hardware, the radar-guided plane, has become

FIGURE 8.
A 1956 National Airlines advertisement, reprinted in National
Airlines, *Annual Report*, 1956. National Airlines Archives, folder
"Archer, Bill: National Airlines Annual Reports, etc." 1990–385,
Historical Museum of South Florida, Miami, FL. Courtesy
HistoryMiami.

domesticated. The ad's text affirms that the technology is actually feminine, as it christens the DC-7 the "Smoothest Sweetheart in the Sky," thereby merging the identity of the mammoth aircraft with the fragile little girl. And hovering over this grand living room is the stewardess, playing ersatz mother to the little girl and doting hostess to the adults. She, too, along with the plane's new technology, plays a vital role in feminizing the plane's persona.

Since flight attendants were the most obvious way to gender the cabin as a feminine domain, it became increasingly imperative for the airlines to hire women over men. In this sense, then, the cold war had profound consequences for stewards and stewardesses. It made stewards undesirable on account of their failure to embody domesticated femininity and to attract women and children as customers. Stewardesses' work, meanwhile, increasingly resembled that of women at home rather than that of nurses or qualified safety professionals. As the airlines' passenger base became more feminized—women went from 25 percent of passengers before the war to 33 percent by the end of the 1950s—so too did the flight attendant corps.[31] The steward in his military-style navy uniform now seemed strikingly out of place.

GROUNDING THE STEWARD

In retrospect, the comments of Eastern CEO Rickenbacker from the first staff meeting after flight attendants unionized were prophetic. He bemoaned to managers: "You have had an election recently of your stewards and stewardesses. Why, I do not know, but I do know there are a lot of smart guys taking advantage of a lot of suckers. . . . They are going to ask for ungodly things—they want this and that— but maybe some day they are going to wake up without anything at all, because you can't get blood out of a turnip."[32] Indeed, in the decade after unionization, Rickenbacker and his fellow airline executives found various ways to keep the career low paying despite collective bargaining. For most men, this meant Rickenbacker's words were spot-on: they ended up "without anything at all."

The first steps toward the complete feminization of the job came when Delta quickly reversed its efforts to introduce male pursers. The airline ceased hiring men by 1949, just a few years into the new policy, after reportedly hiring "a maximum of 19 men . . . at the height of the experiment."[33] Meanwhile, Eastern responded to its rising labor costs in two main ways, both of which adversely affected male flight attendants. First, the airline dispensed with the purser role in the mid-1950s, eliminating the automatic seniority boost and pay bonus that men had enjoyed. Then, from 1954 through 1957, the airline first scaled back, then completely ceased its hiring of stewards. Economics were a key factor in this choice; increased competition from both Delta and Florida-based National Airlines on the lucrative New York–Miami route spurred the airline to improve its service and cut its labor costs by employing more women. By then, executives could cite claims from customers and public relations representatives that stewardesses rendered more effective customer service.

Some airlines with international routes did retain pursers and even continued to hire only men for these positions into the 1960s. Northwest, Braniff, and TWA adopted this policy, choosing to absorb the higher costs of male pursers in an effort to keep a male-dominated hierarchy in their plane cabins. In fact, TWA remained so wedded to this policy that they went to court in New York State in the late 1960s to keep their pursers all male.[34] This placed the airline in an unusual position: they asserted that only men had the necessary qualifications to be pursers, while simultaneously claiming, along with other U.S. carriers, that only women were capable of being regular flight attendants.

Pan Am, meanwhile, forged a mixed stance that was at once progressive and regressive. Alone among international carriers, it always offered women an equal opportunity to become pursers, granting them unique access to higher-paying, more senior positions. Coupling this with its policy allowing women to fly without any retirement age—even if they were married—the airline created an admirable model of relative gender equality in some realms. Yet the carrier also continued to fire women once they became pregnant and enforced strict weight standards that forced many of them out of the workplace. Likewise, men encountered discriminatory attempts to lower labor costs; by 1958 Pan Am had stopped hiring men altogether and ultimately became the defendant who wronged Celio Diaz.

The airlines may have victimized stewards in the most draconian way, but stewardesses encountered a complex web of newly entrenched indignities. Airlines gained a newfound appreciation for stewardesses who married young and thereby cut short their careers. One Braniff recruiting manual even encouraged stewardesses to see quick marriages as a perk: "Where do Braniff Hostesses Go When They Leave Us? You guessed it . . . most of them turn in their wings to get married! The romantic statistics say 98%!"[35] Similarly, Eastern Air Lines, reversing Rickenbacker's earlier disdain for stewardesses who married, now saw this fact as a tolerable annoyance. The airline resigned itself to constantly hiring new flight attendants, noting matter-of-factly: "With larger planes, expanded routes, and the fact that 36 per cent of the Stewardesses resign each year to marry, the company is always on the scout for new talent."[36] The newly created age restrictions placed on stewardesses had a similar effect: forcing women out of the job before they accrued significant seniority and replacing them with younger, lower-paid personnel. Thus the prohibition on new male hires and the age and marriage restrictions placed on women need to be considered together as complementary attempts to circumvent the costs of collective bargaining.

These policies served their purpose well. The unions were unable to overturn the marriage bans and age restrictions on stewardesses. They also could not counteract Eastern's and Pan Am's decisions to stop hiring stewards, which affected only job applicants, not employees. Finally, union leaders were at a loss about whether to defend purser positions, especially at those airlines like Eastern, Northwest, Braniff, and TWA, where the job category drove a wedge between male and female members. By and large, then, the unions had to satisfy themselves with pyrrhic victories. They could boast to their rank and file that they had negotiated higher wages and better pension benefits. But given that these benefits accrued mainly through seniority, the average stewardess—whose career lasted about eighteen months—never benefited from these achievements. Both male applicants for the job and stewardesses facing age, weight, and marriage restrictions were in a "holding pattern," awaiting the 1964 Civil Rights Act to combat the various forms of sex-based discrimination they encountered.

MILITARY-INDUSTRIAL COMPLEXITIES AND THE STEWARD

Under the cold war military-industrial complex, an oligarchy essentially controlled the economic choices of a vast swath of the U.S. economy.[37] Significant authority went to those most centrally tied to the armaments industry, whether politicians, military brass, or industry executives. Unquestionably, though, their decisions had both economic and social ripple effects throughout society. The airlines were just one step removed from the military-industrial complex's epicenter. Like the military, they were customers of Boeing, Lockheed, Douglas, and the other aircraft manufacturers. And they were just as dependent on aeronautical innovations—jet planes, pressurized cabins, more effective radar systems—as those defending the nation.

It makes sense, then, that developments in the cold war affected all levels of the airline industry, even influencing the seemingly apolitical choice of whether flight attendants should be men or women. Economically, the sudden glut of decommissioned aircraft hardened airlines' resolve to both increase their passenger base and cut labor costs. Stewardesses, airline executives soon realized, enhanced both of these prospects. They didn't have the male-privileged economic clout of stewards, who could make a long-term career of the job, often in higher-paying purser roles. Meanwhile, stewardesses also could emulate the doting mothers and living room hostesses of the 1950s American home (who, like stewardesses, were denied a fair wage for their labor). As such, stewardesses were an inexpensive domesticating touch. They reassured new customers that a trip on an airplane—otherwise a converted piece of military hardware piloted, in most cases, by war veterans—would be safe, comfortable, and even enjoyable, and they did so for a fraction of the wages of long-serving stewards.

Both stewardesses and stewards found themselves trapped by increasingly rigid cold war gender norms. Stewardesses couldn't escape the increasing erasure of memories of the war years, when women had been paid the same salary as men and had successfully performed the same work. Meanwhile, stewards rode a wave of male privilege that rose up, then fell apart—at least for them—by the mid-1950s. Their ascendancy immediately after the war entailed a manly makeover: gone were the debonair uniforms of the 1930s, replaced by military dress that put the steward on par (visually, at least) with a pilot or soldier. Unionization in the war's aftermath also bestowed a solid, middle-class wage upon the steward. Yet none of these benefits lasted, save for those who had secured these jobs before almost all the airlines stopped hiring men by the late 1950s. Instead, these enhanced male privileges simply led stewards to become prohibitively expensive. The airlines exploited the rigid gender norms and, as we shall see, the rampant homophobia of the decade to segregate the airplane into two distinct realms: the cockpit, a place that belonged to manly, well-paid pilots, and the cabin, a serene space where services were provided by doting women who had no claim to a family wage.

While stewards' ultimate expulsion from the airlines industry is well accounted for by the economic machinations discussed in this chapter, there is more to the story. I turn next to the joint cultural forces of sexism and homophobia that also helped to eliminate their jobs.

CHAPTER THREE

· "Homosexual Panic" and the
Steward's Demise

The 1950s were arguably America's most homophobic decade of the twentieth
century, even though many people at the time worked to promote greater tolerance
for gays and lesbians. Most famously, sexologist Alfred Kinsey and his associates
laid out the basis for a more inclusive society with their 1948 study, *Sexual Behavior
in the Human Male*.[1] Known simply as the Kinsey Report, the taboo-breaking best
seller had a lot to say about homosexuality that raised eyebrows. Most shocking were
the findings that 10 percent of men preferred sex with men and that 37 percent of
men had experienced same-sex stimulation leading to orgasm at least once in their
lives.[2] In the face of these unsettling findings, Kinsey himself was boldly reassuring.
He recommended that the country simply accept that sexual attractions fluctuate
from person to person and over time in the same person. He also advocated for the
elimination of morality-based sex laws, especially those criminalizing adultery,
prostitution, and sodomy, since upwards of 95 percent of men had broken such
laws at least once in their lives.[3] More specifically, Kinsey called for tolerance of
homosexual behavior, admonishing his readers that "males do not represent two
discrete populations, heterosexual and homosexual. The world is not to be divided
into sheep and goats."[4] Any attempts to criminalize and marginalize homosexuals
would be extremely difficult to enact, implicating far more men than a neatly iden-
tifiable, small minority.

Stewards were particularly invested in whether postwar society would heed
Kinsey's advice. While my research on the 1930s analyzed circumstantial evidence

about "gay" stewards, my work on the postwar era confirms that a decidedly large number of stewards were openly gay. Especially helpful in this regard have been interviews with former flight attendants from the 1940s and 1950s, who estimate that anywhere from 20 percent to more than 50 percent of stewards in the first postwar decade were gay.[5] Moreover, because notions of homosexuality at the time were so easily confused with effeminacy in men, even the stewards who were straight had to worry about how they were perceived. As we have seen, stewards received raises and promotions just like many other men after the war, but they still were on the wrong side of the airplane's demarcated gender line. The profession may have been only a fifth or a half gay, but it was fully queer, simply on the basis of the fact that these men were performing women's work and could therefore easily be read as gender benders and homosexuals.

Unfortunately for stewards and millions of gays and lesbians, the country as a whole chose not to heed Kinsey's words. Instead, following equally esteemed voices of authority, society redoubled its efforts to identify homosexuals and remove them from the workplace and other public realms. Sodomy laws remained in place, continuing to be both a legal menace for those engaging in same-sex sexual activities and a source of potential blackmail. The scientific community also remained largely convinced that homosexuality was a mental illness, despite a minority of voices like Kinsey's urging a reevaluation of the sickness paradigm. Furthermore, as Americans returned in record numbers to churches and synagogues after the war, the voices of religious authorities castigating homosexuality as a sin carried even greater weight than previously.[6]

Politicians, police, judges, juries, and journalists followed these experts in sounding the alarm against the suspected intrusion of homosexuality into the American mainstream. The primary reaction of legal authorities was to create a more extensive framework of laws and policing tactics designed to eradicate homosexuality, especially cracking down against gay nightlife venues. Various cities in the 1950s passed ordinances forbidding the sale of alcohol to homosexuals, outlawing same-sex dancing, and prohibiting cross-dressing.[7] As we shall see, the city of Miami led a particularly zealous campaign against public gay life in August 1954, a consequence of the murder of Eastern Air Lines steward William Simpson in a salacious gay sex tryst.

Simpson's death in Miami also ties into a larger effort begun by the federal government to eliminate homosexuals from employment. This crusade first began with the military (the government's largest employer) just before World War II. As of October 1940, all enlistees were screened to weed out homosexuals, while those already in the military faced expulsion if they were found out.[8] In the

1950s, however, such discrimination expanded rapidly into new realms. President Eisenhower's Executive Order of April 1953—signed within his first hundred days—outlawed the employment of homosexuals in any federal government office. At the height of the cold war, fears ran rampant that the government could be infiltrated by foreign agents or homegrown communists. Homosexuals, because of their perceived mental illness and susceptibility to blackmail, were considered too great of a risk to hire, even in government fields unrelated to national security.[9] The Eisenhower executive order set a precedent for the entire military-industrial complex, as defense firms and other private sector employers whose workers required a security clearance also fired and refused to hire homosexuals. Thus the federal government under Eisenhower, fueled by cold war–era paranoia against all forms of deviance, spearheaded what would become a far broader campaign to eradicate homosexuals from gainful employment.

In fact, the airlines' choice to stop hiring stewards in the 1950s is possibly the most expansive, and arguably the most draconian, application of the Eisenhower precedent. Stewards, after all, were not directly tied to the military-industrial complex. The airlines' refusal to hire stewards therefore pushed the logic of seeing homosexuals as a threat to an extreme, into an industry only loosely tied to the nation's defense. The indiscriminateness of a policy forbidding all men, not just homosexuals, to apply for flight attendant positions also represents a high-water mark of extremism. It is as though airline executives took Kinsey's words regarding homosexuality and ran in the opposite direction. Kinsey used his findings that many men were situationally bisexual to push for decriminalization and normalization of homosexuality. However, the airlines' refusal to hire new stewards suggested a more pernicious model: if no true distinction could be drawn between straight and gay, and if all stewards were suspected of homosexuality, then all men would be kept out of the job.

This chapter considers the William Simpson murder as a pivotal moment for male flight attendants. This is not because the scandal was the singular direct cause of stewards' expulsion from their jobs but rather because it demonstrates the tarnishing of the steward's public image after the 1930s. While prewar stewards were given a potentially alluring and attractive image through Pan Am's advertising of "Rodney the Smiling Steward" and Eastern's creation of stylish uniforms, postwar stewards could not hope to be so positively portrayed. They disappeared from ad campaigns and promotional materials, attracting media attention only as moral pariahs. Eastern responded to Simpson's 1954 murder at the hands of two male hustlers by drastically curtailing its employment of stewards. Delta Airlines also articulated homophobic concerns when questioned about firing its stewards in the late 1940s, and Pan Am had similar concerns when it changed its hiring practices in the late 1950s. Thus postwar homophobia, most vividly exemplified by the Simpson scandal, is partly to blame for the steward's demise. This prejudice worked in tandem with the economic dynamics and sexism of the cold war era to drive men out of the stewarding occupation.

The Simpson murder case also highlights male flight attendants' significant role in legal deliberations that ultimately expanded queer equality. The trial of Simpson's murderers provides a baseline for the following chapters, articulating the desperate legal status of homosexuals in the 1950s, before civil rights innovations improved their lot. In particular, the trial holds an inauspicious role in helping to introduce into U.S. jurisprudence the "homosexual panic" defense, which arose to legally justify, or at least mitigate responsibility for, violence against homosexuals.[10] In the Simpson proceedings and an unknown number of other cases, this meant that murderers were spared the death penalty and even life in prison and were convicted instead of the lesser penalty of manslaughter when their target was gay. Simpson's case thereby illustrates how "homosexual panic" effectively exempted gay men from the promise of equal protection before the law.

Some legal theorists and lawmakers wedded to traditional gender norms were willing to expand further on this logic in the 1960s and '70s, developing additional homophobic legal arguments to thwart moves toward gender-based civil rights. Subsequent chapters profile these attempts to deploy homophobia, from the framing of the sex discrimination clause of the 1964 Civil Rights Act through efforts to ratify the Equal Rights Amendment. As a result, male flight attendants, beginning with Simpson and continuing through the events discussed in the following chapters, became embroiled in crucial civil rights debates on gender and sexuality.

HOMOSEXUALITY AND STEWARDS

My various interviews with former flight attendants confirmed a widely presumed notion: the flight attendant corps in the 1950s harbored far more gay men than was statistically expected. The Pan Am stewards I interviewed contended that roughly half of men working as stewards had been gay. One of them noted, "They would hire four, five, six, seven at a time at the Seattle base—that was the size of the classes—and almost all the men were gay, with few exceptions."[11] Another San Francisco–based steward whose career began in 1951 noted, "I would say at that particular time, that maybe 60 percent were straight and 40 percent of us were gay."[12] When addressing why this preponderance of gay men arose, several men theorized that gay men tended to be better attuned to the job's demands of good grooming and a charming demeanor. Many of these men had "the personalities that they can mix with any kind [of person]," and they were able to serve customers with flair: "That's basically what that job is, wanting to give service."[13]

A similar situation was evident at Eastern Air Lines. Both the straight and gay men I talked to agreed that gays had composed anywhere from 20 to 40 percent of the flight attendant corps, at least at the Miami base where they were stationed. One straight steward, who was among the few men hired after the Simpson murder, remembers, "There were gays when I started [in late 1955]. Of five hundred flight attendants at the Miami base, probably fifty were gay men."[14] Given that only half, or even less, of Eastern's flight attendant corps were men, such a percentage of gays was quite large.

These sizable numbers forced a modicum of tolerance for gays among straight flight attendants and even airline management. Both gay and straight flight attendants largely reported a social ease with each other that was highly uncharacteristic of 1950s society. One straight steward recalls that there were "no problems" with the gay stewards: "We accepted it, and that was it." He even remembered being teamed with a gay steward for the first month of flying, as flight schedules at the time were generated on a monthly basis. In the course of the month, the gay steward was quite open and friendly toward him, even inviting him to "one of their parties." While the straight flight attendant never ended up socializing with the gay stewards, he never felt alienated from them either.[15]

Yet the situation for gays was not entirely open and easy. While some men were forthcoming about their sexuality, others at both Eastern and Pan Am were far more reticent. Attending crew parties with other flight attendants and pilots could mean a risk of exposure: "I didn't like to go to crew parties . . . because there were so many gay stories [being told]," says one former steward who kept his sexuality largely private at work. He added, "The vast majority of the gay male flight attendants were circumspect." For this particular steward, the homophobia of the 1950s was understandable enough: "The gay scene was so raw and behind the scenes and so remote in a lot of people's minds. . . . A lot of people didn't know gay people. . . . So I felt I could understand this [intolerance]. It made sense to me. It was difficult for people to understand this way of life. . . . It was perfectly natural to be negative about it."[16]

Another Pan Am steward, while insisting that his overall experience at the airline had been free of harassment, nonetheless recounted several incidents at the San Francisco base when straight flight attendants had made an issue of homosexuality: "There was a group of 'studs' that . . . were nasty, nasty guys. They were supposedly straight. I remember one guy carried around a list of everyone who was supposedly gay and would show it to his buddies." Still, this steward insisted that management had never followed up on the concerns of these men and said that his female flight attendant peers had tended to be very supportive: "The women liked the gay [stewards] because they knew they could go out on a date and wouldn't get thrown in the sack." For him, life at Pan Am had been a mixed experience of coming out to fellow gay men and some stewardesses, while being much more circumspect around pilots or straight stewards. Around these more hostile audiences, "You just didn't come out. . . . They knew, they suspected. You just kept it quiet."

Others, however, were more open about their sexuality, sometimes because they had no choice. This was especially true of the more effeminate gay men who were more quickly presumed to be gay. Even other gay men at the time referred to these men condescendingly as "gay fags" or "fag ladies."[17] These men, one interviewee suggested, incurred much more harassment from their straight male peers, who "would talk about people that were obvious. And to this day, I've felt guilty because I never stood up for people. I just kept my mouth shut and did my business." Another straight steward at Eastern, whose career began in 1948, suggested that tensions had never boiled over, even with regard to the effeminate stewards: "We had a number of limp-wristed guys. We knew who they were. Their comportment gave them away. But as long as there was no scandal, they stayed on the job. It never got out of hand."[18]

A vignette from former Pan Am steward Roy Orason in his autobiographical novel *Plight of a Flight Attendant* suggests that even effeminate gay stewards could be accepted, at least in limited ways, by their coworkers. The novel describes, from a straight man's viewpoint, the intermingling of all sorts of gay and straight employees at a dinner party of Pan Am personnel at the New Orleans base in 1954:[19] "Every stewardess that was in town . . . showed up. Two of the pilots from the base showed up without their wives, although they too had been invited. . . . Some [non–Pan Am] guys brought girlfriends but most of them wanted to meet the stews who would be there. There was even one of the faggot stewards with his friend there and they turned out to be the life of the party."[20] Orason's account fits into a larger pattern noticeable in my interviews: despite moments of animosity, straight flight attendants knew a good deal about the lives of their gay colleagues, even those "faggots" in the group. And such interactions were usually tolerant, potentially even collegial.

While Pan Am management heatedly denied this a decade later during court proceedings, it is clear that airline executives were quite aware of the homosexual presence in their workforce. In the words of one Pan Am steward, "If there was no scandal involved, I don't think it would be incriminating to be known as gay by a supervisor."[21] The hiring process, management's main mode of controlling the composition of the flight attendant corps, was also devoid of probing investigations into one's sexuality. Applicants weren't asked questions about the subject, and the company did not consult military records to isolate homosexuals who might have avoided or even been kicked out of the services.[22] In fact, not only were gays unafraid to interview for such positions, but an informal gay network in places like San Francisco also circulated word that the job was gay-friendly. One future flight attendant chatted up a gay flight attendant in a coffee shop. The steward, named Kenny, encouraged him to apply and also prevailed on the chief steward doing the hiring: "The guy who was the chief steward was in the closet, and he liked Kenny, and Kenny was able to get him to hire me."[23]

That said, some gay men blamed their interview failures or their poor progress reports as employees on perceived homophobes among the hiring committee and base managers. One man applying with Pan Am in San Francisco noted, "There was a panel . . . of seven for the final interview. And I got one 'no' of the seven, so that blackballed me. And this one [woman] said, 'We all wanted you so much, but we couldn't talk this one guy out of it.' I think [he] was a homophobe and had read my beads."[24] A decade later, a gay purser at TWA made it through the hiring process, only to have major troubles with his first base manager. The manager, according to this individual, "hated gay men" and sought to weed them out of the job. Before releasing a purser from probation, "he would have you walk across the room and smoke a cigarette, to see how you held a cigarette," a decidedly unscientific manner of discovering homosexuals.[25] Overall, however, such incidents seem to be exceptions from the general tendency of hiring committees and managers to be tolerant of gay men and to overlook this aspect of their lives if the men showed potential.

Though scandals were rare, when they did happen relations between management and gay stewards became tense. Pan Am endured a series of gay-related problems in the 1950s, though these never received publicity outside company circles. Most arose from the company policy forcing stewards to double up in hotel rooms while on layovers. While pilots received their own rooms as a consequence of their more lucrative collective bargaining agreements, stewards shared their rooms with another steward, or even with a flight engineer from the cockpit. Placing stewards in this situation when their coworkers often knew them to be gay exposed them to all sorts of potential abuse. "There were a lot of problems for gays on layovers," recalls one Pan Am steward. "We'd double up. And very often there would be someone making moves on you, or you'd hear of a straight guy, ya know, punching out somebody who made a pass at him in the room, trying to get into bed with him." Other stories circulated of gay stewards being forced into sex by chief pursers, who could report them as negligent on the job if they refused. In response, several gay men who attained enough seniority bid on the same routes together, the only way to guarantee that their roommate wouldn't harass them.[26] Interestingly, Eastern avoided such problems, at least in the 1950s. At that time, the airline simply provided each flight attendant with a per diem, which they could spend as they saw fit. This made lodging a completely private decision and gave gay stewards much more security.

The lone Pan Am policy that explicitly addressed problems tied to homosexuality involved the Beirut base in the mid-1950s. This outpost was the hub of Pan Am's extensive Middle Eastern operations tied to the growing U.S. oil interests in the region. Perhaps being so far from corporate headquarters enabled the flight attendants based there to be less circumspect than their U.S.-based employees. According to a few flight attendants I interviewed, the base was well known for its gay stewards, so much so that it drew the attention of the corporate office.[27] In response, the company temporarily refused to transfer any stewards to Beirut—a blanket exclusion on all men, without any attempt to distinguish between gay and straight personnel, much less those with stellar or below-average service records. The company lifted the ban in 1958, apparently in the face of strong union opposition, since it circumvented the collective bargaining agreement stipulating that positions be filled on the basis of seniority, not gender. Nonetheless, the temporary policy followed a pattern for handling homosexual scandals that would recur: when faced with potential embarrassment, the airlines resorted to the draconian measure of excluding all men from certain posts.

While the airlines hiring men dealt with difficult issues tied to same-sex desire, they also faced potential public relations troubles from their stewards' perceived effeminacy. The more the public and other airline personnel perceived the flight attendant job as women's work, the more they harassed men who were employed in it. Several former stewards, both gay and straight, confirmed that humiliating incidents occasionally occurred on the job. One straight ex-steward recalled being asked by a repeat male customer, "Where's your dress?" He initially attempted to defuse the situation with humor, by replying, "I hope you forgive me, sir, but I decided to dress legitimately today." After this response failed to end the customer's abuse, the steward informed the flight captain that he wouldn't work the flight because, as he said, "My masculinity in a very flippant and demeaning way is being questioned." In this case, the captain stuck up for the steward, proceeding back to the cabin and forcing the customer to apologize.[28]

Another steward recalled that pilots were often the source of the most demeaning attacks. "They could make your job miserable," he said of the pilots, some of whom preferred that the women serve their meals in the cockpits. One pilot even ordered a steward to make him coffee in the employee lounge of an airport, since there were "plenty of twenty-year old stewardesses willing to do that for me."[29] The former stewards overall confirmed that problems with the pilot corps, while isolated, were still quite troubling: "We had some wonderful captains. . . . By far I would say the majority were nice guys, but then we had some real bastards." Meanwhile, interactions with customers overall were easygoing and uneventful. But there were occasionally demeaning inquiries from male passengers: "Where are the babes?" or "Why all these men working in first class?"[30] The answer to the last query was simple: men tended to accrue more seniority than women and therefore could claim the more desirable jobs on their assigned flights, including working the first-class cabin.

DELTA'S HOMOPHOBIC PRECEDENT

While Pan Am and Eastern found some sort of modus vivendi with regard to accommodating a gay presence among their flight attendants, Delta found that their male pursers were not worth the trouble of keeping. The airline began hiring men as pursers in 1946 but dismissed all of them by late 1948. Without a labor union in place, the men involved had no recourse when they were terminated, and the event probably would have disappeared from public memory, hidden in inaccessible corporate archives, if, the Equal Employment Opportunity Commission had not questioned Delta about its decision almost twenty years later. The EEOC by 1966 was pursuing the Celio Diaz case and other complaints brought by male applicants to flight attendant positions. To better understand the history of men's exclusion from the job, they asked Delta to explain its short-lived experiment with male pursers.

Delta replied that its experience with men had been "completely unsatisfactory."[31] Foremost among its concerns were sexual issues, especially homosexuality: "While the matter must be delicately stated, it was a fact that the least trace of effeminacy on the part of the purser resulted in the individual being tagged as a sex deviate (in most cases without fault on his part) and, at the other extreme, the least aggressiveness on the part of a more virile steward was subject to misinterpretation by female passengers."[32] Perhaps most significant about this claim is that it confirmed a gay presence among Delta's small corps of pursers, however coyly the company's lawyers framed the letter. After all, the airline noted that the effeminate men were not culpable for being labeled sex deviates "in most cases." This official, though hardly public, admission by an airline that it had gay employees was extremely rare. In fact, I have uncovered only one other admission of this sort from before the 1970s.[33]

Interestingly, the airline's concern that the "more virile" stewards could be misunderstood by passengers suggests a predicament that all stewards—whether straight or gay, effeminate or "virile"—shared. For all of these men, the era's militaristic paradigm of manliness was not reconcilable with the job: effeminate men failed to live up to manly ideals, and virile men followed them too closely, even to the extent of being construed as overly aggressive.[34] It could only beget trouble, from Delta's perspective, to hire either type of steward, as each exposed the company to unnecessary risk: "While Delta was never exposed to public embarrassment or real or threatened litigation as a result of these problems, they did in fact exist and were recognized as such both by the Company and by the stewards themselves." Overall, Delta was simply unwilling to deal with the anxiety unleashed when men worked as flight attendants. Stewards allegedly alarmed passengers, which in turn led managers to worry about the company's image.

A STEWARD'S MURDER

The chasm between the stewardess's fetching public image and the steward's tarnished one is best captured in the *Miami Herald* from November 8, 1954. On page A12 an ad for Eastern Air Lines showed a motherly stewardess bottle-feeding a passenger's baby (figure 9). If the emphasis on femininity seems a little overdone, this effect was needed to counteract the headline of the very next section covering the local news. November 8 was the day that the *Herald* announced the conclusion of the trial of the two young men who had killed Eastern steward William Simpson. The very top of page B1 carried the headline "Youths Guilty of Manslaughter In Fatal Shooting of Steward."[35] Even earlier in the 1950s, neither Eastern, Pan Am, nor any other airline hiring men was featuring stewards in an ad campaign. The days of "Rodney the Smiling Steward" or the dapper Eastern steward leading fashion parades were long gone. By the 1950s, the only time stewards got publicity was when they made the news—scandalous news at that. The announcement of the manslaughter verdict was the culmination of a barrage of news stories arising from the case that played a role in sullying stewards' reputations nationwide.

The story had begun a few months earlier, on August 2, 1954. Twenty-seven-year-old William Simpson had landed at Miami airport that evening around 8:55 p.m. and had quickly raced home. By 10:00 p.m. Simpson had changed clothes and was

FIGURE 9.

Eastern Air Lines advertisement from 1954, as seen in the *Miami Herald*, November 8, 1954, A12. Courtesy Eastern Air Lines.

ready for a night on the town, including a date that he had mentioned to his female coworker before they landed. Just two hours later, however, at 12:09 a.m., a straight couple driving toward a "lovers' lane" eight miles north of Simpson's home found him dead, face down on a gravel road, with a gunshot wound in his side, several hundred yards from his abandoned car.

Whatever his original plans, Simpson seems to have driven barely a block from his home before encountering a young male hitchhiker, who requested a ride northwards toward the suburb of North Miami. At some point, the two agreed to proceed to the deserted stretch known as a lovers' lane, ostensibly because they had arranged to have sex. Yet what seemed to Simpson like a spontaneous, consensual act was actually a well-orchestrated plot by Charles Lawrence and his accomplice, twenty-year-old Lewis Killen, who was secretly trailing the men in his own car.

The two youths had perfected their scheme over a period of five months, luring dozens of gay men to the secluded road, drawing a pistol, and stealing their money. Killen's job was to wait several minutes while Lawrence allowed the victim to perform oral sex on him. Sex was an important ingredient in the ruse, as it rendered the victim more compliant. Once these men had committed an act of sodomy, they would be loath to report the incident to the police. As soon as the men finished, Lawrence would jump out of the car and pull his gun, and Killen would then approach wielding his own gun and demanding the victim's wallet. To make sure they weren't pursued, the youths would then knock the man unconscious and throw his car keys into the weeds or the nearby creek. Such acts were all too familiar to police, gay men, and the tough young men like Lawrence and Killen who made extra money this way. The youths, and even the media, referred to this practice as "rolling" homosexuals.

For whatever reason, however, the robbery of Simpson went wrong. After sex, Lawrence did in fact jump out of the car and pull out his gun. But he later claimed that at that instant he had been spooked (perhaps out of fear that Simpson would quickly drive off). He fired the gun in Simpson's direction, ostensibly without the intent to hit him. But the bullet lodged in Simpson's abdomen. Only then did Killen appear. Despite Simpson's injury, the two youths returned to their original plan and demanded that the injured Simpson step out of the car and give them his wallet. Simpson fell to his knees, holding his wounded side and imploring them, "Leave me alone! Leave me alone!" He handed over his wallet and keys, thereby losing his only chance of escape from the deserted area. He then struggled a few hundred yards up the empty road before finally collapsing. Lawrence and Killen made off with twenty-five dollars, which they split evenly. They reportedly assumed that Simpson would survive the wound and were surprised by news reports the next morning that he was dead.[36]

THE BEGINNINGS OF "HOMOSEXUAL PANIC"

The Miami public first read of Simpson's murder in the afternoon edition of the *Miami Daily News* on August 3, 1954, just a dozen or so hours after Simpson's death. Under the headline "EAL Steward Found Shot Dead: Body Discovered in 'Lover's Lane'" came the first suspicions that there might have been a homosexual angle to the murder. The location of the body strongly suggested a sexual motive. Whether it was because it was statistically unlikely that a woman would commit such a crime or because Simpson was employed in an occupation perceived as gay, police were already suggesting, according to the story, that the murder might have "stemmed from a sex motive by a male." That said, the reporter was quick to add, in the same sentence, that "it was just as likely the slayer was a woman."[37] Similar suspicions arose because Simpson had told a stewardess colleague that he had been "out with a companion until 4 am" on the previous weekend. The reporter noted cryptically, "It is believed that this person—man or girl—may be the same person with whom the victim had a date last night."[38]

By the time the morning edition of the *Miami Herald* appeared on August 4, Simpson's friends were actively attempting to quell suspicions of homosexuality. A fellow Eastern steward and former roommate revealed to readers that Simpson had been engaged before. Indeed, as the *Herald* reported, this friend "described [Simpson] as a good-looking man who dated frequently and confided that Simpson had been 'a man with the ladies.'"[39] Clearly, the case had developed into a two-edged mystery for readers, not only to follow police as they chased down the murderer, but also to determine whether Simpson himself was gay and how his sexual desires might have played into his death.

Regardless of what the papers printed, the police soon came to the conclusion that the case involved homosexuality. On the evening of August 7, five nights after Simpson's murder, North Miami police officers caught up to Charles Lawrence, a troubled youth who was known to police because of rumors that he possessed guns. Under interrogation, Lawrence confessed that he had been at the crime scene, but only to go fishing at the late hour. At this stage, according to the police report, police chief Karl Engel baited Lawrence to come clean about the homosexual nature of the crime. The reporting officer W. H. Thurman recounted that he had "heard the

Chief talking to Lawrence and stating that if he was in trouble that it would be best to tell us about it and that if he had been bothered by a queer, that he should tell us about it, that at one time a queer tried to bother him and that he had hit him because he did not like that type of man himself."

Read generously, Chief Engel's confession that he himself had assaulted men in moments of "homosexual panic" was a street-smart interrogation tactic. It certainly elicited the desired result. Lawrence quickly admitted to shooting Simpson. However, following the chief's lead, he defended his actions as a legitimate response to an unwanted sexual advance: "Simpson had opened his fly and [Lawrence] had told him to stop." After Lawrence tried to leave the car, the report claimed, "Simpson reached up and got hold of him and tried to pull him back into the car and that was when he shot him."[40]

Later that same night, after interviewing Lawrence's accomplice, Lewis Killen, police knew this scenario to be false. Killen revealed that Lawrence had intentionally sought to "roll" homosexuals by posing as a sexually available hitchhiker. They also heard that Lawrence regularly consented to oral sex with his victims. Nonetheless, the notion that Lawrence had killed Simpson in a panicked response to Simpson's unwanted sexual advances did not die. The idea originated with the chief of police, but it would continue to be rehashed over the next few months before the judge and jury. In the meantime, the exposure of the gay-related nature of the murder led to more salacious headlines.

FROM SIMPSON AS VICTIM TO "PERVERTS" AS A MENACE

Both of Miami's newspapers quickly expanded their coverage of the story to implicate the entire gay community as a menacing presence in the city. In his own research into the Simpson murder, media scholar Fred Fejes has chronicled how newspaper editors used it to demand a cleanup drive against Miami's increasingly visible gay venues. Their insinuation was that the murder was the natural offshoot of tolerating such vices as gay bars, cruising venues, neighborhoods, and beaches. They ignored the fact that Simpson did not frequent a bar on the night of his murder; Eastern employees largely avoided gay bars, since police often took license plate numbers or checked IDs of patrons and informed their employers of their actions.[41] It also was immaterial that Simpson's consensual foray at the lovers' lane was hardly different from that of the straight couples who frequented the area on a nightly basis. What ultimately mattered for civic boosters was Miami's reputation as a tourist destination. Just as the *Herald*'s editors fought throughout the early 1950s to clean up the city's gambling and prostitution rackets, they now exploited Simpson's death to clean up Miami's gay underworld.

Thus, on August 9, the first full day after Lawrence and Killen confessed to their roles in the killing, both papers refocused their coverage. For the next several days, they largely neglected further discussion of the case and instead published sensational stories on the size of the gay community in the area. The *Daily News* began by running the front-page headline "Pervert Colony Uncovered In Simpson Slaying Probe" and revealed to the public the bizarre inner workings of this "colony." The article begins, "A colony of some 500 male homosexuals, congregated mostly in the near-downtown northeast section and ruled by a 'queen,' was uncovered in the investigation of the murder of an Eastern Air Lines steward." The article provides even more salacious detail when it quotes justice of the peace Edwin Lee Mason: "I certainly learned a lot during this investigation I never knew before. I not only was surprised at the number of homosexuals turned up . . . but I was amazed to find out that there were distinct classes, not only based on age groups, but also on the ages of the persons with whom they liked to consort and groups based on the type of perversion."[42]

Further shocking the paper's readership was the testimony from various police investigators, who freely implicated Simpson in a steamy underworld of gay sexual and criminal drama. Deputy Sheriff Manson Hill told the paper, "In seeking a motive for the slaying, we theorized that possibly the killing was caused by jealousy. We learned—among other things—that Simpson was bisexual. We also learned that there was a nominal head of the colony—a queen." Investigators even pursued the theory that "the murder might have been for succession of the title, and that Simpson may have been the 'ruler.' "[43] While the article later affirmed that Simpson was not in fact the "queen" of the "colony," the defamation of his character had been accomplished. Additionally, the ground was laid for a monthlong attack by media, politicians, and police designed to drive gays out of the city. Meanwhile, the prospects for justice in the Simpson case were severely compromised by the paper's salacious portrayal of the gay underworld.

As one of the largest campaigns against a gay community in the United States, the harassment drew an acerbic response from the country's lone gay rights group. Known as the Mattachine Society, this organization was based in Los Angeles but had a more national reach, thanks especially to its affiliated publication, *ONE Magazine*.[44] *ONE*'s editorial staff, led by Jim Kepner, made events in Miami a focal point of their reportage. Readers of the November 1954 edition followed a chronology of the unfolding cleanup campaign: bar raids, arrests of gays and lesbians at known gay beaches, collection of files on Dade County "perverts" arrested previously, calls for forced hospitalization or imprisonment of all "deviates," and passage of a new law forbidding bars to serve homosexuals.[45] Kepner, writing under his pseudonym Lyn Pedersen, ended his account by cautioning: "Miami illustrates that corrupt politicians and opportunistic demagogues can herd any community into a pogrom. National policy nowadays makes Negroes and Jews less likely targets for hate orgies. . . . Gays seem top candidates for any new, large-scale witch-hunt in America."[46]

For all of the terror inflicted on the gay community in the month following Simpson's murder, the cleanup campaign could have been much worse. As Fred Fejes notes, it ended quite abruptly, in mid-September, when the newspapers stopped reporting on the story. Indeed, Fejes argues that the overall campaign was orchestrated to achieve somewhat modest goals: overcoming the reluctance of the mayor and chief of police to force the gay scene further underground. Once this had been achieved, the city could present itself as a morally upright town, and the elite could quickly call off the witch hunt. After all, as police chief Walter Headley noted, "If I ran all the homosexuals out of town, members of some of the best families would lead the parade."[47]

THE SIMPSON MURDER AND THE AIRLINES

Consistent with Fejes's thesis is the fact that the press never implicated Eastern or its flight attendant corps as a center of homosexual activity—probably because Eastern and Pan Am were two of the largest employers in Miami and were sources of immense wealth and prestige. Thus never once did either paper run an article that implicated the airlines in the city's homosexual problem. Miami's residential "colonies" of homosexuals were demonized, but there was no mention of what jobs such men held to afford living in a decent neighborhood, nor were there any investigative reports about Simpson's work at Eastern and the preponderance of gay men in the flight attendant corps. The reporting suggested that homosexuality was an identity that manifested itself only in the leisure world—in neighborhoods, bars, beaches, and public parks—rather than at work.

Since the newspapers never attacked the airline, Eastern found a surprising amount of latitude to weather the crisis. While resisting Delta's extreme reaction, managers nonetheless quietly took actions to reduce the number of stewards the airline employed. One former flight attendant claimed that the airline sought to (in his words) "purge" some of its stewards, encouraging them to take jobs elsewhere in the company that were out of the public eye.[48] A second strategy managers chose was even easier to implement, especially given the strength of the flight attendant union at Eastern: they severely curtailed the hiring of new stewards.[49] Whereas men were still being hired at a consistent rate before August 1954, their numbers diminished to a negligible trickle thereafter.

Particularly telling is the plight of Pedro Muniz, whose application was accepted a few weeks before the Simpson murder. Instead of getting called back to start training, however, Muniz received a letter informing him of a freeze on new steward hires. As Muniz writes in his memoirs, "Eastern all of a sudden put a freeze on the hiring of stewards and this was due to a somewhat big scandal that made the headlines of all the Miami newspapers, when an Eastern steward was assassinated in Miami." Muniz waited all of August and September 1954 before finally finding a way to begin flight attendant training. Yet to do so he now needed a special favor. He had befriended an Eastern pilot who "was a very good friend of the Superintendent of In-Flight Services." With the pilot's support, he was allowed to start flight attendant training, the lone man "together with twelve lovely young females."[50]

Muniz's hiring, the first since the Simpson murder, also set a new precedent for subsequent applicants: only men who had connections in the company, especially current employees working in other departments, would be accepted as stewards. Two stewards whose tenures began in late 1955 both had been working at the Miami base before asking for a transfer (one was a security guard, the other worked at the ticket counter). As part of the application process, recalls one of the men, his current boss was called to vouch for his character, including any observed tendencies toward homosexuality.[51] At the same time, the window even for these company men to apply for steward jobs was closing rapidly. The flight attendant training program in Miami, which trained a new class at least once a quarter during busy times, now accepted men just once a year. The men who trained in late 1955 therefore had to wait through several months of female-only classes before finally beginning their training. The flight attendant class of November 1955 contained five men and thirty women.[52]

THE "HOMOSEXUAL PANIC" DEFENSE

In November 1954, Charles Lawrence and Lewis Killen stood trial for the killing of William Simpson. They both faced charges of first-degree murder, since Florida law was clear-cut: if a homicide, even if unintentional, occurred during commission of a premeditated robbery, then the killer and his co-conspirators were guilty of first-degree murder. There was, however, the remote prospect that the jury could find the two young men guilty of manslaughter and prescribe a less severe sentence. For the manslaughter verdict to hold, the jury had to be convinced that Simpson had provoked the killers.[53] Usually provocation involves a violent act, generally a fight between two men, before the murder takes place. In this case, however, there was no scuffle or violence. And only the attackers, not Simpson, were armed.

Yet the jurors were still able to find that Simpson had provoked his own murder by relying on Lawrence's claim during his trial testimony that he had jumped out of the car and drawn his gun on Simpson because "I was afraid he would attack me—make a sexual attack on me."[54] This claim echoed words from Lawrence's conversation with Chief Engel, as well as his written confession that was also read into the trial transcript: "He wanted me to commit an act and I didn't want to. . . . [I] was out to hurt him because I don't like these perverts."[55] Thus, while the Simpson trial predates the creation of the legal term by a full decade, it is clear that the jurors were persuaded by a defense now known as "homosexual panic" or "homosexual advance."[56]

These legal tactics were stretched to the limit to protect Lawrence and Killen from murder convictions. After all, their conspiracy to rob from gay men had required that Lawrence seduce these men while hitchhiking. The jury and newspaper readers also heard that Lawrence's acquiescence to oral sex in the Simpson case was not an isolated event. Yet a juror who shared with the *Miami Herald* the inner workings of the four-hour deliberation was outspoken about the most crucial piece of evidence in their verdict: "He believed the youths' accusations of homosexuality against Simpson 'made a big difference' in the jury's thinking."[57] In sentencing the two defendants to the maximum twenty-year sentence allowed for manslaughter, Judge Grady Crawford added his personal dissent to this application of "homosexual panic," noting that the "record of the trial was such that it would support a first degree murder conviction."[58]

While Eastern's policies toward stewards tightened in the aftermath of the Simpson scandal, it is less clear whether Pan Am's policies also changed in response. For the time being, Pan Am stewards remained securely in their jobs, but the airline ceased hiring men by 1958. A Pan Am steward at the time heard two rival explanations for the policy change. One was that male flight attendants tended to become active in union activities, complicating contract negotiations for management and also potentially driving up salaries, pension costs, and other expensive benefits. The other explanation, however, was that corporate officials and their wives were increasingly disturbed by the number of gay men in the flight attendant corps.[59]

Most clearly, however, the Simpson murder allowed a legal defense unimaginable without homophobia to gain more credibility on its way to becoming an accepted part of U.S. jurisprudence. The notion of "homosexual panic" would ensure that even more men like William Simpson would find second-class status in the courts just for being gay. Simpson's case also foreshadowed a larger smear campaign against gender nonconformists and homosexuals that accompanied sex-based civil rights discourse over the ensuing decades.

HOMOPHOBIA, ECONOMICS, AND THE LAW

There were several reasons behind airlines' choice to effectively end men's access to the steward position in the 1950s. Economic motives, the postwar resurgence of traditional gender norms, and homophobia all played powerful roles. Further, they need to be studied together, for the dynamics of economics, sexism, and homophobia were closely interrelated and worked in tandem to feminize the flight attendant corps.

In the 1950s, workers were easier to underpay if they were black or female, and they were easier to fire (or refuse to hire) as men if they were gay. Airlines had already barred African Americans and other minorities from the flight attendant corps, so they could most effectively lower their labor costs if their flight attendants were young women, not men. Raw economic motives exacerbated the sexism of subjecting women to restrictive work rules and the homophobia of displacing gay-suspected men from their jobs. While the marriage, weight, and age restrictions placed on women entrenched the aviation sector's sexism, Delta's decision in 1948 to jettison all of its higher-paid pursers—coupled with Eastern's and Pan Am's choices to stop hiring stewards in the 1950s—reinforced its homophobia.

The 1950s were an intensely homophobic decade in U.S. culture. For some of this time, airlines like Eastern and Pan Am held their ground against this social stigma, albeit quietly. Public relations campaigns no longer promoted stewards' assiduous service and physical appeal as they had in the 1930s. Yet amid this lack of attention, a sizable cadre of gay men entered the career, a gay community took root at both airlines, and a modicum of tolerance sprang up between gays and straights on the job and even in social situations. The Simpson murder altered this climate. With the public now aware of the scandalous secret that some stewards were indeed "perverts," the airlines increasingly acted in their own economic self-interest. Both Eastern and Pan Am finally embraced the goal of a female-only flight attendant corps, who would be cheaper and more marketable while also supposedly immune to homosexual scandal. Right at the dawn of the civil rights era, the flight attendant corps—already homogenous—was becoming even less diverse: all white, all female, and ostensibly all straight.

The Simpson scandal dissipated somewhat quickly in Miami. The salacious headlines were gone within months, and Eastern weathered the storm without losing its status as a reputable economic leader in the region. Stewards at the airline, of course, fared worse than their employer: many were reassigned to new positions, new hires were more intensely screened, and corporate executives were more resolved to eliminate new male hires altogether. Yet while the business scandal faded, the legal scandal of the Simpson trial endured. Legal teams representing the airlines, including Pan Am and Eastern, did not forget the potency of "homosexual panic." Indeed, in the late 1960s, they would invoke a form of this legal rationale to argue for an exemption from the sex discrimination clause of the 1964 Civil Rights Act. To keep their flight attendant corps all female, they claimed that male customers would be unnerved by male flight attendants and might respond to them in aggressive ways. William Simpson's memory thereby lingered over the next decade's civil rights discourse, as feminists and gay rights advocates fought to renegotiate the relationship between sexism, homophobia, economics, and the law established in the 1950s.

CHAPTER FOUR

Flight Attendants and Queer
Civil Rights

The 1960s were effectively a lost decade for male flight attendants. The historical norm, established in the 1930s and still true into the mid-1950s, of having men compose a sizable percentage of the flight attendant corps had been broken. The career was now preponderantly female, so much so that only 4 percent of flight attendants were men by 1966.[1] This small vestige of men tended to be well-paid, very senior employees at Pan Am and Eastern, men hired back in the post-World War II years. Others were pursers at other international carriers, while the remainder were Hawaiian men hired at United to serve their Honolulu flights and Puerto Rican men working at Trans Caribbean Airways. With stewards' numbers so reduced, many travelers had no idea that any men were working the job or that they had done so since the dawn of aviation. Indeed, in the 1960s almost every flight attendant was young, white, and female.

Workplace developments in the sixties typically served to reinforce sexually desirable stewardesses as the norm. Braniff Airlines led the way in raising stewardesses' hemlines to accentuate their young white bodies. Its "air strip" gimmick from 1965 promised customers that the stewardess would lose an article of her Emilio Pucci-designed uniform every time she walked down the aisle. The television commercial promoting the "air strip" was choreographed to bawdy stripper music and portrayed stewardesses suggestively taking off parts of their ornate clothing ensemble. The male commentator, whose voice eerily resembled that of a strip club emcee, ended the commercial by saying, "The air strip is brought to you by Braniff International, who believes that even an airline hostess should look like a girl."[2] The 1960s also saw the publication of the sassy best-selling book *Coffee, Tea or Me?*, which supposedly revealed the escapades of two real-life stewardesses but was actually ghostwritten by a male author seeking to reinforce the worst stereotypes about stewardesses and their sexual appetites.[3] Stewardess-themed porn films also premiered in the decade, with a naughty 3-D film, *The Stewardesses*, boasting an eleven-month stint in San Francisco theaters in 1969.[4] To state the obvious, the flight attendant career had become a sexist, heterosexist, racially exclusive civil rights nightmare by the middle of the 1960s.

There were some small steps toward redressing these injustices, as the larger social momentum promoting civil rights did occasionally interrupt business as usual in the skies. Most significantly, in 1958 TWA acquiesced in hiring the first African American stewardess, Dorothy Franklin, while a smaller airline hired the first African American pilot. The New York State Commission on Human Rights (NYSCHR) successfully negotiated these concessions by threatening legal action under the state's civil rights laws.[5] By and large, however, breaking the color line in the airplane cabin was not easy, as the airlines by 1965 had hired a meager total of fifty African American stewardesses.[6] The real trendsetting precedent of Franklin's hiring was far more pessimistic: the airlines would change their ways on hiring African Americans, and on retaining married women, mothers, women over age thirty-five, and any man who applied for the job, only begrudgingly and when faced with a court order to do so.

For male flight attendants, the most consequential developments in the 1960s transpired not on the job but rather in the courts and the political discussions involving civil rights. This chapter therefore turns toward Capitol Hill and judicial chambers. The main characters are not stewards themselves but rather the politicians, lawyers, bureaucrats, and judges who interpreted how such men were to be accommodated in the new civil rights-era workplace. And the main male flight attendant character was only an applicant for the job, Celio Diaz, who dreamed of flying for Pan Am while raising his family and working as a truck driver in Miami.

Much was at stake for gay rights in the legal history I sketch, which begins with the crown jewel of civil rights legislation, the 1964 Civil Rights Act. The historical presumption is that gay rights were an unmentioned, unconsidered afterthought of the 1964 moment. The act was instead a victory for the forces of racial justice headed by Martin Luther King Jr., a hard-won legislative triumph of President Lyndon Johnson and his able congressional stewards (Hubert Humphrey in the Senate and Emanuel Celler in the House), and a due homage to the legacy of the recently slain John F. Kennedy. The Civil Rights Act was primarily a race bill, and it unquestionably did more to end Jim Crow segregation in the American public sphere than any other piece of legislation since the close of Reconstruction. Only secondarily did the 1964 Civil Rights Act encompass women's rights. In fact, the path to including a sex discrimination provision in the bill's Title VII, which forbade workplace discrimination in hiring or firing based on race, religion, national origin—and now sex—was one of deeply mixed motives and unexpected legislative maneuverings. But its ultimate impact on allowing women to enter career fields that had previously been off limits was considerable indeed. Thus the second pillar of civil rights, women's equality, made it into the Civil Rights Act and the deliberations leading up to it, but barely.

To date, however, what this chapter asserts has gone unnoticed: the 1964 Civil Rights Act was also a seminal moment for gender nonconformists and even homosexuals. These groups were even coyly referenced—in an admittedly backhanded way—on the floor of the House of Representatives as the sex clause was first added to Title VII in February 1964. Thereafter, queer-baiting became a significant preoccupation of the bureaucrats and lawyers left to interpret the new law after it passed. These considerations took the form of hypothesizing about supposedly absurd gender anomalies who might seek to enter the workplace because of Title VII, including male nurses, female dog catchers, and male Playboy bunnies. When conservatives invoked these anomalies, they sought to limit the act's ability to dismantle gender barriers at work, suggesting that the legislation could not have endorsed such oddities. Raising these queer characters was thus another deployment of homophobia in the legal sphere. As in the Simpson trial, which used "homosexual panic" to affirm that equal protection of the law did not cover sexual perverts, the deliberations on the sex clause of the Civil Rights Act raised the specter of male secretaries—or male flight attendants—to suggest that gender anomalies did not deserve civil rights protection either.

Conventional wisdom suggests that gay rights had its own watershed moments, which came about only in the years after the Civil Rights Act. Stonewall, the riots in New York City in June 1969 when frequenters of a gay bar rioted against police brutality, is considered the foremost of these seminal events.[7] Rightfully so. Stonewall took the previous valiant efforts of fledgling gay rights groups and drastically expanded their intensity and scope. The fights to abolish the sickness model of homosexuality, to eradicate sodomy laws, and to eliminate the exclusion of gays and lesbians from public life—including the workplace—had more momentum after Stonewall than ever before.

But by June 1969, men like Celio Diaz were already using the Civil Rights Act to secure other crucial victories that would ultimately benefit gender nonconformists and homosexuals. Diaz, and other men and women aspiring to careers reserved for the other sex, persevered through years of queer-baiting to carve out a space in the post-civil rights workplace. His victory over Pan Am turned out to be precedent setting, and the court's decision is now effectively the law of the land, forcing a more robust enforcement of Title VII than those who wrote the law originally desired. As a result, *Diaz v. Pan Am* succeeded in preventing all sorts of employers from prejudging a man for his perceived effeminacy or a woman for being butch.

The case also marked, albeit surreptitiously, a key gay rights victory, as it reopened the doors of flight attendant academies to men. Soon thereafter, significant numbers of gay men secured their first unionized, middle-class job, despite continuing efforts in the larger society to keep gays and lesbians out of the workplace. The male flight attendant soon became a representative of a post-Stonewall gay community on its way out of the closet, not just in America's metropolises, but in every city with passenger air service, even in traditionally conservative realms like the South, Midwest, and Mountain West. All of these developments began not with Stonewall but with a series of awkward moments in the House of Representatives during deliberations on the Civil Rights Act.

CIVIL RIGHTS "CONCEIVED OUT OF WEDLOCK"

The history of how the male flight attendant returned to work can be told in a somewhat linear, clear-cut way. It begins with the passage of the 1964 Civil Rights Act and proceeds to the Equal Employment Opportunity Commission, the government agency charged with enforcing Title VII. From 1966 until late 1971, numerous grievances by stewardesses, coupled with a few cases of men seeking to be flight attendants, wound their way through proceedings at the EEOC, which had to rule in a grievant's favor for the case to enter the federal court system.[8] The decisive case for men turned out to be *Diaz v. Pan Am*, which Diaz filed with the EEOC in 1967 and then in Miami's Federal District Court in 1968. Diaz lost his case at the district level but won his appeal in the Fifth Circuit Court of Appeals in 1970. When Pan Am appealed to the U.S. Supreme Court in a final attempt to keep its workforce female only, the Court refused to hear the case and left the appeals decision in tact. Starting in early 1971, then, male flight attendants were once again hired for the job, this time at virtually every major U.S. airline.[9]

Yet this straightforward synopsis only hints at the convoluted path leading to this moment when Title VII worked on behalf of men, gay and straight. While the logic behind the *Diaz* victory flows logically enough from the law's wording, which forbids discrimination based on one's sex, the appellate ruling and the Supreme Court's acquiescence struck many observers as a perversion of the law's original intent. The *Wall Street Journal* accurately encapsulated the bewilderment and consternation of many conservative observers when it noted, "To the extent male stewards replace glamorous stewardesses, the case also may prove to be one of the more controversial interpretations of the 1964 law among members of the male-dominated Congress."[10]

These misgivings from more conservative forces predated the *Diaz* decision. In fact, even when the Civil Rights Act was crafted in Congress, there was little desire to include protection against sex discrimination. Even many supporters of civil rights found the sex discrimination clause troubling. For example, Herman Edelsberg, the man designated to enforce the act's measures in his role as director of the EEOC, considered the sex provision "a fluke . . . conceived out of wedlock" and initially resisted using his agency's resources for sex discrimination cases.[11]

Examining how the sex provision in Title VII was crafted on Capitol Hill exposes a kernel of truth to Edelsberg's claims. As other historians have demonstrated, the sex provision was added by an unexpected coalition led by the conservative southern Democrat Howard Smith of Virginia. Smith's hope in adding sex to Title VII was to peel off votes from the bill's supporters, especially in the Senate, where it was sure to be filibustered. Even when he introduced the sex amendment, Smith could not conceal his contempt for the entire bill, much less the addition of sex as a protected category in employment. "Now, what harm can you do this bill that . . . is so imperfect today," Smith concluded bitterly. "What harm will this [amendment] do to the condition of the bill?"[12]

Yet Smith's amendment—whose supporters were primarily like-minded southern Democrats—also gained traction among the House's most progressive members on women's issues: a handful of Republican and Democratic women members of Congress, such as Republican Katherine Price Collier St. George of New York and Democrat Martha Griffiths of Detroit.[13] Both of these women added their endorsement of the sex amendment to the floor debate, defending the need for fuller equality for women at work. This second basis of support was crucial to approving the amendment, which passed by a very narrow margin. Only 301 representatives cast their vote on Smith's amendment. No roll call was requested, so the counting was conducted by tellers, who recorded 168 ayes and 133 nays. The tellers—Martha Griffiths and Chairman Emmanuel Celler—later confirmed that the amendment's supporters were predominantly southerners and Republicans, an unusual admixture of the House's most conservative and most progressive members.[14] Yet even some of the amendment's progressive supporters assumed that the amendment, along with the rest of Title VII, would not survive the Senate filibuster.

QUEERNESS AND THE BFOQ

Though the House had approved the sex amendment, its work was not complete. Two days after Smith's amendment was accepted, the House was forced to revisit the issue, since Smith, in his haste and halfheartedness, had neglected to add the term *sex* to various places in the bill's wording where it seemed necessary. Smith deferred to Rep. Frances Bolton to propose a second amendment altering Title VII with the additional references to sex. This procedure was meant to be minor, with no design of altering the bill's overall effect. In fact, however, the brief exchange on February 10, 1964—the very day that the Civil Rights Bill finally passed the House—had momentous legal consequences for women and men in various professions, including those seeking to become flight attendants.

While Bolton and Smith moved to add sex to just two places in Title VII, Representative Charles Goodell (R-NY), requested yet another crucial addition. He recommended that sex also be included in the "bona fide occupational qualification" (BFOQ) clause, which read: "It shall not be an unlawful employment practice for an employer to hire and employ employees . . . on the basis of his religion or national origin in those certain instances where religion or national origin is a bona fide occupational qualification reasonably necessary to the normal operation of that particular business or enterprise."[15]

Basically, the BFOQ served as an exemption to Title VII's ban on discrimination at work. It allowed employers the opportunity to either hire or not hire an individual on the basis of his or her religion or national origin. The presumption was that a French restaurant, for example, ought to be able to restrict its hiring search to chefs from France, if it so desired. Yet the wording of the BFOQ certainly provided ambiguity that future employers, labor unions, and judges would find troubling. Especially the clauses "reasonably necessary" and "normal operation" were unclear, and it was uncertain who had legal authority to decide whether an employer's choice to discriminate on the basis of religion or national origin was "reasonably necessary" (did the French restaurant really *need* a chef from France?). This uncertainty was hugely problematic, since if employers were able to decide for themselves what hiring criteria were "necessary," the act would have lost its power to end discrimination. Seemingly aware of how nettlesome the BFOQ could prove to be, legislators consciously chose not to permit any use of a BFOQ based on race. This choice demonstrates how egregious the framers of Title VII found race-based discrimination; employers would *never* be able to claim that hiring members of only one race was "reasonably necessary to the normal operation" of their business.

The fact that Chairman Smith had omitted sex from the BFOQ thereby alarmed Representative Goodell and others interested in minimizing the impact of the sex clause. As the bill stood on the morning of its approval in the House, there would be no justification for an employer to hire only men or only women for any job. The strongly enforced divisions in so many workplaces that allowed sex-segregated careers to thrive were under threat of being dismantled. Thus Goodell rose to add sex to the BFOQ, a move that seemingly caught Representative Bolton off guard. When Goodell proposed the addition, Bolton responded, "I have not studied that. It was not brought to my attention by the staff." Rather than thwart what seemed at the time to be Goodell's innocuous inclusion, Bolton quickly acquiesced with no counterargument: "But if that is the sense of the House, I will be very glad to accept it." With this, Goodell's addition was included with Bolton's proposals and was added to Title VII by unanimous consent.

Goodell's intervention on the House floor comprised just five sentences, and his appearance surely lasted no more than three minutes. He finished his intervention with the most poignant explanation for his actions—and, for gender nonconformists, what may be their most significant inclusion in the civil rights legislative discourse from the 1960s: "There are so many instances where the matter of sex is a bona fide occupational qualification. For instance, I think of an elderly woman who wants a female nurse. There are many things of this nature which are bona fide occupational qualifications, and it seems to me they would be properly considered here as an exception."[16]

Goodell's words are significant in that they subtly raise the specter of gender-transgressing employees. After all, lurking unmentioned in the background of this comment is a rather ominous figure: the male nurse, who might seek to serve, comfort, and even touch the vulnerable elderly woman, all in the name of the Civil Rights Act. Goodell's comment sought to clarify that Congress was not intending, nor would it allow, such forays across the gender divide as embodied in the male nurse. His words were meant to provoke two contrasting responses in his listeners among the Congress and the general public: alarm at the gender bending that Title

VII might allow, and reassurance that the legislation would not be implemented in such an unacceptable way.

Queerness, at least in the form of an almost-but-not-quite-mentioned male nurse, thereby quickly appeared at the heart of civil rights legal discourse. Of course, however, Goodell by no means suggested that such people ought to benefit from the Civil Rights Act. Unlike African Americans and gender-conforming women, whose grievances would now have standing before the EEOC and the federal courts, Goodell foresaw no such protections for queers. If an elderly woman does not want a male nurse, however qualified, she need not have one. And, presumably, if airline customers do not want male flight attendants, they won't be subjected to their presence either.[17] In a loose way, Goodell's interpretation of Title VII and queerness echoed the legal defense of "homosexual panic." Queers might seek redress in the courts under Title VII, but the law would rule against them as long as public opprobrium against them persisted.

PERSISTENT BATTLES OVER QUEERNESS AND TITLE VII

Despite expectations that the Senate would strip all of Title VII from the bill, senators ultimately found enough votes to overcome the filibuster without such significant concessions. During the seventy-five-day southern-led filibuster, the crucial swing votes in the Senate—small-government Republicans—relinquished their opposition to the bill, including Title VII. Headed by Illinois senator Everett Dirksen, they demanded only some small changes to the House version to alleviate fears that the EEOC would become too powerful. The Dirksen compromise was solid enough to garner seventy-one votes, thereby ensuring passage of the bill in the Senate on June 20 and, once again, in the House on July 2. President Johnson signed the bill into law on the very day the House passed the revised version, in a televised signing ceremony that coincided with the start of the July 4 weekend. The Civil Rights Act of 1964 was now the law of the land, along with its quite controversial—but largely overlooked—sex amendment to Title VII.

But the passage of the law was only the beginning of the battle over the BFOQ and the extent to which Title VII would end workplace discrimination. The EEOC and the federal courts now inherited the unresolved issue from the Congress. Even though lawmakers left such an incomplete record, the EEOC's early deliberations followed the same trajectory as the brief discussions in the House. In particular, the EEOC was just as reluctant to embrace the far-reaching call for gender equality in Title VII. Its leaders even reiterated Congressman Goodell's vilification of gender transgressors. Executive director Herman Edelsberg most vividly expressed this line of argument in a November 1965 press conference, noting, "There are people on this Commission who think that no man should be required to have a male secretary—and I am one of them."[18]

While Edelsberg sought to elicit laughter with his comment, EEOC chairman Franklin D. Roosevelt (the son of the former president) pronounced the EEOC's policy in more official tones, though with an equally alarmist stance toward gender bending. When publicizing the commission's guidelines on interpreting sex discrimination, he proclaimed, "Common sense will be the rule in interpreting Title VII." To demonstrate how "common sense" would guide policy, he noted that there would be no "'revolution in job patterns' such as more male nurses or secretaries." Other erotically charged cases of gender bending were out of the question as well: "It is still legal under the Title's ban on sex discrimination to advertise for, and to hire, a masseur for a men's Turkish bath and a masseuse for a women's establishment."[19]

Examining these statements shows that Roosevelt's "common sense" strategy amounted to a mechanism to maintain the status quo. If applied neutrally, "common sense" would recognize vast differences between work as a secretary and work in a Turkish bath. One realm involved a typical workplace of fully clad adults going about routine office tasks. The other was far more intimate, involving undressing and touching of another's body. Meanwhile, the example of nursing was somewhere in the middle; patients might temporarily undress or be touched, but at other times the interactions were more typical of regular offices. Seeing these various workplaces as equivalently deserving of gender segregation might have been common at the time, but it was clearly more phobic than sensible.

Not surprisingly, the EEOC's "common sense" approach translated into a record on sex discrimination that was very timid. More and more women's advocates found the commission to be obstructionist, unwilling to exert the same effort on sex cases as on race cases. Moreover, commissioners seemed preoccupied with the exceptional cases of men desiring to enter women's work rather than the far more numerous cases brought by women facing unequal pay, marriage restrictions, and prohibitions against entering certain fields reserved for men only.

Representative Martha Griffiths, an outspoken advocate of the sex amendment on the House floor, returned there in June 1966 to call the EEOC to task over their neglect of sex issues. "The whole attitude of the EEOC toward discrimination based on sex is specious, negative, and arrogant," she noted, setting the tone for her blistering speech. She then took aim precisely at the EEOC's "common sense" approach and its tendency to highlight gender benders supposedly seeking protection under Title VII: "At the White House Conference on Equal Opportunity in August 1965 they focused their attention on such silly issues as whether the law now requires 'Playboy' clubs to hire male 'bunnies.' . . . The current issue of the EEOC Newsletter, May–June 1966, emphasizes such oddities as whether a refusal to hire a woman as a dog warden, or a man as a 'house mother' for a college sorority house, violates the law." After identifying the ways that the EEOC had shirked their duties, Griffiths laid bare the real agenda behind the EEOC's "common sense" approach: "This emphasis on odd or hypothetical cases has fostered public ridicule which undermines the effectiveness of the law, and disregards the real problems of sex discrimination in employment."[20]

Griffiths's speech was a key moment that galvanized women's advocates to confront the EEOC. Her words circulated through women's networks and directly aided in the formation of the National Organization for Women (NOW), which occurred just a few months later, in October 1966. A key aspect of NOW's original agenda would be to pressure the EEOC to enforce Title VII in a way that supported women. Interestingly, the moment that triggered Griffiths's wrath and thereby also led to the creation of NOW was EEOC inaction on flight attendants' claims of abuse by their employers.

FLIGHT ATTENDANTS AND THE EEOC

To be clear, Griffiths did not criticize the EEOC for their failure to take Celio Diaz's case seriously. She was upset about the EEOC's preoccupation with female dog catchers and male sorority mothers, but not because it correspondingly trivialized the plight of aspirant male flight attendants. Instead, she focused on stewardesses and the age, marriage, pregnancy, and weight restrictions that drastically curtailed their careers. These stewardesses had filed over one hundred grievances with the EEOC in the first year and a half after the agency opened its doors in July 1965.[21] Yet the EEOC, in an unusual set of rulings that incensed Griffiths and many advocates of women's rights, had effectively subordinated these women's cases to Diaz's. Once again, so it seemed, the EEOC was prioritizing an "odd or hypothetical case," in a way that "disregard[ed] the real problems of sex discrimination." A closer analysis reveals why, quite unexpectedly, Diaz's case superseded those of stewardesses.[22]

This unusual scenario started with an encouraging judgment from the EEOC on the question of whether companies could fire women who married, the policy most responsible for keeping stewardesses' careers so brief. In September 1965, the EEOC weighed in on this tricky question and seemingly sided with stewardesses. The judgment stated that "an employer's rule which forbids or restricts the employment of married women and which is not applicable to married men is a discrimination based upon sex prohibited by Title VII of the Civil Rights Act."[23] Flight attendant labor unions had seemingly attained exactly what they needed to combat the airlines' no-marriage policies: a clear pronouncement that unfair treatment toward married women would have to end. After all, even though stewardesses at almost all airlines were fired when they married, married stewards were free to continue working.

However, just twelve days after publishing this marriage guideline, the EEOC baffled the unions in a follow-up to their original pronouncement. In response to a query from the airlines about whether this guideline affected their treatment of stewardesses, the EEOC general counsel replied: "It would be my opinion that the rule announced by Chairman Roosevelt would not apply to airline stewardesses. . . . If an airline may give preference to females only as stewardesses, i.e., if sex is a bona fide occupational qualification for the job of airline stewardesses, it would follow that an airline company could impose further qualifications with respect to such jobs and require that the employee be single and under a certain age."[24] Simply stated, the EEOC was willing to allow the airlines to continue firing stewardesses who married, but only if the airlines could prove that the job was legitimately a female-only career. The airlines had to seek protection under the BFOQ provision of Title VII. Oddly, airlines were told they could continue to fire married women, but only if they could justify excluding men like Diaz from the job.

The EEOC soon thereafter arranged to hold hearings on flight attendants and the BFOQ, with the stakes of tantamount importance not only for men like Celio Diaz but also now for stewardesses fighting their own forms of discrimination. Feminists and the flight attendant labor unions were incensed at the indignity of having to participate in these hearings, not to mention the two-year delay in grievances that resulted.[25] From a feminist view, the case should have been prima facie resolved in their favor, as Representative Griffiths noted in her vitriolic speech on the House floor in June 1966: "The airlines would not be making such a ridiculous argument if the EEOC had not been shilly-shallying and wringing its hands about the sex provision. Since both men and women are employed by the airlines as flight attendants, how in the name of commonsense can it be argued that the employment of either sex alone is 'reasonably necessary to the normal operation' of the airlines?" She ended her critique in disgust: "If any EEOC official believes this kind of foolishness, then the headquarters of EEOC, at 1800 G Street NW, should be called 'Fantasyland.'"[26]

The EEOC hearings hinged on a fairly specific set of questions: whether men could perform certain "nonmechanical" tasks required of flight attendants—and whether these tasks were essential for the job. A supporting document presented to the EEOC aptly summarized the legal argument the airlines developed, which clarified the "nonmechanical" tasks they had in mind. The airlines admitted that men could perform the basic physical functions required on the job: "Men can carry trays, and hang up coats and assist in event of the rare emergency." However, the memo continued, men could not "convey the charm, the tact, the grace, the liveliness that young girls can—particularly to men, who comprise the vast majority of airline passengers."[27] Thus, when the EEOC commissioners ruled in flight attendants' favor, as they finally did in a 3–1 decision dated February 21, 1968, they rejected this argument. They concluded that these "nonmechanical" attributes were not essential to the job: "The most important factor is whether the basic duties of a flight cabin attendant . . . can be satisfactorily performed by members of both sexes."[28] Since the EEOC did not see flight attendants' charm, tact, and grace as a "basic duty," the airlines were not permitted to exclude men on the basis of these criteria. Once the EEOC weighed in on this crucial question, it also granted permission to Celio Diaz to file his grievance against Pan Am in federal court.

ONWARD TO THE COURTS

Diaz v. Pan Am was not the only, or even the most obvious, option for becoming the test case on the BFOQ. In fact, another case against Pan Am brought by a male applicant, Roderick McNeil, began in 1966, three years earlier than *Diaz*. For whatever reason, however, McNeil filed his grievance not with the EEOC but rather with the NYSCHR.[29] The *McNeil* case, therefore, never entered the federal court system, where it could have set precedent for the whole country. Instead, it was litigated under New York State law, so airlines, in theory, could have lost the case and still refused to hire men outside New York State. Yet the priority for all interested parties, even the NYSCHR, was for the federal courts to rule on the BFOQ. Thus, even though the New York commission began its investigation well before *Diaz*, it suspended the *McNeil* proceedings to wait for the *Diaz* ruling.[30]

I mention the *McNeil* case because of its stark differences with *Diaz* in the way it was argued, with the less impactful New York case, ironically, being far more thorough, especially in its arguments favoring male flight attendants. Both cases tackled the same legal questions and arose at approximately the same time. In terms of the proceedings, the evidence presented on behalf of Pan Am was also quite similar in both cases. The New York City law firm Poletti, Freidin, Prashker, Feldman & Gartner represented the airlines in all the discrimination cases that arose after the

Civil Rights Act passed: at the EEOC, in the federal courts, and before the New York commission. The law firm drew from the same roster of witnesses and experts regardless of a case's venue.

But the similarities stopped there. Senior Attorney Alan Saks of the New York commission secured more witnesses on McNeil's behalf than did Robert Burns, the original counsel for Celio Diaz. Saks also was far more thorough in cross-examining the witnesses called by Pan Am. Thus, when the NYSCHR ultimately deferred to *Diaz*, they surrendered their own thorough work on behalf of McNeil to the mercy of a court whose proceedings were heavily skewed in favor of Pan Am. The *Diaz* district-level trial proceedings before Chief Judge Charles Fulton in Miami lasted one day (September 23, 1969), while the NYSCHR proceedings took place over sixteen days (the hearings began in June 1967 and continued sporadically through September 11, 1969). The transcript of the *Diaz* proceedings stretched to 535 pages, which included only about 150 pages generated by Counsel Burns and his witnesses. The NYSCHR proceedings, in contrast, number thousands of pages.

This page imbalance also translated into significant deficiencies in Diaz's claims against Pan Am. Particularly crucial was the failure of Diaz's attorney to address the main legal questions still left over from the EEOC hearings: Could the airlines claim that there were "nonmechanical" aspects of the job that were essential, and were women really far superior to men in performing them? Whereas the NYSCHR had generated a solid case to answer both questions in McNeil's favor, Diaz's attorney failed to do so.

The attorney also failed to counteract what was the most pressing emotional energy behind Pan Am's defense of their female-only policy: a vilification of effeminate and homosexual men. As we shall see, Pan Am's testimony, especially that from a renowned psychologist, exploited society's homophobic fears in justifying the need to hire only women for these jobs. While not quite the same technique as the "homosexual panic" defense used in the Simpson trial over a decade earlier, Pan Am's argumentation clearly sought the same overall effect: to use the stigma against homosexuality against Diaz and McNeil in a way that would trump a blind assessment of the law's merits. Yet while the NYSCHR deployed a variety of means to help counterbalance this homophobia and create a desirable vision of a mixed-sex flight attendant corps, Diaz's attorney failed to do so. Overall, then, when I consider *Diaz v. Pan Am*, I refer quite often to *McNeil v. Pan Am* as well. The former is the case that actually informed U.S. jurisprudence, despite its obvious flaws. The latter is the case for male flight attendants in its more thorough form, the case that ideally should have been argued for the plaintiff.

THE ACTORS BEHIND *DIAZ*

While the law turns on abstract principles and logical application of precedents, it also is heavily influenced by the concrete realities of any given case. With *Diaz*, the reasons for the ruling in favor of Pan Am at the district level become clearer after a consideration of the people involved, the interest groups following it, and the disparity of financial resources between Mr. Diaz and his adversary.

Celio Diaz was not handpicked by feminist groups or labor unions as a model plaintiff for this important test case on the BFOQ. He was not especially good-looking or particularly well-spoken, and he was older—age thirty when he applied for the job in 1967—than most successful flight attendant applicants. Diaz's second lawyer, Eleanor Schockett, who joined the case during the appeals phase, recalls, "As soon as he came into my office, I knew that he wouldn't get the job . . . because he didn't meet the other standards of appearance and so forth that were reasonable [for an employer to require]. . . . You had to be of a slender build. You had to have a very clear complexion, no pockmarks or anything. He tended to a sallow complexion, his eyes were not clear and sparkling."[31] Unlike plaintiffs in other notable civil rights cases, who are selected by advocacy groups for their ability to display the best public relations image, Diaz was not telegenic.

Born and raised in Miami, Diaz still employed a simple manner of speech when I met him at a nursing home toward the end of his life in 2006. He spoke softly and possessed a distinct Cuban American dialect that betrayed his working-class roots. His first foray into the aviation business came as a young man in his early twenties, when he supported his wife and children by working as a caterer for Braniff Airlines at Miami Airport. He had actually met several Eastern Air Lines and Pan Am stewards while working at the airport, and it kindled—better said, rekindled—a persistent dream he carried with him: "I wanted to travel and see as much of the world as I could."[32] Diaz actually wasn't the first man in his family with this dream: an uncle had served as a Pan Am steward in the pre–World War II era, serving as a bilingual liaison for travelers headed to the Caribbean and Latin America. Thus Diaz needed only to spend time with his family to be regaled with stories of hard work combined with opulence and mobility that male stewards used to enjoy in larger numbers than in the 1960s.

A few years after starting at Braniff, Diaz opted for a career change that seemed to put an end to his flirtations with flight. Pursuing better money to provide for his family, he seized an opportunity to become an independent truck driver. This second career allowed Diaz to profit in his own small way from the postwar boom that turned Miami from a sleepy, if somewhat seedy, tourist getaway into a bustling metropolis. But it also seemed to confine him permanently to the city of his birth. And as he approached his late twenties, Diaz the trucker was still dreaming of an alternative career that was more glamorous though far less "manly": he wanted to be a flight attendant and fly the world with Pan Am. He even was willing to take a considerable pay cut to pursue his dreams.

Rather than the unions and feminist groups choosing their model plaintiff, Diaz finally found them. When Pan Am twice refused to consider his applications for a flight attendant position, he sought out a lawyer on his own but could not find one willing to take the case on his modest budget. So he eventually asked for help at the ACLU in South Florida. Note that this was before the ACLU opened its Women's Rights Project under the leadership of future Supreme Court justice Ruth Bader Ginsburg. Ginsburg would later seek out male plaintiffs to challenge interpretations of the Fourteenth Amendment that permitted disparate treatment of women and men. But her work with the Women's Rights Project did not begin until the fall of 1970, two full years after Diaz had filed his case in federal court.[33]

The ACLU referred Diaz to Robert Burns, a lawyer with previous experience in civil rights cases. According to Diaz, Burns had previously been involved in a high-profile case in which a woman won the right to become a professional jockey.[34] Diaz retained Burns as his counsel, with the understanding that he himself, not the ACLU, would pay for the legal fees. He recalls that the case cost him about $3,000 to $4,000, a very modest sum for lawyers in the late 1960s. Burns thereafter helped Diaz file a grievance with the EEOC in April 1967 and proceeded to file on Diaz's behalf in federal court on February 14, 1969.[35] Only after these legal proceedings were under way did the case draw attention from labor unions and feminist groups. Diaz recalled various offers of support from prominent feminist Roxcy Bolton, who helped found the Miami chapter of NOW in 1966 and served as NOW's national vice president in 1969.[36] He did not recall, however, any concrete steps NOW had taken on his behalf.

However interested the labor unions were in this case, they also resisted direct involvement on Diaz's behalf. Lawyers for the Transportation Workers Union, which represented Pan Am's flight attendants, worked intensely on the earlier EEOC hearings. Yet other than writing an amicus brief for the case, the unions did not collaborate with Diaz or Burns in preparing for the case. Likewise, there is no record of interaction between Counsel Burns and either the EEOC or the NYSCHR, both of whom could have provided prescient advice. Even when Eleanor Schockett replaced Burns as Diaz's attorney for the appeal, no direct support came from the unions, NOW, or the EEOC. "No one paid me any attention at all," according to

Schockett. To her surprise, however, the EEOC sent a lawyer to the court of appeals argument. "The EEOC didn't even call me up to say that they were filing a brief, and I met the person that they sent. She was a young lawyer . . . and she stood there and read her brief," Schockett noted with annoyance, even though nearly thirty years had passed in the interim. She continued, "And I think that if she hadn't been a young woman they would have told her to sit down and just submit it."[37]

Schockett's own involvement with *Diaz* again illustrates the disarray of the plaintiff's case. She had no previous experience with sex discrimination law, though the ACLU probably knew of her thanks to her previous work with the South Florida Migrant Workers, where she defended immigrant laborers against intimidation from the police and other authorities. By the time she was asked to replace Robert Burns, however, Schockett had moved on to a position in corporate law. Moreover, the request from the ACLU came at the last minute: "I got a call one day from someone with the ACLU and he asked me if I would file a notice of appeal. And I said, 'Well, can I see the transcript?' And he said, 'That's the problem. The appeal must be filed in two days, and the transcript isn't ready. But if we don't file the notice of appeal, we'll lose all rights.' . . . It must have been a very weak moment. . . . So I said okay."[38]

Schockett personally had never heard of the case before she took it, nor was she deeply involved in the feminist activist groups that had arisen in Miami starting in the late 1960s. However, the tremendous difficulty she had experienced entering the male-dominated law profession had left an indelible mark on her. She had secured her first job via a personal friend, since other firms were reluctant to hire a female lawyer. And when the otherwise all-male coterie of lawyers headed to the back room of the lunch club on Schockett's first day, she was unable to join them. After all, many of the city's finest clubs and dining halls were still segregated by sex in the late 1960s. Feeling very much disadvantaged and underutilized helped shape in Schockett a feminist consciousness that was nonetheless uneasy with the more outspoken activism of NOW: "You know, I came from the generation before . . . I was before that era. But when you can't get a job because of your gender, that was a whole different story."[39] Despite maintaining an ideological distance from NOW, Schockett became a female pioneer in her own right. From the late 1960s to the 1980s, she successfully ascended from a junior lawyer barely able to find work to one of Dade County's first female circuit court judges.

The contrast between the two legal teams in the *Diaz* case was significant. At the court of appeals, the disparity was actually visible to Schockett: "When I walked into the room . . . there's this great big table over there with the lawyers from Eastern, the ATA [Air Transport Association], and the three or four lawyers from Pan Am, and then there's me. And then there's this other [attorney from the EEOC]."[40] Not only did Pan Am and the Air Transport Association have a larger representation of lawyers, they were also very well seasoned on issues of the BFOQ. Herbert Prashker, Pan Am's lead lawyer, knew the strengths of each witness because he argued the same issues at the EEOC and in the *McNeil* case. He was also a fine lawyer who had earned the respect of judges and his fellow lawyers. According to James Armstrong, who represented Pan Am in Miami and worked alongside Prashker during the district court hearings, "He was, you could tell, studious. I liked him and I think the judge [District Judge Charles Fulton] liked him. . . . He could put you on edge if you were in the witness stand. He was rigorous in his examination, very thorough, you'd better be ready when he cross-examined. I don't mean to say he was a bully, but he was good."

Armstrong himself noted the disparity between the two legal teams. "I thought that we were better off. I felt that Pan Am was better represented than [Diaz] was." To some extent, this disparity surprised Armstrong: "Obviously there were people who knew the significance of what [Diaz] was doing. You would have thought that they would have stepped up and said, 'We're going to get you the best.' "[41]

RIVAL INTERPRETATIONS OF THE BFOQ

The immediate questions in the *Diaz* trial, as in the EEOC hearings, involved whether the airlines could require flight attendants to perform "nonmechanical" duties and whether women were innately better at performing these duties. If so, the airlines might legitimately claim that being female was a "bona fide occupational qualification" for the job. Alongside these specific issues, the case also hinged on more abstract legal principles that were vitally important for the future of sex discrimination cases in the country. The central legal question in *Diaz* was how expansive the BFOQ was meant to be, a question that legislators had barely pondered when they hastily wrote the 1964 Civil Rights Act. Recall that Representative Goodell rose up in the House of Representatives to protect the nation against male nurses. In doing so, he suggested that the BFOQ could be invoked quite liberally: "There are so many instances where the matter of sex is a bona fide occupational qualification," he noted when claiming that an older woman ought to be able to have a female nurse. The Senate, however, had written a brief explanatory note on Title VII before passing the legislation. They called the BFOQ a "limited right" to discriminate based on sex.[42] So when the *Diaz* case finally came to arguments, much was at stake: Would sex discrimination be allowed only in "limited" cases, or would there be "so many instances" when it would be allowed? Not only Diaz's and male flight attendants' fates stood in the balance, but also the futures of many women and men seeking access to previously prohibited careers.

Just as in the hearings before the EEOC, Pan Am insisted that their choice to hire exclusively women was driven not by antimale bias but by the wisdom gained from decades of experience managing flight attendants. Their lawyers insisted that the airlines were best qualified—and were legally permitted—to set the prerequisites for a job and to determine who was able to undertake a given job. Since the jet age had required flight attendants to become more customer service oriented and more attuned to an increasingly diverse flying public, women were the best choice over men. Hiring men, Pan Am argued, was problematic because of past negative experiences with stewards: "That [airlines'] service would deteriorate is not a matter of supposition or speculation as the EEOC has suggested—by the unanimous verdict of an entire industry in the United States, it is what has been shown by years of experience with both male and female cabin attendants."[43]

One of the most essential pieces of evidence for the airlines was the testimony of various airlines' executives, especially those who managed the flight attendant corps. A cadre of these men appeared at a variety of these hearings: before the EEOC in 1967, at the NYSCHR from 1967 through 1969, and in the Miami District Court on September 23, 1969. The *Diaz* trial included testimony from Lloyd Wilson, in-flight service director of Pan Am, who testified to the fact that male stewards were increasingly ill equipped for the job. He claimed that jet technology placed greater emphasis on service and less priority on safety and the other auxiliary services stewards used to provide, like handling passengers' bags or rowing passengers from the seaplanes to shore. As more women and children began flying during the jet age, Wilson insisted,

> It became very evident . . . that we needed to give a sense of confidence to the female passenger, to the child traveling for the first time, that it was fun to fly, not just a frightening experience to get safely from "A" to "B." So we found that in all of these areas that *[sic]* the appearance of attractive, well-groomed females in the cabin of the airplane was highly acceptable to our passengers, both male and female, and that many of the duties being performed in that service by a female not only was preferable but was entirely necessary.

As for the tasks that were "necessary" for women to perform rather than men, Wilson included assisting with babies and with elderly passengers, helping with the birth of children, and helping women with toilet or menstrual problems.[44]

Yet a marked contrast appears between *McNeil* and *Diaz* in how the plaintiffs' attorneys countered these arguments. Diaz's first attorney, Robert Burns, raised no objection at all to the claim that women performed the "nonmechanical" work better than men, leaving this potentially damaging aspect of the testimony intact. His cross-examination of Pan Am's Wilson instead pointed to the remaining "mechanical" aspects of the flight attendant job, especially those that required heavy lifting or involved safety. He suggested that male flight attendants would have an easier time opening the aircraft doors or carrying thirty-five-pound wine coolers onto the plane.[45] In each instance, however, Pan Am's Wilson noted that these tasks, even opening the aircraft door, were no longer the flight attendant's responsibility. Burns's only success came in pointing out that customer preference was for a male steward in the case of emergencies.[46]

In the *McNeil* case, attorney Alan Saks went much further in countering Pan Am's claims about these "nonmechanical" tasks. He was able to generate a coherent argument for a diverse flight attendant corps of both men and women, who together would be able to provide more satisfying customer service than women alone. One aspect of this strategy was to show the modest percentage of foreign carriers serving New York City—as well as New York–based Trans Caribbean Airlines, the lone U.S. carrier on the list—that employed a mix of male and female flight attendants without any distinction between their work roles.[47] He also called several witnesses from Trans Caribbean to testify in person at the *McNeil* trial. Overall, on the basis of the practices of this one U.S. carrier and the other foreign carriers, Saks presented a model of flight attendant work roles akin to what was expressed in a 1969 ad for the West German carrier Lufthansa that ran in *Time* magazine:

> WHAT CAN A STEWARD DO THAT A STEWARDESS CAN'T?
> Absolutely nothing, in the line of Lufthansa duty. Our stewards were trained in the same rigorous school as our stewardesses. Which means, for example, that our stewards diaper babies just as well as they serve cocktails. But, if there's no difference in what they can do, why does Lufthansa staff all its flights with both stewards and stewardesses? Because sometimes a woman passenger wants help only from a woman, and a man only from a man. (Can you imagine an eleven-year-old boy, for instance, willingly calling a stewardess to the men's room because he's having trouble zipping up his fly?) When it makes no difference who serves you, the service on most airlines is pretty good. But sometimes it makes a great deal of difference who serves you. And that's when you realize that the service on Lufthansa is pretty special.[48]

The ad very aptly lends itself to an interpretation of the BFOQ that counters the one promoted by the U.S. airlines. It suggests that there are indeed certain workplaces that require members of only one sex, but only where there is bodily exposure, as with a boy needing assistance in the restroom. In all other cases there should be no distinction between the roles men and women could perform. In fact, having a coed workforce arguably is optimal for many service professions, including those on airplanes.

Saks also focused intensively on the work rules implemented at Trans Caribbean Airlines (TCA), which had created an effectively gender-blind workforce by 1967. Note that TCA was a U.S. airline and a member of the Air Transport Association, which was assisting Pan Am in its defense of its female-only flight attendant corps. Yet the airline failed to receive much scrutiny for its uniquely progressive work rules simply because it was relatively small (serving mainly the New York–San Juan route) and because its hub was in Puerto Rico, even though it was officially headquartered in New York City.

When the NYSCHR first interviewed members of Trans Caribbean's management, the airline employed roughly one hundred flight attendants, one-third of whom were men. Men were free to apply for the job, and they did so in modest numbers (about 15 percent of all applications). Meanwhile, stewardesses were permitted to marry and could work as long as they chose. TCA also promoted women to purser positions in the same manner and time frame as stewards. Thus the airline had attained an ideal in which men and women were virtually interchangeable. As a consequence, it became the first U.S. airline in which the two sexes stayed in their jobs for an equal average duration: women served almost four years, rather than the two-and-one-half-year average at other U.S. carriers in the late 1960s. TCA was also the first U.S. carrier to use the term *flight attendant* rather than *stewardess* and *steward*, an innovation that the EEOC in 1977 (nearly a decade later) would apply to the entire profession.[49] Finally, to create an environment in which male flight attendants would not be hampered by complaints regarding their care of children, TCA created rules regarding child care that equalized the workload: "If a child is under 8 years of age, he must be accompanied by a responsible adult. [In cases of children over age eight] when the child is a boy, a male f/a is assigned to watch him; when a girl, a female f/a is assigned. The company refuses to allow a flight attendant to be placed [in charge of a young child]. . . . Flight attendants do not change diapers for infants."[50]

The Trans Caribbean example served McNeil's case very well, offering a vision of a post–civil rights workplace where flight attendants could be treated equally regardless of their sex. Moreover, because TCA's managers vouched for the effectiveness of their work rules, attorney Saks could claim that other U.S. airlines had nothing to fear by embracing such innovations.

Saks used both the Lufthansa and Trans Caribbean examples as a key foundation for a concise interpretation of the BFOQ that would apply to the flight attendant industry and beyond. He advocated that employers should have "a tremendous amount of latitude" to invoke a BFOQ in jobs involving sexual appeal or bodily intimacy. He then added, however, that there should be "limitations" on this practice in service jobs that are not related to sex or nudity: "If the statement were without limitation, an employer could . . . design any public contact job such as cashier or receptionist to have it appeal to ideas of sex." Once this occurred, the employer would then unjustly assert that the job "could only be filled by a woman or a man, as the case may be."[51] According to Saks, since the main duties of flight attendants were not sexual and did not involve bodily contact, the airlines should not be allowed to make gender a prerequisite for the job.

Celio Diaz's attorney, Robert Burns, failed to include any such rationale to bolster his case. He did not introduce the Trans Caribbean example; in fact, the judge's decision makes it clear that he was unfamiliar with TCA's hiring policies.[52] Burns also omitted material from the *McNeil* case about Lufthansa's and other foreign airlines' equal treatment of stewards and stewardesses and failed to offer an alternative vision of the BFOQ from what the airlines were suggesting. These oversights significantly impaired Celio Diaz's case during its first round in Miami.

A "HOMOSEXUAL PANIC" DEFENSE FOR THE BFOQ

On paper, Pan Am was arguing that its female-only policy was due to women's perceived abilities to fulfill certain "nonmechanical" functions better than men. But their defense also hinged on a more emotive argument, as they openly employed homophobia as an excuse not to hire men. Recall once again the reasoning the airlines offered at the EEOC for preferring women for "nonmechanical" tasks, an articulation that remained unchanged in the *McNeil* and *Diaz* testimony: men "cannot convey the charm, the tact, the grace, the liveliness that young girls can— *particularly to men, who comprise the vast majority of airline passengers* [emphasis added]."[53] When defending why men were particularly unreceptive to stewards, the airlines employed a star witness, psychologist Eric Berne. He detailed the ways "homosexual panic" impaired relations between a steward and his male customers, all the while suggesting that catering to this homophobia was a natural and justifiable reaction for the airlines to take. Thus the court in *Diaz* was forced to contemplate a similar legal question from the Simpson murder in 1954 and the deliberations about Title VII's sex clause in the House of Representatives and before the EEOC: Would homophobia trump justice?

Dr. Eric Berne had become a household name in the United States by virtue of his 1964 best-selling book *Games People Play*, which discussed interpersonal communication strategies in a provocative and easily accessible way. He had also published extensively on group dynamics, and his work *The Structure and Dynamics of Organizations and Groups* became the basis for his testimony in the *Diaz* and *McNeil* cases.[54] For the benefit of Pan Am—which paid him about $2,500 for each of his appearances, almost the entire sum Diaz paid his lawyer—Berne analyzed the subconscious interactions between flight attendants and passengers occurring aboard a plane.[55] The overall thrust of his analysis was that the flight attendant, by necessity, must be female. Male flight attendants, according to Berne, dramatically increased the anxiety levels of male passengers, potentially evoking aggressive responses from some men.

Berne's claims relied on the notion that the airplane itself was a particularly anxiety-ridden space for passengers, sealed off from the outside world and then suspended in the air. The experience of being in a levitated, sealed-off "enclave" would "arouse primitive feelings" and trigger a reversion to a childlike assertion of one's egoistic desires.[56] As a result, Berne claimed, flight attendants ended up playing a parental role for passengers, who were exceptionally desirous of special pampering. Thus, rather than seeing mechanical functions as central to flight attendants' work, Berne placed the nonmechanical role of emotional mothering at the core of the job. The flight attendant "really acts like a mommy, even more so than when she is bringing the trays, [when she provides] the pillows, blankets, and tucks them in." He added, "From my experience, as a passenger, they are very appreciative of having the pillow put under their head and having the blanket tucked in a little bit."[57]

Berne's emphasis on tucking passengers in served an additional role in Pan Am's strategy: it highlighted the physical intimacy between flight attendants and passengers, even at moments of vulnerability such as the barely conscious state of near-sleep. This stress was not accidental. As Pan Am attorney James Armstrong recalls, "We knew it was coming, and we knew it would come from [Berne]."[58] Indeed, Berne reiterated the scenario four more times in the next ten or so minutes of his testimony.

The effect of the pillow and blanket scenario was to equate the male flight attendant more to a male nurse than to a maitre d'. As Berne noted, the steward would be "playing a rather female role and . . . might be regarded askance . . . in the same way as male nurses are not entirely accepted." He then added, "I think that there is a good analogy there," since both nurses and flight attendants engage in bed care, of a sort.[59] While women, in Berne's view, would also prefer female flight attendants to tuck them in, this was especially true of men. He characterized the male passenger as constantly needing affirmation of his masculinity and seeking it in his interactions with others: "The thing that makes a man feel most masculine is the attention of a young girl or even the presence of a young girl. Let's say that another man might make him feel unmasculine in some way, and that means uncomfortable."[60]

According to Berne, it made no difference whether the male flight attendant was masculine or effeminate. A masculine flight attendant would make the vulnerable passenger feel less masculine himself, while an effeminate male "might arouse feelings in him that he would rather not have aroused."[61] Berne then offered a more detailed Freudian analysis of how homosexual panic operated in men: "Since it seems that almost every human male passes through a homosexual phase of his development, the effeminacy tends to make almost every man uncomfortable, unless he is an overt homosexual and is accustomed to responding openly to the effeminacy." Thus proximity to effeminate men would "arouse varying degrees of discomfort" in all men, not just latent homosexuals.[62] Because of this panic-inducing effect, Berne concluded that male flight attendants were appropriately disqualified from the job.

In its efforts to counter this famous and well-paid psychiatrist's invocation of homosexual panic, the Diaz team was significantly overmatched. Diaz's lawyer had hired a local Miami psychologist, Dr. Alan Gregg, who had a private practice in the area and had formerly taught as an adjunct professor of psychology at the University of Miami. Given that Gregg's three publications covered issues related to schizophrenia rather than group dynamics, his pedigree for the trial was far from commensurate with Berne's. He also lacked any experience studying or researching homosexuality—though the same was true of Berne, a fact that neither Diaz's lawyer nor the judge objected to.

Gregg did, however, aptly point out the tenuous nature of Berne's various claims. He noted that Berne's "enclave theory" and his assertions about the interactions between passengers and flight attendants were not based on actual scientific research, either in the laboratory or in the field. His fullest critique is incisive but also betrays how poorly versed Gregg was in the facts of the case: "This is not to say that, perhaps, if the research were done, that some of [Berne's assertions] might not be borne out. I suspect that some of it probably would, but when it comes to the matter—I am really not even clear what the trial is today—I think it is about whether or not men should be hired as cabin stewards as opposed to women, or, whatever, but I think when it affects people's lives, and it affects people's livelihoods, that we ought to have much more than just theory to go on."[63]

When the judge's decision came down, it was clear that he placed great credence in Berne's testimony, however speculative it was. Pan Am attorney James Armstrong remembered the Berne testimony to be decisive. "Berne said that in my field, it's a given that women put women and men more at ease than men. Having said that, and on top of that, after having just written a best seller, we thought we couldn't lose. And we didn't lose."[64] This sentiment is borne out in Judge Fulton's opinion. Fulton relied on the Berne testimony to assert that "there are basic psychological reasons" to explain passengers' preference for stewardesses, even citing Berne's assertions that men would "subconsciously resent" and potentially "respond negatively" to a male flight attendant. Fulton's decision also indirectly blamed Diaz's attorney for failing to counter Berne's testimony in a more compelling way. Noting that he had received a copy of Berne's testimony from the *McNeil* case several months before the *Diaz* trial began, Fulton asserted, "[The] plaintiff failed to produce any significant evidence challenging Dr. Berne's conclusions; the plaintiff's psychologist did no more on this point than urge that Dr. Berne's view that an aircraft cabin is a special environment rests on something less than adequate data."[65]

It says a great deal about the tenuous legal status of gender transgressors and homosexuals that Judge Fulton forgave Berne's lack of data. Indeed, in a rhetorical sleight of hand, Fulton excused Berne's lack of evidence—including his reliance on unproven Freudian theories of how "homosexual panic" worked—by citing the Diaz team's own lack of counterevidence. Fulton effectively concluded that the inability to prove stewards were *not* a threat to other men was evidence for the claim—however speculative—that they *did* threaten men.

Of course, the fact that a leading psychiatrist was complicit in entrapping gender transgressors and homosexuals in such a legal conundrum incriminates the psychological community as well. Only in December 1973 (three years after the *Diaz* case was heard in Miami) did the American Psychiatric Association finally remove homosexuality from its manual of illnesses, implicitly admitting that its various Freudian-inspired theories regarding homosexuality needed rethinking. Before that momentous development, however, the psychological community employed its status as scientific professionals in profoundly damaging ways, even when—as in the case of male flight attendants—there was no research-related evidence to do so.

THE *DIAZ* APPEAL: THE FLIGHT FROM
HOMOSEXUAL PANIC

When Eleanor Schockett took over as Celio Diaz's attorney for the appeal, one of her top priorities was to neutralize the testimony of Dr. Berne. Even though the court of appeals was unable to hear new testimony and had to confine itself to the evidentiary record generated in the district court, Schockett sought a way to add more voices from the psychological community that would counter Berne's views. She located two experts with national reputations, Jane Loevinger and Nevitt Sanford, who were willing to write an amicus brief in support of Diaz. At the same time, however, Schockett knew that Pan Am would refuse to grant Loevinger and Sanford standing and that the judges would be compelled to refuse the brief. As Schockett recalls, "We knew what was going to happen." Nonetheless, she had the psychologists submit the brief: "As I figured, they're going to have to read the brief just to throw it out."[66]

Even without the additional evidence to counter Dr. Berne's testimony, Schockett found a very sympathetic hearing in front of the Fifth Circuit Court of Appeals. The judges' goodwill began before the hearing itself. As Schockett recalls, "When I first came in and stood up to introduce myself, the chief judge stood up and turned to the press and said, 'We find it very interesting that this class of men is being represented by a young woman.' That put me at ease." Then, when Schockett began her opening statement, the chief judge again signified his sympathy for Diaz's cause: "The next thing I remember about that hearing was that I said, 'My name is Eleanor Schockett and I represent the plaintiff below and the appellant in this case, Celio Diaz, and the question presented in this case is . . .' And the chief judge stopped me, and he said, 'Isn't the question presented: Just how important are cosmetics in the cabin?' . . . And I said, 'I couldn't have said it better, Your Honor.' "[67]

Schockett was also prepared to address the Berne testimony on the issue of homosexual panic, but the judges expressed very little interest. According to Schockett, "They asked me questions about the homosexuality issue, or I brought that up, and one judge said, 'Well, if that's a concern here, we have more problems in this country than we ever thought of.' "[68] Clearly, the appeals decision was going to be based on something other than the homosexual panic defense employed in the Miami court.

In the end, the court reached a decision that did not explicitly counter the evidence submitted by Berne but nonetheless overturned Judge Fulton's ruling. The judges effectively returned to the conclusion of the EEOC, which minimized the importance of the "nonmechanical" duties that the airlines valued and instead stressed the tasks that were most essential for the job. In the process, the court significantly clarified the confusion surrounding Title VII that had haunted the law since the day Congress added the sex amendment. Rather than heeding the "common sense" approach of the early EEOC, which left vast room for employers to decide for themselves whether sex was a BFOQ, the court of appeals now offered a very strict basis for selecting only one gender for a particular job.

Whereas the law itself stated that a BFOQ would exist in cases when a particular sex was "reasonably necessary to the normal operation" of a business, the court now further clarified this point: "The use of the word 'necessary' in Section 703(e) requires that we apply a business *necessity* test, not a business *convenience* test. That is to say, discrimination based on sex is valid only when the *essence* of the business operation would be undermined by not hiring members of one sex exclusively."[69]

The court then proceeded to assert that the essence of an airline's business is "to transport passengers safely from one point to another." In other words, flight attendants most fundamentally were safety and transportation professionals, and all other work they performed was of secondary importance. Once it had established this more restrictive rubric for understanding the BFOQ, their conclusion in *Diaz* followed logically: "While a pleasant environment, enhanced by the obvious cosmetic effect that female stewardesses provide as well as, according to the finding of the trial court, their apparent ability to perform the non-mechanical functions of the job in a more effective manner than most men, may all be important, they are tangential to the essence of the business involved."[70] Since men were just as capable of performing these mechanical duties, especially those pertaining to safety, the court ruled that Pan Am would have to accept applications from men like Diaz. Likewise, all U.S. airlines would have to treat male applicants equally.

Pan Am now found itself unexpectedly in the position of losing a court case it felt was well argued in its favor. What was most galling to attorney James Armstrong was that the court itself had defined what Pan Am's "essential" business was, rather than allowing the company to do so. Thus, while providing clarity to the BFOQ, the appeals decision smacked of an intrusion into the free market:

> What they essentially said was, "You are in the business of transporting people from place to place." And the whole issue of comfort . . . was beside the point. And I was outraged about that. . . . I remember thinking that had we known it was going to go off on that [the act's wording of "necessary"], we might have developed testimony to show that if we were to have had men flight attendants, we would have risked losing business to railroads or buses. That might have been pretty hard to prove, but there was no thought given to that . . . [since] the district court record was overwhelming.[71]

Pan Am made precisely these sorts of assertions in their brief to the U.S. Supreme Court, hoping that the Court would throw out the appeals verdict and restore the airlines' prerogative to govern their businesses as they chose.

On November 9, 1971, however, the Supreme Court refused to hear Pan Am's appeal. Other circuit courts over time invoked and upheld the Fifth Circuit's interpretation of Title VII and the BFOQ, allowing the ruling to gradually became the accepted law of the land. With the victory in *Diaz*, feminists finally secured the restrictive interpretation of the BFOQ that they had sought, while flight attendant labor unions could finally contemplate the definitive end of age and marriage restrictions on stewardesses, as well as access to the male-only purser corps at TWA, Braniff, and Northwest.

Of course, these victories for women came with an additional prerequisite: that men now enjoy equal consideration and equal standing in this formerly female-dominated career. Pan Am and other airlines opened their flight attendant training programs to men immediately after the Supreme Court's decision, and—as though defying conventional wisdom—large numbers of men applied for the job. Pan Am's first flight attendant class of 1972 boasted an even mix of men and women, a trend that continued for a while before men became a sizable but smaller minority of applicants.[72]

The one man with the most invested in this case, however, never got to fly. Celio Diaz was deemed too old for Pan American, since his application back in 1967 had been filed when he was thirty years old. Pan Am's cutoff at the time, except for those warranting special consideration, was twenty-six. The case was remanded to the district level to assess what damages Pan Am would pay Diaz and the other men whom they previously refused to hire. Diaz hired a new lawyer to fight for a job as a flight attendant, though ultimately to no avail. He instead received an offer to work as part of Pan Am's ground operations, but he turned it down, opting to remain in his career as a trucker. Ironically, the man who played a crucial role in dismantling sex discrimination ultimately fell victim to age discrimination. Diaz returned to his trucking business and raised his children. "I was very disappointed. . . . I always thought if I won the case, I would get to fly for them."[73] Instead, Diaz would satisfy himself with a pyrrhic victory, proud of his role in giving other men a chance to do this work and also quite satisfied that his own daughter became a flight attendant a decade later. She would enter a workplace radically altered from that of the 1960s: far more diverse, less sexualized, more professional, and better paying, thanks in part to her father.

Roderick McNeil had to wait even longer for justice in his case before the NYSCHR. Even though he had filed his case in 1966, two years before Diaz, a final decision was first reached in April 1973. Pan Am then appealed the verdict, forcing McNeil to wait until July 1974 for a final ruling. The commission ultimately sided with McNeil. In fact, unlike the federal courts—which accepted the notion that female flight attendants performed nonmechanical tasks more effectively—the commission refused to admit even this point: "[Pan Am's] argument that in limiting its hiring of flight attendants to females it was entitled to the exception of a BFOQ is frivoulous *[sic]*, to say the least. Respondent failed completely to show that females could perform these duties better than males. As voluminous as this record is, there is no evidence whatsoever presented by the respondent to negate the fact that it discriminated against the complainant because of his sex."[74] Given the far more extensive record in the New York case, including the TCA testimony and the more thorough cross-examining of airline witnesses, it is hardly surprising that the commission sided with McNeil on the basis of the evidence.

Like Celio Diaz, Roderick McNeil also never entered the flight attendant corps. By 1973 he seems to have lost interest in the job, though there is no record detailing exactly why he didn't seek such a position. One thing is clear, however: McNeil, like Diaz, was never in it for the money. Calculations made by attorney Alan Saks in 1968 showed that McNeil would have taken a pay cut to enter the flight attendant corps, compared to the salary he was already earning as a part of Pan Am's ground operations.

QUEER CIVIL RIGHTS, 1964–PRESENT

Congressman Charles Goodell began a new phase of civil rights legal discourse with his brief intervention in the House of Representatives on February 10, 1964. His almost-but-not-quite invocation of a male nurse began an elaborate chain of legal and extralegal moves designed to exclude gender nonconformists from protection under Title VII. The BFOQ became an escape clause from the otherwise too controversial piece of legislation. When used to excess, the BFOQ kept even gender-conforming white women, such as stewardesses, in their proper place. That is, these women were sent home and removed from the workforce, at least once they had a husband or children. Yet Goodell's nurse reference ensured that the brunt of the BFOQ would fall even more harshly upon a less normative class of men and women.

"Common sense," in the parlance of the EEOC's commissioners, dictated that some jobs would remain male only and others female only. But it also meant that arbitrary criteria like customer preference would dictate when this system of gender segregation would be dismantled or remain intact. Thus, as long as the gender-bending queer was ostracized in society at large, redress before the law under Title VII was off limits. "Common sense" dictated that gender pariahs like aspirant male flight attendants or female soldiers were subjected to the court of public opinion, not the law.

Only begrudgingly did the male flight attendant gain access to federal courts. Celio Diaz then won his case, without ever convincing the EEOC or the district judge that men could perform all aspects of a flight attendant's work well, even the "nonmechanical" tasks of comforting and calming customers. Nonetheless, men were back on the job, regardless of the suspicions of queerness that swirled around them—especially fears that they might elicit homosexual panic in other men. Women also were co-victors in Diaz's success. After all, the narrow interpretation of the BFOQ generated by the Fifth Circuit has allowed a wider swath of careers to become sexually integrated since 1971.

Celio Diaz and Roderick McNeil themselves were hardly gender nonconformists. Both were married and raised children. The only thing that made them queer was their desire to be male flight attendants. This transgressive desire nonetheless made both of them, and male flight attendants as a whole, important figures in the civil rights moment of the 1960s. They embody the victory, however tentative, over forces that vilified male nurses, female dog catchers, and stewards offering pillows to air passengers. They also point to a reality that was as true in the 1960s as it is today: the fight for civil rights is *by necessity* a multipronged struggle, combating not only racism and sexism but also homophobia. Finally, these men highlight that queerness was a part of civil rights discourse as far back as the floor debates on the 1964 Civil Rights Act.

CHAPTER FIVE

Flight Attendants,
Women's Liberation, and
Gay Liberation

When a new generation of male flight attendants debuted in the early 1970s, American attitudes regarding gender and sexuality were evolving quickly. Progressive activists worked to introduce concepts like women's liberation and gay liberation into the cultural mainstream, though they were countered by a growing, equally devoted activist base of traditionalists. Both of these movements in the culture war would grow in breadth and sophistication as the 1970s progressed, and their pitched battles continue to this day.[1] Yet for a brief spell at the dawn of the 1970s, it seemed as though feminists, at least, had turned a corner among politicians. The laughter that greeted Congressman Howard Smith's sex amendment to the 1964 Civil Rights Act might still have been typical in some of the Capitol's back rooms, but when Congress voted on the most expansive women's rights initiative to date—the Equal Rights Amendment to the U.S. Constitution—significant majorities from both chambers and both political parties approved it. The Senate's 84-to-8 vote sent it to the states for its likely ratification, and dissenting views like Senator Sam Ervin's of North Carolina were very much the exception. His view that "the physiological and functional differences between men and women constitute earth's important reality" seemed shortsighted, while his warning that "any country which ignores these differences when it fashions its institutions and makes its law is woefully lacking in rationality" failed to convince his fellow lawmakers.[2]

In the same month of this lopsided vote, March 1972, Pan Am's first stewards since the 1950s began their careers. Given such timing, these men were well aware that they were intertwined with the liberation momentum of the day, harbingers of a gender order that was less tied to male privilege. New steward Barry Shelby confessed that his job choice aroused some suspicion. Nonetheless, he humorously claimed for himself the mantle of progress: "When people kid me about my job, I say this is man's liberation."[3] Shelby's joke did expose an important reality: the potential beneficiaries of this liberation moment included all sorts of Americans and all sorts of flight attendants.

Stewardesses unquestionably were better off thanks to court victories like *Diaz*. One flight attendant labor union, the Air Line Stewards and Stewardesses Association (ALSSA), heralded the case as groundbreaking: "We are closer to the day when people will be treated as unique and distinct individuals and not as members of a sexual group."[4] Indeed, by the early 1970s, all U.S. airlines had surrendered their prohibitions on married stewardesses and those who had reached their mid-thirties.[5] While pregnancy bans endured, the ALSSA foresaw that *Diaz* would make this change likely as well: "For if it is not a legitimate job qualification that a cabin attendant be female, it would appear unlikely that the qualification can be imposed to eliminate an entire sexual group in other areas such as . . . [women] with children."[6] By 1974, the policies were being rescinded, with some airlines reinstating stewardesses previously terminated for pregnancy.[7] These changes finally allowed women to contemplate their jobs as a long-term career. At United Airlines, the reality for stewardesses changed quickly. In the 1960s they were all unmarried and childless and kept their jobs for an average of fifteen months. By 1976, over half were married and 15 percent had children. The average stewardess now had six years of seniority, which in turn meant better pay and better pension benefits.[8]

Despite this progressive trend, other sexist employment practices remained in the 1970s. Stewardesses still endured strict weight limits that required them to be twenty-five pounds lighter than a steward of the same height.[9] Before they boarded a flight, a manager would sometimes confirm they were wearing a girdle, and on layovers they shared hotel rooms, while pilots and even stewards got singles. Additionally, the airlines continued to market stewardesses as sex objects. The most crass marketing examples—National Airlines' famous "Fly Me" promotion and Southwest's "Somebody Else Up There Who Loves You" campaign, replete with stewardesses in hot pants and knee-high white vinyl boots—both debuted in 1971 and continued for a few years.[10] But some stewardesses no longer accepted such indignities without a fight and chose to lend their voices to the women's liberation movement. Flight attendant unions increasingly agitated for feminist goals, while a new advocacy group, Stewardesses for Women's Rights (SFWR), organized to promote such priorities even more forcefully. SFWR envisioned transforming stewardesses—given their significant popularity with the flying public—into advocates who would forcefully challenge sexist workplace indignities.[11]

Meanwhile, as became clear over the course of the 1970s, some of the men who had started as flight attendants after *Diaz* had liberationist goals of their own, tied to their status as gay men. A former flight attendant with American Airlines, Sharlene Martin, worked on the New York City hiring committee when the airline employed its first men for domestic service.[12] While it initially did not occur to her that American was hiring gay men in large numbers, this quickly changed: "It became obvious within a year or so that probably 85 percent of the men we hired were gay."[13] These gay flight attendants were not generally politically engaged or even publicly out. But the 1970s saw the first step in a gradual process whereby stewards began to out themselves as gay and demand equal treatment from their unions and employers. These steps were somewhat modest, but they nonetheless opened a new venue in the culture war, especially concerning the fight for LGBT equality in the workplace.[14]

The term *culture war* highlights that these progressive stirrings encountered intense opposition. After conservatives endured what they deemed a series of cultural indignities tied to gender and sexuality—foremost being the loss of gender-segregated public spheres and a denigration of traditional family-oriented values—they began to push back. The controversial *Roe v. Wade* decision in 1973 was a lightning rod for New Right activism, as many across the nation felt profound revulsion toward this court-ordered remedy and organized to overturn it. Ultimately, the rise of a well-endowed and politically active New Right profoundly reshaped the political status quo on social issues. The ERA became more polarizing after *Roe* and the work of activists such as Phyllis Schlafly.[15] Senator Ervin was no longer an isolated voice, and plenty of women like Schlafly assumed the mantle as leading crusaders in the surprisingly successful effort to upend the ERA at the state level.

Singer-turned-activist Anita Bryant emulated for the New Right on gay issues what Schlafly achieved against the ERA. Bryant organized the first coalition of those outraged by gay liberation and the modest political rights gay men and lesbians had won in the 1970s. While originating from a network of evangelical pastors and media outlets, the coalition called "Save Our Children" also drew wider support from Jewish congregations and mainstream Christian churches, as well as from other non-faith-based traditionalists. Most notably, Bryant and her coalition convinced the voters of Miami-Dade County in 1977 to rescind a progay nondiscrimination ordinance passed by the board of aldermen before replicating their success in other cities. Save Our Children's rapid expansion signaled that any sort of progay political or social innovation would encounter fierce opposition.[16]

This chapter explains the 1970s from two complementary perspectives: on the one hand, it discusses flight attendants' lived experiences, looking at how the career evolved, mainly for the better, as the first generation of newly empowered women and gay men found ways to work together. This collaboration suggested some promise for the future: that women and gay men could coalesce to fight employers' sexism and heterosexism, fostering important precedents for workers in other careers along the way. The second focus is on the larger context of American law and politics in the 1970s, when the culture war flared up with acute intensity. The chapter begins with the New Right's and the New Left's reactions to the *Diaz* decision, then considers the legal legacy of the case. As we shall see, key elements in both camps focused on men like stewards—those who aspired to female social roles—in their future strategies. For Schlafly and opponents of the ERA, the male flight attendant became a symbol of the perverse gender bending that needed to be stopped. Meanwhile, advocates of women's liberation and gay liberation at first found hope in the *Diaz* legacy. Ruth Bader Ginsburg of the ACLU's Women's Rights Project was particularly inspired by the potential for men like Diaz to dismantle sexist laws, and she made male plaintiffs a cornerstone of her legal strategy as the 1970s progressed.

Nonetheless, by the close of the decade, advocates of women's rights and gay rights confronted the limitations of the *Diaz* example. What had once seemed like a way to combat gender-based restrictions and to simultaneously bestow greater rights on gays and lesbians through a legal "back door" (opening up spaces for gays and lesbians via Title VII) ended in disappointment. By the end of the decade, the male flight attendant was vilified by the New Right and also orphaned to some extent by the New Left, who found his legal example less fruitful in reforming America's sexist and heterosexist structures than they desired.

STEWARDS AND THE CONSERVATIVE BACKLASH

As the *Diaz* case made its way through the courts, the prospect of male flight attendants created significant negative publicity. An opening salvo occurred when the Equal Employment Opportunity Commission considered the question in 1966: the *New York Times* story ran under the title "A Pillow Please, Miss . . . Er, Mister."[17] The headline itself captured a moment of misrecognition and panic caused by a male flight attendant. It also foreshadowed the testimony of Dr. Eric Berne in the *Diaz* trial that concentrated so intently on stewards positioning pillows for physically vulnerable male passengers. From there on, much of the mainstream press high-lighted the male flight attendant's potential to arouse both fear and derisive laughter among readers. When the *Wall Street Journal* announced the EEOC decision supporting men's claims against the airlines, it opened by noting: "A broad-shouldered six-footer with a crew cut may be serving you inflight martinis in the future and telling you to fasten your seat belts and observe the no-smoking signs."[18]

The *Miami Herald*'s coverage of its hometown son was particularly harsh. Soon after the EEOC decision favoring Celio Diaz, the *Herald's* weekly *Tropic Magazine* ran a full-page image of a burly man in a miniskirt, knee-length stockings, beret, and purse, with the headline, ". . . Is This Any Way to Ruin an Airline?" (figure 10). The article text was just as derisive. Author Jon Nordheimer began his rant by stating: "Here's the worst thing that could happen to commercial airlines. . . . The male stewardess, that's what! Lurking in unemployment lines all over the country are men who are plotting to wrest control of the coffee-tea-or-milk trade and kick those gorgeous girls out of the aisle. Blame the whole mess on Washington." The article then crescendoed with a testosterone-laden diatribe against the EEOC: "Anybody who calls a stewardess a 'sexless attendant' is not a gentleman and deserves a punch in the nose."[19]

An equally churlish critique came from James Kilpatrick, an outspoken critic of race-based and sex-based civil rights.[20] His article on the *Herald's* Viewpoint page of March 4, 1968, was headlined, "Down with Equal Opportunity: Day of the He-Stewardess Is upon Us" and proceeded to attack the EEOC. Embracing William F. Buckley's derisive designation of the agency as the "Equempoppocom" (a play on the word *poppycock*) and his corresponding desire to abolish it, Kilpatrick bemoaned the loss of his "right to girl-watch." He employed outright homophobia directed at the "he-stewardess"—an epithet much like the 1936 *Washington Post*'s "male hostess"—in his most passionate critique of sex-based civil rights: "Can you imagine a male in one of those Braniff costumes? . . . Is there anything less aesthetic than the masculine rear end? But the Equempoppocom has spoken." Kilpatrick's venomous critique successfully concealed the more controversial work rules that the airlines were really defending before the EEOC: the age, marriage, and pregnancy restrictions placed on stewardesses. He offered no defense for why he should be able to enjoy sexual thrills secured by low wages and demeaning work rules aimed at women.[21]

The sleight of hand evident in such articles—supplanting discussions about gender inequality with sensationalized homophobic caricatures—became a central element of conservative politics in the 1970s, especially in the campaign against the ERA. The amendment itself was written to emulate the language of Title VII

FIGURE 10.
The "male stewardess." *Miami Herald Tropic Maga ine*, April 14,
1968, 18–19. Courtesy *Miami Herald*.

and to echo the Fifteenth Amendment to the Constitution, which guaranteed the
right to vote regardless of race. The main clause of the ERA stated quite simply,
"Equality of rights under the law shall not be denied or abridged by the United
States or by any State on account of sex." ERA supporters like NOW stressed that
the benefits of the amendment would principally be economic, finally ensuring that
women would receive "equal pay for equal work."[22] NOW's most popular slogan

supporting ERA was "59¢," a reference to the fact that women earned just 59 cents for every dollar earned by a man.[23]

However, conservatives associated with Phyllis Schlafly's STOP ERA group suggested that more pernicious designs lay behind the amendment. STOP ERA supplanted the debate on economics, diverting the nation's attention to purported gender and sexuality perversions that would take root. They vilified a variety of queer characters, including women desiring military combat roles, advocates of coed bathrooms, and gays and lesbians desiring to marry, all of whom would allegedly get their way under the ERA. Schlafly insisted that the amendment was limitless in how it would dismantle boundaries between men and women (even integrating bathrooms) and secure equal rights for gays and lesbians. In the ratification process in Maine, for example, Schlafly's local organization, Maine STOP ERA, placed a newspaper ad of two men embracing during New York's Gay Pride parade. The text read: "What does the word 'sex' mean? The sex you are, male or female, or the sex you engage in, homosexual, bisexual, heterosexual, sex with children, . . . or whatever? . . . Militant homosexuals from all over America have made the ERA issue a hot priority. Why? To be able finally to get homosexual marriage licenses, to adopt children and raise them to emulate their homosexual 'parents,' and to obtain pension and medical benefits for odd-couple 'spouses.' . . . Vote NO on 6! The Pro-Gay E.R.A."[24] While different in focus, such attacks echoed the deployments of "homosexual panic" in the 1950s Simpson trial and the Berne testimony in *Diaz*. They also tracked the EEOC's initial "common sense" approach to gender desegregation. After all, in each instance, public opprobrium against gender bending or homosexuality supposedly justified a different standard according to which such people did not deserve equal legal protection.

FLIGHT ATTENDANTS AND GAY LIBERATION

It might be expected that the gay community would have been particularly enthusiastic about the *Diaz* victory. After all, thousands of gay men would find gainful employment in a decently paying, unionized career as a result of the court decision. Furthermore, it stands to reason that a job that accommodated a high percentage of gay men in the immediate post-Stonewall moment would become a focal point of gay rights activism. The fact that flight attendants garnered such nationwide visibility and worked in direct contact with growing portions of the U.S. public only enhanced stewards' value to the gay community. Surprisingly, however, the opening of this newly liberated gay career received hardly any notice from the nation's nascent gay media. Rather than becoming a public face for post-Stonewall gays in publications such as the *Advocate*, one of the few news-oriented gay publications with a national audience in the 1970s, flight attendants were mainly invisible. In the occasional mentions of the career, the *Advocate* focused instead on the job's sexualized overtones and resorted to objectifying stewards just as much as the mainstream media objectified stewardesses.

The *Advocate* itself was only beginning publication when the EEOC heard grievances from flight attendants on sex discrimination. It debuted in September 1967 as the *Los Angeles Advocate*, inheriting *ONE* magazine's two-pronged focus on L.A.'s local scene and national gay and lesbian issues.[25] When the EEOC decision was announced in February 1968, the *Advocate* was just an eight-page newsletter composed on a used IBM typewriter. Nonetheless, the editors wrote an editorial entitled "The Only Way to Fly," suggesting that the legal deliberations were of great importance to their readership. The tone, however, replicated the derisive humor of mainstream publications and conservative commentators. Rather than highlight the injustices faced by stewardesses and aspiring stewards, the editors instead welcomed the EEOC decision because it offered gay men a form of libidinal equality: a newfound venue to objectify attractive men.

> All we can say is, "Dammit, it's about time." . . . We who have a different idea of the fair sex have been sorely abused by the airlines. Thousands of miles of bouncing boobies and saccharine smiles. Even the other inmates of those flying tubes don't offer much diversion—fat businessmen who melt over into your precious space, neurotic females who are afraid all conversation inevitably leads to SEX. The occasional serviceman usually winds up not in the seat next to yours, but sandwiched between two elderly matrons intent on sending him cookies (the dirty old hags). All this, we hope, will soon change. . . . Who knows? That trite old bit of humor, "Coffee, tea, or ME?" may soon take on a new, fresh, and exciting meaning.[26]

While certainly scoring points for brazen humor, this take on the EEOC decision nonetheless exhibited the highest danger of gay male camp: its effort to score a self-affirming laugh came at the expense of a fuller critique of sexism.

Later, the *Advocate* almost entirely overlooked Diaz's victory in the court of appeals. The May 26, 1971, edition sandwiched a one-column, eight-line mention of the verdict in an issue otherwise hailing a Los Angeles court victory that allowed strippers at gay bars to go fully nude. The issue's cover showed one of these dancers performing with his hands over his crotch, alongside the gleeful headline:

"Scream and Suck Your Thumb."[27] Both court victories were covered on page 2 of the issue, with the *Diaz* case occupying the far right corner under the disparaging headline "Men Stewardesses." Unlike the more ample article on the stripper case, which included original reporting, the *Diaz* article was entirely drawn from a newswire. It read, quite briefly: "The Fifth United States Circuit Court of Appeals, citing the 1964 Civil Rights Act, has ruled in a case involving Pan American World Airways that airlines must hire 'men stewardesses,' according to United Press International."[28] Why the editors chose to emulate the *Miami Herald*, the UPI, and other mainstream media in calling these men "stewardesses" is unclear. As in the stripper article, however, it seems the headline editors were far more interested in humorously capturing the viewpoint of gay consumers than that of workers.

This reportage illustrates a fundamental tension in gay rights activism in the 1970s. Clearly, gay liberation had very divergent priorities, since certain members of the community—especially the middle-class men who were the most well-heeled gay rights advocates—were often more concerned with liberating their libidos from homophobia than rectifying economic injustices. Such men certainly felt that gay liberation should create more jobs for gays and lesbians, but they also valued greater sexual expression and more freedom for the consumption practices tied to it.[29] In the case of flight attendants, the *Advocate*'s editors therefore followed the mainstream media in stressing the job's sexual overtones.

As a result, women's liberation groups could not count on gay rights activists like the *Advocate* staff as partners in their more all-encompassing critique of the airlines. The concerns of Stewardesses for Women's Rights were actually diametrically opposed on the question of sexuality, as they fought to make the flight attendant career more professional and less prone to the objectification that trapped women in a cycle of poor wages and sexual harassment. Thus, in the political discussions regarding flight attendant discrimination, a chasm between feminism and gay male activism is readily apparent. Feminists could justifiably accuse some gay men of reinforcing patriarchy and sexism, especially in their failure to understand the economic-based injustices that women endured. Likewise, another chasm is equally apparent: feminists risked being perceived as sexually passionless in their attempts to stamp out sexual objectification, while gay liberationists risked the opposite—a reputation as sex obsessed and excessively libertine.

Finally, what to make of the *Advocate*'s failure to cover flight attendants more extensively through the 1970s, neglecting their potential to promote gay priorities? I propose that this neglect betrays a deeper discomfort with male flight attendants. The *Advocate* was actually intensely involved with various other battles to integrate gays in the workplace, especially other unionized jobs such as public school teachers and federal government employees. It also focused heavily on careers with a more "manly" public image: policemen, soldiers, and firemen.[30] For a gay male community battling the stigma of effeminacy, the promise of inclusion in such manly jobs was especially enticing. Meanwhile, important accomplishments gained by flight attendants or male nurses, despite their value for the entire gay community, were often overlooked. Such effeminate careers failed to impress those segments of the gay community interested in asserting masculine virility—their supposed normalcy—to a world that considered them perverted. In this sense, the *Advocate*'s silence on male flight attendants suggests that "male stewardesses" may have been too queer for much of the gay community as well.

FRIENDLY AND UNFRIENDLY SKIES

While their deployment in the culture war suggests a tumultuous existence for the first generation of post-*Diaz* stewards, the actual reality was far less dramatic. In fact, flight attendants whom I interviewed were unable to recall any incident from the 1970s when customers had exhibited the type of antimale phobia posited by Dr. Eric Berne in the *Diaz* trial.[31] Each corroborated the claim of a male member of a 1972 Pan Am flight attendant class: "The passengers were very indifferent [toward stewards]. I never had a problem with a passenger complaining about a gay . . . flight attendant." In fact, my interviewees also recall that the gay presence among these new flight attendants was not entirely obvious in the beginning. Because so many gay men were circumspect in their behavior, especially around managers and customers, the very first men on the job were, according to the same flight attendant, "an invisible minority."[32]

As to why gay men were entering the profession in such numbers, I have no definitive answer from my research, only a telling account of the hiring process offered by former American Airlines recruiter Sharlene Martin. Martin insists that managers never excluded perceived homosexuals and seemingly did not care about their workers' sexual orientation. Instead, they chose men who demonstrated a willingness to work with women, especially since these men would often take orders from American's more senior stewardesses. According to Martin, "We were looking for men who clearly didn't have a problem working with women, who would come into the interview room and have an attitude of cooperation. . . . We looked for listening skills and whether they responded orally to what women said: 'I agree with Susie, that's a great choice.'"[33]

Reporters noted that this cooperation continued through the first gender-integrated flight attendant training sessions. Profiling Pan Am's first post-*Diaz* class, the *Philadelphia Inquirer* found that "trainees, male and female alike, say there was no friction in the classes." One trainee claimed, "There was a great rapport. We got along like brothers and sisters. . . . There was some joking about women's lib, but it was all good natured."[34]

Once on the job, flight attendants tacitly circulated information about each other's sexual orientation, but they typically did so without drawing excessive scrutiny from passengers, management, pilots, or the media. One flight attendant at Pan Am recalled that his training allowed him to connect with other gay men: "The word got around who was gay and who wasn't, and it was almost everybody. So if you flew with someone who was a 1972 hire, you could assume they were gay." According to his own estimate, "about 90 percent" of the men hired in Pan Am's first classes after the *Diaz* decision were gay. For such men, joining Pan Am's flight attendant corps was an opportunity to deepen social networks among fellow gay stewards and numerous gay-friendly stewardesses: "We were like a family, those of us based in New York. We knew everybody very well. And we would socialize with them outside of work."[35]

Media reports did not betray any suspicion that this new generation of stewards was decidedly gay. Instead, in a variety of stories, reporters profiled new stewards who were clearly heterosexual. One husband-wife duo at United Airlines garnered particular attention, as the *New York Times* presented Jerry and Theresa Williams as a progressive civil rights-era married couple. Jerry had initially been a public school teacher who was reluctant to join his wife at United as a flight attendant: "I was apprehensive. A male steward?" It was his wife's increasingly solid wages that fostered his conversion: "I looked at Terry's pay check and I looked at my pay check and I saw that she was earning more money for less education, and for the same amount of work." Jerry nonetheless continued to harbor more notionally manly career goals. The article intimates that "his secret desire is to be a race car driver" but that he would settle for a promotion within the airline. Suggesting a more traditional male-female division within the job, Jerry noted, "A lot of men use it as a stepping stone to get further into the company. . . . I can see jobs ahead that I would like to move into eventually." His wife, seemingly more content in her female-identified profession, did not share such aspirations. In the meantime, the couple crafted a home life that surely struck some readers as revolutionary; in addition to their equal jobs and salaries, "They share all the housework, laundry and cooking. 'One night she'll do the meat and I'll make the salads, or we'll do it together.'"[36]

The *National Observer* even safely heterosexualized the new stewards' erotic potential. While cautioning that the media-inspired stereotype of the profession as sexualized was "almost altogether myth," one reporter nonetheless collected accounts of stewards' experiences aloft. He noted that "most stewards, who are all young and, like stewardesses, picked at least partly for good looks, report similar come-ons [to what stewardesses get]." One United steward had a female passenger leave a note under the coffee cup of her lunch tray: "It was a mash note, with an urgent invitation to call." Even more salaciously, another United steward opted to share his personal issue of *Playboy* with a bored female customer: "[Every magazine] we had was in use, but I told her, 'If you want to read *Playboy*, I'll let you read my personal copy.'" When he returned to collect the magazine, the steward found a note tucked inside the issue. "She had written down her name and the telephone number of the hotel where she would be staying."[37]

Whatever sexual roles straight male flight attendants were performing, gay flight attendants were quickly becoming discreet community builders, including for fellow gay passengers. Stewards shared stories of men seeking them out in the galley and engaging them in conversations that could be motivated by friendliness or sexual interest. They might start off by dropping the names of gay clubs or mentioning other nonobvious markers, then occasionally proceed to sharing a business card or an invitation for dinner. Even a straight steward working for Eastern was impressed by the workings of some gay stewards' informal networks. His gay colleagues, he noted, almost always had connections in far-flung cities. When the airline began new service to Honolulu, some already had phone numbers of men to call for drinks or dinners: "The gays had friends there, even though it was a totally new base." A similar subtle form of networking with gay hotel staff often rendered another privilege: "The gays got nicer rooms than the rest of us," the straight steward playfully complained.[38]

While the overall effect of men entering the career was to significantly desexualize it, many gay men actually embraced the flight attendant's stereotyped role as erotically desirable. Indeed, the long-suppressed 1930s-era notion of the dapper steward, who took part in fashion parades and wore outfits designed to accentuate his slim form, partially returned in the 1970s. As militarized masculinity lost credibility during the 1960s, more space opened up for fashionable men who relied on their appearance to feel empowered.[39] Certain stewards relished the chance to make heads turn:

First, being a Pan Am flight attendant in those days was very prestigious for a gay man, because everyone knew it was very hard to get into Pan Am. . . .

You weren't ashamed to say what you did. . . . And second, we wore the *cutest* outfits! We had Adolfo outfits, our luggage matched, we even had umbrellas, and we all looked fabulous. . . . I used to put my uniform on, and I felt really handsome. And I'd walk through terminals, and I knew if there were gay men, they'd be looking at me. It enhanced you; it gave you self-confidence.[40]

A gay sensibility had returned to the skies, and many stewards were proud to be considered "cute," "fabulous," and "handsome."

Of course, this growing gay male subculture—however discreet it was on one level—had the potential to raise eyebrows among the more conservative elements in the aviation industry. Most suspicious were the traditionally masculine bastions of airline management and the pilot corps. The fact that some managers voiced antigay sentiments in the 1970s certainly provided extra incentive for gay flight attendants to be discreet. Pan Am executive Lloyd Wilson testified before the New York State Division of Human Rights in 1969 that the company would not willingly tolerate gay flight attendants: "If we are aware of homosexuality as a trait or characteristic of an individual that can be made to stand up in a labor hearing with our union, there would be immediate dismissal."[41] His words, while harsh, were outdone by Delta CEO Tom Beebe. In his tell-all book about the inner workings of Delta in the 1970s, former company attorney Sidney Davis recalls an alarming meeting on the issue of male flight attendants: "Beebe started the meeting by telling us, notwithstanding the obvious trend and strong governmental pressure to the contrary, that the company would '. . . no longer hire any more male flight attendants, because they get restless, and restlessness creates unions. Besides . . . they are gay as a three-dollar bill, and we don't need any fags in the Delta family.' "[42] Neither Pan Am or Delta followed through on these threats, though they illustrate that gay flight attendants still risked significant oppression from above in the post-*Diaz* era.

The only moment after *Diaz* when an airline manager actually took a public antigay stand came in 1977. In the heat of the battle to overturn Miami's gay rights ordinance, Colonel Frank Borman, an ex-astronaut who became CEO of Eastern Air Lines, welcomed Anita Bryant to speak at the airline's ground operations facilities. Mechanics, porters, ticket agents, and available flight crew were given the chance to listen to Bryant speak about the evils of homosexuality and the threat posed to children by gays and lesbians. Borman's actions betrayed a corporate resistance to the idea of gay rights, even the basic premise that workers should enjoy protection from being fired on the basis of their sexual orientation (which part of the disputed ordinance covered). At the same time, however, Eastern never moved against its own corps of gay stewards, and the vice president for in-flight services, herself a former stewardess, created a collegial atmosphere for straight and gay flight attendants alike.[43]

Despite working on the same planes and laying over at the same hotels, many pilots were slow to realize how many male flight attendants were gay. Their initial negativity toward stewards actually depended on misrecognizing the majority of them as straight. As a Pan Am steward noted, "The pilots, when we first came on, assumed we were all straight and that we were going to take their girlfriends [from among the stewardess corps] away from them."[44] Former flight attendant Paula Kane, who was active in SFWR, heard this same complaint when she interviewed a group of pilots in 1974. One of them bemoaned, "For a while there you had to knock on the stewardesses' doors. Then it got to the point where they'd knock on our doors. But now, these guys . . . are getting all the action."[45] Only gradually did some pilots discover that most male flight attendants were gay, though this realization did not erase their hostility.

Overall, then, the many gay flight attendants encountered an uneasy status quo during the 1970s. They were dramatically more numerous than they had been in the 1950s, and they had far more freedom to live a rich lifestyle filled with friendship circles, supportive female colleagues, ample opportunities for sexual flings and more lasting relationships, and—most importantly—access to a career that was becoming more professionalized and higher paying as the decade progressed. Yet given society's persistent hostility toward homosexuality, these men remained cautious when dealing with customers, managers, and pilots. They lived a somewhat schizophrenic life of being visible, yet invisible . . . out to some but not to others. The media, despite the homophobic snickering of some conservative commentators, played along, presenting a public image of stewards as men who challenged traditional male roles but remained heterosexual.

STEWARDS AND THE VESTIGES OF SEXISM

Pilots' initial resentment of male flight attendants hints at certain significant improvements brought to the entire flight attendant corps, not just men, as a result of gender integration. For the most part, with some distinct exceptions, stewardesses found a much-desired reprieve from the most sexist aspects of the job in the post-*Diaz* era. Likewise, most men and women working at the time enjoyed a strong sense of collegiality forged through working together. This new reality was particularly evident on layovers, which could last several days on some international routes. While cabin crews had always depended on each other for social companionship, the dynamic rapidly changed to stewardesses' benefit. Previously, stewardesses and pilots had socialized during this time, despite the differences in age, income, and marital status between them. Because these relationships were occasionally tinged with sexual interest on the part of pilots, having gay colleagues offered stewardesses an alternative: "It was very seldom that you would have a whole [crew] dinner anymore. . . . The [male flight attendants] came in and changed the social dynamics of the crew, because the women would do things with the guys and not with the pilots, because the guys were their age . . . and they [would] do fun things with the women: go shopping, go dancing, go out to eat. And the pilots were left out, because they were fuddies-duddies and they were married. And they were conservative, most of them."[46]

The older pattern of socializing tied to a male-privileged hierarchy and the possibility for sex between the pilot and his subordinates gave way to a new form of socializing between largely gay men and largely straight women who interacted as equals. Indeed, the largest flight attendant union in the post-*Diaz* era, the Association of Flight Attendants (AFA), cited men's role in improving all sorts of interactions with pilots, not only on layovers: "Overall, the female flight attendants feel that having men in the cabin has served as a buffer to the hierarchical status formerly established between the cockpit and cabin crews."[47]

That said, the injection of men into this heavily female profession did not immediately dispel more traditional gender notions. A lot of the praise given to stewards came from their ability to undertake more masculine roles, while freeing stewardesses to focus on more notionally feminine activities. In one article, Theresa Williams of United's husband-wife duo noted how her husband's presence influenced passengers' reactions: "Carry-on baggage seems to go under the seat a little faster when Jerry asks than when I do," and "he rarely gets an argument about whether a passenger can put luggage in the overhead rack." Further, Theresa noted, Jerry's presence left her doing more menial work: "If [passengers are] drinking coffee and talking to him, they'll call me to take the empty. They don't want to disturb a man."[48]

Both passengers and flight attendants saw other realms—like safety, money handling, and heavy lifting—where a man's presence supposedly helped but also reinforced separate roles. One passenger expressed approval for stewards in the interest of safety: "I think it's a good thing to have as many guys in the crew as you can, with all the nuts around. You'd appreciate a man's strength in an emergency."[49] Pan Am's vice president of service noted that some stewardesses were also eager to have male coworkers on international routes: "They wonder what strengths the men can bring to the service—such things as the physical strength for lifting, especially on long-haul international flights."[50] Indeed, when American Airlines hired its very first stewards in 1970, it responded to very similar perceived needs. The airline began a short-lived set of routes in the South Pacific, linking Honolulu to Fiji and Australia on particularly long treks. The four stewardesses assigned to the Boeing 707 crews constantly complained about the amount of work on these routes, and a few openly advocated for stewards to relieve them of certain male-identified tasks. One senior stewardess noted her dislike of handling money from liquor purchases: "I, myself, would rather not be responsible for the money at all, as far as taking on & off the airplane. I think a man should be responsible for the liquor & money."[51] When the airline hired men a month later, it gave them precisely these tasks, as well as certain paperwork duties tied to customs and immigration. Overlooked was the alternative solution of hiring an extra woman to do these tasks.

Indeed, such reinforcement of traditional gender norms only exacerbated what was the most contentious issue between male and female flight attendants in the 1970s: access to the purser position on international carriers like TWA and Northwest, which tried to keep these positions male only even after the *Diaz* decision. Starting in 1966 and continuing through the mid-1970s, the purser policies entered the courts, eventually pitting male and female flight attendants against each other. The first women's victory came when Anayat El Schall of TWA sued to become a purser in 1966. She initially won her case, but the airline appealed and was able to delay a final ruling until after *Diaz*. When the court ruled that Title VII required the dismantling of such sex-based distinctions, TWA finally integrated its purser corps, and certain women were granted retroactive seniority for the years they had been denied the job. This decision in turn led a male purser, Pierre Michel, to countersue, claiming a breach of his seniority rights.[52] A New York State court ultimately decided against Michel in 1974, ruling that his loss of seniority did not amount to reverse discrimination.[53] Thus the integration of TWA's purser corps also created the first noticeable rift between male and female flight attendants. That said, such acrimony was largely limited to the couple of airlines—TWA and Northwest—that fought to keep their pursers all male.

Most of all, however, the stewardesses I interviewed stressed one major improvement in their work conditions when men entered the job: skimpy stewardess uniforms were quickly retired when men entered the job. Stewardesses' skirt lines had been rising since the 1950s. And while the 1970s saw the last—and most orgiastic, if you will—throes of this trend, the decade also ushered in a new era of businesslike professionalism in flight attendant uniforms. When the *Diaz* court concluded that the flight attendant corps could not be regarded as an exclusively female realm, it also placed the airlines on notice that its male and female employees would have to be treated equally, even with regard to uniforms. When Sharlene Martin graduated from American's stewardess academy in May 1971, a Bill Blass miniskirt uniform was standard issue: "When you bent over, people could see your [rear end]!"[54] But when men entered American's domestic lines in 1974, the miniskirt was retired. As stewards' uniforms mimicked pilots' military-style outfits, so too did stewardesses' outfits, with their own navy blazers and a stripe on the arms designating their rank. The women also could choose to wear slacks, thus completing a full-scale transition from an exaggeratedly "sexy" style to an androgynous style that placed them in the same symbolic sphere as their male crewmates. As Martin summed up, "I don't think it was a coincidence . . . that we went from miniskirts to professional uniforms. . . . It absolutely parallels the hiring of men."[55]

The finishing touches of American's uniform overhaul came by way of union arguments demanding completely equal treatment of men and women. First, the union argued for the end of American's policy requiring stewardesses to wear nail polish, since the men were not bound by such a requirement. They then succeeded in ending the notorious girdle requirement by facetiously demanding that the airline force all stewards to wear jockstraps when flying to ensure gender parity.[56]

Similar changes were afoot at United Airlines. The January 1973 issue of the airline's publication *Friendly Times* revealed a drastic overhaul of flight attendant uniforms, introducing outfits that concealed much more skin.[57] The stewardesses' 1960s-era Skimmer dresses, designed by Hollywood's Jean Louis, boasted skirt lines six inches above the knee and sleeves that descended only a few inches off the shoulder. The new uniforms, however, covered more of the women's arms and offered them the option to wear slacks. Ironically, it was most likely the Skimmer's high-riding sleeve line that forced United into altering their uniforms so drastically. United originally disallowed their men from wearing short-sleeve shirts, claiming that customers objected to being served by hairy-armed men. Forcing women to wear longer sleeves was their best hope of preventing Title VII-based lawsuits against their antimale bias regarding body hair.[58]

Uniform redesigns were an external manifestation of a deeper set of changes—many of them won through litigation, or the threat thereof—in flight attendant culture. With men now solidly in place as colleagues, female flight attendants had even more legitimacy to continue their struggles against various other sexist policies. The unions, after winning an end to marriage restrictions and age caps by the close of the 1960s, took the next steps in attacking the two other main policies that led to mass firings of stewardesses: pregnancy and weight restrictions. These cases were eventually won, and by the early 1980s the career had attained genuine potential for full gender parity.[59]

The corresponding demographic shifts in the flight attendant corps were evident among all the airlines. Previously, United's flight attendants were all female and all white, save for the handful of Hawaiian men serving the Honolulu flights. By 1976, however, United's flight attendant corps was more diverse racially and had 7 percent men, while the typical stewardess now was twenty-eight years old.[60] AFA president Linda Puchala celebrated this liberation from the restrictive paradigm of the "fly girl": "As flight attendant stereotypes crumbled around us, gradually we began to see our job as a career. . . . Throughout our workforce, the idea was rooting that we were professionals who would work until a normal retirement age, rather than just until management decided arbitrarily that we should stop because of a wedding ring or children at home."[61]

FEMINISM AND THE LEGAL LEGACY OF *DIAZ*

The ACLU enacted a major push in the 1970s that would ultimately help compensate for the absence of a sex-based Equal Rights Amendment. Its lawyers, including future Supreme Court justice Ruth Bader Ginsburg, successfully argued the landmark case *Reed v. Reed* that the Supreme Court decided in 1971.[62] *Reed* was a more conventional women's rights victory than *Diaz*, as it involved a woman seeking to overturn an Idaho state law that automatically gave her husband control of her deceased son's estate. The Supreme Court's decision in *Reed* was also more sweeping than the appeals court victory in *Diaz*, since it ruled that women should enjoy "equal protection under the law," as offered by the Fourteenth Amendment to the Constitution. According to the court's reasoning, no state or federal law could treat women differently simply by virtue of their gender. The ACLU finally saw the beachhead it needed to expand women's legal equality, and it proceeded to establish the Women's Rights Project in 1972 under Ginsburg's leadership to contest other laws that treated women and men disparately.

But Ginsburg's vision for equal protection was even more expansive. In the spirit of *Diaz*, her strategy was to couple the *Reed* victory with another sex discrimination case involving a man.[63] Charles Moritz was a single man who cared for his elderly mother but he could not receive a "caregiver's tax deduction" because he was a man. Ginsburg expended an equal effort on this case, for she saw it and *Reed* as deeply linked. As legal scholar Cary Franklin summarizes, "Although *Moritz* featured a male plaintiff, Ginsburg's brief argued that equality for women would remain a distant goal as long as men were deterred from pursuing traditionally female activities; equal protection thus meant that the state could not prescribe sex roles for either sex."[64]

The Tenth Circuit Court of Appeals ruled on *Moritz* in late 1972, one year after the *Diaz* decision and the better-known *Reed* case. Franklin notes that *Moritz* too was a "historic victory," as the court found that the Fourteenth Amendment protected men as much as women from sex discrimination. History, however, has been less accepting of *Moritz:* "Only *Reed* . . . has become part of the canon of constitutional law."[65]

During her time at the Women's Rights Project, Ginsburg stuck with the unconventional strategy of employing male plaintiffs to expand the courts' enforcement of sex discrimination. Indeed, "by the time Ginsburg's decade-long litigation campaign ended, men far outnumbered women among the ranks of constitutional sex discrimination plaintiffs to appear before the Supreme Court—a ratio that holds true to this day."[66] This strategy had significant successes. Ginsburg considered the 1975 Supreme Court victory in *Weinberger v. Wiesenfeld* to be the cornerstone of her work. When the Court ruled that Stephen Wiesenfeld, a stay-at-home father, deserved equal "mother's benefits" from the Social Security system when his working wife died, it again found that both men and women deserved equal protection. In this case, the Court undid the sexist stereotype that men should work outside the home, while women should stay home and even be compensated in certain circumstances to do so. The government could not grant such benefits only to women "because it believed they should not be required to work" whereas men should.[67] The victory was important to Ginsburg because it affirmed the main legal principle behind employing both men and women as plaintiffs: to eliminate government support—implicit or explicit—of any sex-based stereotypes. Cary Franklin therefore refers to Ginsburg's vision as the "anti-stereotyping" principle.[68]

Nonetheless, as the 1970s progressed, Ginsburg's strategy achieved fewer victories and began to be questioned, even by fellow feminists. Some women plaintiffs were losing Fourteenth Amendment cases on issues like rape, abortion, and pregnancy, as certain judges ruled that these female-oriented hardships did not arise exclusively from their sex or even from damaging stereotypes that women were sexually vulnerable to men or that pregnancy was a desirable state for women. Instead, judges were ruling that such women possessed some additional criteria beyond their female sex that precipitated their unfortunate treatment (their sexual desirability, their status as pregnant) and that these criteria were not grounds for equal protection under the Fourteenth Amendment.[69] In other words, judges were finding—quite controversially—that discrimination based on rape or pregnancy was not sex-based discrimination.

Frustrated by such narrow decisions that hampered progress toward women's equality, certain feminist legal scholars attacked Ginsburg's male plaintiff strategy. There was a growing sentiment, in Franklin's words, that "this theory of equality may have benefited the WRP's male clients, but it did little for women." With judges ruling against women any time their status was different from that of men, the WRP's strategy proved "of little use in combating the forms of discrimination that hurt women most."[70] A few scholars had an even harsher evaluation of this strategy inspired, in part, by Celio Diaz. They saw these men as a reactionary force, equivalent to white plaintiffs claiming "reverse discrimination" to promote the conservative backlash against forced busing and affirmative action brewing in the 1970s.[71] Such sentiments placed Celio Diaz's legacy in jeopardy: Was he a groundbreaking civil rights pioneer who helped dismantle sexist and heterosexist stereotypes, or was he an interloper in the fight for women's liberation?

HOMOSEXUALITY IN THE POST-*DIAZ* LEGAL LANDSCAPE

Gay rights advocates, lukewarm about the *Diaz* case as it was being argued, were similarly unsure in the 1970s whether his victory offered them a way forward. On the one hand, *Diaz* clearly allowed the flight attendant career to become a heavily gay-identified workplace and improved the economic lot of thousands of gay men. At the same time, however, its limitations as an outright gay rights victory were clear. While the decision dismissed (or at least failed to consider decisive) the airlines' "homosexual panic" defense for maintaining a female-only flight attendant corps, it never explicitly granted gays a legal victory in their own name and even theoretically allowed the airlines to continue discriminating against homosexuals as such. Thus the rise of this gay-inflected profession due to Title VII was unhelpfully secretive—an unintended, inexplicit victory—because it failed to concretely invoke the rights of gays and lesbians.

Gay rights advocates in the 1970s did nonetheless seek to build on the legal momentum of *Diaz* and the Fourteenth Amendment victories won by Ginsburg and the ACLU that expanded protections against sex discrimination. After all, these groups could quite lucidly argue that a lesbian, for example, was discriminated against because of her sex when an employer—or the state—discriminated against her for doing something a man could do without penalty (including partnering with, dating, or loving a woman).[72] Soon after *Diaz*, then, such groups pressed other cases to expand Title VII by claiming that homosexuals were implicitly protected under the prohibition against "sex discrimination" in the workplace. Both the EEOC and federal courts heard such cases in the mid-1970s, with the campaign culminating in a May 1979 ruling from the Ninth Circuit Court of Appeals. The judges, however, repudiated these attempts by refusing to " 'bootstrap' Title VII protection for homosexuals under the guise of protecting [sex]. . . . Adoption of this bootstrap device would frustrate congressional objectives. . . . It would achieve by judicial 'construction' what Congress did not do and has consistently refused to do on many occasions [i.e., protect homosexuals as homosexuals]."[73]

Foreclosing this potential loophole forced gay rights activists to pursue a second legal tactic, inspired by Ginsburg's successes starting with *Reed v. Reed* in 1971: seeking explicit protection for gays and lesbians using the Fourteenth Amendment's "equal protection" clause. Of course, this was precisely what alarmed and emboldened the STOP ERA campaign, with Phyllis Schlafly and others arguing that the ERA "would result in the legalization of homosexual marriages" and other similar travesties.[74] Here the campaign relied, not on inexplicit legal victories like *Diaz* for inspiration, but rather on cases that gays and lesbians had won in their own names. For example, gay activist Frank Kameny spearheaded a series of court victories by the late 1960s that forced the federal government to hire gays and lesbians, bringing an end to the Eisenhower-era prohibitions on "sex perverts."[75] Additionally, in 1969 the California Supreme Court invoked the state's equal protection clause to protect gay and lesbian public school teachers from discrimination; a decade later the same court extended this protection to employees of utility companies.[76]

Yet alongside these victories were defeats that severely restricted Fourteenth Amendment protections for gays and lesbians. The most bitter of these involved a librarian who sought employment at a state-run university. James McConnell was originally offered employment at the University of Minnesota in 1970, but the contract was withdrawn when the Board of Regents became aware that he was a gay rights activist and had sought a marriage license in an effort to marry his partner, Jack Baker. The Federal District Court originally sided with McConnell in the case, citing his rights under the Fourteenth Amendment due process clause: "An homosexual is after all a human being, and a citizen of the United States despite the fact that he finds his sex gratification in what most consider to be an unconventional manner. He is as much entitled to the protection and benefits of the laws and due process fair treatment as are others, at least as to public employment."[77]

This apparent victory for gays and lesbians was, however, short-lived. The appeals court overturned the original decision and also employed harsh homophobic rhetoric in its explanation for refusing Fourteenth Amendment protections to McConnell. As far as this court was concerned, the firing was not about denying McConnell his right to employment but rather about the university's right to keep its employees from actively advocating for gay rights. By being outspoken about his homosexuality, McConnell—so the court claimed—sought "the right to pursue an activist role in *implementing* his unconventional ideas concerning the societal status to be accorded homosexuals and, thereby, to foist tacit approval of this socially repugnant concept upon his employer." Vocally supporting gay rights, even to the point of seeking a marriage license with his partner, amounted to forfeiture of one's Fourteenth Amendment protections: "We know of no constitutional fiat or binding principle of decisional law which requires an employer to accede to such extravagant demands."[78] The McConnell precedent, which the U.S. Supreme Court has yet to overrule, suggested that gays' legal protections were forfeited once they outed themselves and publicly advocated such "repugnant" and "extravagant" ideas as a gay rights agenda.

Such legal defeats led gay rights advocates to move beyond the courts in their struggle to gain protection in employment and other public accommodations. To get the sort of workplace security that gays and lesbians needed would instead require legislative action. Alternatively, gay activists, at least for the sake of employment protection, could skirt the legal realm altogether and directly lobby corporations and labor unions to adopt nondiscrimination policies in their hiring and firing practices.

Mainstream gay activists, led by the National Gay Task Force, worked on both of these agenda items in the 1970s, even in the face of an increasingly organized and politically active right wing that targeted homosexuality. The path toward legislative action to protect gay rights took place on various governmental levels. In Congress, a bill adding "sexual orientation" to Title VII of the 1964 Civil Rights Act was introduced in the House of Representatives, securing support from twenty-four co-sponsors.[79] However, attempts on the federal level—and in state legislatures—failed to garner enough support during the 1970s (in fact, federal action has still not been achieved). Instead, activists succeeded primarily in large cities and university towns, securing protection for gays and lesbians from various local legislatures. One of the first such victories came in San Francisco in 1972, when the board of supervisors required all companies doing business with the city to grant equal employment rights to gays and lesbians.[80] While technically not affecting every business in the city, the ordinance nonetheless had the potential to cover a wide swath of corporations, including airlines: "Enforcement could conceivably be extended to cover such diverse firms as retail stores that accept welfare vouchers, airlines using the San Francisco International Airport, public utilities . . . banks in which public funds are deposited, and firms which buy water from the San Francisco Water Department."[81] Thus, despite being pieces of local legislation, the potential effects of such ordinances on corporations across the country were quite significant, especially as more cities followed San Francisco's example.

The backlash against these gay rights victories was intense, once it finally organized into a potent national force. The spark that ignited such a national movement was Miami's passage of a gay rights ordinance in January 1977 and Anita Bryant's deep-felt outrage in response.[82] Bryant's celebrity status, coupled with her strong ties to the evangelical movement, made her a potent spokesperson for those who objected to the expansion of gay rights, and her grassroots "Save Our Children" organization quickly spread throughout the country. Within just two years, Save Our Children had succeeded in overturning not only the Miami ordinance but also those in St. Paul, Wichita, Austin, and Eugene. Furthermore, Bryant helped give evangelical churches a newfound political voice in national politics, illustrating the ability of their impassioned followers to mobilize for political causes and donate sizable sums of money to such endeavors. Coupled with Phyllis Schlafly's STOP ERA, Bryant's Save Our Children ensured that gay rights entered the political sphere in ways that would be bitterly divisive—as a premier battleground in the country's culture war.

CORPORATE GAY RIGHTS

Companies found themselves in an unenviable position as the fight over gay rights progressed in the later 1970s. The country was torn on whether gays and lesbians should be granted equal rights, but gay rights groups were asking them to become alternative guarantors of their work rights. Increasingly, groups like the Mattachine Society and the Gay Activists Alliance placed novel forms of pressure on all sorts of companies—not just those who did business with city governments—to protect lesbian and gay workers. Among other tactics, they began to assemble lists of companies who discriminated against gays and circulated them in gay publications.[83] Corporations were being forced to take a political and moral stand on an issue that they surely would have preferred to avoid. In the process, we see the opening steps in a larger trend regarding LGBT equality in America: a growing discrepancy between the higher levels of equality that economically desirable LGBT employees enjoy at work and the more basic, potentially even nonexistent, equality all LGBT citizens possess in the legal sphere.

Some major corporations in the 1970s resisted countervailing pressure from conservative forces and committed themselves to various gay rights policies. By 1977 the National Gay Task Force was lauding such companies as CBS, AT&T, and Bank of America for their commitment to nondiscrimination in hiring and firing.[84] Even IBM, a company whose fortunes in the 1970s made it synonymous with U.S. corporate power, publicly agreed to grant significant equality to gay and lesbian employees.[85] Often gay rights groups were able to leverage legal pressure from a local ordinance to effectuate a nationwide change in corporate policy, as in AT&T's case: "Previous to passage of the Minneapolis ordinance, Northwestern Bell Telephone in Minneapolis had a written policy against hiring gay people. This policy has changed and contributed to the change in the national policy of the A.T.&T."[86]

No airline in the 1970s was willing as yet to accept a nondiscrimination policy. Instead, the flight attendant unions began the gradual changes in this direction. By 1980 the AFA had amended its own constitution and bylaws to commit the union to nondiscrimination based on "sexual preference."[87] Other correspondence from the AFA archives shows that the union closely followed developments in both state and federal courts that expanded employment protections for gays and lesbians. However, it is not clear whether it was actually filing grievances on these issues on behalf of flight attendants.[88] It took the airlines much longer—until 1993—to begin adding sexual orientation to their nondiscrimination clauses.[89]

Pan Am's flight attendant union, the International Union of Flight Attendants (IUFA), won the largest victory for lesbian and gay aviation workers in the pre-AIDS years. But the policy change also benefited other workers, particularly those who were unmarried and straight. In this sense, the union's success in 1982 at securing so-called "buddy passes" for single employees hearkened back to the *Diaz* case; it was a decisive, yet still inexplicit move toward gay equality. Union files and personal interviews both attest to the displeasure expressed by unmarried flight attendants—straight and gay—regarding the policy that only blood relatives or married spouses could enjoy travel benefits on the airline. One ostensibly straight female purser in 1973 sent off a letter to her union representatives that posed the demand for buddy passes as a question of fairness: "Granted it's wonderful to travel with one's family; however, should we be slighted for not having married?"[90] The union initially was unwilling to fight for this benefit, claiming that the rules for such reduced-fare tickets were set by the Federal Aviation Administration (FAA) and could not be changed.

But the clamoring among unmarried flight attendants continued with such intensity that the union placed buddy passes on the bargaining table during 1977 negotiations. While the demand was dropped during these negotiations, it resurfaced in 1981. The IUFA again polled its constituents that year, and after affirming its broad popularity, fought even harder to insert it in the 1982 contract. Their success that year predated buddy pass privileges at other U.S. airlines by a full decade.[91] Once the FAA finally approved the provisions in January 1983, Pan Am employees could invite their friends or domestic partners to travel with them at a significantly reduced fare. Meanwhile, one Eastern steward recalls how the issue was closely identified as a gay rights issue at his airline. He even noted company gossip that CEO Frank Borman refused extending these privileges to Eastern flight attendants because "I'm not going to let those guys fly their boyfriends around the country!"[92]

WORKING SIDE BY SIDE

In chronicling key improvements to the flight attendant career in the 1970s, this chapter has highlighted how men and women—and gays and straights—now worked side by side, as equal stakeholders in the job. The flight attendant corps became a changed workplace during the decade as men and women worked together to resist, however imperfectly, the two-pronged oppression of a patriarchal system: sexism and heterosexism. Most of this work was done on an informal basis, at both dinner tables (on layovers) and in the workplace itself. Meanwhile, the greatest contract-based accomplishment of this grassroots cooperation was the "buddy pass" victory at Pan Am, which benefited women and men, straights and gays, by forming a collective interest around the idea of equality for the unmarried.

This example contrasts sharply with the presumption that male-female relations in the aviation industry—including relations between stewardesses and stewards—were fundamentally adversarial, pitting men on the side of patriarchal privilege and in opposition to the encroachment of feminism. Of course, there were tensions of this sort among flight attendants, especially regarding pursers at TWA and Northwest.[93] Often, labor union leadership was another point of contention, since many local and national union boards were headed by men who at times seemed unsympathetic to women's concerns. One female candidate in Eastern's 1971 union elections aptly summarized what many stewardesses felt: "This union is approximately ninety percent women, being 'led' by two men. How well do they represent the interests of the majority? . . . Judge for yourself from the experience of the girls in Eastern Airlines."[94]

However, at a majority of the nation's airlines—especially those that had never before hired men—the dynamic between stewards and stewardesses in the post-*Diaz* moment was built on a much deeper sense of equality, especially when compared to the relations between pilots and stewardesses before the 1970s. In fact, it was men at American, United, Delta, and other major carriers who lost out on years of seniority by being barred from employment. As the AFA regretfully noted during the economic downturn in the early 1980s, "Ironically, AFA's male members have experienced the reverse of the condition that usually afflicts women in the workplace: last hired, first fired." Even though men made up just 13 percent of the union's membership, "about 30 percent of AFA's furloughees are men."[95] Uncollaborative male union leaders and senior pursers were the exception to the general rule of relations between the sexes that were now marked by economic parity (maybe even female advantage), workplace cooperation, and free-time enjoyment unencumbered by the threat of unwanted sexual advances from pilots.

The flight attendant corps of the 1970s also ended the virtual invisibility of homosexuality in commercial aviation, marking a greater level of openness than what the stewards of the 1950s achieved. Gay men were now active at all levels of the flight attendant profession. Even certain leaders in flight attendant labor unions were gay or lesbian.[96] In this way, flight attendants' lived experience in the 1970s counteracts the most egregious shortcomings of 1970s-era gay rights and women's rights advocates. The gay men who ran the *Advocate*, for example, tended to ignore women's issues and betrayed an ambivalence toward sexism's effects on stewardesses, asserting instead a desire for gay men to achieve libidinal parity with straight men on airplanes.

Similarly, some feminists in groups like NOW saw LGBT rights as incongruous with their own struggle. Most notoriously, Betty Friedan, the group's founder and first president, decried homosexuality as a "Lavender Menace," thereby echoing the homophobia of the 1950s. Aware of how Phyllis Schlafly and other social conservatives deployed images of mannish women and womanly men for their own gain, Friedan and others calculated that NOW should forsake alliances with lesbians and gay men in order to achieve mainstream respectability.[97] Thus flight attendants at times advocated a fuller vision of liberation than that of the larger women's movement, not only targeting unfair workplace practices and sexual exploitation but also fostering gay liberation and, as Pan Am steward Barry Shelby asserted, "man's liberation."[98]

Meanwhile, post-*Diaz* attempts to foster gender-based and sexuality-based legal equality were still incomplete as the 1970s came to a close. Inspired in part by Celio Diaz, legal activists like Ruth Bader Ginsburg sought to further dismantle laws that harmed women and gender queers. But the New Right activism that grew in part out of controversial court decisions like *Roe v. Wade* helped spawn a new, more conservative generation of justices by the close of the decade. Women's liberation and gay liberation were increasingly frustrated goals, and gay rights advocates became more likely to seek equality in local legislatures and corporate boardrooms.

Even in these corporate venues, gays and lesbians faced intense objections from Save Our Children, Phyllis Schlafly's reconstituted Eagle Forum, and a growing chorus of increasingly active right-wing religious groups. While flight attendants and a handful of other gay-tolerant careers ushered in new potential for queer equality, many other LGBT citizens continued to be exposed to public opprobrium and legally sanctioned discrimination. This combustible status quo, a full-fledged culture war, would continue into the 1980s, and become further exacerbated once gay men started dying in significant numbers to the new and mysterious illness of AIDS. While flight attendants might have enjoyed a certain avant-garde status at the close of the 1970s—as members of a career particularly responsive to the twofold impulses of women's liberation and gay liberation—they were flying headlong into a deeply turbulent era as the 1980s opened.

CHAPTER SIX

Flight Attendants and the
Origins of an Epidemic

AIDS had a devastating impact on the flight attendant corps. As members of one of
America's gayest professions, many of them belonged to the communities hardest
hit when the epidemic officially began in 1981. Flight attendants' experiences with
AIDS extended beyond the sensationalized media reports written for general readers, who typically had no firsthand interaction with the disease.[1] Practically every
flight attendant in these years lost colleagues, friends, or loved ones from among
their coworkers. And it was almost always the gay men who were falling sick in
the prime of their physical health, at the dawn of their adult lives. In my research,
I made only halting attempts to quantify this loss. When I broached the subject
in interviews, former flight attendants' voices grew more hushed, their demeanor
became uncomfortable, their eyes often filled with tears. I addressed the boldest of
such questions to a retired Pan Am steward: "How many people did you know who
were lost to AIDS?" Though years had since passed, his pain was still raw, and he
choked up as he answered, "I stopped counting at 162."[2]

Men like this bemoaned how AIDS seemed to cruelly single out flight attendants, morphing their carefree years of early adulthood into macabre times of
nerve-racking trips to doctors, hospital visits to see sick friends, and far too many
funerals. Their very survival seemed in jeopardy. The disease quickly became not
only a health crisis but a political threat, imperiling the strides toward equality
made by male flight attendants in the 1970s. While flight attendants in the 1950s
and 1960s had fought for a modicum of unofficial gay tolerance and the 1970s had

offered the first prospects of a fuller gay acceptance, the 1980s saw a retrenchment of exclusionary policies and growing social fears directed at these men because of AIDS. Just as flight attendants fought for their physical and political survival, so too did the entire gay community, which was once again the object of intense fear and political scapegoating.

No one better embodies this multifaceted battle for survival than Air Canada flight attendant Gaëtan Dugas, who remains to this day the most infamous steward in history. Having contracted Kaposi's sarcoma (a skin cancer that commonly occurs with untreated HIV infection) in the summer of 1980, Gaëtan was one of the first handful of people diagnosed with AIDS in North America. While few beyond Gaëtan's family and circle of friends followed his plight in contracting the disease, he gained far more notoriety a few years after his death in March 1984. Journalist and author Randy Shilts sensationally resurrected him in his 1987 best-selling book on the AIDS crisis, *And the Band Played On*. What garnered so much attention was Shilts's skillfully framed suggestion—despite ample evidence to the contrary—that Gaëtan was the continent's very first person with AIDS, the "Patient Zero" who brought this African disease to North America.

Planting the story with the *New York Post*, Shilts's publishers started a cavalcade of sensational headlines across the continent, with the *Post* claiming, in a massive bold headline, that it had uncovered "THE MAN WHO GAVE US AIDS."[3] Over the next several months, news stories repeated the most salacious details from Shilts's forthcoming book, including the fact that Gaëtan had had sex with an astounding 250 partners per year. The media frenzy made Gaëtan the scapegoat extraordinaire for America's AIDS epidemic, while his fellow flight attendants—and gay men more generally—were deemed guilty by association for these sexual transgressions.

This progression from hapless victim to demonic scapegoat makes Gaëtan a vital character in the history of HIV/AIDS. A significant portion of the following chapter considers Randy Shilts's and his publisher's complex motives for slandering him and the substantial political consequences of their choice. While Shilts's book to this day rightly earns praise for its detailed account of the early AIDS crisis and its bold incrimination of the Reagan administration and the scientific community for failing to act decisively against AIDS, it also elicits ambivalence from many in the LGBT and HIV/AIDS communities. In essence, Shilts—himself a gay man who would succumb to AIDS in 1994—presented social conservatives with the ultimate political gift: a revolting story of a beautiful, promiscuous, foreign, gay male flight attendant so hedonistic that he introduced a killer virus into North America and then recklessly spread it from coast to coast. The Patient Zero narrative encapsulated for the media and much of the public that AIDS was a disease born of gay immorality, a threat to the nation that came from the post-Stonewall gay credo of unchecked sexual excess.[4] Surely, such tropes existed before Shilts's book, but never with the succinctness and psychological impact of the infamous Patient Zero.

The current chapter examines flight attendants and the AIDS crisis before Gaëtan became the object of AIDS hysteria, in the origin years of the epidemic. At this time, too, flight attendants were central characters in the culture war that dominated America's response to AIDS. Conservatives saw them as the type of gay men who were contagion threats, possessing the potential to transmit this gay disease to otherwise healthy and morally upstanding Americans. In turn, various flight attendants worked to counteract such attempts to marginalize gays and people with AIDS (PWAs) from the social mainstream. United Airlines flight attendant Gär Traynor deserves special acclaim on this front. While the larger public and even historians of the AIDS crisis have completely forgotten him (unlike his Quebecois counterpart), Gär's legacy was no less important.[5] In June 1983, despite being healthy enough to work, Gär was grounded by United because of his AIDS diagnosis. The airline claimed that the public's fears of catching AIDS via casual contact justified their decision. Gär, as well as a handful of other United flight attendants who also lost their jobs because of AIDS, fought the airline in labor arbitration proceedings and threatened the company with further lawsuits.

In December 1984, Gär Traynor became yet another flight attendant-cum-civil rights pioneer, alongside Celio Diaz from the late 1960s. That month he won the right to return to work, quite likely the first PWA in the country to do so. While his arbitration victory was technically not binding for PWAs fired in other industries, it established a precedent that federal and state courts eventually accepted and that Congress also adopted in the Americans with Disabilities Act of 1990: people with HIV/AIDS deserved to be treated just like others with life-threatening, noncontagious illnesses, continuing to work as long as their health permitted. Gär's victory predated the better-known AIDS discrimination case that inspired the 1993 Oscar-winning film *Philadelphia* by a full nine years.[6] It was, in fact, the first in a series of legal steps that enabled many PWAs to remain active in the public sphere, despite widespread beliefs that they were both contagious and morally repugnant.

The stories of Gär Traynor and Gaëtan Dugas together serve to explain how AIDS threatened both the flight attendant corps and the larger gay community. They hardly constitute the entire history of the AIDS epidemic in the United States. Indeed, in recent years, various scholars have written about the disconnect between the treatment of HIV/AIDS as a primarily gay illness and the horrific path the disease has taken—and continues to follow—through poorer communities, both heterosexual and otherwise. I therefore am indebted to historian Jennifer Brier's recent work *Infectious Ideas*, which details how early AIDS outreach in the United States grossly underserved these other victims, especially racial minorities, because of assumptions linking AIDS with white male homosexuality.[7] Nonetheless, focusing on these two flight attendants significantly deepens our understanding of the AIDS crisis. They highlight how AIDS threatened gay-tolerant careers and also illustrate how flight attendants unwittingly assumed key roles in the struggle that conservatives and progressives waged over AIDS and queer civil rights in the 1980s.

GAËTAN AND THE TRUE ORIGINS OF AIDS

The fact that so many people still believe Gaëtan Dugas brought AIDS to North America attests to the impact of Randy Shilts's Patient Zero myth. Yet the myth's power owes far more to the operation of stereotypes about male flight attendants and gay men, coupled with Shilts's own skillfully articulated rendition of the story, than it does to medical facts. Even in 1987, several doctors and prominent AIDS researchers immediately dismissed Shilts's speculation that Gaëtan was North America's first PWA. When asked about the *Post* headline, Dr. Harold Jaffe, a researcher at the Centers for Disease Control (CDC) who worked with Gaëtan when he volunteered for research studies there, called Shilts's claim "preposterous." Jaffe explained, "It's not a correct interpretation to say one person is responsible for introducing [AIDS] to North America."[8] Meanwhile, *Time* magazine, which initially added to the salacious coverage of Gaëtan with an article entitled "The Appalling Saga of Patient Zero," did an about-face just a few weeks later.[9] Highlighting recently published research on a young St. Louis man who had died of AIDS in 1969, the magazine noted, "The case may represent the earliest documented instance of AIDS in North America, predating that of Gaetan Dugas, a Canadian flight attendant." The article ended with a more sober and far more accurate account of the facts about the origins of HIV/AIDS as they stood in late 1987: "Indeed, the history of AIDS in the U.S. may have a much longer prologue than was once suspected." As one of the researchers on the St. Louis case added, "What we're saying is that AIDS has been around for a long time but just wasn't recognized."[10] Later research has affirmed this claim, while also illustrating how far-fetched the Patient Zero myth truly was.

As epidemiologists now know, people have been dying of AIDS since the middle of the twentieth century at the very latest. Preserved blood samples taken in the 1950s at the main hospital in Kinshasa, Congo, show the presence of HIV in patients who died there. Then, at some time around the mid-1960s, HIV successfully traversed the Atlantic and established itself in its first major base outside Africa.[11] But this transmission to America was almost certainly not the by-product of a gay male flight attendant and was definitely not the work of Gaëtan Dugas, who was then just fourteen years old and living with his family on the outskirts of Quebec City. Instead, HIV first came to Haiti, possibly brought there by Haitians who worked for Congo's president, Joseph Mobutu, running the newly independent country's bureaucracies.[12] The latest evidence also suggests that the pandemic subtype of HIV entered the United States quite early, arriving from Haiti around the year 1969. Haiti and the United States have always been linked, but more so since economic globalization began after World War II. Immigrants from Haiti were lured by America's jobs and more relaxed immigration policies starting in the 1960s, trade between the countries grew significantly in the postwar era, and U.S. tourism to Haiti—sex tourism and otherwise—experienced a boom in the late 1960s and 1970s. Yet of the multiple possible HIV infection patterns that surely arose from these linkages, experts who have examined the virus's evolution now claim with virtual certainty that Haitian immigrants planted the pandemic subtype in the United States. Once it was established within these immigrant communities in places like New York and Miami, the disease began to spread, according to epidemiologists, as "the ancestral pandemic clade virus crossed from the Haitian community in the United States to the non-Haitian population there."[13]

Thus, when HIV first appeared in the United States, Gaëtan Dugas was still attending high school in Quebec City and probably had never left Canada for more than a school trip. About to receive his cosmetology license and speaking only French, Gaëtan seemed destined to remain in his hometown or perhaps relocate to more cosmopolitan Montreal, to work as a hair stylist. He was open about being gay and even found a modicum of acceptance from his conservative Catholic stepparents. Yet Gaëtan still dreamed of participating in a larger and more exotic gay world in far-flung places like Paris, Rio, San Francisco, or nearby New York. His first steps in this direction came after his schooling, when he made his way to Vancouver with a specific plan in mind: learn English while working in the city, so that he could join Air Canada's flight attendant corps, which had a strict bilingual admission criterion. The airline—like U.S. carriers after the *Diaz* decision—had by 1973 finally created a gender-neutral hiring practice. Gaëtan was among the thousands of gay Canadian and American men who rushed to fill these jobs. By his early twenties, his hard work learning English, his good looks, and his charming demeanor had finally paid off; Gaëtan earned his wings and began traveling the world.[14]

Just as Gaëtan started at Air Canada, HIV was spreading surreptitiously throughout the United States. With its initial concentration in poorer urban communities, the virus continued to prey on those with inadequate access to health care. This linkage with poverty kept medical authorities from detecting the illness until higher-risk behaviors allowed the virus to move beyond its original foothold. Especially important to HIV's spread were intravenous drug use and male-male sex, both of which became more public and more common in the 1970s. In the post-Stonewall gay community, bars and bathhouses became legal in most American cities for the first time, greatly expanding a nightlife industry that thrived on gays' newfound sexual liberation. Moving almost overnight from a time when even same-sex dancing was illegal to one in which public sex was readily available, many gay men embraced promiscuity. While Gaëtan's self-reported claim of having 250 sexual partners per year was higher than the norm for gay men, he was far from alone.

Thus, despite a much longer and far more complex history, AIDS—a name the CDC finally adopted in late 1982—was now seen as a gay disease and would be treated as such for much of the next decade. Urban gay men in the United States were considered the first and most typical victims of this disease, the epicenter of the epidemic. Meanwhile, the global dimensions of AIDS and the existence of other at-risk groups in the United States were largely ignored. In San Francisco through 1983, 96 percent of AIDS diagnoses were among gay or bisexual men, while this same group made up 93 percent of Los Angeles County's cases as late as 1985.[15]

The first AIDS diagnoses, which Los Angeles physician Michael Gottlieb reported among some of his gay patients in the summer of 1981, were vitally important to Gaëtan's own diagnosis. Then stationed at Air Canada's Toronto base, Gaëtan manifested his first AIDS-related symptoms in December 1979. His swollen lymph nodes would never return to normal, even when he felt well. By mid-1980, he developed a more severe complication that further confused his doctors. They biopsied a skin lesion under his ear in May 1980 and were surprised to discover that Gaëtan had a very rare cancer, Kaposi's sarcoma (KS), that was virtually unknown among French Canadians. Only with Dr. Gottlieb's reports from the following summer did Gaëtan's doctors diagnose him with the new, as yet unnamed, immune disorder. As a result, Gaëtan started commuting to New York University Hospital every month, where doctors were treating other KS patients and working closely with the CDC on this confounding new outbreak. Unquestionably, the early onset of Gaëtan's symptoms establishes him as one of Canada's first cases of AIDS. But his NYU doctors and CDC researchers knew of several other men in California and New York whose symptoms had arisen earlier. As it turns out, Gaëtan wasn't even America's first flight attendant with AIDS, much less the first-ever North American with the illness.

THE HUB AND SPOKES OF AIDS

For gay flight attendants in the late 1970s, their job placed them in a higher-risk category for contracting the disease. One former Pan Am steward saw a deep connection between his work and the prolific gay sex complicit in the disease's transmission. "The whole concept of our job was hedonistic, it really was," he noted. The job's fast pace and rootlessness kept many flight attendants focused on living for themselves without much consideration of the future: "It's that we lived for the moment, and I think [the sex] was part of that." The career appealed to gay men who were young, largely uncoupled, and eager to seek out adventures around the globe. At least at Pan Am, "there weren't too many people in long-term relationships—a few, but I didn't know that many."[16]

Moreover, laying over in fun, far-flung cities from Sydney to Berlin offered these men more opportunities for exposure to the virus. With HIV unnoticed but prevalent in gay bathhouses and discos, minor behavioral choices often meant the difference between life and death. As this ex-steward claimed, "Most of us that [survived the early years], I think we took care of ourselves a little bit better. . . . A lot of them did drugs, and they took uppers to go out partying all night and then they had to fly the next day. A lot of them didn't sleep for, like, three days. These are the ones that died," since this excessive partying often entailed more frequent sexual activity. Several other flight attendants credit their survival even more randomly to their particular sexual interests: a dislike of anal sex or a preference for topping.

Spending time off work was no interlude from the stewards' fast-paced lifestyle. Pan Am stewards and their peers at other U.S. airlines tended to live in major cities like New York and Los Angeles, where the newly won gay freedoms of meeting sexual partners in commercial venues were also readily available. These elements combined to create a lifestyle—both on the job and off—that this flight attendant considered "wild," though he was quick to add, "I'm not passing judgment . . . it was just the times, that's what people did."[17]

All U.S. airlines shared with Pan Am a feature that became increasingly common after deregulation in 1979: flight operations were concentrated at home airports called "hubs," with flights emanating from this base in various "spokes." Hubs were the de facto homes for flight attendants, pilots, and most of the airlines' ground staffs and management. The larger a city, the more likely it was to become a hub. New York

City to this day remains either a primary or secondary hub for several of the United States' top airlines, as do Los Angeles, San Francisco, and Chicago. Coincidentally, thanks to migration and cultural patterns already visible in the 1930s and discussed in chapter 1, these same major cities were also hubs of gay life. As the AIDS epidemic was dawning in these gay metropoles, airline deregulation was driving more flight attendants to relocate to these very same cities. Perhaps not coincidentally, it didn't take long for passengers already suspicious that their male flight attendants were gay to conclude that they were now potential AIDS carriers as well. Such fears turned male flight attendants themselves into the quintessential hub of the epidemic, who then spread the disease along their given airline's spokes into the U.S. heartland.

Figure 11 shows the "hub-and-spoke" flight plan for what was then the largest U.S. airline, United, in the postderegulation years. The concentration of flight activity in America's largest and gayest cities is immediately noticeable: Chicago, San Francisco, Denver, Los Angeles, and New York all were major nodes of activity. By consolidating operations in these cities, the airline found a more cost-efficient way of running its coast-to-coast operations. After all, deregulation (in theory) allowed all airlines to serve any city they chose, without enduring the restrictive route approval process of the Federal Aviation Administration. At their best, hub-and-spoke systems were eminently rational: airlines could focus maintenance and management in just a few cities and also centralize some ticketing, baggage, fueling, and in-flight tasks like catering and cleaning.[18]

Epidemiologists from the CDC published a graph that shows in hub-and-spoke-like fashion the sexual connections among forty of the United States' first 248 gay men diagnosed with AIDS (figure 12). Before they interviewed these men, Gaëtan included, about their sex lives in 1982, the investigators strongly suspected that the disease was sexually transmitted. Yet the finding of so many sexual linkages among the country's first victims exceeded their expectations. Dr. Harold Jaffe, one of the investigators, noted, "Our statistician tells us that the probability of all these [sexual] contacts among men with the same rare disease occurring by some random chance not only approaches zero—it *is* zero."[19] When the authors finally published their findings on this so-called "cluster study" two years later, this graph inadvertently helped give birth to the myth of "Patient Zero."[20] Each circle represented one of the men in the study, along with his location and the order in which he had developed symptoms of AIDS (for example, "NY 17" is the seventeenth man in New York who participated in the study to get sick). The spokes linking these circles represented sexual contact between the men. To reinforce the importance of sexual connections between these men, the researchers selected one person as the "index case"—the

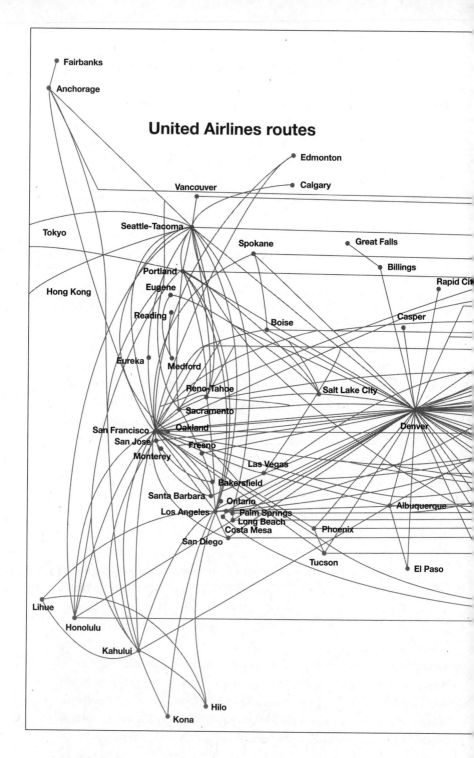

FIGURE II.

This reproduction simplifies the 1985 domestic route system of United Airlines, which at the time was America's largest airline. Even as it omits certain routes, the image none-theless illustrates the intense clustering of United's activities in key cities: San Francisco,

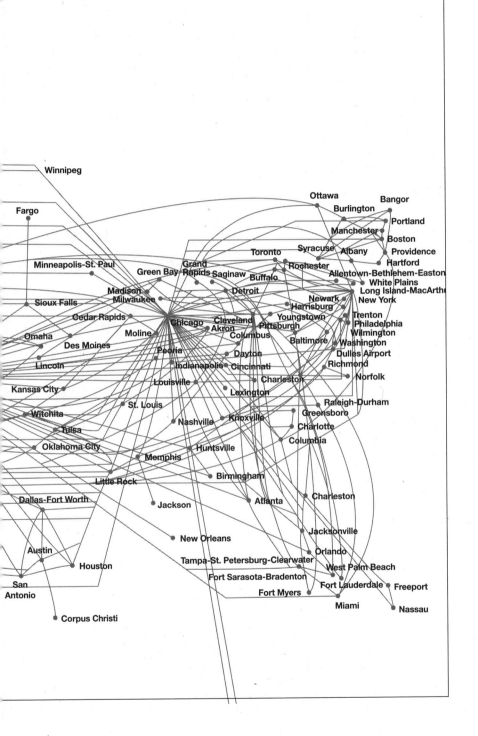

Chicago, Los Angeles, Denver, New York City, and Washington, D.C. As deregulation continued to take hold over the next two decades, United further consolidated its routes in these key cities. *Air Transport World*, September 1985, 20. Courtesy *Air Transport World*.

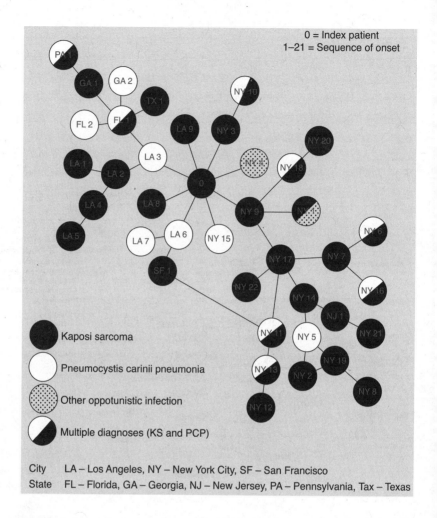

FIGURE 12.
The CDC cluster study graph. Reprinted from David Auerbach
et al., "Cluster of Cases of the Acquired Immune Deficiency
Syndrome: Patients Linked by Sexual Contact," *American Journal
of Medicine* 76 (March 1984): 488, with permission from Elsevier.

hub, if you will—whose sexual activity stood at the center of the graph. Though his
name remained anonymous until Randy Shilts published it in *And the Band Played
On* a few years later, Gaëtan Dugas was the index case.

Placing Gaëtan at the graph's center was an arbitrary choice, since each
man, either directly or indirectly, was linked to everyone else and could therefore

potentially hold this spot. But the CDC researchers felt Gaëtan was a particularly telling case on two fronts. First, he had had sex with eight of the forty men, more than anyone else in the chain (though two other men had sex with five others and *not* with him). Second, he showed how AIDS, if it were indeed sexually transmitted, could potentially jump from coast to coast. After all, as the graph makes clear, Gaëtan had slept with four of the first men with AIDS in Los Angeles and another four of the first men in New York.

While all the other men represented in the graph were assigned a location and a number, Gaëtan was symbolized simply with "o." The researchers denoted him as such not because he was "ground zero," the first in the study to get AIDS. They actually knew that at least five other men in the cluster had gotten sick before him.[21] In fact, the "o" simply designated him as the arbitrarily chosen index case, as the interpretive key makes clear. The researchers also opted not to give Gaëtan a location, given his Canadian citizenship and the fact that he was officially residing outside the United States while they were tracking his sex life. Other than calling him "Patient o," the article referred to him only as a "non-Californian" who was nonetheless connected sexually to some of the original Los Angeles patients.[22] Yet whatever their intent, the researchers made Gaëtan conspicuously stand out in the graph. A quick glance could lead the reader to attribute far greater significance to him than the study itself did. He could easily morph from "o" in this sexual chain to "Patient Zero" for the entire North American AIDS epidemic.[23] However rational the graph was in presenting the cluster study's findings, it left ample room for more irrational interpretations.

The researchers themselves were under no illusions that their "Patient o" was the first North American with AIDS. When questioned by journalists at the time of the study's release in 1984, Dr. William Darrow, a coauthor, bluntly asserted, "Patient o picked up the syndrome from a contact in Los Angeles or New York."[24] Yet this assurance did not stop reporters from focusing on Patient o, even though the researchers stressed the import of the sexual cluster, not the index case. The *New York Times* headlined its story, "US Medical Study Singles Out a Man Who Carried AIDS," while the AP article that ran in the *Los Angeles Times* began similarly: "40 AIDS Cases in 10 Cities Traced to Single 'Carrier.'" The AP even closed with a potentially alarming assertion: "Patient o ultimately did develop AIDS and is still alive, according to Darrow's most recent information," suggesting that this man was still a potential danger.[25] As we shall see, the media's sleight of hand—diverting attention from the cluster to Patient o—later served as Randy Shilts's model when he researched and wrote *And the Band Played On*.

While the media fixated on the index case and his sexual habits, CDC sociologist William Darrow was intrigued by another finding in the interviews: a good number of the men were flight attendants. In fact, of the first nineteen cases in Los Angeles, at least three—not including Gaëtan—were stewards.[26] As they pursued information on the other confirmed cases around the country, Darrow and his colleagues found at least two more flight attendants. Other traveling businessmen were also overrepresented among the early AIDS victims, leading Darrow to write more extensively on the links between travel, homosexuality, and HIV transmission.[27]

Flight attendants were already discovering the same hard truth, quickly realizing that their colleagues were particularly prone to developing the mysterious gay plague. The men I interviewed have vivid recollections of their airline's first casualties from AIDS. Two Pan Am employees recalled that a New York-based friend died very early in the crisis: "He had this mysterious disease, and they only realized what it was about the time he died. . . . This was the first time I ever heard of it."[28] This man's affliction apparently killed him in 1981 or 1982, when the disease was still referred to most commonly as GRID—gay-related immune deficiency—and the term *AIDS* had yet to be coined.

Similarly, in San Francisco, a TWA flight attendant developed mysterious health problems very early on. His friend recalled the man's dire situation: "I remember . . . I was sitting in the JFK terminal when [he] came in from a domestic flight that he had worked from San Francisco. . . . And he saw me there, and he came over crying, and he said to me, 'I don't know what's the matter with me, but I couldn't make the announcements, I couldn't coordinate [anything].' And I [told him] to get to the doctor right away." Compounding the anxiety was that doctors had no forthcoming diagnosis: "They didn't know what was wrong with him, and they eventually gave him a lobotomy" in the unrealized hope of locating the cause of his symptoms. The crude techniques physicians used against this mysterious illness left this steward and others feeling helpless. "It was horrible," was his summation of watching his friend die so painfully and inexplicably.[29]

The TWA flight attendant's case also demonstrates how AIDS began to affect men's work performance, a situation that became more common across the industry. In fact, Pan Am's first Los Angeles-based casualty collapsed while working with a severe case of *Pneumocystis carinii* pneumonia (PCP). He was met by an ambulance at the airport after a flight from Sydney to L.A. and passed away just a few days later.[30]

Fellow flight attendants also noticed that the disease wasn't exactly striking randomly. As the months passed, the younger men—those in their twenties or thirties—composed the majority of those getting sick. One Pan Am employee summed up this depressing observation: "Most of them came from the group hired after 1971. . . . It was mostly the young people."[31] As noted previously, other flight attendants saw connections between their colleagues' partying, drug use, sexual activity, and AIDS. When finally published, the CDC's cluster study began to attach some hard numbers to flight attendants' unempirical observations on these points. It found that the median age for those with AIDS in 1982 was just over thirty-five. Moreover, extensive interviews about the men's sexual habits revealed that a majority had frequented the baths, used poppers (nitrate inhalants), engaged in fisting, and had at least fifty partners in the previous year and over one thousand in their lifetimes.[32] In these early years, at least, AIDS was primarily striking down the more sexually adventurous gay men, and Gaëtan was hardly the only flight attendant in this category.

AIDS HYSTERIA TAKES OFF

Thanks to a growing body of evidence that included the 1982 cluster study, scientists by 1983 were moving toward a consensus that AIDS was transmitted via blood and semen. Indeed, the dramatic rise in cases among sexually active gay men, IV drug users, and hemophiliacs reminded doctors of the infection patterns from viruses like hepatitis B. However, the public's understanding of transmission patterns was less nuanced, especially as scientists still had not located the purported virus causing AIDS (and did not announce this discovery until April 1984). On the one hand, there was enough media coverage of the disease devastating gay men to link AIDS with homosexual behavior. Yet the growth of nongay cases bolstered fears that AIDS could spread indiscriminately among the larger public. This uneasiness flared up with particular ferocity in June 1983, when various media stories reported on a medical study that falsely theorized that AIDS could be contracted via casual contact.[33] Not coincidentally, this was the same moment when some U.S. airlines developed their first exclusionary policies to appease the public's growing hysteria and ground flight attendants with AIDS.

All sorts of media from 1983—the gay press, conservative newsletters, and the mainstream media—reflected this newfound alarm about contracting AIDS from casual contact. An article from Boston's *Gay Community News* catalogued the new impetus to isolate PWAs: some New York hospitals began to segregate AIDS patients, and the city's sanitation workers threatened to walk off their jobs when a colleague developed AIDS and wanted to keep working.[34] Similarly, *Newsweek* detailed the first battles in which worried parents fought school boards to ban children with AIDS from schools. When the Gallup organization polled Americans in the summer of 1983, it found that "a substantial minority of the public at large believes, incorrectly, that mere social contact with AIDS victims may transmit the disease."[35]

Soon thereafter, Phyllis Schlafly's Eagle Forum embroiled flight attendants in the AIDS hysteria of 1983, with a flier entitled "The ERA-Gay-AIDS-Connection."[36] The authors invoke the most familiar tenets of AIDS hysteria, first marking AIDS as a gay disease and then warning that it could cross over into straight society: "If the E.R.A. puts 'sex equality' into the Constitution . . . would police, paramedics, dentists, health personnel and morticians be permitted to take adequate precautions to defend themselves against AIDS and other homosexual diseases?"

The authors then expand the sphere of potential victims beyond isolated professionals exposed to bodily fluids: the general public could contract AIDS as well, via gay employees in the food service industry. "Could we restrict homosexuals from working in the food handling business, such as restaurants and as flight attendants on airlines?," the flier asks.[37] The menacing implication is that any healthy person could conceivably contract the "homosexual disease" simply by frequenting a restaurant or being served a meal by a flight attendant on a plane. Whether coincidentally or not, Eagle Forum's suggestion that gay flight attendants be fired arose just as United Airlines opted to ground long-serving employee Gär Traynor and others suffering from AIDS.

It is not hard to imagine that Gär Traynor would have a good deal in common with the more famous Gaëtan Dugas. They were just five years apart in age, Gär being born in 1947 and Gaëtan in 1952, and both came of age as gay men in relatively small towns. Gär was still known as "Gary" on the outskirts of Eugene, Oregon, where he had been raised as an only child by his mother and stepfather. Like Gaëtan, Gary followed well-trodden migration paths for gay men at the close of the 1960s and the dawn of the 1970s. To perfect his transformation to Gär (he always added the extra panache of an *Umlaut* when signing his name), he made his way to the bigger city of Los Angeles. He joined United Airlines in April 1973, just a year after United first hired men as a result of the *Diaz* case. Thus Gär, like Gaëtan, was part of the influx of gay men who entered North America's various flight attendant teams in the early 1970s.

Gär's AIDS diagnosis came a couple years after Gaëtan's. His health issues first arose in late 1982, when he too developed KS, the sign that alerted his doctors to the fact that he had AIDS. He quickly came under the care of UCLA's Bowyer Clinic, where doctors Michael Gottlieb and Jerome Groopman were forging new treatment strategies for KS and other symptoms. At the time, there were only about fifty AIDS diagnoses in Los Angeles County, confirming Gär as a very early victim of the new illness.[38] On February 8, 1983, Dr. Groopman contacted United on his behalf, explaining his diagnosis and need for weekly chemotherapy.[39] Otherwise, Groopman told the airline, Gär was healthy enough to continue working. Apparently, neither doctor nor patient felt reservations about being candid with United about his condition.

United's initial reaction to Gär's news was sympathetic. His superiors told him to, "stay on [the job] as long as he felt up to it." But this attitude changed as the months went on, especially when the hysteria brewing in 1983 trickled into the flight attendants corps. Gär now noticed that some of his colleagues, on seeing his KS lesions or learning of his AIDS diagnosis, "were quite concerned about even being near me."[40] On May 8, 1983, as headlines trumpeted contagion fears, a flight attendant wrote her superiors about a New York-based colleague with AIDS. In advocating that United rid its workforce of PWAs, she expressed deep anxiety about catching AIDS in the workplace: "I understand (I do not know for fact) there is a FA in JFK with AIDS. With the present facts known that AIDS is transmitted via other means than sexual contact I am concerned. I'm concerned for myself and my small daughter. I must assume there are other FA's who share my concern."[41]

By the end of the month, such fears made their way to Gär's Los Angeles base. A second letter (from a flight attendant to a first-name-only recipient whose job title is unknown, copied to the "AFA [Association of Flight Attendants] LAXSW Safety Committee") expressed concerns about Gär's retention on the job. Unsigned and generated on a telex, it could have been a form letter that was mass-distributed among United's flight attendants at LAX.

Dear [name omitted],

The other day, while in the office area, I was told by another flight attendant (male) that flight attendant Garr [sic] Traynor . . . has AIDS. . . . The subject came up because apparently Garr is bald or has had his head shaven. Garr is currently flying.

On behalf of flight attendants, United customers, and the general public, I feel it is wrong for someone who has a disease such as this for which there is no known cure and about which there is so little known about its transmittal to others, to be out in public knowingly exposing himself to his co-workers and everyone else.

I'm sure it would be appreciated if this matter were investigated, as it would be in everyone's interest, including Garr's, if he were not flying.

Thank you,

[unsigned]

LAXSW F/A[42]

Because their initially tolerant policy toward Traynor and others was creating such concerns, United developed a new, two-pronged strategy that was strikingly self-contradictory. On May 23, 1983 the company distributed its first-ever safety bulletin on AIDS to assure workers they could not contract the disease through casual contact. Then, despite these assurances, they removed Gär Traynor and others from their jobs. Both of these tactics, of course, arose from the same motivation: to assuage workers' fears—and, by extension, passengers' fears—that they could become infected. But one strategy invoked medical facts about AIDS transmission to relieve fears, while the other, purging PWAs from the flight attendant corps, ignored the best medical evidence.

The memo itself exemplifies how society's skittishness toward AIDS hampered efforts to provide accurate information and thereby calm people's fears. Its limited distribution alone reflected this skittishness: United sent it only to the dozen safety coordinators at flight attendant bases, rather than to all employees. The seriousness of the topic was also hidden behind an innocuous title, "A Message from JFKMD," a reference to the airline's New York-based medical director, Dr. George Catlett.[43] In summarizing the disease for the safety coordinators, Catlett was circumspect, describing AIDS as "a mysterious disease which had been reported with increasing frequency among young Americans over the past few years." The closest he got to highlighting the various high-risk groups—beyond the broad allusion to "young Americans"—was his claim that "investigators [have noted] the pattern of occurrences of new cases of the disease among persons with similar life-styles." Explicit mention of homosexuality, not to mention IV drug use, was seemingly too impolitic.

Catlett's counsel to employees varied from vague to more direct. Among the least reassuring claims was "It does appear that for the disease to be transmitted from one person to another, physical contact between the two must occur." Such unspecific language would have only alarmed flight attendants, who worked in the cramped quarters of airplane galleys and aisles and therefore often had "physical contact" with one another and their customers. That said, the memo did later clarify that "sexual contact or mechanical injection of contaminated material into the body tissues" was required to transmit AIDS, and it ultimately asserted, "Risk of transmission of AIDS would seem to be limited to persons who are sexually promiscuous or who submit to improperly prepared drug injections." Somewhat more forceful, but still conjectural, were these claims: "There is *no* evidence that AIDS is spread through the air or by other forms of casual contact that commonly occur in the workplace (such as sitting in the same work area, shaking hands, sharing toilet facilities, etc.). AIDS, therefore, does *not* appear to be a risk to the general public or to those who serve the public in catering professions." By both emphasizing key words to reassure employees but simultaneously using conditional language ("AIDS does not *appear* to be a risk"), Catlett took a tortuous middle path, refusing to definitively quell workers' fears.

This tentative wording provided wiggle room to implement the second prong of United's new AIDS strategy: grounding flight attendants suspected of having AIDS. On the morning of June 28, 1983, Gär's supervisor informed him that he had been placed on a permanent medical leave of absence. No doctors examined him that day, confirming that this was a policy decision, not one based on his actual ability to work. A month after his grounding, Gär received a letter from Dr. C. R. Harper, United's vice president of medical services, explaining the airline's actions. While at first expressing concern for Gär's own health if he continued to work, Harper soon turned to contagion concerns, contradicting Dr. Catlett's message from just two months before. Harper noted, "Although the indications are that the disease is transmitted by intimate physical contact and/or accidental inoculation with blood products, the exact method of transmission is in fact not only controversial but at this point in time conjectural." He then continued to dismantle his colleague's assurances about the lack of contagion risk on planes: "Since the bulk of the duties as a Flight Attendant involve food and beverage handling, it was felt that in the interest of United's flying public that you not perform those duties."[44]

Gär was not the only United flight attendant affected by this new policy. A New York-based flight attendant, Russ Manker, also was grounded, even though he hadn't been diagnosed with AIDS. Instead, Manker was suffering from symptoms that United's doctors presumed were AIDS related: immune deficiency, visibly swollen lymph nodes, and numerous opportunistic infections. At United's encouragement, Manker visited an AIDS specialist in July 1983 to obtain a more definitive diagnosis. After a battery of lab work and other examinations, the specialist concurred with Manker's physician that he "does not, at the moment, fit the case definition for even a prodrome of the AID syndrome. . . . In the present context, I could see no clear justification for denying Mr. Manker his job."[45] Armed with this opinion, Manker arrived at United's Chicago headquarters to be certified for active duty. However, after just a half-day of training, company doctors sent him home. Thus, in a situation arguably even more egregious than Traynor's, United forced Manker onto medical leave because of suspicion that he had AIDS.

Arbitration files from the flight attendants union show that over the following months United grounded at least two other PWAs who were healthy enough to work. In their treatment of Chicago-based flight attendant Bruce Hall, United's medical staff were far more blunt about their reasoning. When Hall reported for work after being diagnosed with AIDS in January 1984, United's physician allegedly told him to "go home, stay home, and don't come back. . . . We don't have people like you working for us."[46] A company doctor examining Hall in July 1984 found he was still healthy enough to work. Nonetheless, the doctor concluded the exam by giving the verdict "PLAN—No flying," with the stated reasoning of "communicability and hyst. concerns."[47] Presumably, the abbreviation "hyst." referenced passengers' and fellow employees' AIDS hysteria.

Not all airlines followed United's example of grounding flight attendants with AIDS. Air Canada offered a more compassionate model, allowing Gaëtan Dugas to remain on active duty as long as his health permitted. He flew as late as January 1984, even with noticeable KS lesions on his arms and face. One of Gaëtan's friends recalled to Randy Shilts how much Gaëtan had valued his work while sick. Then living in Vancouver, he was fighting hard to stave off depression, chronic weakness, and various infections. Gaëtan's friend would sleep over some nights just to accompany him through the fearful night sweats, the chills, the restlessness, and the looming prospect of his death. When Gaëtan managed to get up for work—just months before he finally succumbed to kidney failure—it gave him a "feeling of joy to put on his Navy blue uniform."[48] He came back in the evenings worn out, even from the short day trips to Calgary and Edmonton. But the job did wonders for his mental state, allowing him to retain his sense of pride, of being "strong and in control," despite his grim prognosis.[49]

In the United States, however, at least one other major airline—and possibly more—followed United's example of grounding flight attendants with AIDS.[50] Patt Gibbs, former president of the APFA, the labor union representing American Airlines' flight attendants, confirmed that American undertook such measures in the early 1980s. By Gibbs's account, American's company physician at the time was a former military doctor who had little tolerance for gay men or PWAs and therefore provoked "tons of grievance cases." The first of these cases involved a flight attendant who was fired—not just placed on medical leave, as at United—because of his AIDS diagnosis.[51] Another American flight attendant who later worked on HIV/AIDS issues recalls that the airline's response to AIDS in the earliest years "wasn't pretty." "There were people who were fired, there were people that were harassed, there were people that lost their insurance," he explained.[52] Sadly, Gär Traynor's case was far from an isolated example.

FIGHTING BACK AGAINST AIDS HYSTERIA

Gär Traynor and United's other grounded flight attendants chose to fight their employer in both labor arbitration proceedings and the courts. They thereby invited considerable public scrutiny at a time when many in society dismissed gay men with AIDS as sexually depraved and deserving of their illness. Gär became especially important in these struggles, as he eventually won his case against United in the arbitration process. (Both Manker and Hall eventually reached private settlements outside the labor arbitration mechanism, which explains why I emphasize Traynor's plight from here on out.) His victory established an important precedent for other PWAs. Because the case was a labor union grievance, the decision was not technically admissible in future state and federal court cases. Nonetheless, his victory before an independent arbiter was a sort of dry run for these future cases, complete with expert testimony and a full cadre of lawyers. At the time, the ruling required that United treat its flight attendants with AIDS the same as those with other life-threatening illnesses, like cancer or epilepsy. In the future, this same decision would carry over to other PWAs in other industries, ending their effective banishment from workplaces and the premature loss of their financial independence.

For the flight attendant unions, the choice to devote their limited financial and legal resources to these cases was not easy. The APFA at American Airlines actually struggled quite a bit with this decision. "I took major grief from the APFA board of directors for pursuing our first case," noted former president Patt Gibbs.[53] Their reluctance stemmed not so much from homophobia or AIDS phobia as from financial considerations. The economy at the time was weak, and deregulation was affecting flight attendants' livelihoods for the first time. Massive furloughs had taken place as the airline readjusted its business model. Up to 50 percent of the workforce was affected by the downturn, according to Gibbs. The newly formed APFA was also impoverished compared to other unions and could ill afford pursuing grievances that affected just a handful of flight attendants.

For the union representing United's flight attendants, however, there was apparently no such hesitation. Patricia Friend, now retired from her position as international president of the Association of Flight Attendants (AFA), was in charge of grievances against United during the early AIDS crisis. She claimed that Traynor and the other grounded PWAs received the union's full attention: "There was never any question in our mind what we were going to do, because this was discrimination. And we have fought through our careers and through our history every kind of discrimination that you can think of. . . . It just wasn't open for discussion." Friend added that she and the union's legal staff devoted numerous hours learning about AIDS to defend these men. "I used to tell people, I know more about HIV/AIDS than I ever wanted to know," she noted, "because we had to do that research to defend their right to work."[54]

Despite the union's vigilance, Gär's case encountered numerous delays. A full year had gone by, without a paycheck and with significant medical-related stress, before he chose to open up a new front against the airline. Having moved in late 1984 to San Francisco with his partner, Gär quickly connected with San Francisco's nascent AIDS activist community, especially the newly formed group People With AIDS-San Francisco. PWA-SF was eager to promote his case. John Lorenzini, the group's director, correctly believed it could serve as an important precedent for workers in other industries as well: "People with AIDS are being forced to lie about their health in order to retain [work] positions. It is important to begin now to stem this trend by making United accountable."[55] Thus, when United rebuffed PWA-SF's demands to reinstate Traynor and the other flight attendants with AIDS, the group opted for more dramatic action: a citywide boycott of the airline.

PWA-SF was able to persuade key gay activists to support the campaign. Both the Harvey Milk and Alice B. Toklas Gay Democratic Clubs signed on, and they began pressuring the city's board of supervisors to endorse the boycott as well. For his part, Gär took on a previously unexplored role, as a media personality at the center of the action. He and his partner were on the front page of San Francisco's gay *Bay Area Reporter*, with more articles to come in the *Los Angeles Times* and *Miami Herald*. That said, the boycott overall had only a modest impact. The mainstream media in San Francisco, including the *San Francisco Chronicle*, where Randy Shilts covered the AIDS beat, ignored the story. (Shilts also omitted covering the boycott and Gär's groundbreaking case from *And the Band Played On* a few years later.) Ultimately, however, the action against United was short-lived for a positive reason: the arbitrator in Gär's case announced his long-awaited ruling just a month after the boycott began—and a full eighteen months after Gär lost his job.

A HISTORIC VICTORY

Both United and the AFA knew that Gär's case would hinge on medical evidence about AIDS. Led by neutral arbitrator Martin Wagner, the System Board of Adjustment (the five-member judicial panel that decides labor arbitration cases) was forced to take sides on a very contentious medical and social debate, ultimately choosing between the overwhelming majority of medical experts, who held that AIDS could be transmitted only by blood or semen, and theorists' opinions about more, as yet unproven, avenues of transmission. As the board heard the case throughout 1984, the facts on AIDS were still coming in. Researchers had not even announced their discovery of HIV until mid-1984, halfway through deliberations. Only after this discovery did controversies over transmission patterns finally become settled—at least among medical experts, if not the general public.

To bolster their arguments, both the airline and the union hired top medical professionals as witnesses. United retained Dr. Kevin Cahill of the New York City Board of Health, who had published a cautionary book on AIDS transmission called *The AIDS Epidemic*.[56] The airline particularly highlighted the book's opinion that more avenues of AIDS transmission might still be discovered. Cahill's book at one point offers the opinion, "It would seem prudent to ask that AIDS patients not engage in food preparation or handling for others."[57] In his testimony, Cahill also stressed lingering uncertainty about AIDS contagion, focusing on "what is unknown about the disease and a need to be concerned about the great anxiety about exposure."[58] His testimony, United hoped, would sufficiently justify its decision to ground Gär, especially with a more limited threshold of proof that it outlined for the arbitrators: "The test of the propriety of the action [to ground Traynor] is not whether the medical judgment upon which it was based was clearly correct but whether there was a reasonable medical basis for making it."[59]

For its part, the union stressed the CDC's increasingly assertive claims that AIDS could be transmitted only by direct blood or semen contact with another's bloodstream. They also provided evidence from the health care field, where no doctor or nurse had contracted the disease, a fact that the union correctly attributed to the careful management of patients' bodily fluids in medical settings. Furthermore, the union hired two experts on AIDS from the Chicago area, doctors John Philip Phair and David Ostrow of Northwestern University Medical School. Ostrow was also chair of the Chicago Area AIDS Task Force. Both testified on the known paths of AIDS transmission and the complete lack of evidence for contagion via casual contact.

In his decision, Wagner, the neutral arbitrator, opted for a pragmatic way to navigate this uncertainty regarding AIDS transmission: he followed the AFA's request to examine how the health care professions were handling employees with AIDS. Both the American Hospital Association and a task force at University of California-San Francisco Medical Center (UCSF) had composed guidelines on how to treat nurses and doctors with AIDS, which the AFA had submitted as evidence. Both studies detailed circumstances in which doctors and nurses with AIDS could continue to work. The reports called for treating asymptomatic employees "on an individual basis."[60] As the UCSF report elaborated, physicians "would have to determine that the employee was both free from transmissible infection and not at risk for contracting an infectious disease in the course of performing his or her patient-care duties."[61] Wagner used these examples from the health care industry to conclude the following about flight attendants: "It is the Chairman's opinion that the foregoing observations and conclusions . . . refute a conclusion that an employee afflicted with AIDS should be removed from an attendant position on a *per se basis* [emphasis supplied] and that, if such a conclusion is appropriate in the attendant-patient relationship in a hospital setting, it is equally valid in the flight attendant relationship to the flying public."[62]

Supporting this pragmatic conclusion were two important findings Wagner made about the nature of AIDS. First, like those who drafted the medical guidelines, he was definitively discounting the claim that people with AIDS were always a contagion risk. And second, he was demanding that United's managers trust physicians to determine when an employee was no longer healthy enough to work.

Once Wagner had reached these vital conclusions, he examined how United had grounded Gär, looking for moments when they had sought out and followed physicians' input about his condition. What he discovered significantly weakened United's case. After all, none of their physicians had ever examined Gär, and Wagner had ample evidence from Gär's own doctors that he was, and always had been, healthy enough to work. Dr. Ostrow also recalled for me that United's failure to examine Gär was a highly unusual breach of its contractual obligations: "For any other disease you ha[d] to have a doctor's exam—by a company doctor—to show whether or not you were flight-worthy." Thus "the problem was . . . that the medical director refused to examine [Traynor]. . . . It was very clearly a homophobic, AIDS-phobic thing on their part," Ostrow concluded.[63] Patricia Friend of the AFA recalled United's motives in this way: "The company attorney that we dealt with on the arbitration . . . was not convinced about the medical science. . . . His response to the medical evidence was, 'Well, what if they're wrong? Then what happens?' " For Friend, this attitude disguised a deeper alarm at United that bordered on panic, "They were convinced that, if the people who were buying tickets knew that there were flight attendants working on the airplane who were HIV positive, that they would stay away in droves. . . . So it was all about their image, and [that it] would drive away traffic."[64]

A decisive moment in the hearings came in the cross-examination of United's medical witness, Dr. Cahill. As he was speaking, Dr. Ostrow motioned to the union's lawyer, Marilyn Pearson, that he needed her attention: "I turned to Marilyn and I said, 'Make sure to ask him in cross-examination whether or not you can determine somebody's health status or ability to work from the diagnosis alone.'" Accordingly, the subsequent cross-examination was quite brief: "I don't think it was Marilyn, I think it was a second lawyer . . . and he said, 'I just have one question for you. In your experience, if you have not seen a patient but they have the diagnosis of AIDS, can you from that determine whether they are suitable for work?' He said, 'Of course not.' And all the lawyers on the United side started, you know, twittering. You could see them with horrible anguished looks on their faces. They knew they had lost the case right then and there."[65]

Wagner's written judgment confirms the importance of this scene. He cited Cahill's testimony that a person with AIDS should not be working as a flight attendant but then added that Cahill "also underscored the need for clinical and laboratory data in a case involving an individual's work assignment." A quote from Ostrow's testimony follows, establishing how best to acquire such data: "I think that the most appropriate way to make the determination would be an actual face-to-face physical examination and examination of the laboratory reports."[66] Because United had never taken these steps, Wagner decided the case in Gär's favor, finding that the airline had violated its own collective bargaining contract as well as reasonable procedures in treating PWAs.

Thus, at the end of 1984, Gär Traynor and the AFA had struck a seemingly decisive blow against United's policy of excluding flight attendants with AIDS from active duty. Gär had been awarded a full year and a half of back pay and had won his job back, though he was so embittered with United that he opted not to return. Meanwhile, the AFA now had a precedent that could be cited in its other AIDS-related grievances. Beyond United, other unionized airlines were put on notice that actions to ground PWAs were now illegal. More broadly, possibly for the first time in U.S. jurisprudence, a person with AIDS regained his right to work. Arbitrator Wagner's decision imposing limits on AIDS phobia, especially the excessive fears of AIDS contagion by casual contact, gradually found resonance in other legal venues and eventually became the accepted law of the land.

UNITED'S AIDS-PHOBIC RETRENCHMENT

For a victory that seemed to be unambiguously positive, it is perhaps surprising that Gär's successful arbitration failed to change United's policy of removing flight attendants with HIV/AIDS from active duty. Instead, the airline found a new, albeit more costly solution than placing them on permanent medical leave, since Gär's victory now clearly forbade such a practice. Thus a later case rather than Gär's came to serve as the operative precedent at United.

United learned of Robert Butler's AIDS diagnosis in 1985, almost a year after Gär's case was settled. When Butler was declared healthy enough to continue working as a flight attendant in October 1985, the airline treated him just like the other men before him, refusing to clear him without even examining him. The lone explanation United provided was elusive, avoiding any mention of the contagion fears that arbitrator Wagner had discounted. Instead, a letter to Butler from a United doctor cryptically stated: "The diagnosis of a medical condition has been made by your physicians which is pertinent to your work as a flight attendant." Then, in a particularly demoralizing conclusion, he added, "Because of this, it is necessary for me to remove you from work status and place you on illness leave until your medical condition is resolved."[67] Of course, both United and Butler himself knew how his "medical condition" would be "resolved": his health would further deteriorate until he died. The airline thereby signaled its intention to place Butler on permanent medical leave.

Butler and the AFA quickly filed a grievance. In this case, however, United and the AFA also negotiated a settlement soon thereafter. The agreement absolved United from publicly owning up to its discrimination, as the airline secured a promise from Butler and the union not to publicize the settlement. In exchange, Butler received an even more generous settlement than Gär: he would be paid as though he were still working full time. He received a salary for eighty-five flight hours each month (including his pension, vacation, and sick leave) and even got to bid on promotions and international routes that commanded more money. This agreement—paying Butler to stay off the job and out of the headlines—would last as long as his doctors deemed him healthy enough to work.

As former AFA international president Patricia Friend confirmed, the Butler settlement was open to any flight attendant with AIDS that challenged United's attempt to ground him. Thus, even in 1986, when the facts about HIV transmission had become well established, the company was still holding onto groundless fears that it could be transmitted via casual contact. It was also willing to pay men like Butler to keep them off the job. When I asked Friend how many people were covered by the Butler settlement, she replied, "I'm guessing hundreds. Really, that's how determined the management of United was that these people would not be working on their airplanes." She went on to speculate why the airline might have been so willing to make such a costly settlement: "I hate to put words in their mouth, but my guess is that . . . they didn't think it would go on that long because they would die."[68] It was not until mid-1988 that the airline finally revised its approach to people with HIV/AIDS, a topic covered in the next chapter.

COMMITMENT TO ACTIVISM

Even Gär Traynor saw that his legal victory represented only a modest triumph over the widespread AIDS phobia that predominated at the time. While executives in middle-class career paths might now think twice about removing PWAs from work—or might pay them to stay home, as United had done—various stigmas were still very much entrenched. Health officials, politicians, and others who should have aggressively combated AIDS were instead painfully slow to act. Politicians in Washington failed to fund AIDS research adequately and to expand the health care system into impoverished communities. Meanwhile, officials at all levels of government were loath to break social taboos and educate IV drug users and men having sex with men about ways to avoid AIDS. When AIDS intersected with issues of poverty, race, drug use, prisoners' rights, and homosexual behavior, the response was typically to resist taking necessary action. Thus the fight for true equality in the face of AIDS would require a more radical response than simply holding certain employers accountable for their egregious actions.

Flight attendants were not the ideal candidates to bring these issues to the fore. Their relatively entitled social position shielded them from the ways AIDS exploited poverty, racism, and drug use to become an even more potent killer. That said, Gär himself, as his disease progressed, displayed a growing commitment to AIDS activism, as did several of the flight attendants I interviewed. By the early 1990s, flight attendants at various airlines founded charities and conducted fund-raisers to help their coworkers living with AIDS. Others contributed hours outside work to groups who provided home care to shut-ins, or to activist groups like the NAMES Project, creators of the AIDS Quilt. Numerous others provided countless hours of support to their own friends (often fellow flight attendants) who were sick. Gär was perhaps unusual in the degree and political focus of his involvement in AIDS work, but he was far from alone: many other flight attendants devoted significant time and energy to fight AIDS.

In June 1983, the very month he was forced onto medical leave at United, Gär participated in the first-ever national meeting of PWA activists. At this relatively early stage in the crisis, a variety of AIDS activist groups had already formed around the country, with the largest being the Gay Men's Health Crisis in

New York and the San Francisco AIDS & KS Foundation. But men like Gär perceived these organizations to be inadequate, as they often were a coalition of doctors and gay community leaders whose knowledge of AIDS was secondhand. Increasingly, people living with AIDS in New York and San Francisco fought to be treated as experts alongside these more official voices. Thus the meeting of PWAs in Denver in June 1983 is considered a historic moment of self-empowerment, when patients themselves wrested a certain amount of authority from the established experts. Gär was the lone member from Los Angeles, sitting alongside about fifteen men, primarily from New York and San Francisco.

The Denver Conference introduced Gär to men committed to radical political action. His peers had been weaned on feminism and gay liberation. According to Richard Berkowitz of New York, the lone surviving member of Denver's PWA activists: "[Some of us were] very radical, and I too was very altered by the feminist movement: that you make your own way in the world, and you question everything, and you do things on your own. You don't wait for the government, you don't wait for other people to do things that you need to get done. You organize, you protest, you come up with ideas to supersede governmental inaction. ... That mind-set was the perfect thing for Denver."[69]

In accordance with this principle of self-reliance, the PWAs from New York, including Berkowitz and Michael Callen, had already organized support groups, written the first-ever safe-sex manual, and started to fight the intransigence of doctors and hospitals worried about treating PWAs.[70] Meanwhile, in San Francisco PWA activism dated back to early 1982, when Bobbi Campbell—one of the city's first men to be diagnosed—started an AIDS advice column in the San Francisco *Sentinel*. He and Dan Turner became "star cases," participating in media events and public rallies, conducting information sessions for doctors and nurses about their experiences, and joining boards of organizations devoted to AIDS advocacy.[71] Thus in Denver the men with AIDS who were most engaged with the medical and activist worlds sat at the same table for the first time. As Berkowitz recalled, "Suddenly, when the West Coast and the East Coast came together in Denver, it was like, WOW! It was synergistic."[72]

As their culminating act, the men composed a set of guidelines to enshrine PWAs' dignity, the so-called Denver Principles, and then stormed the main hall of the larger medical conference on AIDS, filled with doctors and nurses, to present their work. The core issue of this intervention was empowerment. Participants called on those with AIDS and their caregivers to resist labels that implied helplessness, such as *victims* or *patients*, and instead to use the term *people with AIDS*.[73] A subsection of the document entitled "Recommendations for Health Care Professionals" called on physicians to move past their stance of neutrality and make an effort to reduce the stigmas of homophobia and AIDS. Another subsection, entitled "Recommendations for All People," asked for support not only in securing basic civil rights but in fighting homophobia and AIDS phobia; it included a call to "not scapegoat people with AIDS, blame us for the epidemic or generalize about our lifestyles." Though the principles reflected their drafters' status as more privileged gay white men with status to health care, the subsection articulating certain "Rights of People with AIDS" expressed a more far-reaching awareness of the role of poverty and racism in keeping people with AIDS from getting adequate care and support. It claimed a right for everyone "to receive quality medical treatment and quality social service provision without discrimination of any form, including sexual orientation, gender, diagnosis, economic status or race." Tied to these concrete rights were more abstract ones, including the right to lead "as full and satisfying sexual and emotional lives as anyone else" and, most fundamentally, the right "to die—and to LIVE—in dignity." Over time, these principles have proven to be inclusive as a paradigm for AIDS advocacy, even as the population with AIDS has become more heterosexual, poorer, and more racially disadvantaged. The National Association of People With AIDS (NAPWA) continues to use the Denver Principles as its mission statement, even as it advocates for a fuller range of issues than did the first generation of gay men.

Despite his presence in Denver, Gär Traynor was not central to framing the Denver Principles. Richard Berkowitz recalls that the more politically savvy members, especially Michael Callen of New York and Bobbi Campbell of San Francisco, "did most of the work." As for the others, "Everyone else contributed little things, and talked about sex and went out and had cigarettes." While somewhat dismissive, Berkowitz's response also illustrated the holistic way these men were fighting the stigma of AIDS. The Denver experience harmoniously combined political activism and friendship building in ways that energized participants. After all, the AIDS crisis was more than a political problem, it was also a deeply felt psychosocial challenge. The companionship built in Denver offered a way forward:

We all came back from [the conference] changed. Before the conference, I mean, first of all you've been handed a death sentence. . . . It was hard not to feel kind of suffocated by the panic . . . to have a new disease, to be really sick, to have [everyone] saying that you're going to be dead in two years. . . . Try to be a functioning person with all that going on! So to meet each other, to see how vibrant and engaged, you know, it was really a wakeup call that you didn't have to lay down and die.[74]

While Berkowitz remembers Gär participating at the dinners and bonding with the group socially, he says Gär's political role was far more limited. "I wouldn't say that he was a forceful personality, or maybe he was either new to politics or was reluctant to get involved," he recalled. "I remember him being like a secondary person there. . . . But, you know, politics had not been everyone's background."[75]

That said, for men like Bobbi Campbell, Gär and the others became an important support system. Campbell appeared on the cover of *Newsweek* on August 8, 1983, and thereby became the most visible PWA in the country, making him an even more effective advocate with Reagan administration officials, health care experts, and PWAs seeking to organize.[76] Yet this prominence hardly spared him from the isolation brought by AIDS. He wrote in his diary in January 1984—about six months before his death: "I slept in, as usual, and woke up feeling tired, as usual. An hour reading the paper, with the kitty sitting by me on the bed, a shower, watering the plants, throwing out the trash. I've begun, slowly, to come to grips with my depression."[77]

In the same entry, however, Campbell found a sort of antidote for his condition. His tone changed considerably when he wrote of his upcoming trip to Atlanta, where he would be reunited with Gär and New Yorkers Artie Felsen and Tom Nasrallah, whom he had befriended in Denver. The men would be presenting at the CDC and also laying the groundwork for the launch of NAPWA. As Bobbi wrote, their companionship was just as vital as the work they would be doing: "I'm starting to get excited about my impending trip to Atlanta. . . . Connecting again with Artie and Tom and Gär is juicing me up again." Clearly, these men now played a dual role for each other: as partners in activism and as friends fortifying one another against the anxieties and uncertainties brought on by AIDS.

Gär's commitment to AIDS activism only intensified after his banishment from United's flight attendant corps. After Denver, he was invited to join the Los Angeles City-County AIDS Task Force, a blue-ribbon committee that advised both Mayor Tom Bradley and the county's board of supervisors on AIDS policies. On the twenty-four-member committee, Gär's credentials stood out for their modesty. He was one of only two members without an advanced degree or a prominent institutional affiliation. Yet in the spirit of the Denver Conference just his status as a PWA gave him a valued perspective. Gär continued to participate on the task force even after he moved to San Francisco in late 1984, where he also joined PWA-SF and helped organize the short-lived boycott of United. In fact, his final letter to his lawyer at the AFA, dated April 2, 1985, reveals someone who was still ambitious about contributing to AIDS activism: "I'm keeping very busy. I'm leaving for Atlanta and the International AIDS conference next week. I have three more conferences this summer in San Francisco, Washington, DC, and New York. I'm looking into going to Paris for treatment. We're finally formalizing the National Association of People With AIDS—a national resources and education system . . . so, as you can see, I'm not without something to do."[78]

LOSING GAËTAN AND GÄR

For someone who gave so much to AIDS activism, it is a bit surprising that Gär Traynor has been forgotten. The legacy of the Denver Conference lives on, but Gär has been overshadowed by bigger contributors like Bobbi Campbell and Michael Callen. His work with the AIDS Task Force in Los Angeles has also gone largely unnoticed, mainly because the group languished in the stalemate between progressives and conservatives that dominated local politics there. Even his precedent-setting legal victory against United, while garnering modest media attention at the time, was swept under the rug shortly thereafter, thanks to United's persistence in grounding flight attendants with HIV/AIDS and the secret Butler settlement.

Personally, Gär Traynor also seems to have disappeared from historical memory. AIDS activists I spoke with in the San Francisco area don't remember him, nor do people working with AIDS groups in Los Angeles. Surely, part of this failure to remember reflects something about Gär's personality (a quietness, perhaps), as well as his decision to pull up stakes from L.A. and resettle in San Francisco. In celebrating his victory over United in a January 1985 front-page story, San Francisco's gay *Bay Area Reporter* noted that "Traynor leads a relatively quiet life in San Francisco. He commented, 'My lover is wonderful and has been very supportive. . . . We have lots of friends and a good support system.' "[79] The article neglects to mention Traynor's continuing role on the L.A. AIDS Task Force and his contributions to PWA-SF.

Most of all, however, Gär has been forgotten mainly because of the tragedy of AIDS itself. Having surrounded himself with friends living with AIDS—men like Bobbi Campbell and John Lorenzini in San Francisco—memories of Gär were lost when these men also passed away. In fact, the closest person in his life, his partner Bob Morana, died just a few weeks before him, also from AIDS. Bob passed away on February 24, 1987, while Gär held on until March 13. Gär's lone claim to immortality is his patch on the AIDS Quilt. Activist Gert McMullin, who has volunteered with the quilt since its beginnings in 1987 at a small storefront in San Francisco's Castro neighborhood, recalled for me the day Gär's patch was made. A man named

FIGURE 13.
Gär Traynor's patch on the AIDS Quilt. Courtesy of the
NAMES Project Foundation.

Brad came in crying. All he could say was "You have to help me. All my friends are
dead."[80] Brad handed over a list of forty names.

The volunteers asked Brad for guidance on how to design each of the patches and
went to work. Besides his name in autograph style, Gär's patch is decorated with
specks of paint: red mostly, but also blue and green (figure 13). The dark background
is a gray mesh screen fabric, while the "T" in his last name is canvas. Gert and the
other volunteers made panels for all forty of Brad's friends that day. But there was
no time to ask about the history or stories of each man, no way for the volunteers
to know that Gär especially had helped breathe life into the sorts of AIDS activism
they were now practicing. The patch they made for Gär, colorful but modest, is all

that is left of his legacy. It was among the first hundred ever displayed. There are now over forty-five thousand alongside it.

Three years before Gär passed away, Gaëtan Dugas finally succumbed to his repeated illnesses. The last straw was kidney failure, and he died in Quebec City on March 30, 1984, at the age of thirty-one. Gaëtan was surrounded by his family, though none of his friends—strewn around the continent, thanks to his jet-setting career and natural wanderlust—were present. Yet his friends were not inclined to forget him. A continent away in Vancouver, Bob Tivey, the first executive director of AIDS Vancouver, planned to memorialize Gaëtan and two of the city's other first casualties of the AIDS crisis. Tivey received permission from the city to plant three cherry trees on the waterfront near the city's Stanley Park.

Thus, on a fall morning in 1985, friends of Gaëtan and the two other men assembled to plant the trees and honor their dead friends.[81] The ceremony was small and somewhat brief, thanks in part to the cold, pelting rain. When the trees were planted, the small crowd dispersed, leaving the trees to fend for themselves in Vancouver's chilly winter as storm clouds burgeoned on the horizon. No plaque was made, nothing written on or carved into the trees. Gaëtan and the others were meant to be memorialized modestly. Their stories would remain only as long as the people who loved them. Then, just like Gär's, Gaëtan's memory would fade away, with little but the beauty of cherry blossoms in the springtime to recall his presence. None of Gaëtan's friends foresaw on that late fall morning in 1985 that he would soon become the world's most horrific AIDS villain.

CHAPTER SEVEN

· The Traynor Legacy versus
the "Patient Zero" Myth

Three and a half years after his death, Gaëtan Dugas figuratively rose from the dead. Thanks to author Randy Shilts, he posthumously became the most fantastical myth of the AIDS crisis, the alleged missing link between an African disease and the American heartland, whose hedonistic sexual cravings spread the disease across the continent. Yet the AIDS crisis that Gaëtan's second persona—Patient Zero—returned to in 1987 was radically different than the one he had left. Actor Rock Hudson's revelation that he had AIDS, and his death soon after, on October 2, 1985, stunned the U.S. public and finally focused the media on the crisis that had been snowballing since June 1981. Shilts, in *And the Band Played On*, aptly called Hudson's news "a demarcation that would separate the history of America before AIDS from the history that came after." Although twelve thousand Americans had already died, Hudson, "riveted America's attention upon this deadly new threat for the first time."[1] The CDC cluster study that first mentioned "Patient 0" in 1984 and Gär Traynor's victory against United that same year both barely registered in the press compared to the attention now devoted to AIDS. Finally, in late 1985, a national discourse had begun.

At first glance, vilifying Gaëtan in *And the Band Played On* seems anachronistic, belonging more to the hysteria of summer 1983 than to fall 1987. After all, in the intervening years, scientists not only discovered more about HIV's spread around the globe but had also definitively dismissed the possibility of contagion through casual contact. Moreover, PWAs had won modest but important victories to retain their civil rights. In 1986 the famous boy with AIDS, Ryan White, in legal proceedings that echoed Gär Traynor's, was allowed to return to school. Meanwhile, courts across the country—including the U.S. Supreme Court in the 1987 decision *School Board of Nassau County v. Arline*—were moving to protect PWAs from being fired because of their illness.[2] With the country gradually overcoming its initial AIDS hysteria, why did Shilts's account of Patient Zero garner so much attention and elicit such panic at such a late date?

The answer has something to do with the increased public attention devoted to AIDS after Rock Hudson. To some extent, Americans were having the same debates in 1987 as in 1983, since many had failed to educate themselves about the disease earlier on. Thus plenty of people still saw PWAs, gay men, and gender anomalies like male flight attendants as contagion threats. But more fundamentally, Gaëtan's resurrection as Patient Zero also laid bare America's lingering animosity toward homosexuality that was at the heart of AIDS hysteria. Shilts's account of Patient Zero reinforced for the public that men who engaged in anal sex and cavorted in bathhouses not only were immoral but also invited plague-like diseases on themselves and the rest of society. Indeed, the will to make the Patient Zero myth about the origins of America's AIDS crisis the truth—despite enormous evidence to the contrary—demonstrated society's deep unease with gays' post-Stonewall sexual freedoms.

The release of Shilts's damning narrative on Patient Zero coincided with a new outbreak in America's culture war over AIDS. Even though PWAs by then had won key civil rights protections, conservatives still aspired to eliminate them from the public sphere. Having surrendered the hope that authorities would require HIV-free schools and workplaces, they instead imposed de facto AIDS quarantines in novel ways, including federal government action aimed at some of society's most surveilled groups: immigrants and prisoners. Thanks to the work of Republican senator Jesse Helms, Congress passed a law in 1987 forbidding immigrants with HIV from seeking citizenship in the United States. Several states also passed new laws to jail those with HIV who spread the disease sexually, while others for the first time explicitly authorized medical quarantines for PWAs who persisted in sexual activity. Finally, just weeks after *And the Band Played On*'s release, Helms and Congressman William Dannemayer, also a conservative Republican, sponsored a new law that cut off federal funding to AIDS groups whose materials promoted homosexuality or male-male sex. The law's passage marked the first time that AIDS policy had been used as a punitive tool against homosexuality itself.

Shilts's salacious story of Patient Zero was ideal propaganda for conservatives because it played into the tenets of their latest campaign to isolate PWAs and gays. As an immigrant with AIDS, Gaëtan stood in for others like him who should be kept out of the country. Meanwhile, as both a gay man with an unchecked libido and an AIDS carrier who recklessly infected others, he embodied those who deserved to be locked up for their sociopathic behavior. Randy Shilts had introduced a poignant new flight attendant scapegoat—one far more menacing than William Simpson of the 1950s or the feared "he-stewardess" of the late 1960s—at a volatile political moment.

The airlines and flight attendants were, admittedly, secondary players in these battles over AIDS, gays, and sex. Gaëtan's status as a scapegoated flight attendant embroiled them in these conflicts, but only as passive instruments of agents like Shilts, conservative politicians, and AIDS activists. However, in terms of the struggle for civil rights, the airlines played a very active and important role, as they effectively switched allegiances in the culture war after Patient Zero. Like other companies, they began to invite PWAs back into the public sphere, no longer ostracizing them as employees who might spread the disease or passengers too panic-inducing to fly. Within months of *And the Band Played On*'s release, United undid the secretive Butler decision and allowed its flight attendants with AIDS to return to work. The airline backtracked, finally accepting the ruling made in Gär Traynor's case a full four years earlier.

In 1993, American Airlines took such tolerance a step further, pivoting from its previous phobic behavior to publicly identify itself as the United States' first "gay-friendly" airline.[3] American improved its treatment of HIV-positive employees and passengers, began to offer LGBT employees new workplace benefits, and openly marketed to gay customers for the very first time. As other airlines quickly followed suit, male flight attendants went from being embarrassing gender deviates to valued corporate ambassadors who could reach out to suddenly desirable gay and lesbian consumers. Thus the industry helped lead the way in a larger corporate movement that welcomed gays and lesbians into the social mainstream, thereby repudiating much of the scapegoating directed at them during the AIDS crisis. This incremental move toward a corporate-inspired queer equality fell far short of the radical politics practiced by activist groups like ACT UP. After all, the airlines weren't in the business of echoing ACT UP's defense of gays' post-Stonewall sexual freedoms. On the whole, however, they did help move society beyond the shame-inducing narrative of Patient Zero and toward the more inclusive legacy set by PWAs like Gär Traynor.

SHILTS'S CONSTRUCTION OF "PATIENT ZERO"

As the beat reporter on AIDS since 1982 for San Francisco's largest newspaper, the *San Francisco Chronicle*, Randy Shilts was one of the most established journalists in the country on the crisis. As Dr. Mervyn Silverman, San Francisco's public health director in the early 1980s, notes, "Randy's writings [on AIDS] were more extensive than the *New York Times*, the *Washington Post*, and the *Los Angeles Times* put together."[4] His job provided him access to virtually every doctor, politician, and activist in the country working on AIDS and also gave him the financial support needed to generate his authoritative account of the early AIDS crisis, *And the Band Played On.*

Shilts's position at the *Chronicle* meant he had very early knowledge of Gaëtan's putative role in the crisis. First, Shilts knew in 1982 that a certain non-American was essential to the CDC's cluster study linking AIDS transmission with sexual activity. In addition, he knew of long-standing gossip that a blond French Canadian flight attendant was creating havoc at bathhouses in San Francisco and elsewhere because he continued to have sex despite having KS and AIDS. As Shilts shared with *Rolling Stone*, "I had known there was a guy [with AIDS] knowingly having sex in the bathhouses, and I did a *Chronicle* story on that in November of '82, and I also knew that there was this study that had linked a lot of the early cases, but I didn't know that the person in that study was also the person who was having sex in the bathhouses. And it was only through people dropping comments that I was able to piece that all together."[5]

Of course, some of the "pieces" Shilts put together to turn Gaëtan into Patient Zero were more accurate than others. The scientific evidence for the claim that Gaëtan was America's first AIDS victim simply did not exist, so Shilts instead resorted to artful writing and outright misrepresentations of the CDC cluster study to bolster this notion. Meanwhile, there was far more evidence about Gaëtan's prolific sex life and his refusal to change his behavior after his diagnosis. Shilts heard about Gaëtan's sexual practices from Dr. William Darrow at the CDC and about his persistence in having sex from Selma Dritz, a public health official in San Francisco. While not interviewed by Shilts, Dr. Alvin Friedman-Kien, Gaëtan's physician at NYU Hospital, later registered his own dismay at Gaëtan's choices: "While [Gaëtan] was in New York, he would go to gay bathhouses and have unprotected sex with a variety of people despite the fact that we warned him against it. I once caught him coming out of a gay bathhouse, and I stopped the car and said, 'What are you doing there?' And he said, 'In the dark nobody sees my spots.' He was a real sociopath. . . . I stopped seeing him. I refused to see him, I was just so angry."[6]

But the most sensational part of the Patient Zero story was the one Shilts could not prove, though he continually tried in his research to establish Gaëtan as the missing link who had brought AIDS to America. One of his primary resources on Gaëtan's sex life was Dr. Darrow from the CDC, who had conducted a series of interviews with Gaëtan about his sex life and had even received from Gaëtan details from his address book filled with names and phone numbers of various men he had slept with. Shilts quizzed Darrow about a variety of ways that Gaëtan might have initiated the epidemic in America. His interview notes show that he asked Darrow about Gaëtan's potential liaisons with infected African men. They also record Darrow's response: Gaëtan had "no sex with Africans."[7] Another theory Shilts raised in his book involved New York's 1976 Bicentennial celebration: sailors from around the world, including Africa, descended on the city to participate in a ceremonial regatta and might have brought the virus with them. Shilts therefore asked Darrow, "Was Gaetan there [in New York] then?" Again, however, Darrow had no such evidence. At most, Shilts's evidence could only reaffirm what Darrow and others at the CDC were consistently asserting: Gaëtan was among the continent's first AIDS diagnoses, but he almost certainly was not the origin of the crisis.

In *And the Band Played On* Shilts carefully obfuscates this reality, never claiming that Gaëtan was the first, while also leading his reader to believe such was the case. The reader begins to develop this impression immediately at the book's opening, where Gaëtan is the first U.S.-based character with AIDS.[8] Later on, in his first mention of the term *Patient Zero*, Shilts is deliberately vague about its meaning. He also fails to clarify the subtle shift he makes from "Patient o"—the "non-Californian" of the CDC study—to his preferred moniker of "Patient Zero." Instead, he simply states, "Later, when the researchers started referring to Gaetan Dugas as Patient Zero, they would retrace the airline steward's travels during that summer [1980], fingering through his fabric-covered address book to try to fathom the bizarre coincidences and the unique role the handsome young steward performed in the coming epidemic."[9] It is difficult to gather from the immediate context just what "unique role" Shilts feels Dugas played in the AIDS epidemic. But this strong choice of words, coupled with the unusual and unexplained term *Patient Zero*, certainly allowed his readers to presume that Gaëtan might have been America's first AIDS victim.

In fact, Shilts fails to elaborate on the CDC's study for the next 124 pages, and the follow-up only further obscures Gaëtan's "unique role." Shilts's analysis blatantly misrepresents the study, starting with his description of the graph that illustrates the sexual connections among forty of the country's first men with AIDS: "At the center of the cluster diagram was Gaetan Dugas, marked on the chart as Patient Zero of the GRID epidemic" (figure 12). Notice that Gaëtan is not just the arbitrarily chosen index case for this limited study; he has now become Patient Zero of the entire "GRID epidemic." In the very next sentence, Shilts continues to mislead his reader: "His role truly was remarkable. At least 40 of the first 248 gay men diagnosed with GRID in the United States, as of April 12, 1982, either had had sex with Gaetan Dugas or had had sex with someone who had."[10] As already noted, there was nothing at all "remarkable" about Dugas's role, since *every* man in the study was sexually linked with *every other man* among the forty. Furthermore, Shilts misread the graph. It simply was not true that all forty men had either slept with Gaëtan or with one of his partners. Indeed, the CDC graph makes it obvious that only *sixteen* of the forty men were so intimately connected to Gaëtan, while one person ("NY 8") was *six* degrees removed from him.

Shilts then compounds this error by employing unclear language to further confuse his readers. Nowhere does he explain that the CDC's moniker "Patient 0" was the innocuous result of Dugas's arbitrary placement at the center of the graph and his lack of a U.S. address. Instead, a few pages later, he replaces the term with one that he seems to use interchangeably, referring to Gaëtan as "the Quebecois version of Typhoid Mary."[11] Recall that Irish immigrant Mary Mallon, known as Typhoid Mary, was not just a person who spread a disease in New York in the early 1900s but actually the first known person in the United States to suffer from asymptomatic typhoid fever.[12] Shilts's embrace of her legacy for Gaëtan suggests that he played a similar role: that he was the foreigner who brought a new disease to the United States before passing it to others.

Much later, on page 439 of the 630-page book, Shilts finally addresses the question of whether Gaëtan brought AIDS to the United States. Recall that researchers knew back in 1982 that he was not the first in the country to develop AIDS-related symptoms and that some Americans had actually died of the disease before 1980, when Gaëtan developed KS. Even the CDC study's coauthor, Dr. Darrow, had shared his view in 1984 that Gaëtan had acquired the virus in New York or Los Angeles. Nonetheless, Shilts embraces a radical form of skepticism to sustain the theory's viability: "Whether Gaetan Dugas actually was the person who brought AIDS to North America remains a question of debate and is ultimately unanswerable." He then provides his best, though strikingly weak, evidence: "The fact that the first cases in both New York City and Los Angeles could be linked to Gaetan, who himself was one of the first half-dozen or so patients on the continent, gives weight to that theory." In lieu of the smoking gun that Gaëtan had sex with

Africans or was in New York City for the 1976 Bicentennial, Shilts employs a further bit of speculation. In this case, he notes that "Gaetan traveled frequently to France, the western nation where the disease was most widespread before 1980."[13] Shilts then drops the issue altogether, leaving his readers to stew in this inconclusive, circumstantial evidence.

Through his omissions of key facts, misconstrual of CDC data, and colorful embellishments, Shilts breathed life into a new myth: that AIDS had entered the United States and spread from coast to coast via Gaëtan, the promiscuous, maniacal flight attendant. Meanwhile, he could claim after the book's publication that he had never smeared Gaëtan in this way and that he had stayed within the realm of legitimate speculation about Gaëtan's role. Indeed, though Shilts passed away in 1994, his friend and publisher, Michael Denneny, still defends him from such attacks: "You have to look very carefully at what's in the book, what Randy actually said. . . . Randy never said that Gaëtan brought AIDS to America."[14] Denneny instead blames the media for misconstruing the book's claims.

THE BENEFITS OF YELLOW JOURNALISM

One thing Denneny does not deny, however, is that both he and Randy Shilts agreed to use the Patient Zero story to promote *And the Band Played On*. Indeed, he contends that the book would have been a failure without the media attention that made Gaëtan infamous. Publishing books on AIDS, according to Denneny, was a risky and unpopular venture in the mid-1980s, and publishers' reluctance nearly sank Shilts's project even before it was written. Presses were skittish about the correlations between AIDS and homosexuality, and many editors assumed that AIDS would be only a temporary crisis. Denneny worked at the time with St. Martin's Press in New York City and had published Shilts's first literary success, a biography of gay San Francisco politician Harvey Milk called *The Mayor of Castro Street*.[15] In the five years that Shilts wrote his book on AIDS, both men, by then good friends, assumed that St. Martin's would publish this work as well.

However, when Denneny pitched the project to the editorial board, "nobody voted for it." As he remembers, some people were uneasy that the book, like the AIDS crisis itself, "had no ending," while others were loath to publish something on AIDS when "there might be a cure tomorrow." After this unexpected failure, Shilts "shopped it at twelve different publishers and then came back to me," recalls Denneny, since no other press would publish it either. Denneny returned to the editorial board and insisted that St. Martin's publish the manuscript. The defining moment came when the head of St. Martin's, Thomas McCormack, finally rallied the board. As Denneny recalls, "McCormack says, 'I want to point out that every one of you has said that you think this is the best proposal ever, and that each of you voted against it [regardless]. Furthermore, Michael is going to kill us if we don't sign it up.' So Tom told them to sign it up." To hedge their bets, St. Martin's offered Shilts an advance of $5,000, nowhere near enough to cover his writing expenses for the exhaustive, 630-page book that took five years to complete. Denneny insists that Shilts, notwithstanding his steady job at the *Chronicle*, "went in the poorhouse to write it. He borrowed from his parents, his brother, everybody he knew. And he had no money. So he really spent himself down, because we didn't give him enough."[16]

Once the book was finished, the editorial board's concerns were proven correct. As the November 1987 release date for *And the Band Played On* drew near, media outlets refused to publicize it. The problem, as Denneny saw it, was Shilts's political message that runs throughout the book: "[Randy] thought he'd written, as he had, this great, sort of classic American reporter's story that basically was a denunciation of the Reagan administration—to some extent the CDC, to some extent the gay community, but much more minor. It really was a massive attack on the Reagan administration." But, as Denneny warned Shilts, "You're not going to get on the 'Today Show' with an attack on the Reagan administration. . . . You're not going to get reviewed in the *New York Times*. . . . That's not going to float." By the summer, the book's publicist was demoralized by the media's lack of interest. As Denneny recalls, "The publicist finally called me down on a Friday afternoon and was totally freaked out and gave me all the bad news." Not a single major media outlet intended to review or promote the book.[17]

As a favor, a friend of Denneny's in the publishing business agreed to read the manuscript over a summer weekend and offer his advice on how to promote it.[18] This was when the myth of Patient Zero finally took off. Denneny visited his friend the following week and received his verdict: "I can tell you how to get it covered if you're willing to do it, if you're willing to get your hands dirty.'" Denneny assured his friend, "I'm willing to get my hands dirty. What do we have to do?" In the face of a media reluctant to report on AIDS, the promoter advocated appealing to reporters' worst sensibilities:

> Essentially, he said we have to use yellow journalism. He said, "I can tell you how to get this on the front page of the *New York Post* and I can guarantee you what the headline will be. . . . You'll get the entire front page of the *Post*, and the headline will read, screamingly, 'The Man Who Brought AIDS to America.' . . .

This story has everything: the beautiful young man, salacious lifestyle, and he's not even American, he's Canadian—the alien who brought AIDS to America!" . . . And he was right, to the point that he called the headline.[19]

Of course, before the infamous headline could appear in the *Post*, as it ultimately did on October 6, 1987, Denneny had to convince Shilts that selling the Patient Zero angle was the right thing. Certainly, Shilts already knew that this was a salacious story, one that he had artfully accentuated through his authorial choices described above. Nonetheless, Denneny claims that Shilts was extremely resistant to promoting the book via Patient Zero: "Randy hated the idea. It took me almost a week to argue him into it. He totally resisted it. He thought this was sleazy." Shilts felt that his integrity was being compromised. But Denneny kept at him: "I know this is yellow journalism. . . . You abhor yellow journalism because you're a journalist. [But] this is the only way we're going to get the journalistic establishment to pick up this story." Denneny also cushioned his hard sell with an incentive for Shilts: "The minute we get you the book reviewed and we get you publicity, you can denounce Reagan up the wazoo. We'll give you the platform. But without this, you're not going to get the platform." He warned Shilts that the book's fate hung in the balance: "If you don't do this, you're going to sell three to four thousand copies, and the five years you spent trying to put this on the map is going to be wasted." After a week of cajoling, including "four days of constant phone calls to sort of force him into it," Shilts acquiesced.[20]

The media circus that followed the *Post* headline was enormous. As Shilts's own newspaper reported, "*Chronicle* reporter Randy Shilts came to work last week and found 34 urgent messages on his desk from newspaper and TV reporters around the country. All of them, he learned, wanted to interview him about a headline that had appeared that day in the *New York Post*." In a fascinating combination of faux naïveté—pretending not to know that the headline effectively came from Shilts himself—and contrived superiority, the *Chronicle* reporter then chided her fellow journalists: "Sensational and misleading though it was, the headline, 'THE MAN WHO GAVE US AIDS,' was flamboyant enough to send the news media of the country running to the telephone."[21] The result of this media frenzy was that Gaëtan Dugas became headline news across the Western world: from the London *Telegraph*, to various Canadian papers, to *60 Minutes* and *Time* magazine in the United States. Meanwhile, the Canadian Broadcasting Company tracked down Dugas's family at their home near Quebec City and broadcast a radio interview with them the very evening of the *Post* story. They expressed anger at the headline and were appalled that his confidential cooperation with the CDC was being rehashed in a tell-all book.[22] The subsequent headlines confirmed the incendiary nature of the claims against Dugas: "The Appalling Saga of Patient Zero" (*Time* magazine), "Patient Zero: The Man Who Brought AIDS to California" (*California* magazine), "The Monster Who Gave Us AIDS" (the *Star* tabloid), "The Columbus of AIDS" (the *National Review*).[23] Most importantly for Denneny, the *New York Times* continued to run articles tied to the Patient Zero story line and also subsequently reviewed *And the Band Played On* in both the Sunday and daily editions.

Yellow journalism was indeed the way to garner media attention for AIDS in late 1987. Shilts and his publisher placed a dead man laid to rest in far-flung Quebec City in the media spotlight, and the news epicenter shifted to both Shilts himself and the offices of St. Martin's Press, where Denneny and other publicists composed a press package highlighting the book's material on Patient Zero.[24] In another premeditated move that reinforced the media frenzy, St. Martin's allowed *California* magazine to publish the book's Patient Zero material in its October 1987 issue. The magazine paid $3,500 to run this material exclusively a few weeks before *And the Band Played On* made it to bookstores on November 7.[25] In the meantime, Randy Shilts himself became a celebrity. As the book reached the *New York Times* best-seller list, he did numerous interviews for television, radio, and print media, including a national spot on CBS television's top-rated *60 Minutes* news program. When Shilts returned to his *Chronicle* office after the *New York Post* broke the story, he found a message from a colleague on his computer screen. It read, "Not only are you going to be a [expletive] multimillionaire, but yer going to cop a Pulitzer too."[26] The latter never came to fruition, but the former claim was somewhat accurate. All told, *And the Band Played On*, which had originally netted Shilts a $5,000 advance, ended up earning him about $1 million.[27]

Of all the interviews Shilts gave in the wake of the Patient Zero story, virtually none of them questioned the veracity of his claims against Gaëtan Dugas. The renowned reporter Harry Reasoner of *60 Minutes* did not challenge his false assertion that Gaëtan or his immediate sexual partners had had sex with 40 of the first 248 AIDS cases. Instead, the report only reinforced the salacious drama surrounding Patient Zero. It opened with footage of a house on Fire Island, a gay beach getaway outside Manhattan. Reasoner voiced over: "In the late 1970's and early '80s, 14 young men shared this summer house on Fire Island east of New York City. At least two of them had been known to have sex with Gaëtan Dugas. Ten of the 14 men have now died of AIDS."[28]

The only media outlet that forced Shilts to clarify his claims was the *Los Angeles Times*. In the course of his interview with reporter Bob Sipchen, Shilts disavowed the main rhetorical emphasis of his book, which suggested that the CDC had implicated Gaëtan as America's first person with AIDS. Shilts admitted to Sipchen, "You couldn't tell from reading the cluster study that [Gaëtan] may have been the person who brought [HIV] into the United States." He then added details from his research that he had inexplicably omitted from the book, noting that he had also interviewed "a New York City public health official who mentioned that the first two patients in that city with AIDS symptoms—perhaps the first two people in the United States—both mentioned a French-Canadian flight attendant for Air Canada as a sexual partner or the partner of one of their past lovers." Of course, without many more details, these claims also provided flimsy evidence that Gaëtan predated these men and all others in the country with AIDS. Yet Shilts made the evidence seem more definitive. He concluded his interview by sharing his own sense of shock when he had heard the deathbed confession of Paul Popham, a founder of the Gay Men's Health Crisis in New York, in 1986. Popham told Shilts that Gaëtan had slept with his ex back in 1980. According to Shilts, "It was one of the most horrible moments of all the horrible moments in doing this story. Paul was emaciated and had lesions all over him. I realized I was looking at somebody who was effectively dying of the virus, and that it was courtesy of Gaetan. . . . That was when the entire scope of the AIDS tragedy just hit me like a bullet between the eyes. Gaetan had slept with somebody on October 31 of 1980 and now I was looking at somebody in 1986 who was dying."[29] Clearly, rather than requiring Shilts to clarify his exaggerated claims about Gaëtan, the vast media attention instead allowed Shilts to capitalize on the unfortunate, easily misrepresented ways that Gaëtan was intertwined with the early AIDS crisis.

That said, Shilts's publisher Denneny was quick to assert that his and Shilts's decision to exploit Gaëtan was not a monetary calculation. Instead, he insisted that their motives were political, as they were convinced that the book's larger story incriminating the Reagan administration and others needed to be told. Both men felt that the book would break through America's silence about AIDS. As Denneny claimed, "I mean, there's no way that a book is going to stop an epidemic, but the book did about as much for the public consciousness as you could hope a book would do." Denneny particularly cited the ultimate impact of *And the Band Played On* on his and Shilts's own professions—publishing and journalism—as it opened up new avenues to cover AIDS-related and gay-related issues. "Many reporters, literally scores of reporters over the years . . . told me how much it changed their lives and their careers. [After Shilts's book] they demanded to cover the gay beat," Denneny claimed. Meanwhile, after seeing a book on AIDS succeed with the public, publishing houses opened their doors to more titles on the subject. Because such good came from their decision to market the book via Patient Zero, Denneny insists to this day, "I don't have any problems with it, and if people want to fault me for it, that's okay with me."[30]

Denneny's final explanation for promoting the book via Patient Zero centers on the devastation AIDS was causing: "Now this is '87. I mean, people are dying left and right. . . . It's very hard to convey to people what it was like at the time." Getting the book ready for publication was itself a process tinged with the specter of imminent death:

> I edited most of that book in hospital rooms at night. I made a deal with one
> of my exes, Tommy, who was dying, and I knew, even when he was in comas,
> he liked to have people there. And I made a deal with the nurses that if I got in
> before 8:30 . . . I could stay till midnight. And I figured, okay, most of the time
> Tommy was in a coma, I can edit in a hospital room just as well as I can edit [at
> home]. So I would get set up and take my shoes and socks off, so that my feet
> would be against his thigh, physically contacting his body. And sometimes he'd
> surface for a few minutes . . .

Denneny paused, visibly emotional, before moving from this intensely personal experience to the book's larger import for the gay community: "It was like being totally embattled. It was a very extreme time. And I don't think people were worrying about money or careers." For men like Denneny, who had lost scores of friends and devoted countless hours to fight AIDS, the Faustian compact necessary to publicize *And the Band Played On* was worth it.[31] The only "bad consequence," according to Denneny, was that the hysteria surrounding Patient Zero "deflected attention from Ronald Reagan's complete unwillingness to cope with, or to even mention the word AIDS."[32]

In fact, however, the negative consequences of the Patient Zero story were more extensive than Denneny acknowledges. AIDS activists were tongue-tied by the ensuing media hysteria, as the horrific headlines attacking Gaëtan and his insatiable sex drive trumped their efforts to support prevention, research, and health care for those with HIV/AIDS. Even more jeopardized were activists' efforts to overturn public perceptions that male-male sex and gay promiscuity were immoral, compulsive, and deadly. The day after the *New York Post* headline, activists and doctors held a press conference in Montreal—the commercial capital of Gaëtan's native Quebec and home to his employer, Air Canada—in an effort to defuse the story. Backing up doctors who discounted the claim that Gaëtan was North America's first AIDS victim, Pierre Gignac, spokesperson for the local "Comité Sida-Aids Montréal," labeled the information on Dugas "futile."[33] He added, "L'information est peut-être vraie, elle est peut-être fausse aussi."[34]

Then, in an indication of how paralyzing the public opprobrium against gay promiscuity could be, Gignac opted to playfully make light of the allegations regarding Gaëtan's torrid sex life: "Pour avoir 250 partenaires par année, il fallait qu'il (M. Dugas) s'envoie vraiment en l'aire, c'est le cas de le dire!"[35] By wittily pandering to the public's anger with humor (and simultaneously making light of Dugas's career as a flight attendant), Gignac demonstrated the true danger of Shilts's Patient Zero narrative. He and other AIDS activists were forced to replicate the same Faustian compact Shilts made to get publicity for his book: playing into the public's opprobrium of gay sex—not to mention gay careers—before hoping to gain acknowledgment of the various injustices that hindered their fight against AIDS.

AIDS UP IN THE AIR

In the history of airlines' responses to the AIDS crisis, such battles over gay sex were nonexistent. Instead, the role that airlines played in the aftermath of the Patient Zero crisis involved more basic civil rights, especially whether PWAs would retain access to jobs as flight attendants and seats as passengers on airplanes. These too were pitched battles. A snapshot of the industry in late 1987, when the story of Patient Zero went public, shows airlines still uncertain about how to handle AIDS. Some continued to pander to AIDS hysteria, while others treated AIDS like any other major illness. Thereafter, all airlines' treatment of PWAs improved significantly. Even those like United and American who had previously discriminated against PWAs changed their policies for the better. Thus, while Shilts's book was a short-term public relations challenge for flight attendants, it failed in the long run to trump the improving situation for PWAs spearheaded by medical evidence, increasingly outspoken AIDS activists, and significant court victories.

Just before the book's release, the issue of transporting passengers with AIDS garnered media headlines. In July 1987 Northwest Airlines refused to transport a U.S. citizen with AIDS back from his end-of-life vacation in China, forcing his family to pay the U.S. Air Force $40,000 to airlift him. Thereafter, Northwest "sent out a memo to employees that virtually banned AIDS patients from the carrier."[36] The airline did so because it still deemed the disease contagious. Yet, illustrating the increasing back-and-forth between conservatives and progressives, the ban lasted just weeks before being partially rescinded. Wearing a T-shirt declaring, "I'm a Human with AIDS" and accompanied by a coterie of news cameras, longtime LGBT activist Leonard Matlovich, who had famously challenged the military's ban on gay service members a decade earlier, went to San Francisco Airport to buy a ticket and board a flight. Fearing a media backlash, Northwest told him that it had changed the policy the day before. PWAs could now fly, though they needed a doctor's note stating they were not contagious.[37] Matlovich left the airport having exposed the airline's hypocrisy. His spokesman ridiculed the airline's contagion fears: "There is no danger to other passengers. If Northwest had done even rudimentary research, it would have known that fact."[38]

When Shilts's colleagues at the *San Francisco Chronicle* investigated other airlines, they found a patchwork of policies regarding passengers with AIDS. United and Delta, like Northwest after Matlovich's efforts, asked PWAs to "voluntarily provide a doctor's release saying they are well enough to travel and do not pose a hazard to other passengers." Meanwhile, "American, Pacific Southwest Airlines, Pan American, World Airways, and Continental, among others, all say they fly AIDS sufferers without . . . a doctor's consent," though it actually took yet another crisis in 1993 to completely change American Airlines' policy, as we shall see. In mid-1987, the most confused airline was USAir. A company spokesperson initially told the *Chronicle*, "The airline does not accept people with AIDS" but called back just an hour later and declared, "We don't have a reason not to accept AIDS passengers."[39]

Issues involving flight attendants with HIV/AIDS had become a global concern by 1987. Indeed, some carriers in other countries followed United's example in grounding such flight attendants. In June 1986, Canada's second largest airline, Pacific Western (which later became Canadian Airlines before merging with Air Canada), enacted such a policy, which led to a repeat of the Traynor case in a Canadian arbitration process. In this instance, however, the situation escalated when the airline failed to hire any new male flight attendants in 1987. As a result, the flight attendants union threatened to file a second grievance on the grounds of sex discrimination. The *Toronto Globe and Mail* quoted union executives about the airline's choice to stop hiring men: "I think they would just as soon not have any male flight attendants flying at this time, because of the AIDS scare. . . . They feel that the passengers would react negatively." Another union official directed blame at pilots as well: "A lot of our pilots don't want the male flight attendants serving them because they figure they can still catch [AIDS] through casual contact."[40] As in the United States, however, such concerns were trumped by the legal system's commitment to equal treatment under work contracts. Pacific Western lost the case, returned PWAs to work, and soon resumed hiring men.

A similarly extreme reaction came from a small carrier named Dan Air in the United Kingdom. The airline admitted that it had stopped hiring male flight attendants in late 1985 because of the AIDS crisis. In justifying its stance before the country's Equal Opportunity Commission, the airline made a three-pronged argument that combined the worst stereotypes about male flight attendants. First, it claimed that "a large proportion—somewhere between 30 and 40 per cent—of men attracted to cabin staff are homosexual." It then added the claim, with rudimentary evidence, that "cabin staff are sexually permissive."[41] Combining these claims with the fact that AIDS was principally transmitted sexually, the airline argued that male flight attendants would be particularly susceptible to contracting AIDS and passing it on to coworkers and fellow passengers. In October 1986, however, Britain's EOC ruled against the airline and forced it to hire men in the future. Executives also hurriedly issued an apology to both its male and female flight attendants for labeling them "sexually permissive" in the legal proceedings.

By mid-1987, a second dimension to the problem came to the fore. Not only were there contagion fears, but increasing immigration restrictions imposed on people with HIV also complicated the situation for flight attendants working international routes. The U.S. government was part of this unfortunate trend once Senator Helms's amendment became law in October 1987. The provision, passed with overwhelming majorities in both houses of Congress, banned immigrants with HIV from acquiring citizenship in the United States, while also granting border officials greater latitude to expel visitors whom they suspected of having HIV.[42] The United States was not the only country to usher in such restrictive policies; others enacted similar measures against permanent residents, and Iraq became the first country to require HIV tests for tourists. Sometimes customs officials in countries that supposedly did not bar HIV-positive foreigners also acted arbitrarily. In February 1987, for example, airport health officials in London refused to allow a Delta flight attendant with AIDS to enter the country despite earlier assurances that there were no such restrictions.[43]

The London incident forced the issue onto the agenda of the International Air Transport Association (IATA), a worldwide trade group for airlines. As IATA's medical advisory committee met in Geneva in March 1987, some harrowing figures were leaked to the press. While no North American newspaper picked up on the story, both British and Australian papers were filled with disturbing numbers: already over one hundred flight attendants worldwide had died of AIDS, with scores of others sick with advanced symptoms. U.S.-based carriers had the largest number of PWAs and AIDS-related deaths. American Airlines allegedly had the biggest crisis, as it "confirmed 50 of its employees had died from AIDS and there were another 60 AIDS sufferers on the staff." Pan American "refused to confirm it had suffered 20 deaths and had a further 30 cases," while United (twelve total cases) and TWA (ten cases) reported more modest numbers. Of course, United's reported number is not at all consistent with the claim from Patricia Friend of the Association of Flight Attendants (AFA), who recalls "hundreds" of flight attendants with AIDS who took the Butler settlement of receiving their full salary and benefits to stay home.[44] Her insights and the reflections from other flight attendants I interviewed suggest that these semiofficial numbers were significantly understated.[45]

The IATA's medical advisory committee expressed concern that the issue might create additional problems for airlines beyond bad publicity. First, it voiced the concern "that health insurance may increase for its staff." It then articulated the fear that international carriers would face service disruptions if "staff with AIDS . . . face immigration problems." Especially to combat the second problem, IATA officials chose to endorse conclusions previously passed by the United Nations' World Health Organization: "that screening of passengers was not justified, useful, feasible or needed; nor that screening crew was any use, or that passengers on airlines are particularly at risk."[46]

As these deliberations confirmed, airlines stood to lose money the longer that AIDS hysteria guided the actions of governments and insurers. This realization further complicated matters for airlines like United. While they feared lost revenue from allowing flight attendants with HIV/AIDS to potentially scare away passengers, they also faced complications when pandering to AIDS hysteria. Thus, just as Randy Shilts was introducing Patient Zero to the world, United was considering lifting its ban on flight attendants with HIV/AIDS and resolutely siding with those seeking to combat AIDS phobia. The timing seemed particularly ironic.

UNITED'S QUIET POLICY CHANGE

To be sure, another major impetus for United's choice to end its AIDS-based discrimination was the increasing number of court decisions won by PWAs. Even the U.S. Supreme Court had weighed in on a case of great importance to AIDS activists, *School Board of Nassau County v. Arline*.[47] *Arline* did not explicitly address HIV/AIDS, but it did involve a schoolteacher with a somewhat similar condition: tuberculosis. In March 1987, the Court ruled that Gene Arline had to be reinstated in her classroom job, which her superiors had previously denied her out of contagion concerns. The ruling made clear that even contagious diseases were covered as a "disability" by the 1973 Rehabilitation Act, which guaranteed that neither the government nor government contractors (like public schools or airlines) could discriminate on the basis of someone's disability.

To side for Arline, the Court also had to determine when a potentially contagious disease like tuberculosis became an actual contagion threat to others. The 7–2 majority's finding was as pertinent to HIV/AIDS as it was to Arline's dormant tuberculosis: in assessing the threat of contagion, Justice William Brennan wrote for the majority, "Courts normally should defer to the reasonable medical judgments of public health officials."[48] This was the standard that the AIDS activist community had been fighting to enshrine in discrimination cases from the beginning of the crisis, and indeed the Court's wording closely tracked the conclusion made in late 1984 by arbitrator Martin Wagner in Gär Traynor's grievance against United. In the course of two-plus long years, this juridical strategy—deferring to the sound judgments of health authorities, not public fears of contagion—made its way from Traynor's modest labor arbitration all the way to the Supreme Court. Airlines like United, which were subject to the 1973 Rehabilitation Act, saw that their modus operandi regarding flight attendants with HIV/AIDS was now even less defensible.[49]

United's new policy was finalized in May 1988. Flight attendants and other employees with HIV/AIDS would be allowed to work as long as they could, and the settlement reached in the Robert Butler case would be rescinded. The men covered by this deal would return to work if they remained healthy enough, or they would go on medical leave. Meanwhile, both the airline and the flight attendants union had a major task before them: educating employees, who previously had received very little information, that AIDS would be a visible part of their workplace. These groups worked together to prepare educational materials for an orchestrated rollout.

The change in tone was significant for an airline that had worked so hard to make such people invisible. The fifty-page manual assembled by the AFA contained the latest medical information on the illness, resource information for those newly diagnosed, and advice on how to talk with someone who was living with HIV/AIDS. It also dealt with a delicate issue that would now resurface: how to handle those fearful about working alongside someone with HIV/AIDS. It clarified that the company would no longer justify such fears. Under the heading, "Must I work with a PWA?" the answer was very direct: "Yes." Such fears could now lead to loss of a job: "In light of the current state of medical knowledge that AIDS is not contagious by casual contact . . . employees who refuse to work put their own continued employment in jeopardy."[50]

The company was equally dramatic in shifting its tone. United's in-house magazine, circulated to all employees, devoted a full page to the issue, including a headline with "AIDS" written in hard-to-miss two-inch letters. The article began by acknowledging the fear that accompanies the illness but insisted that education was the most prudent response: "The best defense against the deadly disease is information." Interestingly, the article itself never mentioned the impetus for this new devotion to a company-wide education campaign. Instead, rather than acknowledging the policy change, it suggested the new status quo had always been in effect. The corporate medical director, Dr. Gary Kohn, stated, "United does not have a written policy per se about AIDS. We have a philosophy about the welfare of our employees: People with AIDS or any other life-threatening disease are treated with respect, dignity and compassion. They can continue to work as long as they are physically able to do so."[51]

The 1988 article was far more detailed than the medical bulletin that had circulated in United offices in 1983, when men like Gär Traynor were first getting noticeably ill. Recall that the 1983 memo used excessively vague and antiseptic language in describing AIDS transmission. It noted, for example, that "for the disease to be transmitted from one person to another, physical contact between the two must occur," while adding that the high-risk groups for AIDS included "persons with similar life-styles," such as those "who are sexually promiscuous or who submit to improperly prepared drug injections."[52] The 1988 notice to employees dispensed with such euphemisms, plainly noting, "As a blood-borne disease, the AIDS infection is spread in only four ways." When detailing the potential for sexual transmission, United's medical team was now very direct: "Semen and vaginal fluids can transmit the virus. . . . The proper use of condoms prevents transmission." Facts on transmission by drug use were also explicit: "Sharing an IV drug needle with someone else can inject the virus directly into the user's bloodstream."[53]

Perhaps the most radical shift between the 1983 and 1988 statements was a frank admission that PWAs were a part of United's workforce. The 1983 memo deflected this admission, claiming that concerns were raised about whether "our employees are at any special risk to contract AIDS by virtue of their wide exposure to the traveling public." In 1988, the focus was now on fellow employees. Noting CDC statistics predicting almost three hundred thousand cases of full-blown AIDS by 1991 and possibly one million more cases of HIV infection, the article bluntly added,

"Some of these statistics will represent United employees. United's population is too large to assume it can defy the odds." It then detailed that the sharing of equipment on the job, food preparation, and exposure to a coworker's saliva or sweat were not possible avenues of transmission. Finally, instead of fear, the 1988 article claimed, a coworker with AIDS "needs the same kind of concern and support that you would want if you had a serious and probably fatal disease."

AMERICA'S FIRST "GAY-FRIENDLY" AIRLINE

As AIDS-related phobia continued to ebb in U.S. society, the airlines readied themselves for yet another significant shift in its handling of queer rights issues. While in some respects a gradual progression, the move toward becoming an outspokenly "gay-friendly" industry can be dated to the year 1993, when American Airlines committed itself to a public relations and marketing campaign addressed directly to LGBT customers. While the appeal from a corporate standpoint was to generate greater loyalty among wealthier LGBT frequent fliers, the impact was considerable on American's employees as well. These workers, over time, found greater acceptance and sensitivity shown toward those living with HIV/AIDS and greater parity for same-sex domestic partners. While still tied to the profit motive, this corporate move toward "gay-friendly" policies nonetheless helped marginalize the right wing's more extreme AIDS-phobic, homophobic agendas.

When American Airlines began this trend, it was actually born out of crisis, not mere goodwill. Actions taken by employees during two events in 1993 demonstrated yet again that the company, like many other corporations, had failed to adequately train their personnel in issues related to HIV/AIDS and homosexuality. The first incident occurred after the gay and lesbian march on Washington in April 1993. Over one hundred thousand people had traveled to the nation's capital to march for queer rights and increased funding for HIV/AIDS. A good number of marchers were heading home on flight 701, a Sunday night flight from Washington's Dulles airport that stopped in Dallas-Fort Worth before continuing on to California. The presence of the marchers was obvious to the crew and various other passengers. A few of them had visible signs of AIDS, as the pilot later confirmed to the press.[54] Yet if anything the mood on the plane was tranquil and even upbeat. As Tim Kincaid, a longtime employee of American Airlines' Corporate Communications Department, told me, "I had some friends who were on that flight, a lesbian couple. . . . They said it was a great flight. . . . Everybody was charged and pumped up. They had had a great day in Washington and just felt really good."[55]

However, the presence of the marchers somehow alarmed the cabin crew. At some point after takeoff, the flight attendants sent a message to the pilot requesting that all of the aircraft's pillows and blankets be replaced at DFW before the plane continued on to California. By the time the pilots conveyed the message to ground operations, the request had taken on an disturbing tone. Employees at DFW registered the message in American's computer system as "inbd crew req complete chg of all pillows blankets due gay rights activits group onbd." Someone on the plane—presumably the flight attendants—had engaged in a profoundly AIDS-phobic, homophobic bit of speculation, perceiving that gay rights activists were equivalent to people with HIV/AIDS, who in turn were a contagion threat if they shared pillows and blankets with other passengers.

When the internal message was leaked to the press in Dallas, a firestorm of criticism erupted. A spokesperson for the Dallas Gay and Lesbian Alliance led the charge, noting the irony that an airline, of all companies, could be so homophobic, "There's no company in this area that employs more gay and lesbian people; that's why this is so appalling." Subtly referring to the presence of gay flight attendants at American, he added, "This crew has to work with gays every day." Then, poking derision at the equation of homosexuality and AIDS, he concluded, "Homosexuality is not something that you catch by touching a pillow."[56] Some flight attendants at American were even more scathing, singling out the all-female flight 701 cabin crew for a vitriolic attack. One person looked up the crew's names on the flight roster and then made a hand-drawn sign: "[Names omitted] ARE IGNORANT HOMOPHOBIC C**TS [letters redacted]."[57] The sign may well have hung in a flight crew lounge; whatever its path, it eventually ended up at the flight attendant union's central offices, presumably because the union feared that the hostility among the airline's flight attendants would continue to smolder.

American chairman and president Robert Crandall was very concerned about the incident. According to Tim Kincaid, "Crandall was outraged by it, saying this is not who we are. . . . We don't discriminate against gay people." When a lawyer informed him that the airline actually had no policy prohibiting discrimination of gays and lesbians, Crandall authorized him to immediately change the policy. Almost as swiftly, American publicly committed itself to treat employees and passengers equally regardless of their so-called "sexual preference."[58] With that, American became one of the first U.S. airlines to commit to nondiscrimination in employment, a trend that was already on the rise elsewhere in corporate America in the late 1970s.[59]

Meanwhile, the airline's Corporate Communications Department was deputized to steer the company through the media crisis. They drafted a letter from Crandall to all employees and to various gay rights groups, apologizing for the incident and insisting that "the Company views these events as deplorable." Though the crew's actions clearly showed a lack of understanding of HIV/AIDS, Crandall's letter stressed American's already implemented commitment to such training. He claimed the airline had a "very active program of AIDS education for employees. We conduct this program in cooperation with the Red Cross, and fly Red Cross people to the cities we serve—at our own expense—when that is necessary."[60] He neglected to mention that such training was voluntary and that a vast majority of frontline employees, including flight attendants, had no HIV/AIDS training at all.

This glaring deficiency again caught up with American just a few months later, on November 14, 1993. Passenger Timothy Holless, who was quite frail with advanced AIDS and KS lesions, boarded a flight at O'Hare Airport and immediately began administering an IV drip before the flight had taken off. Alarmed that he was violating airline policy, a flight attendant ordered Holless to put the drip away and, inexplicably, to cover the lesions on his face. When Holless adamantly refused, the flight attendant called for Chicago police to forcibly remove him from the plane. Though Holless was quite frail and weighed no more than 120 pounds, four policemen arrived to remove him.[61] A fellow passenger described the scene: "The cops dragged him off the plane, leaving his cane and glasses. They dragged him facedown on his belly. He was screaming 'Chicago police abuse, Chicago police abuse' and screaming in pain."[62] By coincidence, a local news television crew also happened to capture the incident.

Coming a few months after the earlier regrettable episode, the Holless incident led gay rights groups and AIDS activists to condemn American more forcefully. The director of the National Association of People With AIDS, the group originally founded by Gär Traynor and his companions from the Denver Conference, led the way, stating, "We are appalled by the actions of American Airlines employees who would ask a man with AIDS to cover his face. The apathetic reaction of the corporation signals a blatant disregard for civil rights and simple compassion."[63] In this case, the airline issued a more muted apology, insisting to Holless that its employees "genuinely felt they were acting in your best interest and in the interest of all passengers on board the flight."[64]

A main reason for American's comparative silence was its fear of legal action, which in fact came quite soon. The Lambda Legal Defense and Education Fund represented Holless in a suit, which other AIDS activists joined as co-plaintiffs. Even twenty-two members of Congress sent a letter to CEO Crandall demanding that the airline implement federal antidiscrimination laws protecting people with HIV/

AIDS. This political intervention from Washington reflected a newly established legal reality as of 1990, when the Americans with Disabilities Act codified the Supreme Court's *Arline* decision and expanded protection from HIV discrimination to even more U.S. companies. Additionally, the company faced a nationwide boycott from gay rights groups. In particular, the organizers of the march commemorating the twenty-fifth anniversary of the Stonewall riots threatened such a move. Because the march, scheduled for June 1994 in New York, was expecting around one million attendees, the airline was quite worried.

Spurred by these threats from the gay and PWA communities, American quickly reached out to a specialized public relations team, Witeck-Combs Communications, based in Washington, D.C. According to Bob Witeck, the firm's co-founder and CEO, American now realized they needed to reach out to the gay community, but they were unsure how to do so sensitively. "[American executives] were outside of their comfort zone and knowledge." Witeck added that American "didn't know whether or not they could even have a conversation with [the Stonewall 25 organizers] in any real sense." Indeed, in the first meeting between Witeck-Combs and American executives, a company lawyer unwittingly highlighted how little attention American paid to such issues. As Witeck recalls, "The attorney . . . said, 'Do you think we have many gay people at American Airlines?'" The comment startled Witeck: "You don't want to answer with a laugh. . . . You want to give him some credit. So I didn't want to say, 'Have you ever been on a flight? Have you ever met flight crews?'"[65]

Counteracting such ignorance was what Witeck deemed a legitimate desire to improve relations with the LGBT and PWA communities: "These were people . . . who said, 'We want to get it right; we don't want to just make [the boycott threat] end.'" At the same time, executives were worried about the financial implications of taking stands to support gay rights, fearing a conservative backlash that could eat into their customer base. Witeck, however, promised that supporting gay and PWA rights would be financially lucrative for the company. Having already seen what he called the "business downside" of the company's actions in the form of a threatened boycott, Witeck assured American that "they also eventually—very quickly—[would see] the business upside."[66] This incentive, however, required sincerity from American when it chose to become gay-friendly. As American employee Tim Kincaid recalls, Witeck and his partner, Wesley Combs, told American executives, "We can help you to address this and achieve a good outcome, but if this is just about window dressing, we're not interested."[67]

Over the next few months, Witeck-Combs and American began to implement a series of changes built on the two-pronged strategy of promoting gay-oriented marketing at American while advancing an LGBT-friendly corporate philosophy and updated workplace policies. One of the first moves was to make peace with Timothy Holless, as the airline accepted an out-of-court settlement that compensated him and also committed itself to more thorough HIV/AIDS training. American agreed to contract with NAPWA to develop new training materials—including a video narrated by a female Pan Am flight attendant with AIDS—that became essential viewing for all flight attendants and gate agents. The video showed how all segments of the population are susceptible to HIV/AIDS and informed employees of the up-to-date scientific facts about HIV transmission and the virtually nonexistent risk of contagion at work. Airline managers also intensified discussions with employees with HIV/AIDS to enable maximal accommodation for flight attendants and others to continue working as long as their health allowed.[68] Thereafter, American also donated cargo space to the NAMES Project to transport the AIDS Quilt free of charge on a variety of occasions and sponsored numerous AIDS Walks across the country.

American agreed to a similarly proactive approach with LGBT organizations like Stonewall 25. Witeck, Combs, and Tim Kincaid flew to New York to meet with the organizing committee in an effort to mediate the impasse and stave off a boycott. American not only was offering improved behavior on HIV/AIDS issues but was also willing to become a sponsor of the march, providing both financial assistance to the organizers and free travel to various LGBT students attending the event.[69] As Kincaid recalls, "There were a lot of people [at Stonewall 25] who just said, 'It's too late!'"[70] But others saw an opportunity to collaborate with American and potentially leverage similar alliances with other corporations. In the end, Stonewall 25 agreed to forego its threatened boycott in the interest of seeing how earnestly American would embrace the LGBT community.

In the run-up to the parade, Witeck-Combs drafted text for an in-house training video at American. One of the company's most senior executives, Robert Baker, narrated the text that explained the importance of the Stonewall riots of 1969, talked about the efforts of gays and lesbians to attain equality, and addressed some of the realities of the AIDS crisis. Though the video was originally intended just for American's frontline employees, Baker insisted that all employees watch it. The main message, as Witeck recalls, was to tell American employees, "These are our customers . . . and these are people that we know you always do your best to treat them equally, with equal respect, and welcome them."[71] Of course, Baker's video was also an attempt to safeguard against a repetition of the pillows-and-blankets fiasco or the Holless incident, especially as so many lesbians, gays, and PWAs were flying to New York. That said, the video was groundbreaking in choosing to address LGBT issues so frankly. Witeck noted the rarity of "a senior executive in 1994 [saying] the word 'gay' out loud to the entire workforce. In '94 no company really had done that. In fact, it was such a big deal that GLAAD [the Gay and Lesbian Alliance Against Defamation], which had been a major critic before, almost did somersaults."[72]

The promised "business upside" of such gay-friendly moves began soon after Stonewall 25. As the gay press highlighted these improvements, Tim Kincaid, even though he was in Corporate Communications, started getting unsolicited calls from gay travel agencies wanting to conduct business with the airline. He eventually forwarded these calls to a colleague in American's sales department, who catalogued these initial proceeds from gay clients and gradually developed compelling data to propose establishing a sales team devoted to LGBT customers. Within a year, the so-called "Rainbow Team" at American was up and running. The innovation has since been copied to appeal to other niche markets, including African Americans and Latinos, but the Rainbow Team was the first such attempt to appeal to diverse customer groups with specifically directed appeals. By doing outreach at LGBT community events and fund-raising banquets for GLAAD, the Human Rights Campaign (HRC), and others, the Rainbow Team increased the company's profile in the gay community. Meanwhile, with the rise of the Internet, online customers could access a portal devoted expressly to LGBT customers. The actual proceeds accrued via the Rainbow Team have been difficult to quantify with precision, but Witeck and Combs observe that the airline has benefited handsomely from this civil-rights-turned-marketing strategy: "Incorporating GLBT issues into the diversity strategy of the company reaped huge dividends for American Airlines. Over the past twelve years, American can attribute millions in revenue from its targeted outreach to gay and lesbian consumers. Doing the right thing is truly good for business."[73]

GAËTAN'S FINAL POSTMORTEM

The year 1993 also marked another turning point in Gaëtan Dugas's posthumous legacy. Having become the most infamous male flight attendant in history thanks to Randy Shilts, he was partially rehabilitated that year, thanks to Canadian filmmaker John Greyson. Also an activist in ACT UP, Greyson's quixotic, campy musical comedy *Zero Patience* allowed movie audiences to connect with a new, more sympathetic Patient Zero.[74] In this account, Gaëtan is transformed from Shilts's stereotype embodying the excesses of gay sexual freedom into an accidental hero who, albeit unwittingly, helped create safe sex and thereby salvaged these same freedoms from the threat of AIDS. In the film's climactic scene, a reincarnated Patient Zero stands over a microscope and examines his own blood sample from the CDC's 1982 cluster study research. Over his shoulder, a character that Grayson loosely based on Randy Shilts tells Zero that the blood sample, like the 1982 cluster study, "establish[es] your guilt" as the man who brought HIV to America. As Zero peers through the lens, he sees a fantastical sight: the blood is now a swimming pool filled with red and white balloons (blood cells), accompanied by people wading around in inner tubes with hats on their heads marking them as "T" cells, "B" cells, and the occasional "anti-body." Finally, floating into the scene is a giant "HIV" cell. The actor playing this role is Michael Callen, a co-framer of the Denver Principles and collaborator with Richard Berkowitz on the first manual advocating safe sex. Callen, appearing just a few months before his death to AIDS-related complications, is in drag, complete with an evening dress, high heels, and a tiara. She looks upward toward Zero's gaze through the microscope's lens and introduces herself as "Miss HIV."

In the course of her ensuing conversation with Zero and his now equally entranced accuser, Miss HIV talks about her worst nemesis, safe sex: "Safe sex is vital. You of all people should know that, Zero." Then Miss HIV proceeds to undo the claim that Zero deserves blame for the epidemic, "For better or worse, that famous flawed cluster soap opera you started back in 1982 convinced everyone that safe sex is crucial." Zero interjects, "That study proved I brought AIDS to North America." But Miss HIV corrected him, "That data merely documents that you slept with some men who slept with some men, etcetera, etcetera, etcetera. . . . They might even have infected you, for all we know." An excited Zero then asks, "Then I wasn't the first?" Miss HIV is now adamant: "Of course not. Scientists have since documented cases of AIDS in North America at least as early as the sixties." Callen then breaks out into song, in a high-pitched falsetto: "Tell a story of a virus, of greed, ambition, and fraud. A case of science gone mad."

When Zero finally raises himself up from the microscope, he delightedly exclaims to his accuser, "*Putain* . . . I'm innocent! I'm not the first, but I'm still the best!"[75] Equally converted is the Shilts-like character, who quickly works to revise his assessment of Patient Zero. He disavows his incrimination of Zero and instead critiques the government's inaction on AIDS and the media-driven hysteria, ending with the claim, "Patient Zero should actually be acclaimed a hero of the epidemic. Through his cooperation in the 1982 cluster study, he helped prove that AIDS was sexually transmitted. Thus, Zero should be lauded as the slut who inspired safer sex."[76]

To say the least, 1993 was a year of odd bedfellows. *Zero Patience* fantastically ends with Gaëtan and the Shilts-like character falling in love and having sex, complete with condoms. By uniting these two characters onscreen, Greyson symbolically expressed the hope that Shilts's efforts to combat AIDS in *And the Band Played On* could join with the more radical vision of groups like ACT UP, who defended gays' sexual dignity against the right-wing condemnation that the Patient Zero narrative empowered. Meanwhile, a second set of odd bedfellows came together that same year. American Airlines, which up to that point had had a poor record on PWA rights, sought an alliance with Stonewall 25 as well as with mainstream LGBT groups like GLAAD and the HRC. The company was actively seeking to become America's first gay-friendly airline, despite never having engaged the LGBT community before, much less its own gay employees. The consequences of this seemingly far-fetched partnership have influenced flight attendants in very significant ways. As the 1990s progressed, gay flight attendants have won significant workplace rights, driving their benefits packages ever closer to parity with their heterosexual peers.

First came corporate nondiscrimination clauses, then flight privileges for domestic partners or a designated friend. By 2001, virtually every airline in the United States had added health insurance coverage for registered domestic partners. Finally, major airlines like American and United also created LGBT employee caucuses, and some—with American in the lead—also extended nondiscrimination clauses to transgender employees.[77] By the year 2000, flight attendants and other airline employees possessed greater economic advantages in their workplace than they did as U.S. citizens and residents of most states, where domestic partner benefits and nondiscrimination laws were (and still are) elusive.

Meanwhile, as the hysteria of AIDS has lessened since the 1980s, Randy Shilts's Faustian compact, in which he slandered a promiscuous gay flight attendant in the interest of garnering a broader readership, is less understood. The headlines that Gaëtan generated in 1987 seem like long-discarded elements from an excessively phobic time, simultaneously making Shilts's motives for slandering him less comprehensible. In offering his rationale for speaking with me and clearing the air about Shilts's role in creating the myth, his publisher Michael Denneny pleaded above all for understanding. Noting his own sense of futility as a publisher and AIDS activist before *And the Band Played On*, Denneny insists, "We spent . . . a good amount of time from '81 to '86 trying to get the media to cover AIDS. And they didn't want to hear about it." He fears that a younger generation would not "realize there was such a resistance" at the time to covering AIDS—one that, in his opinion, warranted the yellow journalism of Patient Zero to overcome it.[78]

CHAPTER EIGHT

· Queer Equality in the Age of
Neoliberalism

While the period since 1993 is heralded by the airlines themselves as gay-friendly, the reality has been more complex for queer flight attendants. After all, the courting of gay consumers and the expansion of LGBT-based employment benefits have coincided with a more advanced phase of airline deregulation that has destabilized the industry. The 1990s and 2000s have seen the dissolution of industry giants like Pan Am and Eastern (both were liquidated in 1991), the disappearance through mergers of other legacy carriers like TWA and Northwest Airlines, and recurrent Chapter 11 filings by every other major network carrier that existed prior to deregulation. For employees, this instability has wrought layoffs, significant declines in wages, and painful benefit givebacks. Consistent with the dictates of neoliberalism, as government regulation of the aviation industry has declined since 1979, so too have ticket prices for consumers. Yet these savings to passengers have partially been attained through reduced wages and benefits for workers. Unions for airline employees, including flight attendants, have been significantly weakened, while corporate executives, business consultants charged with cutting costs, and bankruptcy judges have all gained increasing control of the wage-setting process.[1]

As a result of these changed economic circumstances, the expansion of queer equality for flight attendants since 1993 has been somewhat surprising, marking an uncharacteristic increase in workers' benefits during a time of overall retraction. These changes also came about in significantly different ways than the queer equality victories won by flight attendants in previous years. Celio Diaz's success at forcing the reintroduction of male flight attendants in the early 1970s came by virtue of the 1964 Civil Rights Act. It was an expansion of rights bestowed on all sorts of U.S. workers, crafted (albeit incompletely) by the Congress and eventually affirmed by the federal courts. Over a decade later, the victory won by Gär Traynor to counteract the excesses of AIDS phobia and homophobia was grounded in collective bargaining rights and secured by the vigilance of Traynor's labor union, the Association of Flight Attendants. Still later, the Supreme Court in its 1987 *Arline* decision expanded this victory for HIV-positive employees to more workplaces, and the 1990 Americans with Disabilities Act did so yet again. By 1990 all workers in industries receiving federal aid were largely protected from discrimination based on HIV status, thanks to federal law.

Yet the key LGBT benefits attained since 1993—nondiscrimination clauses and domestic partner benefits—were not anchored in laws or constitutional rights, and they were not secured by collective bargaining. The courts were auxiliary players in bestowing these benefits, as were labor unions. Queer employees certainly lobbied for these benefits, labor unions bargained (unsuccessfully) for them, and the federal courts even belatedly endorsed the bestowal of some (but not all) of them. But airline executives effectively instituted these job perks on their own, as components of more elaborate marketing plans designed to enhance their respective airlines' appeal to wealthy gay and lesbian frequent flyers. Following the advice of public relations firms like Witeck-Combs, who helped develop American Airlines' gay-friendly outreach starting in 1993, the airlines embraced a queer rights agenda in the hopes of seizing a share of the newly cherished LGBT consumer market.

This chapter adds to the growing literature that examines corporations' efforts to court LGBT consumers and its consequences for queer equality. Some of these works take a decisively positive stance toward such developments. One of the earliest books, by gay marketing executive Grant Luckenbill, suggested that companies stood to earn "untold millions" by committing themselves to gay-friendly policies.[2] Corporate strategists like Bob Witeck applied a similar logic to the airline industry by convincing American Airlines that progay corporate policies would yield the "business upside" of loyal gay customers.

Yet some queer scholars who write on such developments are decidedly more pessimistic.[3] Alexandra Chasin, for example, compellingly demonstrates how this collusion of corporate profit seeking and queer rights allows wealthier gays to dictate the queer political agenda. If corporations value LGBT customers mainly for their wealth, then the public voices of the queer community will reflect mainly its white, male, gender-conforming members who already enjoy greater access to economic means. As Chasin notes, "Gay identity politics, in collaboration with gay identity-based consumption, tends to underrepresent women, people of color, poor people, sick people, and very young and very old people." In turn, ignoring these marginalized constituencies within LGBT circles creates a vision of queer equality that stresses only civil liberties (like access to domestic partner benefits, marriage, or the right to serve in the military), while ignoring the deeper need "for political alliance, for a multi-issue, multiconstituency coalition focused on economic justice."[4]

Indeed, in the neoliberal order embodied by the airline industry after deregulation, Chasin's stress on economic justice seems particularly relevant to the plight of flight attendants. As gay flight attendants and their domestic partners now ostensibly possess the equal benefit of reduced-cost travel to far-flung destinations, their diminished take-home salaries decrease the likelihood that they can use it. And while health insurance is increasingly cherished, especially employee-subsidized plans that cover spouses or domestic partners, rising premiums and co-pays diminish the value of this benefit as well. The same problem is found in relation to pension benefits: though domestic partners now stand to inherit from their spouses, they face the distinct prospect of a hollow victory, as more airlines since September 2001 have jettisoned their pension benefits. Indeed, the airline industry's massive layoffs after 9/11 and again since the economic crisis of 2008 only reinforce how tenuous flight attendants' gay-friendly benefits are. When examining the plight of flight attendants since the 1990s, we clearly see how limited the value of queer equality can be when not linked to deeper commitments to economic justice. Service industry workers like flight attendants have seen their prospects for a middle-class livelihood diminish over the past few decades, and the corporate world's nominal commitment to gay civil rights is not a viable solution for remedying this crisis.

To illustrate these points, I concentrate on two key moments in the flight attendant career over the past few decades. The first is airlines' adoption of domestic partner benefits around the year 2000. In particular, I concentrate on how these benefits arose primarily from airlines' LGBT-oriented marketing strategies, not directly from protections guaranteed by laws or fought for by labor unions. This expansion of queer equality thereby arose with diminished support from the two New Deal–era pillars that protected workers' rights and expanded civil rights, though both of these institutions still played an important role in the process. Instead, in the age of neoliberalism, queer equality relied on the more tenuous influence of the gay community as a valued, high-income consumer demographic. While this expansion of benefits was unquestionably positive, it also exposed the underlying danger of diminished legal and labor union clout.

The second moment, from 2010, is flight attendant Steven Slater's dramatic, and much-applauded, exit from his job: a story that illustrates the new, uneasy alliance between queer equality and neoliberal economics. Like "Barney Bullarney," William Simpson, Celio Diaz, Gär Traynor, and Gaëtan Dugas before him, JetBlue flight attendant-cum-momentary celebrity Steven Slater typifies his generation of stewards. In 2010, Slater garnered headlines for an epic workplace tantrum. After landing at JFK Airport, he cursed out a passenger on the plane's public address system and vowed to quit his job before activating the plane's emergency exit slide and tumbling down to the tarmac to head for home, his carry-on luggage and two stolen cans of beer in tow. His exploits struck many working-class Americans as heroic, a full-throated declaration that service sector work had become deplorable as customers' pushiness continued to escalate and workers' salaries shrank.

Slater not only gave up his job but also turned his back on his much-needed health benefits and domestic partner protections. Meanwhile, the many Americans who found him endearing also, somewhat surprisingly, overlooked his status as an out gay man living with HIV. Slater in this sense exemplifies the "liberated" queer flight attendant corps of the present day: a man unabashedly gay, HIV positive, and no longer discriminated against on these counts, who nevertheless shares with other service sector employees a deep-seated disillusionment about his prospects for a career that pays him justly and treats him with dignity.

FLIGHT ATTENDANTS' ASPIRATIONS FOR DOMESTIC PARTNER BENEFITS

In 1983 the flight attendant union at Pan Am successfully bargained for "buddy passes" that both straight and gay unmarried employees could use. This was an impressive but imperfect move toward queer equality, as these "buddy passes" were limited in quantity, unlike the spousal travel passes straight married couples enjoyed, and were more costly to use. Even so, most airlines resisted emulating Pan Am's "buddy passes" until well into the 1990s. In fact, during the peak of the AIDS crisis, no U.S. airline generated new benefits for their queer employees in the mold of the "buddy pass." Instead, AIDS channeled queer rights struggles into grievances like Gär Traynor's designed to retain workplace rights for PWAs. Additionally, when American Airlines exposed itself to AIDS-related public relations calamities in the early 1990s, executives quickly rewrote their corporate policies to include a nondiscrimination clause based on sexual orientation.

This contractual promise to treat LGBT customers and employees on par with heterosexuals quickly spread to other airlines as well.[5] But through 1995 such professions of equality amounted to modest, largely nonmonetary corporate concessions. No flight attendant or other airline employee could take bereavement leave when a domestic partner passed away or extended leave to care for a sick partner. Also lacking were travel perks for domestic partners equal to married spouses'. Equally absent were the most valuable of all benefits, health insurance for domestic partners and pension inheritance rights.

In the mid-1990s, domestic partner benefits were neither a corporate norm nor a legal requirement in the United States, except in smaller, progressively oriented municipalities. The *Village Voice* was the first U.S. corporation to extend a full array of spousal benefits to domestic partners in 1982, while the City of Berkeley was the first municipality to require it from corporate contractors in 1984. By 1993, when the National Gay and Lesbian Task Force and independent researchers working on the book *Cracking the Corporate Closet* interviewed over one thousand major U.S. corporations, they found that only twenty extended domestic partner health benefits.[6] Even in 2002, only 34 percent of Fortune 500 companies offered health benefits to same-sex partners: a figure that has increased to 60 percent in 2012.[7] The airlines, then, were not the first to bestow such benefits when they ultimately did in 2000 and 2001. However, they were within the first one-third of major U.S. companies to do so.

Certainly, gay flight attendants in the early 1990s recognized the disconnect between their company's increasing professions of equality and the unequal benefits packages they were given. By 1992 USAir flight attendant Todd Barr had encountered various frustrations with his employer's travel benefits program. Even after the company granted every employee four "buddy passes" per year, he knew that his partner Jonathan was being treated differently than his coworkers' legally married spouses. He therefore applied for a spouse pass for Jonathan. The airline, not noticing the same-sex nature of the application, initially granted the pass but soon rescinded it. Barr then proceeded with grievances that his union, the AFA, supported, arguing not only for equal travel benefits but for health insurance coverage as well.[8] The case, however, was not successful, and Barr and his partner were left with the modest allotment of a handful of "buddy passes."

The case of United flight attendant John Czyz is also telling, as it demonstrates both the frustration and resourcefulness of queer flight attendants fighting this inequality. Starting in 1992, Czyz used a combination of international law and pressure inside his labor union, the AFA at United, in his efforts to gain equal spousal benefits. Czyz was based at United's flight attendant domicile in London, but he and his partner, Willem Marsman, lived in the Netherlands. Given that Dutch law required employers to bestow equal benefits to same-sex couples residing in the

Netherlands, Czyz in 1992 attempted first, in 1992, to gain spousal travel benefits for his partner and then, in 1996, to get health insurance coverage. He even took his case to the Dutch Equal Opportunities Commission (Commissie Gelijke Behandeling) for a ruling in the summer of 1996, though his case, like Barr's, was unsuccessful.

Correspondence between Czyz and the AFA demonstrates the legal uncertainty that Czyz's requests generated, which in turn left union leaders noncommittal on whether the AFA would support his efforts. Czyz himself picked up on this ambivalence, at one point e-mailing the AFA president at United: "I am the f/a who is living in Holland and filed discrimination charges against UAL for spousal benefits under Dutch law. I know that you don't approve of this action and I am aware of all your concerns as well as the complex attitudes that labor unions also held regarding this issue." He ended his note with a plaintive, "P.S. Please Help."[9]

The response Czyz received from Kevin Lum, president of the AFA at United, was nuanced. As Lum later summarized to the AFA legal counsel: "I've answered to say that I didn't oppose his actions, as much as I was cautioning against proceeding too quickly—and finding ourselves in a representational pickle. I've said I would talk with you regarding what we might be able to issue that would help his situation (as well as ours). As I'm sure you can see, a ruling against United would be another step towards getting 'global' benefits."[10] This summation certainly embodied the hope that such benefits could ultimately be shared by flight attendants systemwide. But even more it expressed a deep uncertainty about Czyz's prospects for success and the potential harm that a loss in the grievance process could inflict on the union's larger collective bargaining priorities.

Thus the AFA soon opted for a guarded strategy of support, not only for Czyz's efforts in the Netherlands, but for all United flight attendants. By October 1996, the AFA was on the verge of adopting a two-pronged strategy: it asked United for a wide range of domestic partner benefits, including travel and health insurance privileges, in its opening offer during collective bargaining that year, while also contemplating a grievance to fight for these benefits. While neither strategy offered certain prospects for success, the option to file a grievance was particularly tenuous. AFA lawyers cited preexisting language in the United-AFA contract outlawing discrimination based on sexual orientation as "provid[ing] at least a colorable basis for such a claim." But filing a grievance was always seen as part of a more elaborate strategy, since the lawyers perceived that it "would add more immediacy to our demands at the bargaining table, and would provide a forum in which we could continue to pursue the issue even if we are unable to resolve the matter in the current negotiations."

The lawyers also cautioned that the grievance itself was likely to fail and could ultimately complicate AFA's larger efforts to attain domestic partner benefits: "By the same token, we should proceed cautiously if we *do* file a grievance since quickly losing the case would only make negotiations more difficult." The lawyers added, "If forced to proceed to decision in such a case, the overwhelming opinion is that we would be unsuccessful at this time." This pessimism came from the lack of legal precedent in the United States to grant domestic partner protections as an extension of provisions protecting gays and lesbians against discrimination. In the end, the AFA's legal team was perhaps most hopeful when reviewing the larger national trend among corporations to bestow LGBT benefits voluntarily: "Last week IBM announced that it is granting domestic partner benefits to its employees. Developments at IBM and other major corporations may signal the beginning of a trend that will spread throughout U.S. industry over the next several years. Even if we do not expect an immediate breakthrough, it may prove important for AFA to keep up the pressure on this issue in order to be positioned to take advantage of these changes in the corporate climate."[11]

As negotiations between United and the AFA became more heated in 1996 and 1997, this hope for corporate largesse became the more likely scenario for attaining benefits parity. The AFA withdrew its opening proposal seeking domestic partner benefits rather early in negotiations, and discussions instead moved toward issues that were more pertinent to the wider majority of flight attendants: wages, retirement benefits, and the use of more foreign-based flight attendants.[12] Another major controversy developed when the airline sought a longer union contract—ten years versus the typical five-year term—as a way to enshrine the wage rates for a longer term and to protect itself against labor agitation as this less generous contract took hold. These issues became so divisive that negotiations dragged on for over a year, until late summer 1997, and even begot an orchestrated campaign by the AFA entitled CHAOS. Standing for "Create Havoc Around Our System," the campaign was designed to frustrate the smooth operation of the airline through employee actions that nonetheless fell short of a full-blown strike.

Despite these deeper preoccupations, the AFA did ultimately pursue a grievance against United on the domestic partner issue. However, it held off doing so until April 1998, once the 1996 collective bargaining contract was finally approved. Even when the grievance was filed, neither United nor the AFA sought to move the case toward hearings, and the process moved no further over the next two years. Instead, a different legal front unrelated to the AFA and the collective bargaining process became the primary venue for contesting these same-sex benefits: the City of San Francisco and United were by that time engaged in an extensive legal battle over whether airlines flying into San Francisco International Airport would have to abide by the city's newly enacted domestic partner law. The case ended up in federal courts, with the City of San Francisco and various LGBT rights groups—such as the ACLU and the LAMBDA Legal Defense and Education Fund—fighting the airlines (and paying the associated legal fees) rather than the labor union itself doing so.

CONTESTING SAN FRANCISCO'S DOMESTIC PARTNER LAW

The City of San Francisco's Equal Benefits Ordinance (EBO) of 1996 thus served as a major catalyst—but still not the decisive one—for expanding full same-sex benefits to flight attendants and other airline employees. The new law forced the issue to the forefront of workplace benefits battles, helped change corporate policies of many employers in the city, and pressured nationwide companies like the airlines to reconsider the issue. Originally drafted in May 1996 by the Harvey Milk Lesbian, Gay, Bisexual Democratic Club, the legislation rapidly gained support from progressive members of the board of supervisors and Mayor Willie Brown. Modeled on similar legislation from smaller cities, the ordinance required all firms doing business with the city to offer the same benefits to domestic partners as they granted to married spouses, including access to health insurance. It passed in late 1996, and firms had a full six months—until June 1, 1997—to change their benefits packages to conform to the new law. By 1998, the city was boasting of the law's success: 91 percent of the three-thousand-plus companies affected by the law had complied.[13]

However, the airlines leasing gates and maintenance facilities from the city at San Francisco International Airport (SFO) were not among those conforming to the law. While all other U.S. airlines failed to comply with the law, United soon became the most publicly visible opponent in the industry. It operated a significant hub at SFO and also was in the process of renewing its lease for maintenance facilities when the domestic partner law was passed. These additional negotiations over facilities gave the city an opportunity to explicitly press United for a commitment to grant its employees domestic partner benefits. In February 1997, the city and United agreed on a short-term lease extension for the maintenance facilities, during which time the city agreed to exempt United from the EBO. By the time the lease was set to expire in summer 1998, according to the agreement, United would then comply "with whatever law was in effect when the lease was up."[14] By early 1997, the city had also opted to extend two other significant concessions to airlines flying into SFO: it would not require airlines leasing just gates to abide by the law, nor would it require the airlines leasing other airport facilities to do so until their leases expired. Thus, except for United and air courier Federal Express (FedEx), whose facilities lease also expired in early 1997, all airlines flying into SFO were legally exempt from the EBO until into the 2000s.

United's role in the airline industry's next legal move is contested. While company executives have denied it, city employees who negotiated with the airline over the EBO were convinced that United played a key role in getting the Air Transport Association (ATA), an umbrella organization representing all US airlines, to sue the city in federal court. The ATA's case, filed in May 1997, sought to exempt the airlines from the EBO for good, and it even raised the prospect of throwing out the entire law on grounds that it unjustly preempted federal law. The airlines' argument was more limited to carving out an exemption for the aviation industry, claiming that the airlines were federally regulated, subject to the Railway Labor Act since 1936 and the Airline Deregulation Act of 1978, and that they therefore enjoyed immunity from locally enacted labor laws like the EBO. In their worst-case scenario, airline executives envisioned having to abide by a troublesome patchwork of local regulations, some of which might be mutually conflicting, in order to operate as a nationwide air carrier. As one airline spokesperson noted, "Local laws have to come secondary to federal laws. It would be difficult if not impossible for airlines to have different regulations at every airport they fly into."[15] Besides the ATA, the only other corporate interests that challenged the EBO were two small companies, both of which were backed by the Reverend Pat Robertson's American Center for Law and Justice. Thus the airlines found themselves in an isolated position of making nuanced legal arguments about federal and local labor laws, while standing as the only major industry to oppose the city's gay-friendly ordinance.

United felt this pressure most acutely, since SFO was an important hub. It was the airport's largest carrier, leasing forty-three gates and paying $40 million each year in rent and fees to the city.[16] By not extending domestic partner benefits, United consequently risked losing more than its maintenance lease and alienating its LGBT customers; it also was contemplating a major disruption at one of its most important nodes of activity. Despite these stakes, United deemed exemption from the EBO important enough to fight for. While it is unclear whether the airline motivated the ATA's lawsuit against the city, it fully supported it. In fact, when its lease extension expired in late 1998, United joined the case as a plaintiff in its own name, thereby fortifying the efforts to exempt the airlines from the law.

While its external actions displayed a consistent position of pursuing its grievance against the city, United's internal deliberations were actually more unsteady. In fact, executives seriously considered granting total benefit parity to domestic partners quite early in the legal procedures. In late September 1997, United executives received word that its main rival, American Airlines, was about to extend domestic partner benefits to their employees nationwide. United then quickly resolved to match whatever benefits American granted "within hours," with the justification that United would "need to be able to respond to protect our market," a prescient admission of the importance of LGBT customers to its financial considerations.[17]

These hurried discussions involved at least five executives and CEO Gerald Greenwald, who encouraged his staff to prepare for quickly implementing the new benefits. According to notes taken during a meeting with Greenwald, the CEO instructed the following: "1) Get unions involved 2) Start-up right away. No roadblocks."[18] In late September 1997, United executives thus made a series of nine phone calls to the various unions, including AFA officials representing United's flight attendants. Each union expressed no opposition to the extension of domestic partner benefits as long as no concessions were required to compensate for this benefit expansion. Yet once United received word that American had reversed course and no longer intended to extend these benefits, United also opted to hold off. The airline never went public with its flirtation to end the standoff with the city and continued to participate in and even redouble its involvement in the ATA lawsuit to receive an exemption from the EBO. In strategizing about domestic partner benefits, the airline seemingly feared activity from its competitors more than legal coercion from the city, the courts, or an AFA grievance.

In the meantime, advocates for the EBO in San Francisco turned up the pressure on United and the ATA for their decision to challenge the law in court. Activists quickly formed an umbrella group called Equal Benefits Advocates and laid the groundwork for a boycott of United as early as 1997. They singled out United partly because of its size and partly because its negotiations with the city on a lease extension for its maintenance facilities seemed to precipitate the lawsuit. The activists particularly stressed United's hypocrisy in claiming to be a gay-friendly airline while also spending significant sums of money on legal actions designed to resist providing its employees with domestic partner benefits. Shops in the predominantly gay Castro neighborhood began displaying "United Against United" stickers, banners, and pins, and numerous marchers burned their United frequent flyer cards during street protests in front of United ticket offices.[19]

On the one hand, United continued its support for LGBT philanthropic causes, a tactic it had begun several years earlier after American's success courting the gay market. United continued to donate to the San Francisco Gay Men's Chorus, the

NAMES Project that displayed the AIDS Quilt around the country, AIDS Walk events, and various other LGBT charities and rights groups. Yet when a local AIDS charity called Academy of Friends accepted a United donation to cover a fund-raiser in March 1999, it stirred controversy within the LGBT community. One community newspaper accused Academy of Friends and other LGBT nonprofits of "being used to cover up United Airlines' homophobia" and of "tak[ing] money from a corporation that discriminates against its gay employees."[20] Simultaneously, activists kept up their occasional street protests. In one major action in July 1999, they seized upon the Tinky Winky controversy inspired by the Reverend Jerry Falwell, who suggested that year that the plush purple toy with a triangle on its head was gay propaganda directed at children. Protestors assembled at United's ticketing headquarters in downtown San Francisco with a full array of Tinky Winkies. The crowd was headed by protesters dressed head to toe as the purple doll, who subsequently were arrested when they blocked the office's entrance. The protests also found sympathy from members of the city's board of supervisors, who informally supported the boycott and encouraged city employees to steer business away from United and FedEx whenever possible.[21]

Even some United employees publicly broke with their employer's actions on the EBO. One employee group, "United at United," tried to walk a fine line of advocating a change in domestic partner benefits while also resisting calls for boycotts against the company. While flight attendants were not the main organizers of the group, many of them were active in it. Meanwhile, some members of the AFA based in San Francisco opted for a far more aggressive strategy against their employer, reinvigorating the CHAOS operation designed to pressure United during the 1997 negotiations. This time they used the same tactics to protest the airline's challenge to the EBO.[22]

Several flight attendants from United and other carriers also provided sworn affidavits to the city's lawyers highlighting the disparate treatment they endured by not having domestic partner benefits. In his testimony, American Airlines flight attendant Patrick Galbreath singled out his employer's hypocrisy of reaching out to the LGBT community while still denying equal benefits: "It distresses me and other gay and lesbian employees that American refuses to provide domestic partner benefits to its employees but is happy to take the 'gay and lesbian dollar.' We wish American would fulfill in economic terms the non-discrimination policy it purports to follow."[23]

The airlines' intransigence on bestowing domestic partner benefits was resulting in more of a focus on the various rulings that came from the federal district court on the airlines' challenge to the EBO. These proceedings dragged on for two years, starting in mid-1997. The court first registered a verdict in April 1998, then a very similar one in May 1999. Both of these decisions were, in effect, stalemates, as they affirmed the legality of the EBO and the right of the city to require its contractors to provide domestic partner benefits whenever it offered them to married spouses. However, the court also recognized the validity of the airlines' core concerns about the preemption of federal benefits laws. In a nuanced decision, the court argued that the airlines were indeed exempt from providing some—but not all—of the benefits covered under the EBO. Since federal laws, especially the Employee Retirement Income Security Act of 1974 (ERISA), provided nationwide guidelines for benefits like health insurance and pension benefits, airlines were exempted from offering these elements to employees' domestic partners. But other non-ERISA benefits—including spousal travel privileges, bereavement leave, and family medical leave—would have to be offered to employees. Also, even though the EBO contained language recommending that city contractors extend domestic partner benefits to all of their employees nationwide, the district court ruled that the law could cover only San Francisco–based employees.

Both sides clearly attained some of their objectives in these decisions. The city and the larger boycott movement saw most aspects of the EBO upheld in federal court and also greeted the partial demand that airlines conform to the law as a victory. They especially welcomed the extension of equal bereavement leave and travel benefits to employees' domestic partners. However, the airlines gained immunity from two of the largest and most desirable employee benefits: domestic partner health insurance and pension benefits. The city's legal team opted to accept this decision. It regretfully saw the EBO curtailed to non-ERISA benefits only, at least for the airlines, and also acquiesced to the court's choice to vacate the ordinance's clause that would have forced changes at "any of a contractor's operations elsewhere within the United States."[24]

Yet the ATA and United were not content even with this mixed decision. Instead of acquiescing in 1999, they quickly asked for a stay of the decision and appealed the verdict to the federal court of appeals. Their reasoning was the same as their original legal concerns they articulated when first filing the case in 1997: they believed the airline industry should be governed by federal laws, like the Railway Labor Act and Airline Deregulation Act, rather than municipal ordinances. Thus the case continued for another two years after the district court's final decision in May 1999. This action secured for United and the other airlines a reprieve in bestowing these benefits, but it also kept them—especially United—in protesters' sights as the main target of criticism.

SEPTEMBER 11, 2001

September 11, 2001, was anticipated as a momentous day in aviation history and LGBT equality. That was the day, after all, that the Ninth Circuit Court of Appeals in San Francisco chose to release its verdict in the case between the airlines and the city. Especially given the status of the case in mid-1999—with a neutral verdict generating an appeal—this decision was supposed to determine once and for all whether airline employees, including flight attendants, would receive benefits for their domestic partners.

Of course, as events transpired, September 11 ended up altering the aviation industry and the flight attendant career in ways unforeseen before that morning. The choice of Al Qaeda operatives to use United and American planes as weapons of terror led to the most tragic day in the history of civil aviation. Dozens of flight attendants and pilots were lost in the tragedy, as were hundreds of passengers. In all, the four hijacked planes led to the loss of over three thousand lives and countless millions of dollars of property. With U.S. air space closed for days, passengers suddenly loath to fly, and the economy temporarily floundering, U.S. airlines entered a period of unprecedented financial losses. A month before the attacks, U.S. airlines flew a record number of passengers: they had 65.4 million customers in August 2001. Overnight, the number of passengers was nearly cut in half, as fewer than 40 million people flew in September 2001.[25] From 2001 until 2005, U.S. airlines cumulatively lost more than $40 billion.[26]

It took a full four years for passenger numbers to recover to the pre-9/11 numbers. But the airlines flying these same numbers of passengers had changed significantly: worst affected were the so-called network carriers (who worked on a hub-and-spoke system and had a global reach), who accrued most of the billions of dollars of losses after the tragedy, shrank their domestic route networks to shed costs, shed thousands of employees, and renegotiated labor contracts to slash wages. Before the attacks these airlines had employed over 465,000 workers, but by July 2005—even with passenger numbers back to the pre-9/11 level—there were only 309,000 workers at these same airlines.[27] Understandably, then, the release of the U.S. Appeals Court ruling on the morning of September 11 was almost completely overlooked and decidedly anticlimactic. The expectation that this long-awaited decision would be somehow at the forefront of the aviation world's agenda that morning was not fulfilled.

Long before that morning, however, other events transpired to make the court's ruling less pertinent—even to the flight attendants and other airline employees with domestic partners, as well as to the LGBT activists on the streets of San Francisco. As United's legal team continued to appeal the district court decision, the company did something wholly unexpected on July 30, 1999. United's new CEO, James Goodwin, announced that day that the airline was bestowing a full panoply of benefits on employees with domestic partners. In addition to the non-ERISA benefits that the district court had ruled for (travel passes, bereavement leave, and family medical leave), the airline went a step further and bestowed the most prized benefits of all: domestic partner health coverage and pension inheritance. Goodwin explained his reasoning thus: "As we have said from the very outset, this case has never been about gay and lesbian rights. What we oppose . . . are local municipalities intruding upon the federal domain by attempting to legislate the employee benefits package of companies like airlines doing business nationwide." Goodwin then stressed the breadth of the company's policy change: "We are not merely complying with the San Francisco ordinance . . . but are offering a broader package of domestic partner benefits to our employees and retirees."[28] Meanwhile, the LGBT press in San Francisco, after two years of hounding the airline and its decision to challenge the EBO, was gleeful about the turn of events. "FINALLY!" ran the front-page headline in the Bay Area Reporter. A companion editorial noted the remarkable turn of events: "United Airlines, decidedly, won the 'Most Abrupt Policy Shift' Award for a corporation." It went on to credit community activists and airline employees for the victory: "The company's decision . . . demonstrates that persistence pays off for the gay community, which banded together in a way that's not seen much anymore. It was the activists who kept the issue in front of the public and the queer United employees who came forward to offer depositions who deserve a lot of the credit."[29]

Interestingly, United's decision on domestic partner health benefits marked a subtle competitive shift in the airlines' race to garner gay customer loyalty through extending such benefits. Since 1994, American Airlines had had a reputation of leading the way on LGBT rights. It bested United and its competitors by including the first nondiscrimination clause covering sexual orientation in its corporate bylaws back in 1994. It also was the first to follow Pan Am's 1983 precedent in the mid-1990s by offering "buddy passes" to its unmarried employees. Because American had been working closely with the gay public relations firm Witeck-Combs since 1994, the assumption was that it would set the standard in the industry, as it nearly did one more time in 1997 by seriously contemplating the introduction of full domestic partner benefits. On this occasion, however, United actually moved beyond all of its competitors, becoming the nation's first airline to extend health insurance and the other benefits that San Francisco's board of supervisors originally sought to require.

Not to be outdone, American Airlines announced within hours that it would match United's moves. Over the next several months, the main network carriers followed: TWA, US Airways, Continental, and Delta soon acquiesced. What the entire aviation industry had been fighting through the courts was thereby bestowed unilaterally on employees once the marketing and public relations departments prevailed on United's executives. By the time the tragedy of September 11 took place and the court of appeals decision came out that same morning, almost all the airlines flying into SFO had already come into compliance with the EBO as written, even though they had successfully attained immunity from key tenets of the law. Importantly, the airlines did so, not at the command of the courts, but rather by following the dictates of marketing analyses, particularly those highlighting the value of gay and lesbian customers, who continued to enjoy an exalted reputation as a wealthy and travel-happy niche market.

The court's actual decision on September 11, anticlimactic though it was, only reinforced the district court's rulings back in 1998 and 1999. Rather than accepting the airlines' view that the EBO infringed on the free operation of their business, the court emphasized the civil rights nature of the EBO and its very low implementation costs. First, the court likened the EBO to a 1966 California law that required the airlines not to discriminate against nonwhite pilots. Such laws might implicitly impose costs on the airlines themselves, the court argued, but they did so to end a larger social ill of discrimination, making them legitimate costs that employers should be expected to bear.

The judges then took up the larger question of whether the Airline Deregulation Act of 1978 precluded a city like San Francisco from requiring such extra costs. As in the airlines' own justifications, the court's reasoning was primarily about cost considerations. Concerning the airlines' major criticism of the law, the judges noted: "They point out by way of example that United employs 17,000 people at SFO, operates over 500 daily flights and has invested tens of millions of dollars in facilities. They argue that because of this economic situation, the City has extreme bargaining power and leverage over the Airlines and can force them to accept the Ordinance's nondiscrimination provisions in the Airport leases. This, they contend, is preempted by the ADA."

In countering this claim, the court offered a free market justification of its own. It embraced the neoliberal underpinnings of deregulation, but in this case to support San Francisco's prerogative to promote queer equality: "Whatever leverage the City has in its negotiations over the Airlines is created by the market conditions that were allowed to blossom through the passage of the ADA"" If airlines still desire, by their own free choice, to fly into San Francisco, "the Airlines will have to agree to abide by the Ordinance's non-discrimination requirements as a 'cost' of maintaining their leases at SFO." Thus the court placed limits on airlines' pursuit of cost efficiency: if a local government perceived a civil rights issue to be pressing enough, they could still prevail on corporations to conform to some of these standards, within reason.[30]

The appeals court decision thereby created an interesting counterdynamic to the tragedy of 9/11. As the aviation industry entered very turbulent years and thousands of employees stood to lose their jobs, gay and lesbian employees had secured important new benefits. These were attained through a combination of San Francisco law, federal court decisions, and, most decisively, corporate actions designed to appeal to LGBT customers. The overall result was impressive: queer employees now enjoyed virtual parity in the workplace, with employers treating their domestic partners on par with married spouses, even as all states at the time refused to recognize same-sex marriages as legally valid. Amid the aviation industry's subsequent round of layoffs, wage cuts, and benefits givebacks, these new LGBT-friendly perks have thus far remained, even though they are guaranteed (in most jurisdictions outside San Francisco) by no more than easily modified corporate policies. Thus, while impressive, these benefits remain tenuous—as do flight attendant jobs more generally in the post-9/11 era.

THE JETBLUE FLIGHT ATTENDANT

Unlike the network carriers, JetBlue was a post-9/11 success story. It was one of just a handful of U.S. airlines that posted a profit in 2001, and it continued to do so for every year through the downturn in air traffic that ended in 2005. When it began operations in 2000, JetBlue brought the Southwest Airlines model of a low-fare, low-cost airline to the Northeast corridor, establishing a hub at JFK Airport in New York City. JetBlue promised to be significantly different from the start-ups that had come and gone on the East Coast since deregulation. It was exceptionally well financed, boasting a $150 million nest egg that came from deep-pocketed investors like George Soros and Chase Bank. This capital allowed JetBlue to purchase an all-new aircraft fleet boasting leather seats, more legroom, and individual television screens for each passenger. JetBlue customers could enjoy both lower fares and more comfort than their counterparts flying a traditional network carrier.

While the new fleet was one key aspect that lowered JetBlue's costs (fuel costs were lower and maintenance costs were virtually nonexistent), another major factor was lower labor costs. In the years before JetBlue's debut, CEO David Neeleman had started up low-cost carrier MorrisAir in Utah, which he sold to Southwest Airlines for a sizable profit, and West Jet in Canada. Key to both of these companies' successes was their nonunion workforce, which allowed them to keep wages lower than their competitors. Neeleman emulated this strategy at JetBlue, designing a workplace that allegedly felt more egalitarian than a union airline. Flight attendants were referred to as "crew members" (on par with pilots, at least in title), the human resources department was known simply as "People," and Neeleman himself kept his take-home pay at a modest $200,000 in the beginning to promote a sense of solidarity with his workers.

While JetBlue flight crews took home lower wages than their peers at a network carrier, they also were more productive. Both flight attendants and pilots were expected to chip in with cleaning the aircraft during layovers, a chore that labor unions at the network carriers had successfully bargained away decades earlier, and pilots were given financial incentives to work longer hours. Workers were also expected to be available for impromptu changes to their schedules and to take on extra work hours that union contracts largely protected against. As the *Financial Times* reported in 2002, these different work rules and wage rates made JetBlue crew members far cheaper and more productive than workers at the nation's largest carrier, United. JetBlue pilots flew "about 80 hours a month against about 50 hours at United," and the airline's overall labor costs "represented 25 per cent of JetBlue's second-quarter revenues, compared with 47 per cent for United."[31] The ever-important industry barometer of success, the cost to fly one seat one mile, placed JetBlue in a very enviable position: while network carrier US Airways' costs peaked at 12.9 cents per seat-mile before 9/11 and Southwest enjoyed a modest 7.48 cent cost, JetBlue was situated even more enviably, with a 6.5 cent cost per seat-mile through 2001.[32]

JetBlue worked hard to create an environment for their flight attendants and other employees that would motivate workers to invest more effort for less earnings than their unionized peers. They typically hired employees in their early twenties who were enthusiastic about receiving their first career-oriented jobs. They also tended to select social extroverts, who were more likely to be energized by social situations and to be engaging with customers and coworkers. The airline trained all employees at their own "JetBlue University" to acquaint them with the company's expectations and unique corporate culture. Indeed, the culture was intended to break with the formality of the United States' network carriers, going even further than Southwest's playful and informal culture to become what one employee called "a huggy, fuzzy company." As one manager explained, "Every employee greets everyone with a kiss. . . . If that's not who you are coming in the door, shortly afterwards that is who you will become. You will become upbeat. It's almost like you're floating."[33] Executives expected that this collegiality and goodwill would lead their employees to undertake tasks that were not in their job descriptions, making them more flexible and more productive overall.

Of course, once the network carriers began purging upwards of one hundred thousand employees immediately after 9/11, JetBlue workers had an additional incentive to work hard without wage parity: they enjoyed job security and the prospect of promotions, while many of their peers elsewhere were losing their jobs. Indeed, JetBlue's most infamous flight attendant, Steven Slater, would come to the company in the late 2000s after experiencing multiple job losses after 9/11. The Los Angeles native had gotten his first job in aviation as a nineteen-year-old in the early 1990s, working at regional carrier Sky West. He later worked part of the decade at an international carrier, remembering these years as the best in his career: "I was fortunate to fly during a very good time for the airline industry. . . . Pre 9/11 747's to Europe, Chateaubriand, caviar, and escargot. Seventy-two-hour layovers in Frankfurt and Zurich. It was an amazing time."[34] The years after 9/11 were, however, far less glamorous. Slater endured various bouts of unemployment, as well as layoffs or furloughs from airlines like Delta and Business Express.

By the time he landed a job at JetBlue later in the decade, Slater was relieved. His MySpace page referred to his gratitude for returning to work at JetBlue: "Chances are I am flying 35,000 feet somewhere over the rainbow on my way to some semifabulous JetBlue Airways destination! Truly, some are better than others. But I am enjoying being back in the skies and seeing them all."[35] That said, Slater was under considerable stress during the entirety of 2009 and 2010. JetBlue denied his January 2009 request for a hardship transfer to Los Angeles so that he could care for his mother, who had been diagnosed with terminal lung cancer. Thus he and his partner, Ken Rochelle, began arduous cross-country runs from New York City to take care of his mother, and Slater was forced to reduce his flying schedule. In the course of 2009, Slater earned just $9,700. "In my twentieth year in the business . . . I earned less than I did in my first," a statement that was probably true for thousands of flight attendants beyond Slater. Indeed, the major reason Slater kept his job was for the free travel that he enjoyed and Ken's spousal travel passes, which allowed both of them to commute between their home in Queens and his mother's in Los Angeles.[36]

Slater's time at JetBlue certainly had its unique traits: not every flight attendant dealt with the same stress of caring for a sick family member or had Slater's own history of alcohol and drug abuse or his HIV status (Slater tested positive in 2002). In other ways, however, Slater's relationship to his job was not uncommon. His wit and perkiness endeared him to some coworkers and passengers and surely was one reason that managers opted to hire him at JetBlue. One frequent traveler on Slater's routes recalled him as someone "who is always so nice. He makes your flight enjoyable."[37] His money troubles were also quite familiar to many flight attendants, who likewise faced bouts of unemployment and furloughs, significant wage cutbacks, and work rules that forced them to undertake more tasks unrelated to passenger safety or hospitality. Finally, Slater's own growing disenchantment with passenger-related stress, carry-on luggage hassles, and more invasive security screenings made him typical of flight attendants and passengers in the post-9/11 years. The precrisis era of Chateaubriand and escargot had been replaced with fuller flights, cramped overhead storage bins, and increasingly irritable customers.

AUGUST 9, 2010

In a way reminiscent of how many Americans refer to the Al Qaeda terrorist attacks as "September 11th," Steven Slater calls his famous incident simply "August 9th." The full set of events that transpired on JetBlue flight 1052 from Pittsburgh to JFK that day are still contested. Slater claims the boarding process was chaotic and included a scuffle between two passengers vying for luggage space in an overhead bin. He had gone over to resolve the issue, telling one of the passengers to surrender her bag: "That's not going to fit. We're going to have to check it up front." As the passenger explained that she did not want to surrender the bag because its contents were important, she inadvertently let go of the door to the overhead bin, which proceeded to hit Slater on the head and leave a bleeding gash. The gossipy tabloid *New York Daily News*, which took the lead in reporting the most salacious details of the events, then described how Slater's behavior changed for the worse: "Passengers on the 46-minute flight said he acted like an unstable diva" for the remainder of the flight. The report continued: "Things took a turn for the weird when Slater stood up to give the safety instructions. . . . The bottom button of his shirt was unbuttoned, revealing his paunch as he held the oxygen mask and life jacket—briefly. 'He sort of threw them on the floor after demonstrating,' said [a passenger]. The display prompted nervous laughter among several passengers."[38]

When the flight landed, Slater was still stewing. This is when his tirade took on memorable proportions. As passengers were deplaning, one who had been involved in the carry-on scuffle allegedly lashed out at Slater again. Slater grabbed the intercom and announced, "To the passenger who called me a motherfucker: Fuck you . . . I've been in this business for twenty years. And that's it. I've had it. I'm done."[39] He proceeded to the galley of the plane, grabbed two beers, and then sought out his carry-on luggage before deploying the plane's emergency exit slide. He slid down the slide with beers in hand, traipsed across the tarmac, sought out his car, and drove away. The *Daily News* added one last outrageous point: he "then headed home to have sex with his boyfriend."[40] Another reporter who followed up on the Slater story several months later recalls this detail as "one of the most vivid, and badass, details of the Slater legend," especially as some reports claimed the couple were caught *in actu* as the police arrived to arrest Slater.[41]

Like all popular legends, some of the details of the Slater account are truer than others. For instance, Slater's actual exit from the plane was quite a bit more awkward than the first news reports suggested. In fact, he originally forgot to bring his bags with him on his descent down the emergency exit slide. As he later detailed: "I'm looking back up at the airplane, and I'm like, *Shit, now what?* . . . Obviously it was a moment of adrenaline, and I wasn't planning any of this. I can't exactly yell, 'Hey, guys, you want to throw down my bags?'"[42] So Slater shimmied his way back up the slide, "as baggage handlers around him guffawed and took cell-phone pictures." He then had only about fifteen feet to walk from the slide to a service door leading into the terminal. He eventually emerged in the JetBlue baggage claim quite disheveled, but with "the biggest deranged smile on my face because I am feeling so free and light and unencumbered."[43]

While Slater's escape from the plane was therefore more awkward in reality than in subsequent news reports, his arrest was decidedly less so. There was no basis for the *Daily News* report that he and his boyfriend Ken were having sex after the episode. Instead, this embellishment fit with the common stereotype of male flight attendants as gay and overly sexual, the same sort of stereotypes deployed in more heinous ways against William Simpson and Gaëtan Dugas in earlier years. Such social expectations allowed the *Daily News* to portray Slater as an in-flight "unstable diva" and also gave them license to place him in bed with his partner as the cops knocked on their door. Slater himself sees the seeds of prejudice running through the media accounts about his arrest: "Of course, they immediately put us where they always put the gays, in bed." Rochelle was in fact wearing just his underwear when Slater came back from the airport, and he proceeded to chastise Slater for giving up his job. As a devout Catholic, Rochelle then proceeded to the bedroom to pray. He reappeared, still half-dressed, when the police arrived at the door. Says Slater, "I just think it's funny—they're imagining this sex romp, and he's back there actually praying the Rosary. Like a little choirboy."[44]

These sexual elements make Slater's rise as a popular hero all the more remarkable. In the succeeding days, Slater became headline news, with the *Daily News* hailing him as an "icon for frustrated wage earners everywhere." Within hours, enterprising entrepreneurs were selling "Free Steven Slater" T-shirts, and numerous segments on talk radio and late-night television were devoted to the flight attendant's plight. The *Daily News* interviewed a local psychologist to dissect the public's fascination with Slater: "People are making a folk hero out of Slater, because we've all been there," he said. "Long hours, no raise or possibly a salary cut. Couple that with a difficult customer or client, and he did what we all wanted to do, he told the customer to shove it! And stormed off."[45] One *Daily News* headline included the quip "Forget Sully!," a reference to the heroic US Airways pilot, Chelsey Sullenberger, who landed a packed jet on the Hudson River eighteen months earlier and saved dozens of lives. That Slater attained such public esteem—albeit with a fair share of irony from the likes of the *Daily News*—was unprecedented for a gay male flight attendant. While press coverage found ways to emphasize his queerness (as a petulant diva, an overly dramatic escape artist, and a sex-starved gay man), people across the country identified with the intensity of his protest.

That Slater's status as a gay male flight attendant did not disqualify him from this public esteem says something about the state of queer equality in 2010. Even later revelations by the *Daily News* about Slater's HIV status (and the fact that he worked part of the flight with an open cut on his forehead) failed to arouse deep public disapproval. This embrace of Slater suggests that the LGBT community's political and economic struggles for benefits parity and other queer equality initiatives had deeper public traction. Not only were workers growing accustomed to queer men and women enjoying workplace equality, they also were developing a capacity for empathy, at least an ability to identify with the anger and frustration of a gay man fed up with the indignities of his neoliberal workplace.

NEOLIBERAL PUSHBACK

From the perspective of JetBlue executives, there was nothing heroic about Slater's actions on August 9. He had transgressed the norms of professional behavior, damaged property by deploying the slide, forced the plane to be removed from service for the remainder of the day, and endangered the airline's grounds workers, who could have been seriously injured by the deploying slide. Moreover, Slater's tirade exposed the frustrations of JetBlue flight attendants, whom the airline consistently promoted as a contented, hardworking group that did not need or want the protection of a labor union. The company stayed silent for several days after the incident as their legal teams worked through the implications of a potential criminal case against Slater. Finally, at the end of August, CEO David Barger broke his silence, saying Slater was "not a hero in my book" and adding that he was "disheartened to think that so many people would call him a hero." From Barger's perspective, Slater's outburst was an "egregious act" that had endangered fellow employees, delayed flights, and left the airline with a $25,000 cost of restoring the slide.[46] Slater was immediately placed on leave after the August 9 incident and resigned from the company soon after.

The ensuing legal proceedings against Slater involved charges of criminal mischief, reckless endangerment, and trespassing. More generally, however, the case fell along familiar fault lines in the neoliberal legal order: Slater claimed diminished culpability for his actions given the stressful workplace conditions that he had endured, while JetBlue stressed Slater's personal responsibility for his actions. The company was demanding reimbursement from Slater for at least $10,000 of the costs it had incurred thanks to the slide deployment, and Slater faced jail time for trespassing onto the JFK tarmac, even if he had traversed only fifteen or so feet on his way from the base of the slide to the staff door. In this phase, JetBlue gained the upper hand, as key aspects of Slater's defense began to unravel.

First, when the Queens police interviewed forty of the flight's passengers, no one corroborated Slater's claims of two altercations with the same female passenger, and the passenger was never located. In fact, none of those interviewed saw Slater get hit in the head at the beginning of the flight, nor did anyone hear the passenger use forceful language at the flight's conclusion. Further investigation and interviews with Slater revealed his previous history of alcohol abuse and drug addiction, and in time Slater also admitted that he had been drinking before the August 9 flight. Thus media accounts moved away from portraying Slater as a hero and toward dismissing him as an out-of-control drunk. By August 13, the *Daily News* included a new version of Slater as a man on a drinking binge: "After he slid out of the plane, Slater went home, where cops found him drunk and in bed with his boyfriend—his eyes bloodshot and reeking of booze, sources said. When cops asked him if he had been drinking, Slater said, 'Yes, while waiting for you to show up.' "[47]

After gradually revealing other details of Slater's personal struggles over the next several weeks—his HIV status, his long history battling addiction, and his role as primary caregiver to his dying mother—the media further challenged Slater's role as a heroic everyman. Instead, he increasingly came across as unstable and overwhelmed by conditions beyond JetBlue's control— a discredited man who had overreacted because of his own shortcomings. By the time Slater appeared before a judge in October 2010, his status had diminished considerably. Queens district attorney Richard Brown was still willing to reach a plea bargain with Slater, claiming that some of his culpability was mitigated by work-related stress: "Mr. Slater felt somewhat humiliated by what he perceived as degrading working conditions," Brown said.[48] But Slater agreed to plead guilty to some of the charges against him— attempted second-degree and fourth-degree criminal mischief—while also reimbursing JetBlue $10,000 for the costs tied to his outburst. "At the end of the day, I'm a grown adult and I must take responsibility for my actions," Slater commented.[49]

Rather than face jail time, Slater was offered an alternative sentencing program available to defendants with mental health issues. In advocating for sparing Slater prison time and offering him instead a yearlong probation with court-supervised alcohol treatment, his lawyer noted that his client had "snapped under the pressure of his work, the death of his father, his mother's illness and his own health problem," a reference to his HIV status.[50] With this deal in hand, Slater avoided prison, while JetBlue avoided perhaps the most unwelcome consequence of the episode: the airline was assured that Slater would not seek out incendiary publicity throughout 2011, since in doing so he would violate the conditions of his parole. Plus, as one now known to be personally compromised, Slater posed less of a risk to the JetBlue flight attendant corps' reputation. As Slater explained, after the incident "people wanted me to slide into everything. Slide into a bar! Slide into a club! Slide into a New Year's party at the stroke of midnight in a baby diaper!" But with the threat of jail time hanging over his head, "the closest Slater has allowed the media to get to the undocumented central image of his fame was to be filmed sitting at the bottom of a playground slide once, accepting a Resignation of the Year award from Bravo."[51] As such, Slater's fifteen minutes of fame were largely over, and JetBlue still benefited from its decidedly positive reputation as a hardworking and customer-friendly airline. The company had weathered a public relations disaster: instead of exposing the pressures placed on their workforce, the Slater saga become one of personal culpability fueled by alcohol addiction and emotional overreaction.

EQUALITY IN THE MIDST OF UPHEAVAL

Sadly, Steven Slater's descent from working-class hero to a compromised and culpable perpetrator of malfeasance replicates a similar nosedive in the livelihood of flight attendants since deregulation. The era since 1979 has been shaped most by corporate reorganizers like Frank Lorenzo and Carl Ichan. These men took the lessons of low-cost start-ups—especially their emphasis on lowering salaries while changing work rules to increase productivity—and applied them to the traditional network carriers that had thrived in the decades before deregulation. Lorenzo's small Texas Air was able to resuscitate Continental Airlines in the 1980s, primarily by using bankruptcy laws to void labor contracts and lay off thousands of employees, while nonetheless growing the airline into a legitimate hub-and-spoke carrier. The airline's return to profitability and its ascent from a small-scale airline centered in Texas to one with a thriving New York–area hub was attained primarily on the backs of pilots, flight attendants, and mechanics. However, Lorenzo's similar strategy at Eastern Air Lines as well as Ichan's attempts at TWA in the late 1980s and early 1990s were less successful. When unions at Eastern failed to buckle under pressure and went on strike in 1989, Lorenzo opted to liquidate the company after selling off its most lucrative routes to competitors. Ichan's era as head of TWA was equally contentious and ultimately unsuccessful. While the airline survived his tenure, which ended in 1995, it did so as a mere remnant of its previous self, with drastically scaled-back operations in both its international and domestic networks.

Male flight attendants were caught in these upheavals. Their introduction in the 1970s came at the peak of the career's splendor; the legacy carriers still enjoyed viability, even as labor unions succeeded in increasing wages and the courts diversified the workplace to include men and women, nonwhites and whites, and (subtly) gays and straights. The first generation of male flight attendants after the *Diaz* decision in 1971 thereby enjoyed legitimate prospects of making this job a lifelong career that offered them a solidly middle-class lifestyle. Even when the upheavals at Continental, Eastern, TWA, and Pan Am in the 1980s signaled harder times ahead—and lowered some flight attendants' wages or even forced them out of their jobs—other network carriers like United, American, Delta, and US Airways forged ahead with few alterations to their wage scales. Thus male flight attendants at these airlines witnessed the 1990s' embrace of gay customers as a uniquely promising moment when their job security and high wages could combine with an openness to queer equality. The hope existed, at least at the deep-pocketed network carriers, that corporate promises of nondiscrimination would take the shape of economic enhancements to their contracts, including domestic partner health and pension benefits and unlimited spousal travel privileges.

Yet the lessons of deregulation for many aviation executives included the belief that labor unions, progressive judges, and prolabor legislatures were the primary obstacles to attaining profitability in the new era of low-cost operations. These actors were inclined to credit Frank Lorenzo's shrewd use of bankruptcy, which defanged employee labor unions, as the key to Continental's ascendance, just as they were apt to blame Eastern's labor unions—not Lorenzo or his predecessors in the boardroom—for the airline's ultimate demise. This meant that men like Steven Slater who started flying in the early 1990s enjoyed greater visibility and respectability as gay men on the one hand, while also being more hamstrung than their male colleagues from the 1970s in their ability to demand new or improved benefits through collective bargaining.

That the airlines as a whole, and United Airlines in particular, fought to marginalize their flight attendant labor union, the courts, and the San Francisco Board of Supervisors by fighting the extension of domestic partner benefits from 1997 onwards should, therefore, come as no surprise. Benefits, in the postderegulation mind-set of neoliberalism, should be extended only when justified by a potential revenue stream—like appealing to prosperous LGBT customers—rather than dictated by civil rights principles or union perseverance. Hiring male flight attendants like Steven Slater had, quite fortuitously, become good business for the airlines, as their marketing departments discovered the gay dollar in the early 1990s. Yet the dictates of increasingly cutthroat pricing strategies across the industry also counseled caution when extending potentially costly benefits to such gay men and their less visible lesbian colleagues.

Sadly, then, both "September 11th" and "August 9th" embodied the sorts of fleeting victories (or outbursts, as it may be) that LGBT airline employees would have to content themselves with, especially since 9/11 further exposed the vulnerabilities of America's higher-cost network carriers. The court of appeals decision on the morning of September 11, 2001, rightly did not even warrant a headline compared to the tragedy of that day, which altered the airlines' financial calculus for the worse. The benefits that gay flight attendants were assured that morning—and that had already been attained with United's dramatic about-face two years earlier—became instantly less valuable. Spousal travel benefits are less usable when planes are filled to capacity with revenue-paying passengers; health insurance is still cherished, but inherently less valuable as co-pays go up and coverages go down; and pension benefits are increasingly worthless, as more airlines shed their plans in bankruptcy. Of course, the newly furloughed and unemployed enjoy even fewer, or none, of these benefits.

Meanwhile, Steven Slater's brief few days of fame as a nationwide working-class hero also dissipated nearly as quickly as the unrealized euphoria of the court of appeals decision on 9/11. His act of resistance on August 9, 2010, originally struck a deep chord with workers, who happily overlooked—maybe even embraced—his playful campiness and well-publicized alleged sexual exploits with his male partner. Yet by the time of his trial just two months later, Slater had effectively been discredited as an alcoholic with deep personal shortcomings that had motivated his eccentric outburst. While the district attorney did permit his stressful working conditions to count as grounds for a plea bargain, he also resorted to legal tools that branded Slater mentally ill in order to avoid jail time. In addition, after earning a total of $9,000 in 2009, Slater was forced to repay JetBlue $10,000 for his outburst in 2010. Thus both September 11th and August 9th highlight the profound limitations placed on queer equality that flight attendants have fought for in their careers. Ostensibly, they have won tremendous equality; yet their status as service employees in a neoliberal workforce has deprived them of the full economic fruits they have gained.

Conclusion

Plane Queer has analyzed the deep intersections of sexism and homophobia in the flight attendant profession. While these two modes of discrimination have always plagued this workplace, the male flight attendant's legacy illustrates that they have been particularly acute at select moments in U.S. airlines' nearly ninety-year history. The intensity of sexism and homophobia has corresponded not only with shifting cultural norms but also with evolving economic and legal factors. Sexism and homophobia, instead of operating as independent cultural variables or predictably moving along a consistent trajectory (from, say, being very intense in the beginning of the profession to declining consistently thereafter), have followed economic and legal cues to move erratically over time. Thus, while periods like the 1930s, 1970s, and 1990s stand out as less homophobic, the 1950s and 1980s were decidedly antagonistic for gay men working as flight attendants.

The 1930s saw the first expectations that flight attendants be young, middle-class white women rather than white men. When airlines like Pan Am and Eastern defended men as viable employees for these jobs, media outlets like the *Washington Post* belittled them as "male hostesses," and even the in-flight magazine at Pan Am portrayed the comic strip steward "Barney Bullarney" as a wimpish man who couldn't hold his own against male mechanics and managers. Thanks to the exclusion of African Americans and a growing expectation that only women would hold these jobs, the male flight attendant corps started to stand out as *plainly queer* even in the 1930s. Their status as white men doing servile "women's work" or "colored work" compromised them as failed men and suspected homosexuals.

Yet for the most part queer-baiting of the steward was largely still inchoate and somewhat tame in this decade, especially compared to the post–World War II moment. That this modicum of tolerance coincided with stewards' lower labor costs compared to stewardesses' was not accidental. Indeed, this cost differential provided executives like Eastern's Eddie Rickenbacker the incentive to withstand the belittling attacks on stewards and even to promote them as desirable public relations ambassadors. For Rickenbacker, the extra expenses tied to stewardesses' high turn-over—due mainly to sexist work rules that required women, but not men, to quit their jobs upon marrying—were prohibitive. While admitting that stewardesses were more appealing to the businessmen who composed Eastern's core customer base, he bluntly defended his use of stewards with a mixture of sexist and economic reasoning: "If passengers want to fool around with girls, let 'em do it at their expense, not mine."[1]

While Rickenbacker stressed the cost-savings potential of stewards in the 1930s, neither Eastern nor Pan Am dismissed stewards' significant marketing potential. Countering the sexism and homophobia of the day, both of these airlines crafted their stewards into stylish public relations tools for the so-called "gay" (sexually libertine, over-the-top, opulent) upper-class culture based in the country's largest cities. This was, after all, the same social milieu from which most airline customers at the time came. Along these lines, Pan Am developed promotional materials like "Rodney the Smiling Steward," while Eastern adorned its stewards in sharp outfits that highlighted their sexual appeal in an effort to court new customers—both female and male. As long as airline customers were drawn from very rich clientele accustomed to the gender fluidity of Prohibition-era nightlife, the steward could plausibly, though tenuously, lay claim to around one-third of America's flight attendant positions. This trend, however, would not last through the 1950s.

Media reports of the death of Eastern Air Lines steward William Simpson in 1954 betrayed strong social disapproval of the effeminate and sexually deviant steward that was typical of the cold war era. Reporters characterized Simpson's sexual tryst with a young man on a lovers' lane as morally alarming and proceeded to recraft Simpson into a perpetrator rather than a victim of a crime. Meanwhile, as media outlets published salacious speculation that William Simpson might have been the "queen" of the city's extensive "pervert colony," stewards on the job occasionally encountered similarly derisive abuse from customers or pilots. The men I interviewed recalled customers occasionally chiding them ("Where is your dress?") or pilots demeaning them in airport lounges between flights ("Fix me coffee, like the girls do.").

William Simpson's death—and the partial exoneration of his killers thanks to a "homosexual panic" legal defense—occurred during an economically lucrative moment for stewards. Many of the men who worked alongside Simpson and others at a wide variety of other U.S. carriers found the profession increasingly attractive for men and aspired to make it their lifelong career. The airlines, like other industries, prioritized male hiring in the wake of World War II, and all flight attendants were now better paid thanks to successful unionizing efforts. However, stewards, who could keep working even after marrying and without any age limit, accrued more seniority (and consequently even higher salaries and more extensive benefits) than their female peers. Also unlike stewardesses, many stewards received automatic promotions to the more senior position of purser, which most airlines reserved for men only.

While airline executives were complicit in crafting these male privileges, they were not fully content with the more costly status quo that resulted. Short-serving stewardesses were far cheaper, even if their turnover—as in the 1930s—added to the costs of training new hires. Stewardesses also were more convincing as public relations ambassadors by the 1950s, since they could better coddle tired businessmen and reassure traveling women that airplanes could be as comfortable as one's own living room. Thus airlines now had a strong financial incentive to capitalize on the sexism that kept stewardesses underpaid and the homophobia that made stewards stand out as failed men and deviant sexual predators (as in the publicity surrounding the Simpson case). Airlines now viewed feminizing the entire flight attendant corps as the most viable way to domesticate the airplane and neutralize the costs of collective bargaining and male privilege.

A decade later, when Celio Diaz won his court victory over Pan Am in 1971, one significant economic consequence stands out: as the courts, thanks to Title VII, forced all U.S. airlines to accept men as flight attendants, they also effectively transformed the job into a solidly middle-class profession. After *Diaz v. Pan Am*, airlines could no longer treat stewards and stewardesses differently. The marriage bans, weight rules, and uniform disparities that kept stewardesses economically (and sexually) vulnerable would no longer be tolerated.

By legal fiat, the courts had effectively ushered in a more queer workplace, as thousands of gay men quickly signed up for the job. But they also forged a less sexist workplace that both men and women—and gays and straights—found increasingly high paying and free of discrimination. In an industry still regulated by the government and bolstered by relatively strong unions, the workforce grew increasingly diverse and stable financially. The service sector profession of flight attendant had become a pathway into the middle class for men and women of all races. Meanwhile, gay men's growing presence in this career in turn increased the visibility of the entire gay community, just as Stonewall marked a new era of increased assertiveness in queer rights struggles. These men had effectively made the *plane queer*, and customers across the United States—even in culturally conservative realms like the South, Midwest, and Mountain West—could see this gay presence with their own eyes.

AIDS challenged this short-lived era of growing queer equality for flight attendants. Rather quickly, the compassionate responses of airlines like Air Canada and United Airlines to Gaëtan Dugas's and Gär Traynor's illnesses were replaced, at least at most U.S. carriers. After six months of flying with AIDS, Traynor was placed on permanent medical leave, as United executives responded to growing public consternation (albeit unfounded) about potential AIDS transmission in the workplace. People with AIDS serving food were deemed a contagion risk, and visible signs of sickness like KS lesions marked flight attendants like Gaëtan and Gär as gay, diseased, and a threat.

The subsequent demonization of Gaëtan Dugas shows the irrational potential of AIDS hysteria to fashion untruths into truth: that the epidemic was reducible to one man, a consequence of gays' moral failings, and an imminent health threat to anyone in the public sphere. Randy Shilts's choice to scapegoat Dugas had significant financial consequences; his book went from potential obscurity to the best-seller list. In turn, airlines like United made a similarly pessimistic financial calculation: that there was more money to be made pandering to AIDS hysteria by removing flight attendants with AIDS from active duty, even if it meant continuing to pay them their full salaries.

Yet Gär Traynor's legacy ultimately offered the airlines a more attractive financial calculus that took hold by 1988. Backed by his union and the National Labor Relations Board, Traynor became one of America's first PWAs to regain his right to work, at the early date of December 1984. When the U.S. Supreme Court in 1987 made a similar decision in *School Board of Nassau County v. Arline*, a wider swath of employees—indeed, any employees with HIV working for the federal government or a government contractor—won the same right. Since the airlines were included in this decision, they needed to undo their previous policies of exclusion. The subsequent return of flight attendants and customers with HIV/AIDS helped significantly reduce the stigma of AIDS by normalizing the presence of PWAs in the public sphere.

Events in 1993, especially American Airlines' infamous "pillows and blankets" episode and its rough treatment of passenger Timothy Holless, demonstrated that such inclusion was still haphazard and incomplete. Yet the fact that executives at American reacted to these incidents with genuine concern testifies to the changing calculus regarding homophobia and AIDS phobia that the corporate sphere now considered. As Bob Witeck, a gay marketing specialist hired that year by American, noted, the company regretted the so-called "business downside" of these incidents: threatened boycotts by LGBT groups, criticism broadcast in the wider mainstream media, and scrutiny from members of Congress for their insensitive, potentially illegal policies.[2]

The year 1993 consequently marks a key moment when the relationship between sexism, homophobia, economics, and the law changed considerably. Before this moment, key progress to combat discrimination came about via civil rights laws and legal decisions that assured women and men of equal treatment and minimized, at least in cases like *Diaz v. Pan Am*, the potency of "homosexual panic" legal defenses. These progressive legal actions were then complemented by important investments by labor unions, as in the Traynor case. Thus, up until the 1990s, the courts and organized labor played crucial roles in forging a more equitable workplace for women and men, as well as gays and straights. Starting in 1993, however, this New Deal–era coalition was supplanted. Conservatives' commitment to strict constitutionalism neutralized courts' willingness to interpret civil rights laws expansively, while neoliberal economic policies—including the deregulation of the airline industry—helped neutralize the power of labor unions.

Instead, customers gained in prominence over employees, and the locus of supporting campaigns against homophobic discrimination shifted from the courts and unions to corporate marketing departments. The airlines, with American in the lead, began committing themselves to a "gay-friendly" civil rights agenda that ultimately included nondiscrimination clauses for gays, lesbians, bisexuals, and even transgender employees. By 2001, the airlines had also extended benefits to domestic partners, including both health insurance and travel vouchers. While all of these benefits were geared toward workers, the airlines enacted these steps toward queer equality because of the alleged "business upside" that would result: they hoped to attract a larger share of the supposedly wealthy and travel-happy LGBT consumer base.[3] The courts and unions were largely bystanders in this process, even though the Federal Court of Appeals in San Francisco ultimately upheld the need to bestow some (but not all) of these benefits to comply with the City of San Francisco's domestic partner legislation.

Symbolically speaking, JetBlue flight attendant Steven Slater is the present-day successor to "Rodney the Smiling Steward," William Simpson, Celio Diaz, Gaëtan

Dugas, and Gär Traynor. He has personified for the media the male flight attendant of his day. In Slater's case, he enjoyed nearly total parity in terms of civil rights protections: neither his homosexuality nor his HIV-positive status was grounds for adverse treatment on the job. Yet his plight has become emblematic not just of flight attendants but of all sorts of service sector employees in the age of neoliberalism. Slater's dramatic departure from his job by emergency slide expresses many employees' deep-seated frustration with the customer-first policies of today's companies that expose them to workplace indignities. Slater also lacked union representation at JetBlue, another common characteristic of the neoliberal age. A strong labor union might well have provided him more support as his work conditions worsened and more legal counsel during the subsequent proceedings that threatened him with jail time and financial penalties.

Instead, Slater became a churlish media celebrity, embodying for some a justifiable degree of job-related frustration and for others a condemnable degree of personal culpability. Neither audience, however, made an issue of Slater's private life. The fact that he was arrested at his home, allegedly in bed with his boyfriend, made for a great story. But neither his homosexuality nor his HIV status was a basis for his legal problems or negative moral reputation, as the case had been years earlier with William Simpson or Gaëtan Dugas. Instead, for some observers, Slater's irresponsible actions were at fault, especially his choice to endanger others by deploying the emergency slide. For others, however, the neoliberal economic order was on trial: decades of cutting airline fares at the expense of workers' wages and on-the-job protections had devolved to a point at which Slater resorted to desperate, but understandable, measures to assert his dignity.

Slater's plight serves as a provocative end point for *Plane Queer* and its investigation of sexism, homophobia, and AIDS phobia in the flight attendant corps. Like the male flight attendants covered in previous chapters, Slater is just as dependent on economic and legal factors in his search for queer equality. But his status relies on a novel relationship of these various factors: gone is the most overt sexism and homophobia of previous decades, but gone as well are the prospects for flight attendants—whether male or female, straight or gay—to attain a middle-class standard of living. The state of the postderegulation flight attendant is, therefore, a cautionary one for queer equality: true parity cannot be attained through "gay-friendly" corporate policies alone but depends instead on a combination of civil rights efforts and economic and legal structures that protect the aspirations of service sector employees.

NOTES

INTRODUCTION

1. "Court Lets Stand Order That Airlines End Anti-Male Bias in Hiring Cabin Attendants," *Wall Street Journal*, November 10, 1971, 2.

2. I use the term *queer* in this book, even as I recognize it is fraught with potential for misunderstanding. The most helpful aspect of the term is that it implies a twofold transgression: one is "queer" when one transgresses established gender norms, as in the case of transgendered individuals or, more aptly for my project, when one assumes social roles that belong to the other gender. Additionally, *queer* refers to homosexuality. In the case of male flight attendants, this dual significance is especially helpful: all male flight attendants were gender queers in that they were performing a job that was *women's work*. Additionally, as we shall see, a disproportionately high percentage were also gay, making them queer in this sexual sense as well.

Since the 1990s, *queer* has had an additional meaning, especially for certain activists and academics writing in the tradition of "queer theory," as a challenge to the established socioeconomic order of neoliberal democratic capitalism and the hetero-normativity it is entwined with. Queer actions are meant to unsettle this status quo, and this is where certain scholars may begrudge my application of the term to male flight attendants. Many flight attendants have not been particularly politically engaged, much less revolutionary. Indeed, through the years these men and their female colleagues have been selected for their conservatism: white, male (at least the ones I focus on), normatively good-looking, and accommodating to the whims of customers and managers alike.

Moreover, the "queer equality" victories I profile in this book are decidedly progressive but by no means politically radical: the career's workplace has clearly improved through efforts to rid it of racism, sexism, homophobia, and AIDS phobia, but employees are still at the mercy of the neoliberal economic order. I take to heart the concerns of those who wince at my ascriptions of *queer* to these men and *queer equality* to their legacy. But I also suggest that such readers will find more to agree with at the ending of this book, where I call into question the genuineness of the equality that straight and queer flight attendants have supposedly attained since the 1990s.

For those seeking further clarity on the contours of queerness and queer theory in today's academia, I recommend Annamarie Jagose, *Queer Theory: An Introduction* (New York: NYU Press, 1996).

3. Kathleen Barry, *Femininity in Flight: A History of Flight Attendants* (Durham: Duke University Press, 2007), 11.

4. "Brief Amicus Curiae on Behalf of Air Transport Association of America and Its Member United States Carriers," November 21, 1969, 5, in *Diaz v. Pan Am* Federal District Court Documents, National Archives, Southeast Region, Atlanta, GA. The statistics assembled by the Air Transport Association showed that 22,306 of the 23,259 flight attendants hired by U.S. carriers were women. That left only 853 men on the job.

5. The term *gay-friendly* is not my own but rather comes directly from an American Airlines company spokesperson. Jeordan Legon, "Tension at American Air," *San Jose Mercury News*, January 30, 1997, 1C.

6. Randy Shilts, *And the Band Played On: Politics, People, and the AIDS Epidemic* (New York: St. Martin's Press, 1987).

7. Barry, *Femininity in Flight;* Georgia Panter Nielsen, *From Sky Girl to Flight Attendant: Women and the Making of a Union* (Ithaca, NY: ILR Press, 1982).

8. In addition to Barry and Nielsen, others who have covered stewardesses' contributions to the women's equality movement include Paula Kane, *Sex Objects in the Sky: A Personal Account of the Stewardess Rebellion* (Chicago: Follett, 1974); Cathleen Dooley, "Battle in the Sky: A Cultural and Legal History of Sex Discrimination in the United States Airline Industry, 1930–1980" (PhD diss., University of Arizona, 2001); and Carney Maley, "Flying the 'Unfriendly Skies': Flight Attendant Activism, 1964–1982" (PhD diss., Boston University, 2011).

9. *Homosexual panic* and its closely related spin-off *homosexual advance* pertain to cases where a man assaults or even kills a gay man. In the "homosexual panic" defense, lawyers argue that their client acted violently because he had deeply repressed homosexual desires of his own. "Homosexual advance" makes no such judgment on a man's own sexual orientation. Instead, it presumes that any man would react violently when hit on by another man. The following articles describe the terms and also offer critiques of these defenses: Gary David Comstock, "Dismantling the Homosexual Panic Defense," *Law and Sexuality Review* 2 (1992): 81–102; and Robert Mison, "Homophobia

in Manslaughter: The Homosexual Advance as Insufficient Provocation," *California Legal Review* 80, no. 1 (1992): 133–41.

10. The most thorough legal discussion of Ginsburg's work on behalf of male plaintiffs at the ACLU is Cary Franklin, "The Anti-Stereotyping Principle in Constitutional Sex Discrimination Law," *NYU Law Review* 85 (April 2010): 105–14.

11. Without reducing queer history in an overly facile manner, it does hold that most key works in the field are rooted in these respective sets of archives. Those who write of homosexuality's medical origins include Michel Foucault, *The History of Sexuality*, vol. 1, *An Introduction* (1976; repr., New York: Vintage Books, 1990); and Henry Minton, *Departing from Deviance: A History of Homosexual Rights and Emancipatory Science in America* (Chicago: University of Chicago Press, 2002).

Those who look at early homophile activism as the foundation for a modern gay identity include John D'Emilio, *Sexual Politics, Sexual Communities: The Making of a Homosexual Minority in the United States, 1940–1970*, 2nd ed. (Chicago: University of Chicago Press, 1998); Martin Meeker, *Contacts Desired: Gay and Lesbian Communications and Community, 1940s-1970s* (Chicago: University of Chicago Press, 2006); and Daniel Hurewitz, *Bohemian Los Angeles and the Making of Modern Politics* (Berkeley: University of California Press, 2007).

Margot Canaday has opened up a fresh vein of analysis, looking at how the federal government "help[ed] to produce the category of homosexuality through regulation." Margot Canaday, *The Straight State: Sexuality and Citizenship in Twentieth-Century America* (Princeton: Princeton University Press, 2009), 3.

Those who instead focus on nightlife as the point of origin for the LGBT community include George Chauncey, *Gay New York: Gender, Urban Culture, and the Making of the Gay Male World, 1890–1940* (New York: Basic Books, 1994); Elizabeth Lapovsky Kennedy and Madeline D. Davis, *Boots of Leather, Slippers of Gold: The History of a Lesbian Community* (New York: Routledge, 1993); and Nan Alamilla Boyd, *Wide Open Town: A History of Queer San Francisco to 1965* (Berkeley: University of California Press, 2003).

12. To date, only historian Allan Bérubé has a published account of a gay-identified career. Like my work, his essays, released by John D'Emilio and Estelle Freedman after his death, discuss the importance of gay-identified workplaces to the larger lesbian/gay/bisexual/transgender (LGBT) community and the larger civil rights movement in the United States. See especially Allan Bérubé, "No Race-Baiting, Red-Baiting, or Queer-Baiting! The Marine Cooks and Stewards Union from the Depression to the Cold War," in *My Desire for History: Essays in Gay, Community, and Labor History* (Chapel Hill: University of North Carolina Press, 2011). Bérubé's archives are held at the GLBT Historical Society, San Francisco.

13. Boyd's *Wide Open Town* is particularly effective at tracing this progression in the San Francisco bar scene.

14. Allan Bérubé, " 'Queer Work' and Labor History," in *My Desire for History*, 265.

15. Ibid.

16. Sharlene Martin, former American Airlines flight attendant and member of the New York City hiring team, phone interview by author, December 5, 2006.

17. Anonymous A, interview by author, December 31, 2004.

18. Douglas Crimp, "How to Have Promiscuity in an Epidemic," *October* 43 (Winter 1987): 237–71. Scholars who have analyzed Shilts's work include Priscilla Wald, *Contagious: Cultures, Carriers, and the Outbreak Narrative* (Durham: Duke University Press, 2008), 213–63, and Richard McKay, "Imagining 'Patient Zero': Sexuality, Blame, and the Origins of the North American AIDS Epidemic" (DPhil diss., Oxford University, 2011).

19. These scholars include Alexandra Chasin, *Selling Out: The Gay and Lesbian Movement Goes to Market* (New York: Palgrave Macmillan, 2000); Amy Gluckman, *Homo Economics: Capitalism, Community, and Lesbian and Gay Life* (New York: Routledge, 1997); Katherine Sender, *Business, Not Politics: The Making of the Gay Market* (New York: Columbia University Press, 2004); Lisa Duggan, *Twilight of Equality: Neoliberalism, Cultural Politics, and the Attack on Democracy* (Boston: Beacon Press, 2003); and Rosemary Hennessey, *Profit and Pleasure: Sexual Identities in Late Capitalism* (New York: Routledge, 2000).

1. THE PRE–WORLD WAR II "GAY" FLIGHT ATTENDANT

A version of this chapter also appeared as an article: Phil Tiemeyer, "Technology and Gay Identity: The Case of the Pre-World War II Male Flight Attendant," *History and Technology* 27 (June 2011): 155–81.

1. Kathleen Barry provides a succinct overview of Church's and Boeing's interactions. She also notes that the very first U.S. flight attendants began work in 1926, when Stout Air Services of Detroit hired male "aerial couriers." Barry, *Femininity in Flight*, 14–23. "Legacy carriers" are the airlines, like Pan Am, Eastern, TWA, United, and American, that incorporated in the late 1920s and would dominate U.S. air travel until after deregulation in 1979. In the 1920s, the four domestic-only carriers (excluding Pan Am, which flew only international routes) were known as the "Big Four." The term *"legacy carrier"* dates to the postderegulation period, when these same carriers, accompanied by other long-serving companies like Delta, Continental, Braniff, and Western, still dominated the industry before bankruptcy and consolidation began.

2. Ibid., 11.

3. Henry LaCossitt, "Adventures of the Air-Line Stewardesses," *Saturday Evening Post*, June 26, 1954, 96.

4. "Feminists Aroused by Airline Plan to Hire Male 'Hostesses,'" *Washington Post*, October 11, 1936, X8.

5. No airline actually hired both men and women as flight attendants before World War II. Instead, most airlines opted for a female-only corps, while a few chose only men.

The percentage of men in the career comes from "Contact," *New York Times*, July 11, 1937, XI, 6. This article places the number of male flight attendants in 1937 at 105 and the number of females at 286. In all likelihood, 1937 was a bit of a nadir for stewards, since their percentages were probably much higher at the very beginning of the decade and even at the end of the decade. In 1930, for example, Pan Am's male-only flight attendant corps was one of the largest contingents of flight attendants in the United States, outnumbering United's first eight stewardesses hired that same year. Then, by 1938, Eastern's expanding service on the East Coast, anchored by a male-only steward corps, would have increased the percentage of stewards vis-à-vis the figure from 1937. That said, I have no exact numbers for men and women working as flight attendants in any other year besides 1937.

6. Margery Davies, *Woman's Place Is at the Typewriter: Office Work and Office Workers, 1870–1930* (Philadelphia: Temple University Press, 1982), 179, 183.

7. Margot Canaday, who succinctly traces the ways that gay identity was still being solidified in the 1930s, adds that federal bureaucrats were also helping to shape the nation's sense of gay identity at the time. See Canaday, *Straight State*.

8. I do so because the line between discrimination based on sexual orientation and gender discrimination has always been porous. In reference to the Progressive era, Margot Canaday notes that the homosexual's "perversion was defined primarily by gender inversion . . . rather than by sexual behavior per se. . . . It was that perverts wanted to be penetrated *like women*, rather than the fact that they had sex with men, that made them perverse." Ibid., 11.

9. On the clientele of 1930s air travel, see David Courtwright, *Sky as Frontier: Adventure, Aviation, and Empire* (College Station: Texas A&M University Press, 2005), 91–109.

10. I have more to say on my use of *gay* later in this chapter. Note for now that the term was used in ways that were both sexual and more generic, illicit and more innocent, to describe the nightlife of the Prohibition era. For a fuller analysis of how the meanings of *gay* as both "homosexual" and more generally "enjoyable" at times converged in 1920s and 1930s urban life, see Chauncey, *Gay New York*.

11. A seminal work in the field of gender and technology is Ruth Schwartz Cowan, "The 'Industrial Revolution' in the Home: Household Technology and Social Change in the 20th Century," *Technology and Culture* 17 (1976): 1–24. The term *mutual shaping* is discussed in Nina Lerman, Ruth Oldenziel, and Arwen Mohun's "Introduction: Interrogating Boundaries," in *Gender and Technology: A Reader*, ed. Nina Lerman, Ruth Oldenziel, and Arwen Mohun (Baltimore: Johns Hopkins University Press, 2003), 2.

12. Lerman, Oldenziel, and Mohun, "Introduction," 4.

13. Courtwright discusses the growing feminization of the cabin in *Sky as Frontier*, 107.

14. "Pansy shows" were burlesque shows emphasizing male performers in drag, and they most often were hosted by a master of ceremonies, also a man in drag. For a

discussion of their immense popularity and rather rapid demise in New York City, see Chauncey, "'Pansies on Parade': Prohibition and the Spectacle of the Pansy," in *Gay New York*, 301–30.

15. Ibid., 328.

16. Chauncey's work is also the most informative in describing fairies' appropriation of the term. See especially his introduction to *Gay New York*.

17. Thomas Waugh, *Out/Lines: Underground Gay Graphics from before Stonewall* (Vancouver, BC: Arsenal Pulp, 2005), 41.

18. Carl Solberg, *Conquest of the Skies: A History of Commercial Aviation in America* (Boston: Little, Brown, 1979), 111.

19. Judy Klemesrud, "Stewardess, 1930-Style," *New York Times*, May 15, 1970, 41.

20. Linn, "He Earned His Wings as First of His Kind," *Miami Herald*, June 10, 1980, 4B.

21. Albert Rogell, dir., *Air Hostess* (Los Angeles: Columbia Pictures, 1933). See imdb.com.

22. "Rodney," *Pan American Airways Magazine*, March 1933, 3.

23. Tom McCarthy, "Tom McCarthy Interviews a Flight Steward," *Washington Post*, March 2, 1938, X9.

24. Larry Tye, *Rising from the Rails: Pullman Porters and the Making of the Black Middle Class* (New York: Henry Holt, 2004), 25.

25. Kathleen Barry's research leads me to note an important exception: one small northeastern airline hired African American stewards in 1930. After that year, however, the airline discontinued service, and the only African American flight attendants until 1958 were forced out of the job. See Kathleen Barry, "Femininity in Flight: Flight Attendants, Glamour, and Pink-Collar Activism in the Twentieth-Century United States" (PhD diss., New York University, 2002), 44.

26. Marcia Winn, "Cupid Is Great Plane Hazard for Stewardess," *Chicago Daily Tribune*, November 2, 1939, 22.

27. "Actress Tells Way to Date Up Airline Hostess," *Los Angeles Times*, April 9, 1936, 10.

28. The various features of the Pan Am Clipper are profiled in "Regular Air Route to the Orient Opens," *Washington Post*, November 17, 1935, B6.

29. Helen Stansbury, director of United's women's traffic division, 1937, quoted in Courtwright, *Sky as Frontier*, 107.

30. By the end of the 1930s, women had gone from a very modest percentage of passengers to about 25 percent of the flying public. Clearly, however, they were still significantly outnumbered. Solberg, *Conquest of the Skies*, 275.

31. McCarthy, "Tom McCarthy Interviews," X9.

32. In the early 1930s, Eastern hired a handful of stewardesses to serve their routes. Thanks, however, to a legal and financial scandal in 1934, the airline was forced to

reincorporate and laid off all of its flight attendants. For the few years before the debut of their stewards in late 1936, Eastern actually had no flight attendants, assigning the task of serving coffee or boxed lunches to the copilot. This was not an unusual practice at smaller, cash-strapped airlines. See Robert Serling, *From the Captain to the Colonel: An Informal History of Eastern Airlines* (New York: Dial Press, 1980).

33. "Hostesses Soon to Be Replaced by Men on Eastern Air Lines," *Washington Post*, October 18, 1936, M6.

34. "Feminists Aroused."

35. "Mrs. Roosevelt Praises Flight-Steward Service," *Great Silver Fleet News*, April 1937, 4.

36. Serling, *From the Captain*, 122.

37. Ibid., 170.

38. The guaranteed monthly minimum salaries for flight personnel respectively in 1933 were $250 for pilots, $150 for copilots, $100 for stewards and stewardesses, and $80 for field mechanics or radio men. Each type of personnel could expect to double this wage, since they were also paid by the hour on top of this minimum. "Pilots Forecast Dispute on Pay in Airline Code," *Washington Post*, August 12, 1933, 3.

39. "Hostesses Soon to Be Replaced."

40. Serling, *From the Captain*, 122.

41. "Eastern Carries the Male!," *Great Silver Fleet News*, Spring 1941, 42. Married women actually encountered increased work restrictions during the Depression years. Historian Barbara Melosh writes about changing laws for state and federal government employees: "A number of state legislatures, and then the federal government, passed the so-called married person's clause, mandating that the civil service could employ only one member of a family; many women were dismissed under the law." See Barbara Melosh, *Engendering Culture: Manhood and Womanhood in New Deal Public Art and Theater* (Washington, DC: Smithsonian Institution Press, 1991), 1.

42. Miami-based National Airlines would eventually become Eastern's strongest competition on this route, but as of 1938, it still held a Florida-only route system. By the 1950s, National's in-flight service and slick ad campaigns made it more formidable as a competitor. The CAB also awarded Delta the New York-Miami route in the early 1950s.

43. Robert Daley, *An American Saga: Juan Trippe and His Pan Am Empire* (New York: Random House, 1980).

44. A thorough discussion of streamlined design and its importance to Depression-era culture is found in Jeffrey Meikle, *Twentieth Century Limited: Industrial Design in America, 1925–1939* (Philadelphia: Temple University Press, 1979).

45. "Gilbert Rohde Revolutionizes Future Men's Clothes and Revives Long Beards," *Vogue*, February 1, 1939, 138.

46. "Fashion Preview," *Great Silver Fleet News*, November 1936, 8.

47. "What We've Heard," *Great Silver Fleet News*, December 1936, 6.

48. On the history of fashion shows, see Amanda Fortini, "How the Runway Took Off," *Slate*, February 8, 2006, www.slate.com.

49. Chauncey, *Gay New York*, 349.

50. "EAL Invades Gotham P.M. Life," *Great Silver Fleet News*, June 1937, 3.

51. "Flight-Steward Reveals Drama," *Great Silver Fleet News*, April 1937, 10.

52. The term *screwball* has gained most acceptance in the film genre, where it describes antiheroes who embody irrational, often loony behavior but nonetheless are the film's protagonists. Media critic Wes Gehring notes, however, that film screwballs have their antecedents in newspaper comic strips, among other comedy genres. Wes Gehring, *Screwball Comedy: A Genre of Madcap Romance* (Westport, CT: Greenwood Press, 1986), especially 20–21.

53. Bugs Bunny did not debut under that name until 1940, but a rabbit character in the film *Hare Hunt* from April 1938 shared Bugs's trademark Brooklyn accent and witty sense of humor. Meanwhile, Elmer Fudd also did not crystallize as a character until around 1940, but his predecessor, Egghead, co-starred with Daffy Duck in the 1938 film *Daffy Duck and Egghead*. Both films were Warner Brothers productions under the direction of Tex Avery. See imdb.com.

54. For greater detail on gender-based assumptions tied to war and the roles gay men and women played in World War II, see Allen Bérubé, *Coming Out under Fire: The History of Gay Men and Women in World War Two* (New York: Free Press, 1990).

55. "Eastern Carries the Male!," 41.

56. Genevieve Baker, "The Service That Leaves a Smile: Meet PAA's First Flight Stewardess," *New Horizons*, October–December 1944, 24.

2. THE COLD WAR GENDER ORDER

1. These statistics come from Courtwright, *Sky as Frontier*, 127–28.

2. For an account of benefits bestowed on veterans after World War II, see Glenn Altschuler and Stuart Blumin, *The GI Bill: The New Deal for Veterans* (New York: Oxford University Press, 2009).

3. Elaine Tyler May, *Homeward Bound: American Families in the Cold War Era* (New York: Basic Books, 1988).

4. If we consider just two recent media productions regarding Pan American Airways, we find that the existence of male stewards has been completely erased from them. The 2002 film *Catch Me if You Can*, depicting con artist Frank Abagnale impersonating a Pan Am pilot in the 1960s, suggests the airline had an all-female flight attendant corps at the time. More egregious is ABC television's 2011 series *Pan Am*, which chronicles the lives of Pan Am stewardesses in the early 1960s. The show portrays all-female crews even on inaugural 707 flights to European capitals. In reality, these lucrative spots were assigned by seniority and would have included at least two, if not three, long-serving stewards as part of the crew.

5. "Hearings before the Select Subcommittee on Labor of the Committee on Education and Labor," House of Representatives, 89th Cong., 1st sess., September 2, 1965, 484. Only a few airlines, including Eastern and Pan Am, opted out of this trend to force retirements at a certain age. Pan Am also allowed married stewardesses to continue working, though only until they became pregnant.

6. D'Emilio, *Sexual Politics, Sexual Communities: The Making of a Homosexual Minority in the United States, 1940–1970*, 2nd ed. (Chicago: University of Chicago Press, 1998), 24.

7. Eddie Rickenbacker, "Remarks Made by Captain Eddie V. Rickenbacker at Staff Meeting, September 14, 1945," in EAL Staff Meeting Talks, vol. 1, in Record Group 101, Accession 96–66, Box 3, Eddie Rickenbacker Archive, Auburn University Special Collections, Auburn, AL.

8. "'We Can Hire 1000 Veterans,'" *Great Silver Fleet News*, May 1945, 6.

9. Eddie Rickenbacker, "Remarks made by Captain Eddie V. Rickenbacker at Staff Meeting, March 3–7, 1947," in EAL Staff Meeting Talks, vol. 1, in Record Group 101, Accession 96–66, Box 3, Eddie Rickenbacker Archive, Auburn University Special Collections, Auburn, AL.

10. Serling, *From the Captain*, 239.

11. Photo "Twenty-Fourth Class of Flight Attendants," *Great Silver Fleet News*, January-February 1946, 34. An article from a 1946 issue of the same magazine noted that Eastern at the time employed "240 Flight Attendants of whom 60 were Stewards." But it also mentioned that the number of attendants would expand to 600 in the coming months, with no breakdown of this future hiring based on sex. John Stickney, "It's the Little Things," *Great Silver Fleet News*, May-June 1946, 11.

12. These statistics cover only the New York-based Atlantic Division, where there were sixty-one stewards and fifty-four stewardesses working on January 1, 1947. The Latin American Division based in Miami, as well as the divisions headquartered in San Francisco and Seattle, hired and trained flight attendants independently. "Flight Service Personnel, January 1, 1947" and "Flight Service Personnel, November 1, 1946, Training Group," Box 291, folder 4, Pan American Archives, Otto Richter Library, University of Miami, Miami, FL.

13. "Stewards in Spotlight at Miami Graduation," *Clipper: Latin American Division*, February 1951, 1.

14. Koren ultimately enjoyed a forty-year career as a flight attendant with Pan Am. His memoirs offer a fascinating and significant firsthand history from a male flight attendant whose career spanned the entire cold war. Jay Koren, *The Company We Kept* (McLean, VA: Paladwr Press, 2000), 32.

15. Detailing the purser's paperwork on Pan Am circa 1947, the *Saturday Evening Post* noted, "There were quarantine and immigration forms, baggage declarations and landing cards, the mail book and valuable-receipt form (pursers are responsible for

the mail and air express courier), the ship's manifest, reservation cards, the weight-and-balance sheet and several special forms for the [host country's] authorities." Richard Thruelsen, "Women at Work: Airline Hostess," *Saturday Evening Post*, May 24, 1947, 70.

16. Koren, *Company We Kept*, 39.

17. While other airlines hiring men are mentioned elsewhere in this chapter, I should add that both Piedmont and Allegheny Airlines also were hiring men during these years. Their hiring practices also changed by the late 1950s.

18. Stickney, "It's the Little Things," 12.

19. Ibid., 11.

20. Ibid., 10.

21. For details on early unionizing efforts among flight attendants, see Barry, *Femininity in Flight*, 63–74. The AFL and the CIO would merge in 1955 to form the AFL-CIO.

22. M. L. Edwards to All Stores Personnel, October 28, 1946, Box 97, Folder "August- December 1946," TWU Archives, New York University, New York.

23. TWU Air Transport Division, "Survey Report to Flight Service Personnel," issued January 24, 1961, Box 56 (unprocessed), folder "Pan Am Contracts," TWU Archives, New York University, New York, NY. This leaflet provides the wage scales for the various airlines in 1961. At every airline hiring pursers, the pursers with five years' experience were paid 60 percent more than stewards or stewardesses with no experience. Pan Am's pay was the highest in the industry, with veteran pursers earning $640.53 per month for jet plane service, while their entry-level stewardesses earned $379.48 on jet service.

24. May, *Homeward Bound*, 10.

25. For an analysis of the military's role as a catalyst of pre-World War II aircraft manufacturing, see Jacob Vander Meulen, *The Politics of Aircraft: Building an American Military Industry* (Lawrence: University Press of Kansas, 1991).

26. Air Force Historical Research Agency, *Army Air Forces Statistical Digest: World War II* (Washington, DC: Office of Statistical Control, Headquarters, Army Air Forces, 1945), 127, table 79, www.usaaf.net/digest/index.htm. .

27. These C-47s, the same plane as the DC-3 civilian aircraft, could be purchased from the military for $25,000, or just $4,000 a year. Solberg, *Conquest of the Skies*, 323, 328.

28. Quoted in Justine Harari, "Madeline Cuniff: Pioneer of Trans-Atlantic Routes," *Flight Attendant Magazine*, September/October 1986, 22. Pan Am had introduced a "tourist class" even on its lucrative trans-Atlantic routes by 1952. Yet while these tickets were dramatically cheaper than the full-fare rate, their price was maintained at a high level (prohibitively high for most Americans), thanks to an international price-setting scheme under the aegis of the International Air Transport Association.

29. Two-thirds of the five million migrants from Puerto Rico during the 1940s and 1950s—flying Pan Am, Eastern, Trans-Caribbean Airlines, and a sundry of charter carriers—came to the mainland United States by air. They usually arrived in the early morning hours, having flown on low-fare overnight coach tickets from San Juan to New York. See Jorge Duany, *The Puerto Rican Nation on the Move: Identities on the Island and in the United States* (Chapel Hill: University of North Carolina Press, 2002), and Courtwright, *Sky as Frontier*, 130.

30. Boeing's first 707 prototype was so dependent on the military version of the plane, the KC-135, that it didn't even have windows in the fuselage. This was another visual image that provoked consternation in some first-time travelers uneasy about the militaristic overtones of air travel. Ann R. Markusen and Joel Yudken, *Dismantling the Cold War Economy* (New York: Basic Books, 1992), 57.

31. Female customers composed 25 percent of air passengers before the war and just 15 percent during the war itself. Solberg, *Conquest of the Skies*, 275. This increased to 33 percent in the 1950s. Courtwright, *Sky as Frontier*, 128. This significant rise in the percentage of women travelers coincided with the substantial increase in the sheer number of airline passengers discussed earlier, meaning that the airlines carried roughly 1.25 million women in 1941 and about 5 million in 1958.

32. "Minutes of Staff Meeting," March 3–7, 1947, EAL Staff Meetings, vol. 1, Box 3, Record Group 101, Accession 96–66, Eddie Rickenbacker Papers, Auburn University Archives, Auburn, AL.

33. J. A. York, Assistant to Vice President—Personnel, Delta Airlines, to Equal Employment Opportunity Commission, May 24, 1966, Box 1, folder 1, *Roderick McNeil v. Pan American World Airways* case file (CS-12975–66), New York State Division of Human Rights collection, New York State Archives, Albany, NY.

34. The policy was eventually overturned by the New York State Commission on Human Rights in the case of *Pearl Nelson v. Trans World Airlines* (Q-CS-16–66), filed in 1966.

35. Braniff Airways, "How You Can Be a Braniff Airline Hostess," n.d., Box 26, Folder 2, Braniff Airways Collection, University of Texas at Dallas Archives, Richardson, TX.

36. Stickney, "It's the Little Things," 11.

37. By 1965, 10 percent of personal income in the United States and 20 percent of manufacturing output was directly tied to the cold war economy. Approximately twelve to fourteen million Americans gained their livelihood from defense-related industries. Markusen and Yudken, *Dismantling the Cold War Economy*, 44.

3. "HOMOSEXUAL PANIC" AND THE STEWARD'S DEMISE

1. I do not intend to suggest that Kinsey was America's foremost advocate for gay rights. This distinction fell to the gay rights (homophile) organizations that first

organized in the 1950s, including the Mattachine Society and the Daughters of Bilitis. Kinsey, in fact, shied away from being a more outspoken supporter. Certainly, his surveillance by the FBI and close scrutiny from other right-wing groups made him reticent to support the homophiles publicly. See Minton, *Departing from Deviance*.

2. Alfred Kinsey et al., *Sexual Behavior in the Human Male* (Philadelphia: W. B. Saunders, 1948), 650–51.

3. Ibid., 392.

4. Ibid., 639.

5. My interviews involved seven former stewards who had worked for either Eastern or Pan Am. The earliest start date was 1948, the latest 1955. These interviews were conducted either by phone or in person between 2004 and 2008. These men were located via word of mouth and with the assistance of online communities of former flight attendants. We have mutually agreed to keep their identities anonymous.

6. John D'Emilio offers a thorough analysis of the many obstacles facing gays and lesbians in the postwar era in his book *Sexual Politics, Sexual Communities*.

7. Fred Fejes covers this general trend, while also focusing more specifically on Miami's antigay campaign. As such, his work has been of great assistance to my own. Fred Fejes, "Murder, Perversion, and Moral Panic: The 1954 Media Campaign against Miami's Homosexuals and the Discourse of Civic Betterment," *Journal of the History of Sexuality* 9, no. 3 (2000): 305–47.

8. Canaday traces this progression from World War I through World War II in *The Straight State*. See also Bérubé, *Coming Out under Fire*.

9. Presumably, Eisenhower's motives were consistent with those documented in a Senate report from 1950, which articulated the risks to national security and the illness paradigm of homosexuality as motives to exclude homosexuals from government work: U.S. Senate, Committee on Expenditures in the Executive Departments, Subcommittee on Investigations. *Employment of Homosexuals and Other Sex Perverts in Government*, 81st Cong., 2nd sess., Doc. No. 241, December 15, 1950. The Truman administration deferred implementing these recommendations, leaving the task to Eisenhower.

10. The term *Homosexual panic* and its closely related spin-off *homosexual advance*, pertain to cases like the Simpson homicide, where a man assaulted or even killed a gay man. The aggressor could invoke either of these defenses, claiming that he had experienced a form of temporary insanity that arose from being hit on by a gay man. In the "homosexual panic" defense, lawyers would argue that their client had acted violently because he had deeply repressed homosexual desires of his own. "Homosexual advance" makes no such judgment on a man's own sexual orientation. Instead, it presumes that any man—whether a latent homosexual or not—would react violently when hit on by another man. Comstock's "Dismantling the Homosexual Panic Defense" and Mison's "Homophobia in Manslaughter" describe the terms and also offer critiques of these defenses as illogical and homophobic.

11. Anonymous A, interview by author, December 31, 2004.

12. Anonymous B, interview by author, August 8, 2008.

13. Ibid.

14. Anonymous C, interview by author, August 18, 2005.

15. Ibid.

16. Anonymous A, interview.

17. Anonymous B, interview.

18. Anonymous D, interview by author, March 15, 2006.

19. Orason recounts many of his own personal memories from the point of view of a fictional character, Rob Orlon. Roy Orason, *Plight of a Flight Attendant* (Citrus Heights, CA: Sierra, 1994).

20. Ibid., 141.

21. Anonymous A, interview.

22. At least one applicant acknowledged that he had avoided the military by admitting to recruiters his homosexuality. While this information would have been accessible in public records, the airlines he flew with never sought out this information.

23. Anonymous B, interview.

24. Anonymous A, interview.

25. Anonymous E, interview by author, August 5, 2008.

26. Anonymous A, interview.

27. All three individuals who shared this information with me did not reveal particular details of the behavior that had attracted such attention from the company. Instead, one noted, "Beirut Base got pretty scandalous. There were several gays out there and [the company] wanted to tone that down. In fact they refused to transfer any males there for a while . . . because it got to be too much." Anonymous A, interview.

28. Anonymous D, interview.

29. Anonymous F, interview by author, October 10, 2005.

30. Anonymous A, interview.

31. It may be that Delta's 1966 letter includes some moments of applying later rationales onto a previous historical moment. However, none of the reasons provided in the letter sound strikingly out of sync with prevalent notions of masculinity in the late 1940s. Letter from J. A. York, Assistant to Vice President—Personnel, Delta Airlines, to Equal Employment Opportunity Commission, May 24, 1966, Box 1, folder 1, *Roderick McNeil v. Pan American World Airways* case file (CS-12975–66), New York State Division of Human Rights collection, New York State Archives, Albany, NY.

32. Ibid.

33. The other admission was from Trans Caribbean Airways; it and numerous denials from other airlines can be found in the New York State Commission for Human Rights case file of *McNeil v. Pan Am*.

34. For an account of the extreme social controls placed on male sexuality, whether heterosexual or homosexual, during this time period, see Estelle Freedman, "'Uncontrolled Desires': The Response to the Sexual Psychopath, 1920–1960," *Journal of American History* 74, no. 1 (1987): 83–106.

35. Richard Rundell, "Youths Guilty of Manslaughter in Fatal Shooting of Steward," *Miami Herald*, November 8, 1954, B1. The airline, when making its ad buys for the week, would have been aware that the Simpson trial was concluding and would receive either front-page headlines or coverage on the first page of the local news section. For two very fine published accounts of the murder and its significance, see James Sears, "Purging Perverts in Paradise," in *Lonely Hunters: An Oral History of Lesbian and Gay Southern Life, 1946–1968* (Boulder, CO: Westview Press, 1997), 12–47, and Fejes, "Murder, Perversion."

36. The most thorough description of the murder events appears in Milt Sosin "Confession Is Given in Air Steward's Death," *Miami Daily News*, August 8, 1954, 1A. I have added certain details from the original police report: North Miami Police Department, Case #54–13737, Concerning the Homicide of William T. Simpson, North Miami, FL.

37. Sanford Schnier, "EAL Steward Found Shot Dead," *Miami Daily News (Home Edition)*, August 3, 1954, 1A.

38. Milt Sosin and Sanford Schnier, "'Lovers' Lane' Killer Hunted," *Miami Daily News*, August 3, 1954, 1A.

39. Bryan Donaldson, "Man Seen Jumping into Car before Air Steward's Slaying," *Miami Herald*, August 4, 1954, 1A. Though his name is part of the public record, I have chosen not to reveal the identity of Simpson's friend. Now deceased, the man was an EAL steward known to be gay by his fellow employees, who served another thirty years as a flight attendant. He was called to testify in the Simpson trial, presumably because he was a good friend of Simpson and among the last people to see him alive. Other flight attendants suggest that this steward was nearly fired as a result of the Simpson murder and had to fight through the union to maintain his job, though I have been unable to substantiate this claim.

40. North Miami Police Department, Case #54–13737, Concerning the Homicide of William T. Simpson, North Miami, FL.

41. Anonymous F, interview.

42. Milt Sosin, "Pervert Colony Uncovered in Simpson Slaying Probe," *Miami Daily News*, August 9, 1954, 1A.

43. Ibid., 8A.

44. The history of the Mattachine Society and other early gay rights (homophile) groups and publications can be found in John D'Emilio's *Sexual Politics, Sexual Communities*.

45. Jim Kepner, "Miami Hurricane," in Jim Kepner, *Rough News—Daring Views: 1950s' Pioneer Gay Press Journalism* (New York: Haworth Press, 1998), 49–55, originally

published in *ONE Magazine*, November 1954. Further details of the campaign are found in both Sears, "Purging Perverts," and Fejes, "Murder, Perversion."

46. Kepner, "Miami Hurricane," 55.

47. Quoted in ibid., 51.

48. Anonymous F, interview.

49. Eastern stewards were very active in the union. In fact, steward Rowland Quinn was elected president of the Air Line Stewards and Stewardesses Association in 1953, and he would serve in that capacity into the 1960s. Nielsen, *From Sky Girl to Flight Attendant*, 60.

50. Pedro Muniz, *My Book: Tales of Travels and Tribulations* (Santo Domingo: Editora Corripio, 1987), 77.

51. Anonymous F, interview.

52. Anonymous C, interview.

53. The other way of justifying a manslaughter verdict in the case was to find that the slaying was accidental (or provoked) *and* that it did not take place during the commission of a robbery. The jury, however, clearly found that the two youths had in fact been engaged in robbery, since they convicted Killen, who was uninvolved in the shooting itself, along with Lawrence.

54. J. L. (Dixie) Smith, "Jurors Weighing Verdict in Slaying of Air Steward," *Miami Herald*, November 7, 1954, 2A.

55. J. L. (Dixie) Smith, "Confessions Put in Record at 2 Youths' Slaying Trial," *Miami Herald*, November 6, 1954, 1B.

56. Simpson's case is quite early in the development of "homosexual panic" as a legal defense. Scholars have noted its rise as an explicit tool in U.S. jurisprudence only during and after the late 1960s. See Scott McCoy, "The Homosexual-Advance Defense and Hate Crimes Statutes: Their Interaction and Conflict," *Cardozo Law Review* 22 (2000–2001): 639. If the case had been tried in later years, lawyers would more likely have employed a "homosexual advance" defense, though "homosexual panic" was also a possibility. After all, Lawrence exhibited some signs of repressed homosexuality, since he allowed Simpson—and others before him—to perform oral sex on him before allegedly getting spooked by Simpson's advances.

57. Richard Rundell, "Youths Guilty of Manslaughter In Fatal Shooting of Steward," *Miami Herald*, November 8, 1954, 1B.

58. "Youths Get 20 Years in Slaying," *Miami Herald*, November 11, 1954, 1D.

59. Anonymous B, interview: "Some of the wives of the corporate officers made some decisions for their husbands . . . [and] they thought the stewards were gay. You know, there were too many gays and they should not be hired. That was the rumor, the wives who caught on . . ."

4. FLIGHT ATTENDANTS AND QUEER CIVIL RIGHTS

1. "Brief Amicus Curiae on Behalf of Air Transport Association of America and its Member United States Carriers," November 21, 1969, 5, in *Diaz v. Pan Am* District Court Documents, National Archives Southeast Region, Atlanta, GA. The statistics assembled by the Air Transport Association showed that 22,306 of the 23,259 flight attendants hired by U.S. carriers were women. That left only 853 men on the job.

2. The website of the Dallas Historical Society features a solid overview of Braniff's promotional campaigns from the 1960s and '70s, including the "air strip" debut in 1965. "Color in the Sky: 1965—The Air Strip," 2002, www.dallashistory.org/history/dallas/1965_uniforms.htm. The television commercial has been posted on YouTube: "The Air Strip," uploaded July 19, 2006, www.youtube.com/watch?v=MKiVCkEodDw.

3. Trudy Baker and Rachel Jones, *Coffee, Tea or Me? The Uninhibited Memoirs of Two Airline Stewardesses* (New York: Bartholomew House, 1967). The ghostwriter was Donald Bain.

4. The film was rereleased in 2009 in a fortieth anniversary edition. See imdb.com.

5. "TWA Will Hire a Negro Hostess," *New York Times*, February 10, 1958, 44.

6. Christina Kirk, "Negro Girls Win Their Wings," *Sunday News*, September 5, 1965, II: 8.

7. Historian Martin Duberman's oral history-based account of Stonewall is an excellent resource for understanding the event's significance to gay rights. Martin Duberman, *Stonewall* (New York: Penguin Press, 1994). That said, earlier milestones in gay rights history should not be overlooked. A small but significant activist movement scored significant victories as early as the 1950s. By 1966, gays and lesbians were marching every year at the Liberty Bell in an effort to fight homophobia, and a transgender riot occurred at Compton's Cafeteria in San Francisco in the same year. See the documentary film, *Screaming Queens: The Riot at Compton's Cafeteria*, directed by Victor Silverman and Susan Stryker, written by Susan Stryker and Victor Silverman, produced in association with ITVS and KQED, 2005.

8. Male cases that passed through the EEOC and went to the federal courts included *Diaz v. Pan Am* (1969), *Schrichte v. Eastern* (1970), and *Hailes v. Pan Am* (1968). In the *Hailes* case, court papers were filed, but the plaintiff withdrew the case before a hearing was made. *Schrichte* would have been ruled upon but was preempted by the *Diaz* decision, which moved through the courts more quickly.

9. Southwest Airlines was a peculiar exception, as it refused to hire male flight attendants until forced by a federal court in 1981. The airline claimed that its branding as the "love airline" required a young, attractive female-only cadre of flight attendants, despite the precedent in *Diaz* that ostensibly forbade such reasoning. See *Wilson v. Southwest Airlines Co.*, 517 F. Supp. 292 (N.D. Tex. 1981). As a consequence of the Wilson case, Southwest established a fund of $1 million for back pay to men previously denied

employment. This fact is noted in a subsequent court case, *Wilson v. Southwest Airlines Co.*, 880 F.2d 807 (5th Cir. 1989).

10. "Court Lets Stand Order That Airlines End Anti-Male Bias in Hiring Cabin Attendants," *Wall Street Journal*, November 10, 1971, 2.

11. Ruth Rosen, *The World Split Open: How the Modern Women's Movement Changed America* (New York: Penguin Press, 2000), 72.

12. 88th Cong., 2nd sess., *Cong. Rec.* 110 (February 8, 1964): 2577.

13. Indeed, Congressman Smith did not come upon the idea of a sex provision in Title VII on his own. The National Women's Party had lobbied him to include it, thereby providing a feminist origin for the provision beyond Smith's own more petulant motives. See Jo Freeman, "How 'Sex' Got into Title VII: Persistent Opportunism as a Maker of Public Policy," in *We Will Be Heard: Women's Struggles for Political Power in the United States* (Lanham, MD: Rowman and Littlefield, 2008), 171–90.

14. Carl Brauer, "Women Activists, Southern Conservatives, and the Prohibition of Sex Discrimination in Title VII of the 1964 Civil Rights Act," *Journal of Southern History* 49, no. 1 (1983): 51.

15. Civil Rights Act of 1964, Title VII, Section 703(e). See EEOC, "Laws and Guidance," www.eeoc.gov/policy/vii.html.

16. 88th Cong., 2nd sess., *Cong. Rec.* 110 (February 10, 1964): 2718.

17. More specific discussions of male nurses and their plight in future court cases based on Title VII and the BFOQ are found in Jillian Berman, "Defining the 'Essence of the Business': An Analysis of Title VII's Privacy BFOQ after *Johnson Controls*," *University of Chicago Law Review* 67 (Summer 2000): 749–76; and Sharon McGowan, "The Bona Fide Body: Title VII's Last Bastion of Intentional Sex Discrimination," *Columbia Journal of Gender and Law* 12 (2003): 77–80.

18. Elizabeth Shelton, "Title VII Will Referee Sex by Common Sense," *Washington Post*, November 23 1965, B1.

19. Ibid.

20. Martha Griffiths, "Women Are Being Deprived of Legal Rights by the Equal Employment Opportunity Commission," 89th Cong., 2nd sess., *Cong. Rec.* 112 (June 20, 1966): 13689.

21. Barry, "Femininity in Flight," 440. In the first year of its existence (through June 1966), the EEOC had received over nine thousand grievances, a modest number of which involved discrimination based on sex. Thus flight attendants accounted for a significant number of the sex-based grievances before the commission (447).

22. A fuller discussion of the EEOC's treatment of the *Diaz* case is found in Phil Tiemeyer, "'Male Stewardesses': Male Flight Attendants as a Queer Miscarriage of Justice," *Genders*, Spring 2007, www.genders.org.

23. "Sex as a Bona Fide Occupational Qualification for Stewardesses: Statement of United Air Lines," April 22, 1966, 72, in Box 13, Accession 8/18/72, Air Line Pilots

Association—Stewards and Stewardesses Division Archives, Wayne State University, Detroit, MI.

24. Quoted in Barry, "Femininity in Flight," 451.

25. The delay would not have been nearly as long except for the intransigence of the airlines. In November 1966, as the EEOC was first poised to rule that sex was not a BFOQ for the job of flight attendant, the airlines sued to throw out the decision. Their basis for this request was that one commissioner on the three-member panel, Aileen Hernandez, was a feminist and had even recently joined NOW. The court sided with the airlines and forced the EEOC to reevaluate the question without Hernandez, beginning with entirely new evidentiary hearings, which finally took place in September 1967.

26. 89th Cong., 2nd sess., *Cong. Rec.* 145 (June 20, 1966): 13694.

27. "Sex as a Bona Fide Occupational Qualification." 11.

28. U.S. Equal Employment Opportunity Commission, "Flight Cabin Attendant: Opinion That Sex Is Not a Bona Fide Occupational Qualification for Position." *Federal Register* 33 (February 21, 1968): 3361.

29. The commission changed its name to the New York State Division of Human Rights in 1968, when it also gained increased judicial powers. It is now known as the NYSDHR.

30. The *McNeil* case began in 1966, while *Diaz* was tried on the district level in 1969. Yet the Supreme Court had ruled on *Diaz* by the end of 1970, whereas McNeil waited until April 1973 for resolution of his case in New York. Pan Am would actually appeal parts of the *McNeil* decision, thereby delaying full resolution of the case until July 1974.

31. Judge Eleanor Schockett, interview by author, March 14, 2006, Miami, FL. Diaz's first lawyer, Robert Burns, elected to withdraw from the case after the district decision.

32. Celio Diaz, interview by author, March 16, 2006, North Miami, FL.

33. For more on the ACLU's Women's Rights Project and Ginsburg's involvement in it, see Franklin, "Anti-Stereotyping Principle."

34. Diaz did not recall the details of the jockey case that Burns was a part of, and it may have been a local Miami case. Regardless, female jockeys were a cause célèbre of the feminist movement in 1968. In that year, Olympic equestrian Kathy Kusner began a successful legal process to become the first licensed female jockey. Kusner's victory, followed closely by those of other women, made them the first professional female athletes in a formerly all-male sport. "Kathy Kusner Gets Jockey License," *New York Times*, October 30, 1968, 56.

35. The long lag between Diaz's grievance with the EEOC and his filing in federal court was due to the EEOC's moratorium on rulings regarding flight attendants. Diaz's case was put on hold until the EEOC's February 1968 ruling that sex was not a BFOQ.

36. Bolton became the most prominent women's rights advocate in South Florida. Her activism led to several key victories in the 1960s and 1970s, including forcing the integration of male-only dining rooms in Miami (1969), establishing South Florida's

first Rape Treatment Center (1974), and successfully lobbying the National Hurricane Center to stop naming all hurricanes after women (1979).

37. Schockett, interview.

38. Ibid.

39. Ibid.

40. Ibid.

41. James Armstrong, interview by author, March 17, 2006, Coral Gables, FL. Armstrong was a partner at Smathers & Thompson in Miami, the law firm that handled all legal work for Pan Am's Miami-based Latin American Division. His involvement in *Diaz v. Pan Am* was limited, since his main work involved corporate law, antitrust, and some labor issues.

42. The Senate's "Interpretive Memorandum of Title VII" stated that the BFOQ was "a limited right to discriminate on the basis of religion, sex, or national origin. . . . Examples of such legitimate discrimination would be the preference of a French restaurant for a French cook, the preference of a professional baseball team for male players, and the preference of a business which seeks the patronage of members of particular religious groups for a salesman of that religion." "Interpretive Memorandum of Title VII of H.R. 7152 Submitted Jointly by Senator Joseph S. Clark and Senator Clifford P. Case, Floor Managers," 88th Cong., 2nd sess., *Cong. Rec.* 110 (April 8, 1964): 7213.

43. "Brief Amicus Curiae on Behalf of Air Transport Association of America and its Member United States Carriers," November 21, 1969, 8, in *Diaz v. Pan Am* District Court Documents, National Archives Southeast Region, Atlanta, GA.

44. Testimony of Lloyd Wilson, Trial Proceedings of *Diaz v. Pan Am*, September 23, 1969, 99, in *Diaz v. Pan Am* District Court Documents, National Archives Southeast Region, Atlanta, GA.

45. *Diaz v. Pan Am*, 311 F. Supp. 559 (S.D. Fla. 1970), transcript of trial proceedings, 161–64, *Diaz v. Pan Am* District Court Documents, National Archives Southeast Region, Atlanta, GA.

46. Ibid., 166–67.

47. This survey became Complainant's Exhibit 23 in the *McNeil v. Pan Am* hearings. "Alan J. Saks Survey of Practices on Foreign Airlines," in Box 1, folder 2, *McNeil v. Pan Am* papers (CS-12975–66), New York State Division of Human Rights Collection, New York State Archives, Albany, NY.

48. This ad originally appeared in *Time*, Latin American ed., April 8, 1969. Respondent's Exhibit TT "Lufthansa Ad," Box 3, folder 1, *McNeil v. Pan Am* papers (CS-12975–66), New York State Division of Human Rights Collection, New York State Archives, Albany, NY.

49. Pan Am hurriedly amended their contract in February 1977 to strike out the terms *Stewardess* and *Steward* and replace them with *Flight Attendant.* The reason for this

change was feared legal action: "Enclosed are . . . Letters of Agreement . . . modifying certain job titles in order to eliminate a formal complaint which will be filed by the Equal Employment Opportunity authorities because the current titles are considered to be sexist in nature." Wyatt Fisher to Ernest M. Mitchell, February 8, 1977, box 67 [unprocessed], folder: "Pan Am Agreements other than Basic Agreement 1977," TWU Collection, New York University, New York, NY.

50. Memo from Alan Saks, re: *Nelson v. TWA* and *McNeil v. Pan Am*, August 10, 1967. *McNeil v. Pan Am* files, box 1, folder 1, New York State Division of Human Rights Records, New York State Archives, Albany, NY.

51. Testimony from March 3, 1969, pp. 1519ff, in Box 2, folder 1, *McNeil v. Pan Am* papers (CS-12975–66), New York State Division of Human Rights Collection, New York State Archives, Albany, NY.

52. *Diaz v. Pan Am*, 311 F. Supp. 559 (S.D. Fla. 1970), n. 6. This is the part of the judge's ruling in which he admits that United Airlines hired a few Hawaiian male stewards. However, this is the only exception to the female-only flight attendant policy he cites from the United States, leaving TCA out completely.

53. "Sex as a Bona Fide Occupational Qualification," 11.

54. Eric Berne, *Games People Play* (New York: Grove Press, 1964); Eric Berne, *The Structure and Dynamics of Organizations and Groups* (Philadelphia: Lippincott, 1963).

55. When testifying before the NYSCHR, Berne received $1,500 plus travel expenses, while for the Diaz trial he received $2,500 and paid his own expenses.

56. *Diaz v. Pan Am*, transcript of trial proceedings, 320.

57. Ibid., 331.

58. Armstrong, interview.

59. *Diaz v. Pan Am*, transcript of trial proceedings, 337.

60. Ibid., 334–35.

61. Ibid., 369.

62. Ibid., 370–71.

63. Ibid., 407.

64. Armstrong, interview.

65. *Diaz v. Pan Am*, 311 F. Supp. 559 (S.D. Fla. 1970).

66. Schockett, interview.

67. Ibid.

68. Ibid.

69. *Diaz v. Pan Am*, 442 F.2d 385 (5th Cir. 1971). Emphasis in original.

70. Ibid.

71. Armstrong, interview.

72. Pan Am's very first flight attendant class after the *Diaz* decision graduated on March 30, 1972, with a contingent of sixteen men and eighteen women. See "Male

Stewards, Then and Now," *Clipper*, April 10, 1972, 1, in Box 292, folder 19, Pan Am Archives, Otto Richter Library, University of Miami, Miami, FL.

73. Diaz, interview.

74. Albert Pacetta, Presiding Member, State Human Rights Appeal Board, July 18, 1974, *McNeil v. Pan Am* files, Box 1, folder 1, New York State Division of Human Rights Records, New York State Archives, Albany, NY.

5. FLIGHT ATTENDANTS, WOMEN'S LIBERATION, AND GAY LIBERATION

1. A thorough account of the culture war is found in David Courtwright, *No Right Turn: Conservative Politics in a Liberal America* (Cambridge, MA: Harvard University Press, 2010).

2. Senator Sam Ervin, quoted in *Cong. Rec.* 116 (1970): 29672.

3. Robert Lindsey, "U.S. Airlines Seek Stewards to Work Aloft," *New York Times*, April 7, 1972, 37.

4. Gilbert Feldman, "Supreme Court Prohibits Limiting Cabin Attendant Positions to One Sex," *Intercom* (Newsletter of ALSSA Local 500, TWU, AFL-CIO), December 1971, in Box 87 (unprocessed), no folder, Transportation Workers Union Collection, New York University Library, New York, NY.

5. For example, American Airlines rescinded its marriage and age restrictions in 1968, offering back pay to stewardesses fired for marriage reasons and recalling any stewardess fired upon attaining age thirty-two or thirty-three after July 1, 1965. See "Summary of Stewardess Agreement," August 26, 1968, in Box 57 (unprocessed) "Re. Negotiations with American Airlines," no folder, Transportation Workers Union Collection, New York University Library, New York, NY.

6. Feldman, "Supreme Court."

7. For example, reinstatement offers came to Pan Am stewardesses in August 1974. See Barney Spera, President, TWU Local 505, to Mrs. Sally Whitehouse, August 5, 1974, in Box 90, folder "ATD-E.M. Mitchell-PAWA-Corresp.-Flight Service Personnel, Jan-Dec 1974," Transportation Workers Union Collection, New York University Library, New York, NY. TWA and American Airlines also allowed mothers to return to work around the same year; see Gail Toes, "F/A Fights Back," *Stewardesses for Women's Rights*, March/April 1976, 9. United lost a key legal case in 1975 before the New York State Division of Human Rights that challenged their firing policy at week 27 of a pregnancy. See "Highlights: A Decade in Review," *Flightlog (AFA Newsletter)*, Fall 1983, 13.

8. Steven Rattner, "Activist Hostesses Nettle Airlines with Demands." *New York Times*, February 9, 1976, 44.

9. This figure comes from Pan Am's June 1972 weight chart for flight attendants, reproduced in Lyman Randall, *A Definitive Study of Your Future As an Airline Steward/Stewardess* (1973; repr., New York: R. Rosen, 1979), 56.

10. On National's "Fly Me" campaign, see Leonard Sloane, "Advertising: New 'Fly Me' Spots," *New York Times*, August 30, 1972, 56. On Southwest, see "New Texas Airline 'Loves' Its Passengers," *New York Times*, August 8, 1971, 56.

11. A firsthand account of SFWR's activities is found in Kane, *Sex Objects in the Sky*. Kathleen Barry's work also provides thorough details on how female flight attendants became more vocal in their advocacy of women's rights. See Barry, "Fly Me? Go Fly Yourself!," in *Femininity in Flight*, 174–210.

12. These men would not, however, be the first male flight attendants for American. The airline had hired Polynesian men starting in late 1970 for their short-lived flights in the South Pacific, and it had inherited a larger corps of male flight attendants when it purchased Trans Caribbean Airlines in March 1971.

13. Sharlene Martin, former American Airlines flight attendant and member of the New York City hiring team, phone interview by author, December 5, 2006.

14. Details of other workplaces that saw a growing focus on LGBT issues, especially within labor unions, can be found in Kitty Krupat and Patrick McCreery, *Out at Work: Building a Gay-Labor Alliance* (Minneapolis: University of Minnesota Press, 2001), and Gerald Hunt, ed., *Laboring for Rights: Unions and Sexual Diversity across Nations* (Philadelphia: Temple University Press, 1999).

15. Historian Donald Critchlow provides a thorough account of Schlafly's career as a New Right advocate opposed to feminism in Donald Critchlow, *Phyllis Schlafly and Grassroots Conservatism: A Woman's Crusade* (Princeton: Princeton University Press, 2005).

16. Media scholar Fred Fejes offers a book-length discussion of Bryant and Save Our Children, including an especially insightful chapter on the Miami-Dade County vote against gay rights in 1977. Fred Fejes, *Gay Rights and Moral Panic: The Origins of America's Debate on Homosexuality* (New York: Palgrave, 2008).

17. "A Pillow Please, Miss . . . Er, Mister," *New York Times*, May 29, 1966, S20.

18. "'Coffee, Tea or Milk' Can Be Served Aloft by Men, Agency Rules," *Wall Street Journal*, February 26, 1968, 15.

19. Jon Nordheimer, "Is This Any Way to Ruin an Airline?" *Miami Herald: Tropic Magazine*, April 14, 1968, 18–20.

20. Historian Nancy MacLean discusses Kilpatrick's opposition to civil rights in *Freedom Is Not Enough: The Opening of the American Workplace* (Cambridge, MA: Harvard University Press, 2008).

21. James Kilpatrick, "Down with Equal Opportunity: Day of the He-Stewardess Is upon Us," *Miami Herald*, March 4, 1968, 7A.

22. Political scientist Jane Mansbridge compellingly questions NOW's central claim that ERA would rectify the wage differential between men and women. There was nothing in the amendment itself that would have rectified women's wage disparity beyond the legal protections already offered by Title VII of the Civil Rights Act and the

1963 Equal Pay Act. Instead, the impact of the ERA, according to Mansbridge, would have been more indirect, providing women an additional constitutional support when they articulated demands before the courts and in the realm of public opinion. See Jane Mansbridge, *Why We Lost the ERA* (Chicago: University of Chicago Press, 1986), 36–44.

23. NOW had settled on the "59¢" slogan by the late 1970s. Ibid., 36.

24. Quoted in ibid., 137.

25. The details of the *Advocate's* early history can be found in Mark Thompson, ed., *Long Road to Freedom: The Advocate History of the Gay and Lesbian Movement* (New York: St. Martin's Press, 1994), especially the book's introduction, xvii–xxvi. *ONE*, the nation's first gay publication, whose coverage of the 1954 William Simpson murder was treated previously, stopped publishing the year after the *Advocate* began. Key members of *ONE*, including Jim Kepner, eventually joined the *Advocate*.

26. "The Only Way to Fly," *Los Angeles Advocate*, March 1968, 4.

27. "Scream and Suck Your Thumb," *Advocate*, May 26, 1971, cover.

28. "Men Stewardesses," *Advocate*, May 26, 1971, 2.

29. A vivid account of the rising gay capitalism in America's largest cities that began already before the 1970s is offered in Boyd, *Wide Open Town*.

30. In a one-year period between February 1975 and March 1976, the *Advocate* ran several major stories on the Los Angeles Police Department's intense resistance to hiring gay officers (see, for example, "L.A. Police Department's Position on Gay People," February 26, 1975, 8–9) and an in-depth interview with the nation's first openly gay officer ("Law Enforcement First: Openly Gay Deputy Sheriff," March 24, 1976, 6). As a counterargument to my claim that the lack of interest in the victory of male flight attendants was tied to the stigma of effeminacy, note that all of the occupations mentioned, as well as that of teachers, are also held by government-contracted employees, thereby making them especially inviting targets for court cases by gays and lesbians seeking equal accommodation in such jobs. As will be discussed later, federal courts held the government to a higher degree of rigor than private employers in granting equal protection to gays and lesbians.

31. The interviews discussed in this chapter involve eight former flight attendants—six men and two women—who flew for various U.S. airlines during the 1970s. Some of these interviews were conducted in person, others via phone, from December 2004 through December 2006.

32. Anonymous G, interview by author, December 31, 2004.

33. Martin, interview.

34. Quoted in Don Bedwell, "Come Fly Me," *Philadelphia Inquirer*, June 1, 1972, 15.

35. Anonymous G, interview.

36. Judy Harkison, "Wife's Job Appealed to Him, Now He's a Flight Attendant," *New York Times*, February 4, 1973, 56.

37. Wesley Pruden Jr., "Airline Stewards Return," *National Observer*, December 2, 1972, in Box 291, folder 6, Pan American Airways Collection, Otto Richter Library, University of Miami, Miami, FL.

38. Anonymous C, interview by author, August 18, 2005.

39. Indeed, large segments of the gay male subculture, though they were largely kept out of the public spotlight during the postwar years, had always identified closely with this more feminine sensibility. For consideration of the associations between gay men and aesthetics, especially fashion, see Shaun Cole, *"Don We Now Our Gay Apparel": Gay Men's Dress in the Twentieth Century* (Oxford: Berg, 2000).

40. Anonymous G, interview.

41. Testimony from February 14, 1969, Lloyd Wilson, Director of Flight Service, Pan American Airways, 1190, *McNeil v. Pan Am* files, Box 2, Folder 1, New York State Division of Human Rights Records, New York State Archives, Albany, NY.

42. Sidney Davis, *Delta Air Lines: Debunking the Myth* (Atlanta: Peachtree, 1988), 138.

43. An account of Bryant's visit to Eastern facilities was shared in a personal interview with a former Eastern steward. Anonymous F, interview by author, October 10, 2005.

44. Anonymous G, interview.

45. Paula Kane, "What a Stewardess Is Really There For," *Midwest: The Chicago Sun-Times Magazine*, August 11, 1974, 8.

46. Anonymous G, interview.

47. The AFA was the successor to the Air Line Stewards and Stewardesses Association (ALSSA), which had been the main flight attendant labor union since the 1950s. The AFA was established late in 1973 to grant the flight attendants complete independence from the pilots' union, the Air Line Pilots Association. The quote comes from Joan Volpe, "Who We Are: The Flight Attendant Subculture," *Flightlog*, Fall 1983, 15.

48. Pruden, "Airline Stewards Return."

49. Ibid.

50. Bedwell, "Come Fly Me."

51. Harriett Jacobs, to unnamed officials in labor union, September 22, 1970. Box APFA 30A.3, folder 30A.3.3, Transportation Workers Union Collection, New York University Archives, New York, NY.

52. See *Trans World Airlines v. State Human Rights Appeal Board*, 46 A.D.2d 138 (1974).

53. A review of the case is provided by Marsha Krossner, "TWA v. Michel—Sex Discrimination???," *Stewardesses for Women's Rights (Newsletter)*, February 1975, 5.

54. Martin, interview. Martin notes that stewardesses did have the option to wear slacks underneath the miniskirts.

55. Ibid.

56. Patt Gibbs, former president of the Association of Professional Flight Attendants, interview by author, August 30, 2005, Euless, TX.

57. Carole Metschke, "New Inflight Wardrobe Debuts," *Friendly Times*, January-February 1973, 8. Even though United was among the first airlines to hire men after the *Diaz* decision (beginning in early 1972, thereby complementing their Hawaiian-only steward corps on Honolulu-bound flights that had existed since 1950), this issue of *Friendly Times* is the first to mention stewards.

58. Patt Gibbs remembers that fighting for stewards' right to wear short sleeves was among the first male-oriented grievances that the APFA pursued against American Airlines. Gibbs, interview. United also had a grievance on whether men could wear short-sleeved uniforms. Steward Don Bartley actually lost this case in 1975, though the judgment noted that United was again changing its uniforms to resolve the issue: "Uniform changes for female flight attendants are now being made which will no longer permit the use of short sleeves for such employees." See "System Board Decision," Case "ORD 28–74 Don Bartley," Box 1, Folder "Beards," Accession AFA Legal 10–3-94, Association of Flight Attendants Collection, Reuther Labor Archives, Wayne State University, Detroit, MI.

59. Both Kathleen Barry and Georgia Panter Nielsen thoroughly discuss these legal battles. See Barry, *Femininity in Flight*, and Nielsen, *From Sky Girl to Flight Attendant*.

60. Linda Puchala, "We're All in This Together," *Flightlog*, Fall 1983, 4.

61. Ibid.

62. *Reed v. Reed*, 404 U.S. 71 (1971). For the legacy of *Reed v. Reed* in winning for women nearly equal coverage under the Fourteenth Amendment as racial minorities, see Gretchen Ritter, *The Constitution as Social Design: Gender and Civic Membership in the American Constitutional Order* (Stanford: Stanford University Press, 2006), 215–60.

63. Ginsburg was very aware of the *Diaz* case, though it is unclear just how much Diaz's example influenced her own choice to use male plaintiffs. She even wrote about *Diaz* in the first textbook on sex discrimination law that she coauthored in 1974. See Kenneth M. Davidson, Ruth B. Ginsburg, and Herma H. Kay, *Sex-Based Discrimination: Text, Cases, and Materials* (Minneapolis: West Publishing, 1974), 675–80. Cary Franklin, discussed below, suggests that Ginsburg's time in Sweden was likely the main catalyst for this legal strategy, as she was heavily influenced by Swedish philosophy of *jämställdhet*—or gender equality—that saw men's imprisonment in gender roles as troubling as women's. For an account of Ginsburg's Swedish influences, see Franklin, "Anti-Stereotyping Principle," 100 ff.

64. Franklin, "Anti-Stereotyping Principle," 123. I depend heavily on Franklin's thesis throughout this section, as her scholarship analyzes the impact of Ginsburg's use of male plaintiffs while at the Women's Rights Project.

65. Ibid., 124.

66. Ibid., 84.

67. *Weinberger v. Wiesenfeld*, 420 U.S. 636 (1975).

68. Franklin, "Anti-Stereotyping Principle," 88.

69. Ibid., 130.

70. Ibid., 129.

71. See, for example, Ann Scales, "Feminist Legal Method: Not So Scary," *UCLA Women's Law Journal* 2 (1992): 1–34.

72. Interestingly, current-day legal scholars like William Eskridge are seeking to rekindle a similar legal argument for same-sex marriage. They argue that Ginsburg's victories on the Fourteenth Amendment should be the basis for this legal change, since same-sex marriage ultimately treats people differently based on the sex of the person they love. See Franklin, "Anti-Stereotyping Principle," 173.

73. Three separate cases brought on behalf of gays and lesbians arguing for Title VII protection based on sexual orientation were clustered together in this decision. The cases were *De Santis v. Pacific Tel. & Tel. Co.*, *Strailey v. Happy Times*, and *Lundin v. Pacific Tel. & Tel. Co.*, 608 F.2d 327 (1979).

74. Quoted in Allison Walzer, "Who Are They?," *Advocate*, March 24, 1976, 11.

75. For details on Kameny's decades-long struggle against federal government discrimination, see David K. Johnson, *The Lavender Scare: The Cold War Persecution of Gays and Lesbians in the Federal Government* (Chicago: University of Chicago Press, 2004).

76. *Morrison v. Board of Education*, 1 Cal. 3d 214 (1969), and *Gay Law Students Ass'n. v. Pacific Tel & Tel. Co.*, 24 Cal. 3d 458 (1979). The 1979 decision was novel in granting gays and lesbians equal protection at a privately owned company. However, the company in question, Pac Bell, was a state-regulated monopolistic provider of essential services.

77. *McConnell v. Anderson*, 316 F. Supp. 809 (1970).

78. *McConnell v. Anderson*, 451 F.2d 193 (1971).

79. National Gay Task Force, *"Heard Any Good Fag Jokes Lately?,"* brochure, [1977], in folder "National Gay Task Force and Gay Activists Alliance," Alternative Literature Ephemera, Special Collections, Northwestern University Archives, Evanston, IL.

80. Don Jackson, "Rights Law in San Francisco," *Advocate*, April 26, 1972, 1.

81. "S.F. Hiring Law Goes into Effect," *Advocate*, May 24, 1972, 3.

82. In addition to Fred Fejes's account of Save Our Children in *Gay Rights and Moral Panic*, there is Bryant's own account of her political and religious activities in her book, *The Anita Bryant Story: The Survival of Our Nation's Families and the Threat of Militant Homosexuality* (Old Tappan, NJ: Revell, 1977).

83. An example of such undertakings comes from the Buffalo-based Mattachine Society of the Niagara Frontier. They distributed a survey to various companies in 1972 asking about their practices toward homosexuals, especially whether the companies knowingly hired or fired homosexuals. The cover letter mailed with the survey made it

clear that "as an aid to the better than 54,000 homosexual men and women living in the Niagara Frontier, it is . . . our aim to compile a list of employers and renters that express a spirit of cooperation in non-discrimination toward gays." Donald Michaels, Chairperson Jobs and Housing Committee, Mattachine Society of the Niagara Frontier Inc., n.d., in folder "Homosexuality and Employment," Box 34, Record Series 19280–02, New York State Division of Human Rights Collection, New York State Archives, Albany, NY.

84. National Gay Task Force, *"Heard Any Good Fag Jokes Lately?"*

85. IBM's reputation as America's most influential company in the 1970s is treated in Nancy Foy, *The Sun Never Sets on IBM* (New York: Morrow, 1975).

86. Sue Chrislotleson, quoted by Randy Shilts, "City Rights Laws: Are They Just Toothless Paper Tigers?" *Advocate*, March 10, 1976, 7.

87. "Highlights: A Decade in Review," *Flightlog*, Fall 1983, 12.

88. In particular, AFA lawyer Jules Balkin corresponded with the Gay Rights Advocates in 1979 to discuss rulings involving Pacific Telephone and Telegraph, which I have treated above. Lew Lasher to Jules Balkin, June 13, 1979, in folder "Homo-sexuals," Box 1, AFA Legal 10–31–94, AFA Archives, Walter Reuther Labor Archives, Wayne State University, Detroit, MI.

89. The country's two largest carriers after deregulation, American and United, both first adopted nondiscrimination clauses in 1993. Much more will be discussed on American's decision to become the first such airline to do so in chapter 7. See Daniel B. Baker, Sean O'Brien Strub, and Bill Henning, *Cracking the Corporate Closet* (New York: Harper Business, 1995), 201, 204.

90. Jo Ann Neil, "Cabin Attendant Report," January 19, 1973, in folder "ATD-E.M. Mitchell-PAWA-Correspondence-Flight Service Personnel (Locals 500, 504, 505) Jan-May 1973," Box 90 (unprocessed), TWU Archives, New York University Library, New York, NY.

91. Letter 5 of Preliminary Draft of Flight Attendant Agreement, February 27, 1982, from Martin Mueller to Alice Flynn, "Letter of Understanding: Travel Privileges," in folder 15 "Bargaining 1982," Box 1, IUFA Collection, New York University Library, New York, NY.

92. Anonymous F, interview.

93. Because male pursers like TWA employee Pierre Michel, who filed the previously mentioned court case in New York State, risked loss of their seniority through no fault of their own, their animus was arguably less an indication of sexism and more a matter of economic self-interest. Nonetheless, their actions certainly seemed to pit them against female flight attendants aspiring to their positions.

94. Bernice Dolan, quoted in Barry, *Femininity in Flight*, 562.

95. Pamela Casey, "The Way We Were," *Flightlog*, Fall 1983, 9.

96. Patt Gibbs, who was active in American Airlines' union in the 1970s and later became president of the APFA, came out in the 1980s. Meanwhile, Robert Wagner of

TWA was one of the founding officers of TWA's independent local in 1974. While neither of these flight attendants openly discussed their sexuality, they also didn't deny it. Both claim that their orientation was known to most of their peers.

97. A firsthand account of these tensions within NOW is offered by Del Martin and Phyllis Lyon, the original founders of America's first lesbian activist organization in the 1950s and longtime members of NOW as well. Del Martin and Phyllis Lyon, *Lesbian/ Woman* (1972; repr., Volcano, CA: Volcano Press, 1991).

98. Lindsey, "U.S. Airlines Seek Stewards," 37.

6. FLIGHT ATTENDANTS AND THE ORIGINS OF AN EPIDEMIC

1. An August 1985 poll published in *Newsweek* found that 96 percent of respondents did not know anyone who had AIDS. David Gelman, "The Social Fallout from an Epidemic," *Newsweek*, August 12, 1985, 28.

2. Anonymous H, interview by author, January 3, 2005. The flight attendant was careful to explain that this number included other social contacts of his, not just fellow flight attendants.

3. "The Man Who Gave Us AIDS," *New York Post*, October 6, 1987, 1.

4. I refer quite often to post-Stonewall gay sexual freedoms in the following two chapters. I am borrowing heavily from Jennifer Brier and her use of similar phrasing. Among these post-Stonewall freedoms, Brier cites the rise, especially among gay men, of commercialized gay sex venues (bars, bathhouses, and pornographic print media), an increase in nonmonogamous sexual practices, and a proliferation of sexual acts (not only anal and oral sex, but also fisting and other nontraditional sexual practices). See Jennifer Brier, *Infectious Ideas* (Chapel Hill: University of North Carolina Press, 2009).

5. While no academic has written on Traynor, a handful have written on Dugas. For the most recent published account of the Patient Zero myth, see Wald, *Contagious*, 213–63. Richard McKay has also generated a dissertation on Patient Zero, and I look forward to its eventual publication: McKay, "Imagining 'Patient Zero.'"

6. The film was inspired by Manhattan lawyer Geoffrey Bowers and his complaint against the law firm Baker & McKenzie. It was argued before the New York State Division of Human Rights. See Mireya Navarro, "Vindicating a Lawyer with AIDS, Years Too Late," *New York Times*, January 21, 1994, B1.

7. Brier, *Infectious Ideas*, 45–77. Other scholars have examined similar topics: see Meredith Raimondo, "Dateline Atlanta: Place and the Social Construction of AIDS," in *Carryin' On in the Lesbian and Gay South*, ed. John Howard (New York: NYU Press, 1997), 331–69; Michelle Cochrane, *When AIDS Began* (New York: Routledge, 2004); Cindy Patton, *Inventing AIDS* (New York: Routledge, 1990); and Paul Farmer, *AIDS and Accusation* (1992; repr., Berkeley: University of California Press, 2006).

8. "First AIDS Patient Story Dismissed," *Gazette* (Montreal), October 17, 1987, A3.

9. William Henry III, "The Appalling Saga of Patient Zero," *Time*, October 19, 1987.

10. Christine Gorman, "Strange Trip Back to the Future," *Time*, November 9, 1987.

11. M. Thomas Gilbert et al., "The Emergence of HIV/AIDS in the Americas and Beyond," *Proceedings of the National Academy of Sciences*, early ed., 104, no. 47 (November 20, 2007): 1–5.

12. Ibid., 3.

13. Ibid.

14. I have used Randy Shilts's own research to provide these details of Gaëtan's life. Shilts interviewed various friends, coworkers, and doctors of Dugas while composing his book. Some of these details made it into *And the Band Played On*, while others remain in his notes, now available at the San Francisco Public Library. See Randy Shilts Archive, And the Band Played On Collection, Box 9, folder 23, "Shilts: And the Band Played On: Patient Zero," James Hormel Gay and Lesbian Center, San Francisco Public Library, San Francisco, CA.

15. San Francisco's figure was reported by the San Francisco AIDS Foundation in September 1983; Brier, *Infectious Ideas*, 211 n 24. The Los Angeles figure comes from Claire Spiegel, "AIDS Epidemic: A Scramble for Funds in Bid to Combat It," *Los Angeles Times*, July 22, 1985, B1.

16. Anonymous G, interview by author, December 31, 2004.

17. Ibid.

18. For coverage of the motives for and impact of the hub-and-spoke system after deregulation, see George Williams, "The Impact of Hub and Spoke Networks," in *The Airline Industry and the Impact of Deregulation* (Brookfield VT: Ashgate, 1994), 18–27; and Elizabeth E. Bailey, David R. Graham, and Daniel P. Kaplan, "Routes and Industry Performance," in *Deregulating the Airlines* (Cambridge, MA: MIT Press, 1985), 67–90.

19. Ann Fettner and William Check, *The Truth about AIDS: Evolution of an Epidemic* (New York: Holt, Rinehart and Winston, 1984), 87.

20. David Auerbach et al., "Cluster of Cases of the Acquired Immune Deficiency Syndrome: Patients Linked by Sexual Contact," *American Journal of Medicine* 76 (March 1984): 487–91.

21. William Darrow, E. M. Gorman, and B. P. Glick, "The Social Origins of AIDS: Social Change, Sexual Behavior, and Disease Trends," in *The Social Dimensions of AIDS*, ed. Douglas Feldman and Thomas Johnson (New York: Praeger Press, 1986), 103. Of course, as research would later clarify, the onset of sickness is not a strong correlate with the timing of one's infection with HIV. Individuals progress toward perceptible illness at their own unique pace.

22. Auerbach et al., "Cluster of Cases," 489.

23. Priscilla Wald traces this misleading development in her chapter on Patient Zero. See Wald, *Contagious*, 213–63.

24. "US Medical Study Singles Out a Man Who Carried AIDS," *New York Times*, March 27, 1984, A25.

25. "40 AIDS Cases in 10 Cities Traced to Single 'Carrier,' " *Los Angeles Times*, March 26, 1984, A1.

26. Darrow shared this recollection when interviewed by Randy Shilts. Shilts, "Shilts: And the Band Played On: People—Darrow, William W.," 5.

27. Darrow, Gorman, and Glick, "Social Origins of AIDS," 95–107.

28. Anonymous A, interview by author, December 31, 2004.

29. Anonymous E, interview by author, August 5, 2008.

30. Anonymous A, interview.

31. Anonymous B, interview by author, August 8, 2008.

32. Auerbach et al., "Cluster of Cases," 489–90. *Fisting* refers to rectal stimulation with the hand.

33. James Oleske et al., "Immune Deficiency Syndrome in Children," *Journal of the American Medical Association* 249 (May 6, 1983): 2345–49. This study found that children living in households with adults with AIDS also tended to contract AIDS. In addition to correctly theorizing that perinatal transmission was occurring between mother and child, the researchers speculated that household exposure might be causing these children's infections. This incorrect speculation generated panic-driven headlines about the possibility of contracting AIDS without sexual contact or IV injection.

34. Bob Nelson, " 'Casual Contact' Theories Incite AIDS Panic," *Gay Community News* (Boston), June 18, 1983, 3.

35. Tom Morganthau, "Gay America in Transition," *Newsweek*, August 8, 1983, 30.

36. The flier, entitled "The ERA-Gay-AIDS Connection," is detailed in Ellen Goodman, "For the Wastebasket," *Washington Post*, January 17, 1984, A15.

37. Quoted in Ellen Goodman, "At Large," *National NOW Times*, January–February 1984, 9.

38. This is an estimate based on other available statistics. In April 1982, the CDC knew of nineteen cases in Los Angeles County. In May of 1983, that number had risen to eighty-one. Traynor's diagnosis in January 1983 occurs closer to the later date, though the rate of new infections surely accelerated over time. The May 1983 figure is in "3,000 Marchers Seek More AIDS Research," *Los Angeles Times*, May 27, 1983, 18.

39. United Airlines System Board of Adjustment, "Grievance of Gar M. Traynor, LAX 47–83, AFA Case 64–12–2–270–83," p. 1, in ILIR Library, Martin Wagner Arbitration File (record Series 35/3/411), Box 13, folder "United Airlines and Assoc. of Flight Attendants, 1984," University of Illinois Archives, Champaign, IL.

40. Marc Fisher, "No Friendly Skies for Flight Attendant Who Caught AIDS," *Miami Herald*, February 3, 1985, 8A.

41. [Name omitted] to [names omitted], May 8, 1983, in Association of Flight Attendants Archive, Wayne State University, Detroit, MI, Accession 2–20–04 AFA Chicago (5sb), Box 3 of 5, folder "Gar Michael Traynor v UAL (LAX 47–83)." Throughout this section, I have redacted all names, except for those such as Traynor's that entered the public record through media accounts or are otherwise accessible to the public in venues other than the AFA archive.

42. Anonymous LAX flight attendant to [name omitted], May 31, 1983, in Association of Flight Attendants Archive, Wayne State University, Detroit, MI, Accession 2–20–04 AFA Chicago (5sb), Box 3 of 5, folder "Gar Michael Traynor v UAL (LAX 47–83)." The abbreviation LAXSW designates a United employee's home base (LAX) and his or her department. SW is the department of United for service workers such as flight attendants.

43. Dr. George Catlett, "A Message from JFKMD," May 23, 1983, in Association of Flight Attendants archive, Wayne State University, Detroit, MI, Accession AFA Chicago 2–20–04, Box 1, folder "MEC 6–83, Nancy Coopersmith (MEC) v. United Airlines."

44. C.R. Harper, MD, Vice President, Medical Services, United Air Lines, to Mr. G.M. Traynor, July 25, 1983, in folder "United Airlines," Box 13, Henry Wilson Papers (1996–2002), GLBT Historical Society Archives, San Francisco, CA.

45. The HIV virus had first been isolated in Paris in May 1983 but had not been widely noticed in North America until a full year later, when Dr. Robert Gallo replicated the discovery. Thus, even though Manker may well have been HIV-positive at the time, doctors had no way of diagnosing him with AIDS until he demonstrated more severe symptoms, like a more severe drop in his white blood cells, KS, or PCP pneumonia. Dr. [name omitted] to Dr. George Catlett, August 29, 1983, in Association of Flight Attendants archive, Wayne State University, Detroit, MI, Accession 2–20–04 AFA Chicago (4sb), Box 4, folder "(DEN 21–83) Russ Manker v. United Airlines."

46. George Mendenhall, "United Has Unfriendly Skies For Employees with AIDS," *Bay Area Reporter*, November 15, 1984, 1.

47. Handwritten note in Association of Flight Attendants Archive, Wayne State University, Detroit, MI, Accession 2–20–04 AFA Chicago (3SB), Box 3, folder "(ORD 19–84) Bruce Hall—Medical (AIDS)."

48. Shilts, "Shilts: And the Band Played On: Patient Zero," 7.

49. Ibid.

50. The lack of either archival material or oral histories with people in positions of authority at other U.S. airlines has prevented me from establishing whether airlines besides United and American grounded their employees with AIDS. Flight attendants I interviewed from Pan Am and TWA unanimously claimed that their airline treated colleagues with AIDS very sympathetically, though they didn't recall men working very long after their diagnosis or seeing men with KS lesions on the job.

51. Patt Gibbs, former president of the Association of Professional Flight Attendants, interview by author, August 30, 2005, Euless, TX.

52. Anonymous I, interview by author, January 9, 2009.

53. Gibbs, interview.

54. Patricia Friend, interview by author, Washington, DC, November 23, 2009.

55. Mendenhall, "United Has Unfriendly Skies," 1.

56. Kevin Cahill, ed., *The AIDS Epidemic* (New York: St. Martin's Press, 1983).

57. Ibid., 135.

58. "United Airlines Flight Attendant System Board of Adjustment, United Airlines and Association of Flight Attendants, Grievance of Gar M. Traynor LAX 47–83, AFA Case 64–12–2-70–83," signed by Chairman and Neutral Member Martin Wagner, December 20, 1984, 8, in Martin Wagner Arbitration File (Record Series 35/3/411), Box 13, folder "United Airlines and Association of Flight Attendants, 1984," ILIR Library, University of Illinois Archives, Urbana-Champaign, IL.

59. Ibid., 4.

60. Advisory Committee on Infections within Hospitals, American Hospital Association, "Personnel with AIDS or Suspect AIDS," December 1983, quoted in "United Airlines Flight Attendant System Board of Adjustment: Grievance of Gar M. Traynor, LAX 47–83, AFA Case 64–12–2-270–83," 8.

61. Task Force at the University of California, San Francisco, "Direct Patient-Care Responsibilities for Employees with AIDS," Sept 1983, quoted in "United Airlines Flight Attendant System Board of Adjustment: Grievance of Gar M. Traynor, LAX 47–83, AFA Case 64–12–2-270–83," 9.

62. "United Airlines Flight Attendant System Board of Adjustment: Grievance of Gar M. Traynor, LAX 47–83, AFA Case 64–12–2-270–83," 10.

63. Dr. David Ostrow, phone interview by author, December 23, 2009.

64. Friend, interview.

65. Ostrow, interview.

66. "United Airlines Flight Attendant System Board of Adjustment: Grievance of Gar M. Traynor, LAX 47–83, AFA Case 64–12–2-270–83," 12.

67. Dr. Robert McGiffin Jr. (United Airlines Regional Flight Surgeon) to Robert Butler, October 9, 1985, in Accession 7–2-04 AFA Chicago (4sb), Box 1, folder "(ORD 99–85) Robert Butler," Association of Flight Attendants Archives, Wayne State University, Detroit, MI.

68. Friend, interview.

69. Richard Berkowitz, interview by author, New York, NY, October 22, 2009.

70. Richard Berkowitz and Michael Callen, *How to Have Sex in an Epidemic: One Approach* (New York: News from the Front Publications, 1983).

71. Michael Callen and Dan Turner, "A History of the PWA Self-Empowerment Movement," originally published in the *1988 Lesbian & Gay Health Education Foundation Program Booklet*, in the personal papers of Richard Berkowitz, New York, NY.

72. Berkowitz, interview.

73. The following quotes come from "The Denver Principles," as reproduced in National Association of People With AIDS (NAPWA), *Strategic Plan, 2010–2012* (self-published, 2010), 2, www.napwa.org.

74. Berkowitz, interview.

75. Ibid.

76. "Gay America: Sex, Politics, and the Impact of AIDS," *Newsweek*, August 8, 1983, cover.

77. Bobbi Campbell, personal diary, entry from January 26, 1984, in Collection MSS 96–33, "Bobbi Campbell Diary 1983–1984," University of California San Francisco Archives, San Francisco, CA.

78. Gär Traynor to Marilyn Pearson, April 2, 1985, in Accession 2–20–04 AFA Chicago (5sb), Box 3, folder "Gar Michael Traynor v UAL (LAX 47–83)," Association of Flight Attendants Archives, Wayne State University, Detroit, MI.

79. George Mendenhall, "Flight Attendants Win Bias Case in United Airlines AIDS Firing," *Bay Area Reporter*, January 17, 1985, 2.

80. Gert McMullin, phone interview by author, December 1, 2009.

81. Details of the ceremony come from Guy Babineau, "Gaëtan Dugas and the 'AIDS Mary' Myth," *Capital Xtra*, November 9, 2007.

7. THE TRAYNOR LEGACY VERSUS THE "PATIENT ZERO" MYTH

1. Shilts, *And the Band Played On*, xxi.

2. *School Board of Nassau County, Florida v. Gene Arline*, 480 U.S. 273 (No. 85–1277, March 3, 1987).

3. American identified itself as "gay-friendly" in various statements. Note, for example, the comment of company spokesperson Andrea Rader in 1997: "This is a very gay-friendly company." Jeordan Legon, "Tension at American Air," *San Jose Mercury News*, January 30, 1997, 1C.

4. Quoted in Carrie Lozano, producer/director/editor, *Reporter Zero*, documentary film (Free History Project, 2006).

5. Gary Wills, "The Rolling Stone Interview: Randy Shilts," *Rolling Stone*, September 30, 1993, 46 ff. Interestingly, the column Shilts references, supposedly from November 1982, made no mention of a French Canadian. And its actual release date was a year later, after Dugas had left San Francisco for good. See Randy Shilts, "Some AIDS Patients Still Going to the Baths," *San Francisco Chronicle*, November 15, 1983, 4.

6. Ronald Bayer and Gerald Oppenheimer, *AIDS Doctors: Voices from the Epidemic* (New York: Oxford University Press, 2000), 61.

7. Randy Shilts Archive, And the Band Played On Collection, Box 1, folder 18, "Shilts: And the Band Played On: People—Darrow, William W.," 5, James Hormel Gay and Lesbian Center, San Francisco Public Library, San Francisco, CA.

8. Shilts, *And the Band Played On*, 11.

9. Ibid., 23.

10. Ibid., 147. *GRID* was the term most often used before the name *AIDS* was decided upon in late 1982. GRID stood for "gay-related immune deficiency," signaling the relationship between the illness and the gay community where it was first discovered by physicians in the United States.

11. Shilts, *And the Band Played On*, 158.

12. I again recommend Priscilla Wald's *Contagious*, in this case for her chapter on Mary Mallon and the work in her chapter on Patient Zero that further examines Shilts's attempts to link Gaëtan Dugas with Mallon's legacy.

13. Shilts, *And the Band Played On*, 439.

14. Michael Denneny, interview by author, New York, NY, August 14, 2008.

15. Randy Shilts, *The Mayor of Castro Street* (New York: St. Martin's Press, 1982).

16. Denneny, interview.

17. Ibid.

18. According to Denneny, the promoter in question wishes to remain anonymous. Ibid.

19. Ibid.

20. Ibid.

21. Patricia Holt, "Behind the Tragedy of AIDS," *San Francisco Chronicle*, October 18 1987, 1.

22. These details are recounted in "Un Québécois responsable de la propagation du SIDA en Amérique? IMPOSSIBLE DE L'AFFIRMER," *Journal de Montréal*, October 8, 1987, 2.

23. The collection of headlines was gathered and published by Guy Babineau, "Gaëtan Dugas and the 'AIDS Mary' Myth," *Capital Xtra*, November 9, 2007, www.xtra.ca

24. The press packet is described in Crimp, "How to Have Promiscuity," 241–42.

25. "St. Martin's Press Subsidiary Rights Sales Info.," August 10, 1987, in Randy Shilts Archive, And the Band Played On Collection, Box 8, folder 3, "ATBPO Editors Correspondence, Death Certificates, Misc.," James Hormel Gay and Lesbian Center, San Francisco Public Library, San Francisco, CA.

26. Bob Sipchen, "The AIDS Chronicles," *Los Angeles Times*, October 9, 1987, 1.

27. Denneny, interview.

28. "Patient Zero," in *60 Minutes* (transcript), *CBS News*, November 15, 1987.

29. Sipchen, "AIDS Chronicles," 1.

30. Denneny, interview.

31. Denneny's work as a gay activist began long before the AIDS crisis, as a graduate student in Chicago. His main involvement with AIDS was as a member of the editorial

board of various New York gay publications, especially the *New York Native*, during the epidemic's early years. Denney, interview.

32. Quoted in Lozano, *Reporter Zero*.

33. The French term *futile* is a cognate in English and would most accurately translate as "useless" in this context. Andre Noel, "Le sida aurait été introduit en Amérique par un Montréalais," *La Presse* (Montréal), October 7, 1987, A1.

34. "The information could be true, but it also could be false."

35. "To have had 250 partners each year, he [Mr. Dugas] must have truly gotten 'flung up in the air', you could say!" To get "flung in the air" is a colloquial expression referring to the orgiastic joy of having sex. In this case, it is also a playful pun referring to Mr. Dugas's career as a flight attendant, who also gets launched into the air as part of his job.

36. Fran Golden, "AIDS Victims Grapple with Travel Curbs," *Travel Weekly*, September 24, 1987, 81.

37. Allyn Stone and Jeff Pelline, "Airlines' Confusing Policy for AIDS Passengers." *San Francisco Chronicle*, August 15, 1987, 1.

38. Golden, "AIDS Victims Grapple," 81.

39. Stone and Pelline, "Airlines' Confusing Policy," 1.

40. Robert MacLeod, "Airline Accused of Not Hiring Male Cabin Crew," *Toronto Globe and Mail*, March 16, 1987.

41. John Fraser, "Major British Air Carrier Told to Hire Male Staff Despite Worries of AIDS," *Toronto Globe and Mail*, February 3, 1987.

42. Ever since early 1986, the Reagan administration had expressed the intent to implement this new policy. However, the Helms Amendment compelled the administration to follow through on its plans. Jonathan Fuerbringer, "Senate Votes to Require Test of Aliens for AIDS Virus," *New York Times*, June 3, 1987, B8. See also Brier, *Contagious Ideas*, for background on the Helms Amendment.

43. "Crewmember with AIDS Barred at Gatwick," *Aviation Week and Space Technology*, February 23, 1987, 36.

44. Patricia Friend, interview by author, Washington, DC, November 23, 2009.

45. "Airline Staff AIDS Toll 'More Than 100,'" *Courier-Mail* (Brisbane, Australia), March 30, 1987. The story originally broke in the *Sunday Express*, published in London.

46. "Airlines Study AIDS Effect," *Flight International* (Surrey, UK), April 18, 1987, 5.

47. *School Board of Nassau County, Florida v. Gene Arline*, 480 U.S. 273 (No. 85–1277), March 3, 1987.

48. Opinion of Justice William Brennan, *School Board of Nassau County, Florida v. Gene Arline*, 480 U.S. 273.

49. More details of the investment of AIDS activists in the *Arline* case are found in Stuart Taylor, "Justices Support Disease Victims," *New York Times*, March 4, 1987, A1.

50. Association of Flight Attendants, "AIDS Manual," July 1988, II-1, in folder "AIDS Manual," Box 7 (of 15), Accession AFA Chicago 2–20–04, Association of Flight Attendants Collection, Walter Reuther Labor Archives, Wayne State University, Detroit, MI.

51. "A Special Report on AIDS," *United Times*, June 1988, 9, republished in Association of Flight Attendants, "AIDS Manual."

52. Dr. George Catlett, "A Message from JFKMD," May 23, 1983, in Association of Flight Attendants Archive, Wayne State University, Detroit, MI, Accession AFA Chicago 2–20–04, Box 1, folder "MEC 6–83, Nancy Coopersmith (MEC) v. United Airlines."

53. "Special Report on AIDS."

54. Peter Finn, "American Airlines Memo on Gay, Lesbian Fliers Touches Off Furor," *Fort Worth Star-Telegram*, April 29, 1993, A7.

55. Tim Kincaid, phone interview by author, April 26, 2010.

56. Finn, "American Airlines Memo," A7.

57. In folder "AIDS," Association of Professional Flight Attendants Archives, Euless, TX.

58. Kincaid, interview.

59. See Baker, Strub, and Henning, *Cracking the Corporate Closet*, 201, 204.

60. "American Airlines Issues Statement on Flight 701 Incident," *PR Newswire*, April 29, 1993, www.lexisnexis.com.

61. "AIDS Patient Arrested after Disturbance on Plane," *CNN*, November 16, 1993, www.lexisnexis.com.

62. Quoted in John Gallagher, "Flight Risk," *Advocate*, December 28, 1993, 31.

63. "NAPWA Condemns American Airlines' Actions in Holless case," *PR Newswire*, November 16, 1993, www.lexisnexis.com.

64. "American Airlines Apologizes for Removing AIDS Patient from Plane," *Associated Press*, November 18, 1993, www.lexisnexis.com.

65. Bob Witeck, interview by author, Washington, DC, April 17, 2010.

66. Ibid.

67. Kincaid, interview.

68. Anonymous I, interview by author, January 9, 2009.

69. Queer scholar Alexandra Chasin stresses that such largesse also imposes corporate-friendly conditions on LGBT organizations, such as agreements to include American's name in the organization's materials and an exclusivity agreement forbidding cooperation with other airlines. Chasin details the conditions that American included in a late agreement with another LGBT rights group, the International Gay and Lesbian Human Rights Commission, in Chasin, *Selling Out*, 197.

70. Kincaid, interview.

71. Witeck, interview.

72. Ibid.

73. Robert Witeck and Wesley Combs, *Business Inside Out* (Chicago: Kaplan, 2006), 21.

74. John Greyson, writer and director, *Zero Patience* (Montreal: Alliance Atlantis Communications, 1993).

75. *Putain* is a French exclamation meaning "fuck."

76. Greyson, *Zero Patience*, 1:12:00–1:20:00.

77. American's first-of-its-kind nondiscrimination policy for gender identity was developed in 2001 and includes guidelines on how to protect workers' rights as they undergo the gender transitioning process.

78. Denneny, interview.

8. QUEER EQUALITY IN THE AGE OF NEOLIBERALISM

1. Neoliberalism refers to the weakening of government regulation and labor union power in the economy over the last several decades. Globalization of production (also referred to as outsourcing) is closely intertwined with this dynamic, as companies seek to skirt North American or European labor and environmental laws by moving production to less regulated countries. While a service industry like commercial aviation is somewhat immune to outsourcing, the U.S. aviation industry has nonetheless seen ample restructuring along neoliberal lines since deregulation in 1979. Some of the critiques of neoliberalism that I consulted while composing this chapter are found in note 3 below.

2. Grant Luckenbill, *Untold Millions: Gay and Lesbian Markets in America* (New York: Harper Business/HarperCollins, 1995).

3. These include Chasin, *Selling Out;* Gluckman, *Homo Economics;* Sender, *Business, Not Politics;* Duggan, *Twilight of Equality?;* and Hennessey, *Profit and Pleasure.*

4. Chasin, *Selling Out,* 27.

5. For a detailed list of the expansion of airlines' nondiscrimination policies regarding sexual orientation in the early 1990s, see Baker, Strub, and Henning, *Cracking the Corporate Closet,* 195–205.

6. Ibid., 19.

7. James O'Toole, "Best Companies List Hits Gay Rights Milestone," *CNNMoney,* January 20, 2012, http://money.cnn.com/2012/01/20/pf/jobs/best_companies_gay_rights/.

8. Baker, Strub, and Henning, *Cracking the Corporate Closet,* 195.

9. John Czyz to Kevin Lum (United Airlines MEC president), e-mail, June 23 1996, included in a fax from Kevin Lum to David Borer, General Counsel, AFA, June 24, 1996, in folder "UAL—Domestic Partners/Benefits—1996," Box 10 of 28, Accession "8–6-04 AFA Legal," Association of Flight Attendants Archives, Wayne State University, Detroit, MI.

10. Kevin Lum to David Borer, fax.

11. David Borer, General Counsel AFA, to Kevin Lum, United Airlines MEC President, memo re: Domestic Partner Benefits, October 8 1996, in folder "UAL—Domestic Partner Benefits—1996," Box 28 of 28, Accession "8–6–04 AFA Legal," Association of Flight Attendants Archives, Wayne State University, Detroit, MI.

12. Among the controversial elements of the proposed agreement were a wage freeze for flight attendants from 1997 until 2001 (with year-end lump sum bonuses partly compensating for the stagnant wages); a commitment to use foreign-based flight attendants, who were less experienced and therefore cheaper, on 40 percent of international flights; and resolution of a dispute involving retirement benefits for around seven thousand senior flight attendants. One AFA spokesperson summed up: "There is something in this for everyone and something not to like." Judith Crown, "United Flight Attendants' Pact under Fire," *Crain's Chicago Business*, September 8, 1997, 1.

13. Cynthia Laird, "Landmark DP Law Is a Success, Mayor Says," *Bay Area Reporter*, January 8, 1998, 1.

14. City of San Francisco Supervisor Leslie Katz, quoted in Bruce Mirken, "Battle with Airlines over Domestic Partner Benefits Continues," *San Francisco Bay Times*, March 19, 1998, 3.

15. FedEx spokesperson Jess Bunn, quoted in ibid., 3.

16. *Air Transport Association of America v. City & County of San Francisco*, 266 F.3d 1064, (9th Cir. 2001).

17. Quoted in "Defense Reply Brief in Support of Cross-Motion for Summary Judgment," January 22, 1999, 1, *Air Transport Association of America, et al. v. City and County of San Francisco, et al.*, Case number C97–1763 CW (U.S. District Court, Northern District of California, Oakland Division), National Archives and Records Administration Archives, San Bruno, CA.

18. Ibid., 9.

19. Details of the protests are covered in Nicole Christine Raeburn, *Changing Corporate America from Inside Out: Lesbian and Gay Workplace Rights* (Minneapolis: University of Minnesota Press, 2004), 118 ff.

20. Gil Criswell, "Community Must Remain United!," *San Francisco Spectrum*, March 5 1999, 1.

21. Fear of negatively affecting their court case against the ATA led the city's board to refrain from an official, full-fledged boycott of the two companies.

22. I look forward to the eventual publication of Ryan Murphy's book on flight attendant activism tied to the San Francisco domestic partner law. His dissertation is Ryan Murphy, "On Our Own: Flight Attendant Labor and the Family Values Economy" (PhD diss., University of Minnesota, 2010).

23. "Declaration of Patrick Galbreath in Opposition to Plaintiff's Motion for Injunction Pending Appeal," June 18, 1999, 6, *Air Transport Association of America, et al. v. City and County of San Francisco, et al.*, Case No. C97–1763 CW (U.S. District

Court, Northern District of California, Oakland Division), in National Archives and Records Administration Archives, San Bruno, CA.

24. *Air Transport Association of America v. City & County of San Francisco*, 266 F.3d 1064, (9th Cir. 2001).

25. U.S. Department of Transportation, Research and Innovative Technology Administration, Bureau of Transportation Statistics, "Airline Travel since 9/11," *Issue Brief*, December 2005, 1.

26. Massachusetts Institute of Technology, Global Airline Industry Program, "Airline Industry Overview," http://web.mit.edu/airlines/analysis/analysis_airline_industry.html (accessed February 25, 2012). The original statistic was provided by the Air Transport Association in its "ATA 2007 Economic Report."

27. Ibid., 2. While so-called budget carriers like Southwest and Jet Blue did grow between 2001 and 2005, their increased employment numbers added a total of only 5,600 jobs—far too few to compensate for the loss of over 150,000 jobs from the network carriers. Simply put, the airlines were flying the same number of passengers in July 2005 as before 9/11, but with considerably fewer employees and even slightly fewer available seats than before.

28. Cynthia Laird, "FINALLY! United to Give DP Benefits," *Bay Area Reporter*, August 5, 1999, 20.

29. "The Friendlier Skies," *Bay Area Reporter*, August 5, 1999, 6.

30. *Air Transport Association of America v. City & County of San Francisco*, 266 F.3d 1064, (9th Cir. 2001).

31. Caroline Daniel, "Start of a Longer Haul into the JetBlue Yonder," *Financial Times*, August 26, 2002, 8.

32. The 1999 costs for US Airways and Southwest are reported by David Coburn, "Heading for a Hard Landing?," *Philadelphia Inquirer*, March 23, 2000, D1. The JetBlue statistic comes from Laurence Zuckerman, "JetBlue, Exception among Airlines, Is Likely to Post a Profit," *New York Times*, November 7, 2001, C3.

33. Daniel, "Start of a Longer Haul."

34. Michael Idov, "Steven Slater's Landing," *New York Magazine*, January 30, 2011.

35. Quoted in Andy Newman and Ray Rivera, "Fed-Up Flight Attendant Makes Sliding Exit," *New York Times*, August 9, 2010.

36. Idov, "Steven Slater's Landing."

37. Barry Paddock et al., "Out to Launch! Wacky Steward Says He Wants to Fly Again," *New York Daily News*, August 13, 2010, 10.

38. Christina Boyle et al., "Rage Just Took Off: JetBlue Jumper's Fuse Lit before Flight Left Gate," *New York Daily News*, August 12, 2010, 5.

39. Idov, "Steven Slater's Landing."

40. Alison Gendar, Oren Yaniv, and Dave Goldiner, "Coffee, Tea . . . or Flee! As JetBlue Flight Lands, Attendant Goes on Rant Grabs Beer & Slides Down Emergency

Exit to Tarmac Heads for Home, Where Cops Find Him & Beau in Bed," *New York Daily News*, August 10, 2010, 2.

41. Idov, "Steven Slater's Landing."

42. Ibid.

43. Ibid.

44. Ibid.

45. Lore Croghan et al., "New Hero Takes Flight. Forget Sully! Slater Earns Nation's Admiration for 'Grand Exit,'" *New York Daily News*, August 11, 2010, 4.

46. Bill Hutchinson, "JetBlue Big Says Slater 'Not a Hero in My Book,'" *New York Daily News*, August 31, 2010, 23.

47. Paddock et al., "Out to Launch."

48. Thomas Zambito and James Fanelli, "Runway Rage 'Hero' Avoids Prison Time," *New York Daily News*, October 20, 2010, 10.

49. Tamer El-Ghobashy, "Sorry for Rough Landing—JetBlue Attendant Who Left Flight via Escape Chute Pleads Guilty, Apologizes," *Wall Street Journal*, October 20, 2010, A3.

50. Ibid.

51. Idov, "Steven Slater's Landing."

CONCLUSION

1. Serling, *From the Captain*, 170.

2. Bob Witeck, interview by author, Washington, DC, April 17, 2010.

3. Ibid.

BIBLIOGRAPHY

ARCHIVES

AIDS Collection, Quebec Gay Archives, Montreal, QC.

Airline periodicals, various, Transportation Library, Northwestern University, Evanston, IL.

Alternative Literature Ephemera, Special Collections, Northwestern University Library, Evanston, IL.

Association of Flight Attendants Collection, Walter Reuther Archives of Labor and Urban Affairs, Wayne State University, Detroit, MI.

Association of Professional Flight Attendants Archives, APFA Headquarters, Euless, TX.

Braniff Airlines Papers, Special Collections, University of Texas at Dallas Library, Richardson, TX.

Diaz v. Pan Am files, Federal Court Records, National Archives, Southeast Region, Atlanta, GA.

Eddie V. Rickenbacker Papers, Special Collections, Auburn University Library, Auburn, AL.

Independent Union of Flight Attendants Collection, Robert F. Wagner Labor Archives, New York University, New York, NY.

National Airlines Papers, Historical Museum of Southern Florida, Miami, FL.

New York State Division of Human Rights Collection, New York State Archives, Albany, NY.

ONE National Gay and Lesbian Archives, Los Angeles, CA.

Pan Am Archives, Special Collections, University of Miami Libraries, Coral Gables, FL.

Randy Shilts Papers, James C. Hormel Gay and Lesbian Center, San Francisco Public Library, San Francisco, CA.

Smithsonian National Air and Space Museum Archives, Washington, DC.

Stewardesses for Women's Rights Collection, Special Collections, Northwestern University Library, Evanston, IL.

Transport Workers Union of America Collection, Robert F. Wagner Labor Archives, New York University, New York, NY.

Wilson v. Southwest Airlines files, Federal Court Records, National Archives, Southwest Region, Fort Worth, TX.

PUBLISHED WORKS

Altschuler, Glenn, and Stuart Blumin. *The GI Bill: The New Deal for Veterans.* New York: Oxford University Press, 2009.

Auerbach, D. M., W. W. Darrow, H. W. Jaffe, and J. W. Curran. "Cluster of Cases of the Acquired Immune Deficiency Syndrome: Patients Linked by Sexual Contact." *American Journal of Medicine* 76 (March 1984): 487–91.

Bailey, Elizabeth E., David R. Graham, and Daniel P. Kaplan. "Routes and Industry Performance." In *Deregulating the Airlines*, 67–90. Cambridge, MA: MIT Press, 1985.

Baker, Daniel B., Sean O'Brien Strub, and Bill Henning. *Cracking the Corporate Closet.* New York: Harper Business, 1995.

Baker, Trudy, and Rachel Jones. *Coffee, Tea or Me? The Uninhibited Memoirs of Two Airline Stewardesses.* New York: Bartholomew House, 1967.

Barry, Kathleen. *Femininity in Flight: A History of Flight Attendants.* Durham: Duke University Press, 2007.

———. "Femininity in Flight: Flight Attendants, Glamour, and Pink-Collar Activism in the Twentieth-Century United States." PhD diss., New York University, 2002.

Bayer, Ronald, and Gerald Oppenheimer. *AIDS Doctors: Voices from the Epidemic.* New York: Oxford University Press, 2000.

Berkowitz, Richard, and Michael Callen. *How to Have Sex in an Epidemic: One Approach.* New York: News from the Front Publications, 1983.

Berman, Jillian. "Defining the 'Essence of the Business': An Analysis of Title VII's Privacy BFOQ after *Johnson Controls*." *University of Chicago Law Review* 67 (Summer 2000): 749–76.

Berne, Eric. *Games People Play.* New York: Grove Press, 1964.

————. *The Structure and Dynamics of Organizations and Groups*. Philadelphia: Lippincott, 1963.

Bérubé, Allan. *Coming Out under Fire: The History of Gay Men and Women in World War Two*. New York: Free Press, 1990.

————. *My Desire for History: Essays in Gay, Community, and Labor History*. Chapel Hill: University of North Carolina Press, 2011.

Boyd, Nan Alamilla. *Wide Open Town: A History of Queer San Francisco to 1965*. Berkeley: University of California Press, 2003.

Brauer, Carl. "Women Activists, Southern Conservatives, and the Prohibition of Sex Discrimination in Title VII of the 1964 Sex Discrimination Act." *Journal of Southern History* 49, no. 1 (1983): 37–56.

Bray, Alan. *Homosexuality in Renaissance England*. London: Gay Men's Press, 1982.

Brier, Jennifer. *Infectious Ideas*. Chapel Hill: University of North Carolina Press, 2009.

Bryant, Anita. *The Anita Bryant Story: The Survival of Our Nation's Families and the Threat of Militant Homosexuality*. Old Tappan, NJ: Revell, 1977.

Cahill, Kevin, ed. *The AIDS Epidemic*. New York: St. Martin's Press, 1983.

Canaday, Margot. *The Straight State: Sexuality and Citizenship in Twentieth-Century America*. Princeton: Princeton University Press, 2009.

Chasin, Alexandra. *Selling Out: The Gay and Lesbian Movement Goes to Market*. New York: Palgrave Macmillan, 2000.

Chauncey, George. *Gay New York: Gender, Urban Culture, and the Making of the Gay Male World, 1890–1940*. New York: Basic Books, 1994.

Christian, Paula. *Edge of Twilight*. Greenwich, CT: Fawcett Publications, 1961.

Cobble, Dorothy Sue. *Dishing It Out: Waitresses and Their Unions in the Twentieth Century*. Urbana: University of Illinois Press, 1991.

————. *The Other Women's Movement: Workplace Justice and Social Rights in Modern America*. Princeton: Princeton University Press, 2004.

————. *Women and Unions: Forging a Partnership*. Ithaca, NY: ILR Press, 1993.

Cochrane, Michelle. *When AIDS Began*. New York: Routledge, 2004.

Cole, Shaun. *"Don We Now Our Gay Apparel": Gay Men's Dress in the Twentieth Century*. Oxford: Berg, 2000.

Comstock, Gary David. "Dismantling the Homosexual Panic Defense." *Law and Sexuality Review* 2 (1992): 81–102.

Corber, Robert J. *In the Name of National Security: Hitchcock, Homophobia, and the Political Construction of Gender in Postwar America*. Durham: Duke University Press, 1993.

Courtwright, David T. *No Right Turn: Conservative Politics in a Liberal America*. Cambridge, MA: Harvard University Press, 2010.

————. *Sky as Frontier: Adventure, Aviation, and Empire.* College Station: Texas A&M University Press, 2005.

Cowan, Ruth Schwartz. "The 'Industrial Revolution' in the Home: Household Technology and Social Change in the 20th Century." *Technology and Culture* 17 (1976): 1–24.

Crimp, Douglas. "How to Have Promiscuity in an Epidemic." *October* 43 (Winter 1987): 237–71.

Critchlow, Donald. *Phyllis Schlafly and Grassroots Conservatism: A Woman's Crusade.* Princeton: Princeton University Press, 2005.

Daley, Robert. *An American Saga: Juan Trippe and His Pan Am Empire.* New York: Random House, 1980.

Darrow, William, E. M. Gorman, and B. P. Glick. "The Social Origins of AIDS: Social Change, Sexual Behavior, and Disease Trends." In *The Social Dimensions of AIDS*, edited by Douglas Feldman and Thomas Johnson, 95–107. New York: Praeger Press, 1986.

Davidson, Kenneth M., Ruth B. Ginsburg, and Herma H. Kay. *Sex-Based Discrimination: Text, Cases, and Materials.* Minneapolis: West Publishing, 1974.

Davies, Margery W. *Woman's Place Is at the Typewriter: Office Work and Office Workers, 1870–1930.* Philadelphia: Temple University Press, 1982.

Davis, Sidney. *Delta Air Lines: Debunking the Myth.* Atlanta: Peachtree, 1988.

Dean, Robert D. *Imperial Brotherhood: Gender and the Making of Cold War Foreign Policy.* Amherst: University of Massachusetts Press, 2001.

D'Emilio, John. "Capitalism and Gay Identity." In *The Lesbian and Gay Studies Reader*, edited by Henry Abelove, Michèle Barale and David Halperin, 467–78. New York: Routledge, 1993.

————. *Lost Prophet: The Life and Times of Bayard Rustin.* New York: Free Press, 2003.

————. *Sexual Politics, Sexual Communities: The Making of a Homosexual Minority in the United States, 1940–1970.* 2nd ed. Chicago: University of Chicago Press, 1998.

Dooley, Cathleen. "Battle in the Sky: A Cultural and Legal History of Sex Discrimination in the United States Airline Industry, 1930–1980." PhD diss., University of Arizona, 2001.

Duany, Jorge. *The Puerto Rican Nation on the Move: Identities on the Island and in the United States.* Chapel Hill: University of North Carolina Press, 2002.

Duberman, Martin. *Stonewall.* New York: Penguin Press, 1994.

Duggan, Lisa. *Sapphic Slashers: Sex, Violence, and American Modernity.* Durham: Duke University Press, 2000.

————. *Twilight of Equality? Neoliberalism, Cultural Politics, and the Attack on Democracy.* Boston: Beacon Press, 2003.

Ehrenreich, Barbara. *The Hearts of Men: American Dreams and the Flight from Commitment*. Garden City, NY: Anchor Press/Doubleday, 1983.

Engle, Karen. "The Persistence of Neutrality: The Failure of the Religious Accommodation Provision to Redeem Title VII." *Texas Law Review* 76, no. 2 (1997): 317–433.

———. "What's So Special about Special Rights?" *Denver University Law Review* 75 (1998): 1265–1303.

Evans, Joan. "Cautious Caregivers: Gender Stereotypes and the Sexualization of Men Nurses' Touch." *Journal of Advanced Nursing* 40, no. 4 (2002): 441–48.

———. "Men Nurses: A Historical and Feminist Perspective." *Journal of Advanced Nursing* 47, no. 3 (2004): 321–28.

Evans, Sara M. *Personal Politics: The Roots of Women's Liberation in the Civil Rights Movement and the New Left*. New York: Knopf, 1979.

Farmer, Paul. *AIDS and Accusation*. Berkeley: University of California Press, 2006.

Fejes, Fred. *Gay Rights and Moral Panic: The Origins of America's Debate on Homosexuality*. New York: Palgrave, 2008.

———. "Murder, Perversion, and Moral Panic: The 1954 Media Campaign against Miami's Homosexuals and the Discourse of Civic Betterment." *Journal of the History of Sexuality* 9, no. 3 (2000): 305–47.

Fettner, Ann, and William Check. *The Truth about AIDS: Evolution of an Epidemic*. New York: Holt, Rinehart and Winston, 1984.

Foss, Rene. *Around the World in a Bad Mood! Confessions of a Flight Attendant*. New York: Hyperion, 2002.

Foucault, Michel. *The History of Sexuality*. New York: Vintage Books, 1990.

Foy, Nancy. *The Sun Never Sets on IBM*. New York: Morrow, 1975.

Franklin, Cary. "The Anti-Stereotyping Principle in Constitutional Sex Discrimination Law." *NYU Law Review* 85 (April 2010): 105–14.

Freedman, Estelle. "'Uncontrolled Desires': The Response to the Sexual Psychopath, 1920–1960." *Journal of American History* 74, no. 1 (1987): 83–106.

Freeman, Jo. "How 'Sex' Got into Title VII: Persistent Opportunism as a Maker of Public Policy." In *We Will Be Heard: Women's Struggles for Political Power in the United States*, 171–90. Lanham, MD: Rowman and Littlefield, 2008.

Freeman, Joshua Benjamin. *In Transit: The Transport Workers Union in New York City, 1933–1966*. New York: Oxford University Press, 1989.

Gallagher, John, and Chris Bull. *Perfect Enemies: The Battle between the Religious Right and the Gay Movement*. Lanham, MD: Madison Books, 2001.

Gehring, Wes. *Screwball Comedy: A Genre of Madcap Romance*. Westport, CT: Greenwood Press, 1986.

Gerson, Kathleen. *No Man's Land: Men's Changing Commitments to Family and Work.* New York: Basic Books, 1993.

Gilbert, James Burkhart. *Men in the Middle: Searching for Masculinity in the 1950s.* Chicago: University of Chicago Press, 2005.

Gilbert, M. Thomas, Andrew Rambaut, Gabriela Wlasiuk, Thomas J. Spira, Arthur E. Pitchenik, and Michael Worobey. "The Emergence of HIV/AIDS in the Americas and Beyond." *Proceedings of the National Academy of Sciences* 104, no. 47 (November 20, 2007): 1–5.

Gluckman, Amy. *Homo Economics: Capitalism, Community, and Lesbian and Gay Life.* New York: Routledge, 1997.

Graham, Hugh Davis. *The Civil Rights Era: Origins and Development of National Policy, 1960–1972.* New York: Oxford University Press, 1990.

Greider, William. *Fortress America: The American Military and the Consequences of Peace.* New York: Public Affairs, 1998.

Hansen, Miriam. "Of Mice and Ducks: Benjamin and Adorno on Disney." *South Atlantic Quarterly* 92, no. 1 (1993): 27–62.

Harrison, Cynthia Ellen. "A 'New Frontier' for Women: The Public Policy of the Kennedy Administration." *Journal of American History* 67, no. 3 (1980): 630–46.

———. *On Account of Sex: The Politics of Women's Issues, 1945–1968.* Berkeley: University of California Press, 1988.

Heins, Marjorie. *Not in Front of the Children: "Indecency," Censorship, and the Innocence of Youth.* New York: Hill and Wang, 2001.

Hennessey, Rosemary. *Profit and Pleasure: Sexual Identities in Late Capitalism.* New York: Routledge, 2000.

Hochschild, Arlie Russell. *The Managed Heart: Commercialization of Human Feeling.* Berkeley: University of California Press, 1983.

Hollander, Anne. *Sex and Suits.* New York: Knopf, 1994.

Hunt, Gerald, ed. *Laboring for Rights: Unions and Sexual Diversity across Nations.* Philadelphia: Temple University Press, 1999.

Hurewitz, Daniel. *Bohemian Los Angeles and the Making of Modern Politics.* Berkeley: University of California Press, 2007.

Huxley, Aldous. *Brave New World: A Novel.* Garden City, NY: Garden City Publishing, 1932.

Jagose, Annamarie. *Queer Theory: An Introduction.* New York: NYU Press, 1996.

Jarvis, Christina S. *The Male Body at War: American Masculinity during World War II.* DeKalb: Northern Illinois University Press, 2004.

Jeffers, H. Paul. *Ace of Aces: The Life of Captain Eddie Rickenbacker*. New York: Ballantine Books, 2003.

Johnson, David K. *The Lavender Scare: The Cold War Persecution of Gays and Lesbians in the Federal Government*. Chicago: University of Chicago Press, 2004.

Kane, Paula. *Sex Objects in the Sky: A Personal Account of the Stewardess Rebellion*. Chicago: Follett, 1974.

Kardiner, Abram. *Sex and Morality*. Indianapolis: Bobbs-Merrill, 1954.

Keller, Yvonne. "'Was It Right to Love Her Brother's Wife So Passionately?' Lesbian Pulp Novels and U.S. Lesbian Identity, 1950–1965." *American Quarterly* 57, no. 2 (2005): 385–410.

Kennedy, Elizabeth Lapovsky, and Madeline D. Davis. *Boots of Leather, Slippers of Gold: The History of a Lesbian Community*. New York: Routledge, 1993.

Kepner, Jim. *Rough News, Daring Views: 1950s' Pioneer Gay Press Journalism*. New York: Harrington Park Press, 1998.

Kessler-Harris, Alice. *In Pursuit of Equity: Women, Men, and the Quest for Economic Citizenship in 20th-Century America*. New York: Oxford University Press, 2001.

———. *Out to Work: A History of Wage-Earning Women in the United States*. New York: Oxford University Press, 1982.

Kimmel, Michael S. *Manhood in America: A Cultural History*. New York: Free Press, 1996.

Kinsey, Alfred C., Wardell Baxter Pomeroy, and Clyde Eugene Martin. *Sexual Behavior in the Human Female*. Philadelphia: W. B. Saunders, 1953.

———. *Sexual Behavior in the Human Male*. Philadelphia: W. B. Saunders, 1948.

Knauer, Nancy. "Domestic Partnership and Same-Sex Relationships: A Marketplace Innovation and a Less Than Perfect Institutional Choice." *Temple Political and Civil Rights Law Review* 7, no. 43 (1998): 337–45.

Koren, Jay. *The Company We Kept*. McLean, VA: Paladwr Press, 2000.

Krupat, Kitty and Patrick McCreery. *Out at Work: Building a Gay-Labor Alliance*. Minneapolis: University of Minnesota Press, 2001.

Lerman, Nina, Ruth Oldenziel, and Arwen Mohun. "Introduction: Interrogating Boundaries." In *Gender and Technology: A Reader*, edited by Nina Lerman, Ruth Oldenziel, and Arwen Mohun. Baltimore: Johns Hopkins University Press, 2003.

Lewis, W. David. *Eddie Rickenbacker: An American Hero in the Twentieth Century*. Baltimore: Johns Hopkins University Press, 2005.

Lichtenstein, Alex. "Putting Labor's House in Order: The Transport Workers Union and Labor Anti-Communism in Miami during the 1940s." *Labor History* 39, no. 1 (1998): 7–23.

Luckenbill, Grant. *Untold Millions: Gay and Lesbian Markets in America*. New York: Harper Business/HarperCollins, 1995.

Lynd, Robert Staughton, and Helen Merrell Lynd. *Middletown in Transition: A Study in Cultural Conflicts*. New York: Harcourt Brace, 1937.

MacLean, Nancy. *Freedom Is Not Enough: The Opening of the American Workplace*. Cambridge, MA: Harvard University Press, 2008.

Maley, Carney. "Flying the 'Unfriendly Skies': Flight Attendant Activism, 1964–1982." PhD diss., Boston University, 2011.

Mansbridge, Jane J. *Why We Lost the ERA*. Chicago: University of Chicago Press, 1986.

Markusen, Ann R., and Joel Yudken. *Dismantling the Cold War Economy*. New York: Basic Books, 1992.

Martin, Del, and Phyllis Lyon. *Lesbian/Woman*. 1972. Reprint, Volcano, CA: Volcano Press, 1991.

May, Elaine Tyler. *Homeward Bound: American Families in the Cold War Era*. New York: Basic Books, 1988.

McCoy, Scott. "The Homosexual-Advance Defense and Hate Crimes Statutes: Their Interaction and Conflict." *Cardozo Law Review* 22 (2000–2001): 629–63.

McGowan, Sharon. "The Bona Fide Body: Title VII's Last Bastion of Intentional Sex Discrimination." *Columbia Journal of Gender and Law* 12 (2003): 77–80.

McKay, Richard. "Imagining 'Patient Zero': Sexuality, Blame, and the Origins of the North American AIDS Epidemic." DPhil diss., Oxford University, 2011.

Meeker, Martin. *Contacts Desired: Gay and Lesbian Communications and Community, 1940s–1970s*. Chicago: University of Chicago Press, 2006.

Meikle, Jeffrey L. *Twentieth Century Limited: Industrial Design in America, 1925–1939*. Philadelphia: Temple University Press, 1979.

Melosh, Barbara. *Engendering Culture: Manhood and Womanhood in New Deal Public Art and Theater*. Washington, DC: Smithsonian Institution Press, 1991.

———. *"The Physician's Hand": Work Culture and Conflict in American Nursing*. Philadelphia: Temple University Press, 1982.

Mezey, Susan Gluck. *In Pursuit of Equality: Women, Public Policy, and the Federal Courts*. New York: St. Martin's Press, 1992.

Minton, Henry. *Departing from Deviance: A History of Homosexual Rights and Emancipatory Science in America*. Chicago: University of Chicago Press, 2002.

Mison, Robert. "Homophobia in Manslaughter: The Homosexual Advance as Insufficient Provocation." *California Legal Review* 80, no. 1 (1992): 133–41.

Muniz, Pedro. *My Book: Tales of Travels and Tribulations*. Santo Domingo: Editora Corripio, 1987.

Murphy, Ryan. "On Our Own: Flight Attendant Labor and the Family Values Economy." PhD diss., University of Minnesota, 2010.

Musbach, Alice, and Barbara Davis. *Flight Attendant: From Career Planning to Professional Service*. New York: Crown, 1980.

Nast, Heidi J. "Queer Patriarchies, Queer Racisms, International." *Antipode* 34, no. 5 (2002): 874–909.

Nielsen, Georgia Panter. *From Sky Girl to Flight Attendant: Women and the Making of a Union*. Ithaca, NY: ILR Press, 1982.

Oleske, James, et al. "Immune Deficiency Syndrome in Children." *Journal of the American Medical Association* 249 (May 6, 1983): 2345–49.

Orason, Roy. *Plight of a Flight Attendant*. Citrus Heights, CA: Sierra, 1994.

Patton, Cindy. *Inventing AIDS*. New York: Routledge, 1990.

Raeburn, Nicole Christine. *Changing Corporate America from Inside Out: Lesbian and Gay Workplace Rights*. Minneapolis: University of Minnesota Press, 2004.

Raimondo, Meredith. "Dateline Atlanta: Place and the Social Construction of AIDS." In *Carryin' On in the Lesbian and Gay South*, edited by John Howard, 331–69. New York: NYU Press, 1997.

Randall, Lyman. *A Definitive Study of Your Future as an Airline Steward/Stewardess*. 1973. Reprint, New York: R. Rosen, 1973.

Ritter, Gretchen. *The Constitution as Social Design: Gender and Civic Membership in the American Constitutional Order*. Stanford: Stanford University Press, 2006.

Rosen, Ruth. *The World Split Open: How the Modern Women's Movement Changed America*. New York: Penguin Press, 2000.

Rotundo, E. Anthony. *American Manhood: Transformations in Masculinity from the Revolution to the Modern Era*. New York: Basic Books, 1993.

Rozen, Frieda Shoenberg. "Turbulence in the Air: The Autonomy Movement in the Flight Attendant Unions." PhD diss., Pennsylvania State University, 1988.

Rydell, Robert W. *World of Fairs: The Century-of-Progress Expositions*. Chicago: University of Chicago Press, 1993.

Savage, William W. *Comic Books and America, 1945–1954*. Norman: University of Oklahoma Press, 1990.

Scales, Ann. "Feminist Legal Method: Not So Scary." *UCLA Women's Law Journal* 2 (1992): 1–34.

Schiller, Herbert I., and Joseph Dexter Phillips. *Super-State: Readings in the Military-Industrial Complex*. Urbana: University of Illinois Press, 1970.

Sears, James T. *Lonely Hunters: An Oral History of Lesbian and Gay Southern Life, 1948–1968*. Boulder, CO: Westview Press, 1997.

Sedgwick, Eve Kosofsky. *Between Men: English Literature and Male Homosocial Desire, Gender and Culture*. New York: Columbia University Press, 1985.

———. *Epistemology of the Closet*. Berkeley: University of California Press, 1990.

Sender, Katherine. *Business, Not Politics: The Making of the Gay Market*. New York: Columbia University Press, 2004.

Serling, Robert. *From the Captain to the Colonel: An Informal History of Eastern Airlines*. New York: Dial Press, 1980.

———. *The Only Way to Fly: The Story of Western Airlines, America's Senior Air Carrier*. Garden City, NY: Doubleday, 1976.

Shilts, Randy. *And the Band Played On: Politics, People, and the AIDS Epidemic*. New York: St. Martin's Press, 1987.

———. *The Mayor of Castro Street*. New York: St. Martin's Press, 1982.

Solberg, Carl. *Conquest of the Skies: A History of Commercial Aviation in America*. Boston: Little, Brown, 1979.

Stackhouse, Max L. *The Ethics of Necropolis: An Essay on the Military-Industrial Complex and the Quest for a Just Peace*. Boston: Beacon Press, 1971.

Suzik, Jeffrey Ryan. "'Building Better Men': The CCC Boy and the Changing Social Ideal of Manliness." *Men and Masculinities* 2 (October 1999): 152–79.

Thompson, Mark. *Long Road to Freedom: The Advocate History of the Gay and Lesbian Movement*. New York: St. Martin's Press, 1994.

Tiemeyer, Phil. "'Male Stewardesses': Male Flight Attendants as a Queer Miscarriage of Justice." *Genders*, Spring 2007, www.genders.org.

———. "Technology and Gay Identity: The Case of the Pre-World War II Male Flight Attendant." *History and Technology* 27 (June 2011): 155–81.

Tye, Larry. *Rising from the Rails: Pullman Porters and the Making of the Black Middle Class*. New York: Henry Holt, 2004.

Vander Meulen, Jacob A. *The Politics of Aircraft: Building an American Military Industry*. Lawrence: University Press of Kansas, 1991.

Wald, Priscilla. *Contagious: Cultures, Carriers, and the Outbreak Narrative*. Durham: Duke University Press, 2008.

Waugh, Thomas. *Out/Lines: Underground Gay Graphics from before Stonewall*. Vancouver, BC: Arsenal Pulp, 2005.

Williams, George. "The Impact of Hub and Spoke Networks." In *The Airline Industry and the Impact of Deregulation*, 18–27. Brookfield, VT: Ashgate, 1994.

Wilson, Richard Guy, Dianne H. Pilgrim, Dickran Tashjian, and Brooklyn Museum. *The Machine Age in America, 1918–1941*. New York: Brooklyn Museum / Abrams, 1986.

Wilson, Sloan. *The Man in the Gray Flannel Suit*. New York: Simon and Schuster, 1955.

Witeck, Robert, and Wesley Combs. *Business Inside Out*. Chicago: Kaplan, 2006.

Zelman, Patricia G. *Women, Work, and National Policy: The Kennedy-Johnson Years*. Studies in American History and Culture. Ann Arbor: UMI Research Press, 1982.

INDEX

ACT UP, 170, 191, 193

Advocate magazine, 116–18, 134, 249n25, 249n30

AIDS (Acquired Immune Deficiency Syndrome). *See* HIV/AIDS

AIDS Quilt (NAMES Project), vii, 161, 165–67, 190, 204

Air Canada, 3–4, 11, 137, 140, 141, 154, 178, 179, 181, 223

aircraft technology: DC-3, 17, 24–26, 28, 29, 34, 42, 47, 52; Ford tri-motor, 19; and influence on flight attendant gender roles, 17–18, 20, 24, 33, 41, 54, 56, 97; innovations during World War II and immediate aftermath, 20, 47, 52, 54, 56, 58; jet airplanes, x, 52, 54, 58, 97; Pan Am Clipper, 17, 24–25, 52

Air Line Pilots Association (ALPA), 50

Air Line Stewards and Stewardess Association (ALSSA), 50, 110

Air Transport Association (ATA), 95–96, 99, 202, 203, 205

American Airlines: bestowal of queer-friendly employee benefits, 187, 189–90, 193, 197, 203, 204, 208, 224; embrace of "gay-friendly" public relations strategy, 12, 170, 186–91, 193, 195, 197, 203, 204, 207, 224; stewardesses at, 29, 44, 125; hiring of first stewards in 1970s, 10, 111, 118, 124, 125, 134; route network, 28; target of 9/11 terrorists, 206; treatment of HIV-positive employees and passengers, 154, 155, 170, 180, 181, 183, 186–89, 190, 193, 197, 223, 224; wages for flight attendants, 217

American Civil Liberties Union (ACLU), 5, 94, 95, 112, 126, 128, 201. *See also* Ginsburg, Ruth Bader

Americans with Disabilities Act, 11, 138, 189, 195

And the Band Played On: events surrounding publication of, 169, 170, 174, 175, 177, 178, 179, 193; portrayal of Patient Zero in, vi, 4, 11, 137, 138, 139, 146, 147, 168, 169, 171–74; profile of the early AIDS crisis in, 156, 168, 171. *See also* Patient Zero myth; Shilts, Randy

181, 182; male stewards after *Diaz*, 134; as non-union, 50, 68, 121; routes, 28, 57, 233n42

Denneny, Michael, 11, 174–79, 193

Denver Conference of PWAs (1983), 162, 163, 164, 165, 188, 192

deregulation of airline industry: contemporaneity with bestowal of queer benefits, 12, 194, 196; creation of hub-and-spoke networks, 142–45; financial repercussions for airlines, 53, 194, 209, 217–19; impact on flight attendant employment and wages, 155, 194, 196, 216, 217–19, 225; impact on flight attendant labor unions, 194, 217–19, 224; invocation in Equal Benefits Ordinance case, 202, 205, 208–9; strikes by flight attendant unions, 217

Diaz, Celio, Jr.: personal history, 10, 81, 93–94, 106, 108; portrayal in media, 113, 116–7; role in *Diaz v. Pan Am*, 1, 5, 9, 57, 68, 83, 89–92, 94, 96, 97, 98, 100–108, 112, 128, 134, 138, 194, 197, 222, 224. See also *Diaz v. Pan Am*

Diaz v. Pan Am: as a case brought by a male plaintiff, 5; as compared to *McNeil v. Pan Am*, 91–92, 98–100, 103, 106–7; and EEOC, 1, 83, 89–91, 92, 94–96, 97, 100, 104, 108, 113; and federal appeals court, 83, 94–96, 104–5; and federal district court, 83, 91–103; importance to gender-based civil rights law, 1, 3, 5, 9–10, 83, 89, 90, 106–8, 112, 126–28, 134, 222, 224; importance to queer equality movement, 10, 83–84, 100–8, 115–18, 132, 134; interpretation of Title VII of Civil Rights Act, 84, 91, 96–103 (*see also* bona fide occupational qualification); media coverage of, 1–2, 5, 112–15, 115–18; opposition to decision, 1–2, 10, 84, 112–15;

personalities involved in, 93–96; queer press reaction to decision, 115–18; role in allowing male applicants for flight attendant jobs, 2, 3, 8, 106, 109–11, 119, 140, 150, 217, 222; role in overturning discrimination against stewardesses, 90, 106, 110, 124–5, 217, 222; use of homophobic defense by Pan Am, 92, 100–104, 108, 112, 118, 128, 224; and US Supreme Court, 83, 106.

disability rights. *See* HIV/AIDS

domestic partner benefits and airlines: bestowal by US corporations, 196, 198; buddy passes as precursors, 132–33, 197, 198, 207; challenge of Equal Benefits Ordinance by airlines, 201–9, 224; conservative resistance to, 202, 204; extension of full benefits, 3, 4, 12, 186, 193, 195, 196, 197, 207–9, 211, 217, 218, 224; flight attendant labor unions' stance on, 195, 196, 197–201, 203, 204. *See also* Association of Flight Attendants; United Airlines

Dugas, Gaëtan: impact on flight attendants' reputation, 11, 12, 137, 170, 197, 213, 224–25; impact on perceptions of queer sexual freedoms, 11, 137, 138, 169, 170, 179–80, 193, 213, 223; as Patient Zero, 4, 11, 137, 139, 146, 167, 168, 169, 170, 172, 174, 176, 177–78, 180, 193; personal history, 137, 140, 141–42, 150, 154, 165, 167, 171, 223; portrayal in *And the Band Played On*, 168, 171, 172–74, 177, 223; portrayal in *Zero Patience*, 191–93; role in CDC cluster study, 139, 143, 146, 147, 148, 171, 172–73; sexual activity, 137, 141, 143, 147, 148, 171, 173–74, 177–78, 179–80; treatment by Air Canada, 154, 223. *See also* Patient Zero

queer equality (LGBTQ rights): airline support for, 4, 12, 186–91, 193, 194–219, 224–25; and *Diaz v. Pan Am*, 10, 83–84, 100–108, 115–18, 132, 134; and the EEOC, 87–91, 107–8, 129; efforts to expand Title VII for homosexuals, 128–31; growing public acceptance of in 2000s, 214; importance of 1964 Civil Rights Act to, 81, 82–83, 86–87, 108, 130, 195; military service rights for gays and lesbians, 196; and neoliberalism, vi, 4, 12, 194–219, 224–25; nondiscrimination laws, 111–12, 121, 130–31, 132; nondiscrimination policies (corporate), 130, 131–32, 187, 193, 195, 197, 198, 204, 207, 217, 224, 252n83, 253n89, 263n77; same-sex marriage 115, 196; sexism amongst gay male activists, 116–18; trajectory of in flight attendant history, 3, 4, 5, 6, 8, 10, 12, 13, 63, 135, 223. *See also* domestic partner benefits; HIV/AIDS; homophobia

racial discrimination (racism): African American pilots, 81, 208; and Civil Rights Act of 1964, 9, 81–82, 87; and flight attendant corps 7, 23, 78, 81, 220; Hawaiian stewards, 7, 44, 80, 126, 246n52, 251n57; Latino flight attendants, 7, 16, 44, 80, 93; professions dominated by African Americans (*"colored work"*), 3, 7, 16, 82, 221; train porters (Pullman porters) 7, 16, 22, 23

Rickenbacker, Eddie: response to unionization, 56, 57; role in hiring stewardesses, 40, 57; role in hiring stewards at Eastern, 15, 26–28, 39, 47, 51, 221; role in hiring World War II veterans, 45–46; role in World War I, 26, 39

"Rodney the Smiling Steward." *See* Pan American Airways

Sanchez, Amaury, 14–16, 20, 41

San Francisco AIDS (KS) Foundation, 162

Schlafly, Phyllis, 111–12, 115, 129, 131, 134–35, 150

School Board of Nassau County v. Arline. See *Arline*

September 11, 2001: as decision day in EBO court case, 206, 208–9, 218; impact on airlines, 196, 211, 212, 218–19; terrorist attacks, 206

sex-based discrimination (sexism). *See* gender discrimination

Shilts, Randy: career as journalist, 156, 171, 181; death, 137; difficulties publishing *And the Band Played On*, 174–75; figurative portrayal in *Zero Patience* 191–93; interviews conducted by for *And the Band Played On*, 154, 171, 172; portrayal of AIDS crisis in *And the Band Played On*, 137, 168, 175, 193; role in constructing Patient Zero myth, 4, 11, 12, 137–39, 146–47, 168–74, 183, 223; role in publicizing *And the Band Played On* via Patient Zero, 174, 176, 177, 178, 180, 193. See also *And the Band Played On;* Patient Zero myth

ship stewards, 7, 19, 27, 29

Simpson, William: consequences of murder for stewards, 62, 63, 75–76, 77, 78, 222; exploitation of murder to enact gay panic, 9, 61, 73–75, 77, 79, 221; legacy as victim of "homosexual panic," 5, 9, 63, 77–78, 79, 82, 92, 101, 115, 170, 197, 213, 222, 224, 225, 241n56; murder of, 69, 71–72, 73; personal history, 72; police investigation into murder of, 72–73; trial of murderers of, 63, 69, 76–77.